金岳霖全集

第五卷

人民出版社

# Articles

Tao, Nature and Man

本文是作者 1943—1944 年访问美国期间撰写,生前未发表,标题为编者所加。

——编者注

# Preface

During the academic year of 1943—1944 I accepted the invitation of the State Department of Washington D. C. to visit America. It was a great pleasure to me to meet many persons whom I would not otherwise have met and to be acquainted however haphazardly with the climate of America opinion. But whenever the idea that something was also expected of me in return managed to emerge above the level of my consciousness, I was preyed by a guilty sense of woeful inadequacy for the job on hand. Although a professor merely professes, and needn't profess more than Protestants nowadays protest, yet there should be a subject which he could offer as a sort of cultural barter. I have taught logic and epistemology in China for a number of years, but to talk about either in America would be merely carring coal to Newcastle. I am not a Sinologist; and to settle problems of Chinese history in term of the West System would be quite beyond my capacity. I was interested in introducing Chinese ideas to America, but here again I was hardly the person to do it, people much better suited to the work either could be persuaded to do so, or else like Dr. Hu Shih had already been doing so for quite a number of years. I have certain ideas. It is distinctly immodest of me to air them anywhere; fairness however requires me to pass them as my own rather than to attribute them to the thinkers of the past merely to burden them in the end with perhaps untenable thought. In the following pages I am giving in English a much abridged version of a book published some years ago under such was conditions in China that not only it is not found in libraries, but also I myself haven't a single copy. The bulk of this following was done in the peace and quiet of Lowell House, Cambridge, and in the Oriental Institute, Chicago. I have added a chapter on Nature and Man which is not in original book in order to bring ideas somewhat out of the unpopular level. Whether or not the book is worth writing or publishing, it gives me at any rate an opportunity to express my gratitude to Harvard University, to the University of Chicago, and above all to the Department of State of America.

# Stuff[*]

## I

Let us take what we ordinarily call a particular thing or object, for example, the magnolia in the side palace of Lo Saio T'an, near to the lake, in the Summer Palace in Peking. We have already described and located for you a particular object; it is located in a well known Palace in a well known City and it is classified under the catalogue of magnolia. Those who had paid special attention to that tree will recall its "shape" and "character" and the place it is located; to them nothing further need be said. They may take an excursion into their past experiences, and if their recollections were vivid, they would see that tree in their mind's eye. But to those who do not remember or never have seen the tree before, nothing avails so far as a substitute for direct experience is concerned.

Suppose that some of them do not know what a magnolia is

---

  ＊ 原稿没有第一章的标题，也没有第一节的标号，这里的标题和第一节的标号"Ⅰ"为编者所加。——编者注

or how it looks like. We might say a lot of things which are trees of this particular tree since it does belong to the family of magnolias. But while these statements are true of that magnolia, they are not uniquely true of that magnolia. There are ever so many magnolias for which these statements are equally true, for example, the two magnolias in front of The Library of Congress. Thus while these statements tell us what a magnolia is like, they do not indicate the shape of that magnolia, or its age or its size, or how many trunks it has or whether its trunks are straight, etc. To get at that particular magnolia, something else is needed. If we were scientists or literary men we might describe that tree in greater detail, not merely in anwser to the questions listed, but also to questions that might be asked along other lines. If words fail, we might be tempted to draw, and if drawings are inadequate, we might resort to photographs. But how are we to be sure that the picture was taken in Peking other than in Hollywood. It seems obvious that no matter what we do, we are doomed to failure so long as revealing the "thatness" of that magnolia is concerned. While we are convinced that as a matter of fact there is no other tree exactly suited to the description or the drawing or the photograph, we are at least equally convinced that the possibility if there being one can not be denied. The question of possibility is not one that is contingent before a conglomeration of related facts; any thing that is not contradiction is possible. The minutest description of an x may possiblly be equally adequated for y; x is $\varphi$, $\psi$, $\theta$,... and y is $\varphi$, $\psi$, $\theta$,... are not contradictions.

Americans who are so accustomed to mass production will grasp the point more easily than the Chinese.

We were speaking of describing that magnolia tree. Description is made of abstract ideas which are instruments for segregating one universal or a set of universals from any universal or any set of universals. To say that a fine apple is red may be perfectly true, and if true, it rules out certain possibilities such as for instance that it is green. It keeps you in ignorance about other possibilities, for instance it may be large compared to other apples, or almost perfectly spherical unlike other apples. Neither size nor shape is revealed by the proposition that it is red, its function is to single out one universal, to leave the rest untouched and to rule out certain possibilities. The usefulness of abstract ideas should not be minimized, they are the basis of communicability of experiences. Particular experience can not be communicated. I can not ask you to meet at the station a friend of mine whom I have known for years but whom you have never met or seen by just mentioning his name; I have to describe him in abstract terms, to say for instance that he is tall, has a lot of white hair, or that he stoops and is a bit lame, etc.... and trust to the probability that there is not another man of the same description at the train. Discriptions are eminently useful, but they do not always prepare you for your experience of the described objects. To say that a certain tree is a tall magnificent magnolia does not prevent you from having surprises when you are confronted with that tree and see it to be "that" tall and "that" magnificent.

A particular thing or object is never merely either one universal or a set of universals. The Winston Churchill is one of the most colorful personalities of their age, but describe him as much as you like, and no matter how adequate and full you aim your description to be, you merely arrive at a combination of universals, a sort of Churchillianity which may possibly be shared by another Englishman or American. Neither is Aristotle the sum totle aristotelianness. The usual reaction to the joke that all Aristotle's books were written by another man of the same name is that no difference is made; this is so because we are merely his readers not for instance his wife in a monogamous society; if we were we would pay more attention to one of them than to the other. And though it is hardly imaginable that there could be two Aristotles exactly alike, it is by no means impossible that aristotleness is shared by many, each one of whom is a particular individual.Since each one of them is a particular object sharing a common set of universals, no particular object in so far as its particularity is concerned is ever merely a set of universals. Hence no description in terms of abstract ideas will ever reveal the particularity of a particular object.

Besides description we employ other means to get at particular objects. The very first sentence with which we started our discussion makes use of proper names in order to get at the particular magnolia we have in mind. Particular objects might be named or pointed to or refered to in terms of ordered frames. To point things out is probably the easiest, the most convenient since with regard to most things we don't bother to give names. But pointing to is an operation that requires co-temporal and cospatial experience. You can not point to the past any more than you can point to an unnamed and unrefered tree and ask a friend in a distant city to appreciate its shape and color. Naming has certain advantages; names stick faithfully to the things named. John Doe might have been thin and now he may be fat; but fat or thin, he remains John Doe. When a particular thing can not be pointed to or is not named, it is often refered to in terms of ordered frames. The most frequently used ordered fames are that of time and space. A thing at such and such time and place particularizes the thing mentioned. In particularization, sometimes one implement alone is used, but more often a combination of these implements together with descriptions is necessary. This is what we have done with the particular magnolia tree in our very first sentence.

But implements of particularization are only applicable to a particular or a name of particulars and strictly speaking not applicable to particular things or objects. A particular is different from an universal only from the point of view of its particularity, not from the point of view of its being an object. Even a pattern of particulars is only a pattern of aspects. As aspects, particulars do not have the substantiality, the actuality and the potentiality of particular things or objects: A set of universals does not constitute an object, neither does a set of particulars, since, neither has got what we ordinarily call "body". Perhaps if we invoke the aid of time, we can see more easily that a particular is different from a particular thing or object. Particulars do not repeat, once they are gone, they are gone for ever; whereas in particular things or objects there is something that persist endurance. Implements of particularization merely enable us to get of particulars and strictly speaking not particular things or objects. Let us return to that magnolia with which we started. It is forever changing. And yet in so far as its particular shape and character at any particular moment are concerned, they can not change, since they don't endure. A succession of different sets of particulars has indeed taken place and may even serve as a criterion for our observation of change, but none of the sets has changed into any other. There is something that has changed and so far that thing has been illusive.

When we describe we are segregating universal or universals, when we point to or name or refer to ordered frames, we indicate particular or particulars. As we have already said there is in that magnolia something that is neither an universal or a set of universals, nor a particular or a name of particular. There is a certain "thatness" that eludes both description and indication which for the sake of convenience let us call expression. There is then something in every particular thing or object, a "thisness" or "thatness" or an x that can not be expressed. Mt. Everest is comparatively permanent, but ever in this case it is constantly and continually undergoing a series of changes which is simply another way of saying that in or around or about "it" there is a succession of different sets of particulars or of different realizations of sets of universals. I am smoking now, the cigarette in my hand is extremely mysterious; its paper came from a factory out of materials that were plant life receiving nourishment from the sun, the water and the earth, its tobacco could be similarly traced, but surely waterness or sunshineness or earthness have not been transformed into cigaretteness; there is something that went through are these as if a man changes from his uniform into his business suit. As I know, the cigarette gradually disappears, some of it takes the form of smoke and soon merges into the air, some of it has turned to ashes, and the remaining becomes crumbled up in my ash tray. The "identity" of the cigarette seems to have disappeared and yet if the situation were as simple as that we would find in quite meaningless to say that "this" ash was a part of "that" cigarette. There must be something that goes through cigaretteness and ashness almost as if a student changes from a sophomore into a junior.

Some of you may think in terms of modern physics and interpret the inexpressible x as electrons. You may say that what constitutes this or that particular object is a particular bunch of electrons and is therefore expressible. But this evidently is not what is meant. A particular collection of particular electrons is indeed expressible; in so far as it is particular, it can be indicated, and in so far as it realizes an universal, if can be described. But what underlies both the collection and each of the particular electrons is stilt the inexpressible x. In urging the above argument you have mistaken the analytical procedure from the expressible to the inexpressible for the scientific procedure from the macroscopic to the microscopic. In the physical sciences there is a reduction of the big to the small, or the complex to the simple, it is an attempt to explain or to describe the macroscopic in terms of the microscopic; it is not the concern of the sciences to tackle the problem that no matter how big a star is or how small an electron is, there is in both an x that is inexpressible. An electron is eminently expressible, and if in future it is to be described in terms of entities a million times smaller yet, these entities are equally expressible. But underlying both there is still that inexpressible x.

Some of you may suggest what is here called an inexpressible x may be a sort of gestalt, a pattern, an unique form or a freak configuration of accidental properties. A particular thing or object is indeed that, but if it were merely that, it would have nothing inexpressible. However freakish a configuration is, may be, it is describe in terms of universals and could be named or pointed to or refered to in terms of ordered frames. Practical difficuties there are bound to be, we may not have adequate ideas or terms to describe the configuration, or we do not know enough to say anything definite about it, we are liable to fumble and fail. But theoretically it is expressible. If it were described, the description would be to it somewhat as what Aristotleness is to Aristotle and if we were to point out the configuration we would be doing hardly anything more than to point out Aristotle in relation to Aristotleness. If we call Aristotleness or Rooseveltness as synthetic possibilities ( a synthetic possibility is such that its constituent possibilities are conjoined but not inferable from each other ) they are merely classes for which so far as we know each has only one member. But having only one member to such a class is a question of fact, not of theory. The same is true of freak configurations. Howerer freakish or unique a configuration may be, it is not the inexpressible x.

## II ①

The world with which we are familiar in common sense including that of history and science belong to the realm of expressibles, even though we are often confronted with experiences which we are at a loss to express. The implements for expression from the point of view of language are symbols, words and sentences. I shall ignore whatever difficult problems there are of language and proceed straight to what is expressed by language usually called meanings. It is necessary to distinguish the content from the object of what is meant. The simplest way of making this distinction clear is to take a simple sentence such as "The desk is low". On the one hand you have the intended meaning of the person who uttered the sentence, and on the other you have a state of affairs usually called a fact which the person who uttered

① 原稿中"Ⅱ"下面有一个标题"The Realm of Expressibles",为了统一体例,现删去。——编者注

the sentence experienced in some context or others. The former is the content and the latter the object. While both are expressed by the sentence, neither is the sentence. We need not concern ourselves with what is expressed by exclaimation or questions, for one purpose only what is expressed by declarative sentences need by considered. These sentences are usually made up of nouns or pronouns or proper names, adjectives, demonstratives and verbs, or other qualifiers or quantifiers. From the point of view of content, some of these stand for ideas and some such as pronouns and names designate sense-data or images. The special content of a sentence in which we are interested is what is now often called a proposition. A proposition is distinguished from the sentence that expresses it as well as from the fact or object asserted by it. The constituents of a proposition are ideas, images, or sense-data.

Images and sense-data are concrete-like or particular like entities in the eminently synthetic process of thinking. In the analytical structure of thought, they are absent. Although they are mental or sensual, they are not ideas. They are in some sense private, hence they can not be communicated except through the instrumentality of ideas. They are the things that afford us the richness and variety of one sensual and mental life. While they are in some sense private, they are not devoid of objectivity, for they are the basis of communicability of experiences even though they are not themselves the instruments of communication. This can be seen from the words that express them. A string of proper names or pronouns or demonstratives without experiential content express nothing unless they are interwoven with nouns, adjectives and verbs. The location of that magnolia tree is done not merely in terms of propes names, but also in terms of descriptions. If without descriptions we can not communicate, without ideas we can not either, in spite of the fact that we have images and sense-data.

It is the abstract ideas that are the agencies for communication. Abstract ideas as contents have universals for their objects. Whatever else any given universal may be, it is at any rate something distinguishable and distinct from other universals. Each universal is just itself, it includes everything that is itself and excludes everything that isn't. This you can easily see can not be said of any concrete object, for instance, the red fommegranite on the fire-place shelf is neither merely red, nor merely fommegranite, nor merely both. Naive as the idea may be, it is yet not easily expressed. Perhaps it is its naivete that prevents it from being readily intelligible. What is insisted here is that there is a separability or discreteness in universals which in terms of ideas is the basis of abstraction of any one of them from synthetic and concrete wholes. To say that this apple is red singles not redness for consideration quite irrespective of its roundness or sweetnesss or sourness which presented in the concrete are inseparable. An idea merely articulates an aspect, not a whole, an abstract, not a concrete. Whatever differences there may be in grammar between nouns and adjectives, they are the same one respect, the ideas expressed by them only articulates aspects not wholes. Whenever we say this chair or that desk, we are accustomed to regard expression as pointing to whole concrete objects. It does so indeed in the content of our early day life, but if you analyse it, you will find that it is the particular context that furnishes you with the feeling of wholeness or concreteness, and that apart from the context the "this" and "that" become variables and the only information supplied by them is that whatever they point to are describable in terms of chair or desk quite irrespective of their being red or green or made of steel or wood.

What is true of ideas is also true of propositions. The latter too only articulate certain aspects of our experience. It is only through leaving an enormous lot unsaid that certain other things can be said. We may achieve a certain degree of completeness by saying things in turn (hence also leaving things in turn) and arriving at making the summary almost a complete description of an object. But no proposition by itself can ever achieve wholeness. If we aim at saying everything we succeed in saying nothing. Such a statement as "After all F. D. R is F. D. R" may aim at comprehensiveness and conclusiveness, but it really says nothing, however conclusive it may be. Roosevelt couldn't be any body or anything else. The name is a proper name and unless it is legally changed, it sticks to the particular individual named irrespective of changes, and whatever he is, he simply is. If as a result of a quick turn either to the extreme right or to the extreme left, some one says of him that "untrue to himself, he has betrayed his cause", one is not talking of Roosevelt the concrete individual person from birth to death, but of Rooseveltness definable in terms of political ideas and beliefs formerly describable of that person and now no longer describable of that person. If the statement is true, Roosevelt is still Roosevelt though in certain aspects in politics, he is no longer Rooseveltness. The statement does say something because it leaves certain things unsaid.

Propositions have this property of discreteness. This quality of articulating certain aspects which are abstractly distinguishable and separable from other aspects. This is so irrespective of particular or general or universal propositions or whether they are true or false. The sum total of our knowledge is simply the sum total of true propositions which we can assert. If we know a good deal of history we can assert a rather comprehensive set of particular and general propositions. If we know a lot of natural science, we can assert a rather comprehensive set of universal propositions. Having common sense is also having the capacity to assert a body of propositions some of which are true while others are believed by large number of people to be true. Knowledge is synthetic or unified in the knower, not in any one of the true propositions which in knowing we can assert. But our knowledge is limited, there are any number of true propositions which we have never been concious of, have never entertained and never asserted. The sum total of true propositions reflect the kind of world as well as the particular world in which we live our sensual and mental lives. Even when we are often at a loss to express our sensual and conceptual experiences, the whole world of those experiences is yet within the realm of expressibles. We live synthetically, but the fact that we can express how we live is due to the fact that our synthetic lives can be taken successively in aspects, the sum total of true propositions assertable of the whole world is a sum total of aspects which are abstractly distinguishable from each other. Through the abstract distinctiveness of aspects the whole sensual and conceptual world belongs to the realm of expressibles.

It it not merely true propositions with which we are here concerned. A false proposition is different from a true one only in that it is false, it does not cease to have that property of discreteness through its falsity. Whether true or false, propositions are either particular or general or universal. A particular proposition is a content of thought supposedly assertable about a particutar object or an event expressed by such sentences as "this is a desk" or "Mr Huang is a hero". The demonstrative and the proper name indicate sets of particulars and the predicates describe universals. An universal proposition is a content of thought assertable of the relatedness and connectedness of universals such as what is expressed by the sentence "Whatever x may be, if it is a man, it is a mortal". In this case it is quite clear that whether true or false the proposition deals with distinguishable aspects. A general proposition occupies a midway position, it is neither particular nor universal, it summarizes a collection of particular objects in terms of the ordered frames of time and space such as is expressed by "The people in America before 1492 were Red Indians" or " the Chinese under the Manchu Dynasty wear queues". One of the difficulties of the social sciences compared to the natural is that up to the present the latter has been able only to discover true general propositions while incapable of inferences beyond its limits of time and space. Obviously we can't expect a Chinese to wear a queue now that he is no longer under the rule of the Manchu Dynasty. Inspite of time and space limitations, a general proposition still deals with distinguishable aspects.

Before a proposition can be true or false, it has to satisfy certain conditions for significance in order that it is capable of having any meaning. I shall not discuss those conditions from the point of view of pure logic. From that point of view we needn't concern ourselves with epistemology and it is in conjunction with epistemology that our attention is centred at present. Take the so-called laws of identity and contradiction. Both are different aspects of the same condition. The law of identity is the positive aspect, that of contradiction is the negative aspect. These aspects together require the identity of every abstract idea with itself and difference of each from every other. These aspects form the very core of analytic abstraction from the synthetic and the concrete, the very basis of separate distinction of the inseparable or unseparated distinguishables. A proposition can have no meaning, that is, it can not be a proposition at all, if it isn't itself or can be others than itself. Obviously this condition for significance takes precedence over the problems of truth and falsehood. It is not merely the true propositions that are significant, false propositions are equally significant. And yet as will be mentioned in the next section, the condition itself can not be expressed in its lumpy completeness. The condition for the significance of expressions is itself werely expressed in terms of its aspects.

The realm of expressibles is the realm of that which can be described in terms of universals or described and pointed to or named or refered to in terms of particulars. As we have already seen, an inexpressible x is neither a particular or a set of particulars, nor an universal or a combination of universals. It can not be the subject or predicate of ordinarily true or false propositions whether particular or general or universal. In the sense in which we are said to know history and natural phenomena in their various branches, our inexpressible x can not be known. Although it is intellectually arrived at, that which is arrived at is yet incapable of being the object of conceptual knowledge or sensual experience. What is required in order to grasp it is a sort of intellectual projection, a recognition of intellectual limitations accompanied by a leap out of intellectual processes with a proposition into the great beyond instead of returning to the essence of intellectuality. In this I am maintaining a distinction between intellectual projection and intellectual reflection, for whereas the latter is a return to pure intellectuality such as a study of logic, the former is a dashing at a tangent into the inexpressibles making it nagatively intelligible and therefore also non-sensually experiencible.

# III

There are inexpressibles which through intellectual ingenuity succeed in getting presented for humman contempletion. Incredible as it may seem, logic the object to be studied as distinguished from the content of our studies can not be expressed either in its entirety or in its essence. The content does not quite correspond to the object in at least two ways. In the first place, you have the logo-centric predicament. Any attempt at dealing with logic in any way always assumes it. Try to squeeze logic as much as you can into a system and you discover that some of it remains outside. This is more easily felt when we examines the beginnings of any system of logic. Take the primitive ideas and the propositions of the *Principia Mathematica*. If one recognizes them to be the beginnings of a system of logic, one assumes their related ideas and propositions which as yet are outside the system, and if one does not assume them, one wouldn't recognize them to be the beginnings of system of logic. I am not talking now of the problem of alternative systems of logic. The admission of alternative systems automatically also admits some logic to be outside any one system. Our point is rather that even admitting one system to be the unique system, one has to assume logic and the logic that is assumed is yet outside the supposedly unique system. To express logic in any way seems to be essentially to leave it unexpressed in other ways and attempts at completeness in this sense have been failures.

We may also examine the sequence of a system of logic. Implication is different from inference, and bearing the distinction in mind, you discover two sequences in *Principia Mathematica*. The horizontal sequence is one of implications, and the vertical one is that of inferences. From the point of view of the organization of the system, inference is more important in the sense that without it the system can not unfold itself. And yet inference is not formally a part of the system. Although the principle of inference is listed as one of the primitive propositions, it isn't like any of the others, and what is more important, every inference in the system is formally outside the system, for whereas every horizontal sequence is a formal expression of implication( or equivalence etc. )no vertical sequence is a formal expression of inference. In the former, it is not the reader's business to "imply", something implies something, but in the latter, it is eminently his business to infer, for it is he who infers. Every inference in the latter sequence is a datum very much as this patch of color on my desk is a datum to be expressed by me. The bracket reference to the principle merely enable me to recognize the datum to be inference very much as experience teaches me to recognize that patch of color to be brown. There is nothing formal about it. Returning to expressions, we may say that while implicatives are formally expressed, inferences are not, for while the horizontal lines express implications, the vertical line is itself a sequence of events or activities. Thus a very important element in the unfoldment of a system is yet outside of the system.

In the second place, from the point of view of essence, logic can hardly be expressed either. Suppose we take the different systems of logic, ignoring for our purpose the question as to whether there are merely different systems of the same logic or different systems of different logics or even whether they or some of them are systems of logic at all. Take the principle or the law of identity. We have in PM $p \supset p$, in the socalled three valued system $p \subset p$, in a four valued system $p > p$ and in the fine valued system of Prof. Lewis $p \prec p$. They are not the same, and yet they are all of them claimed to be principles or laws of identity. Since according to the claim every one of them expresses the principle, none expresses it uniquely. No expression has grasped all its essence so that given any expression one feels that although it expresses some aspect of the principle, others are left out. You may say that this is so under the assumption that the different systems innumerated are systems of logic. While the assumption is not discussed, it is yet made, and making it we feel that we succeed only in expressing aspects of the principle of identity. This may very well be, but if we take any one system, we have the same phenomenon. In *Principia Mathematica* for instance, we have $p \supset p$, $p \equiv p$, $x = x$, $A \subset A$, $R \supset R$... What are we to think of these as the expressions of the principle of identity? All of them are in some sense the same, and in other senses different. If we were logicians we could probably resort to an expression variable for which the listed expressions are values and say that the expression-variable embodies the essence of the principle of identity without any of its inconsequential aspects. But an expression variable is neither any nor all of its values, and what is more important, being an expression for expressions, it expresses nothing on the same level of any of its values. It does exhibit something, namely the form in which the principle of identity is to be expressed, but it is not itself an expression of the principle of identify. The latter is illusive so far as complete and essential expression is concerned.

The above merely point out the presence of inexpressibles even in the sphere of logic. But if we do not aim at essence or completeness, we have no fault to find with the current expressions of propositions of logic. By granting the essential separateness of expressions and what is expressed and projecting ourselves intellectually beyond them we can transcend them and arrive at what is expressed in its essence and entity. As logicians we must remain at the analytical level and look at $p \supset p$, $p \equiv p$, $A \subset A, \ldots$ separately so as to be fully conscious of their difference. It is desirable that we should remain at the analytical level and be fully conscious of distinctions and differences. But as philosophers, we should also be able to look at these expressions or any one of them and through them grasp the essence and the entity of what is expressed. The logician helps the philosopher. The advance in logic during the last half century or so has made logical expressions clearer, much less lumpy and much more integrated than they were before, and while it has not enabled us to express the inexpressible in logic, it has enabled us to grasp it more firmly than before. So far as the expressible is concerned, the recent advance in logic has made its expression extremely articulate in terms of the inter-relatedness of ideas.

It is now a part of the common sense of the philosophical world to regard a tautology as being that truth function of propositions which asserts no fact and entertains every possibility. It can not be false on the one hand and must be true on the other. That it can not be false need not be dwelt on at all, exhibitions of this aspect abound in text books on logic. The more important aspect to a philosopher is rather that a tautology must be true. There are even so many things which can not be false and yet can in no sense be said to be true. But this is not what we have in mind. We are not concerned with how a tautology must be true, since the reasons why it can not be false also account as to how it must be true. The question upper most in our minds is rather: what is it that a tautology is true of? It is true of Reality with a capital R, or underlying reality, or to use Professor Spaulding's intentionally non-descript phrase, a state of affairs? Or is it true of a transcendental mind? Perhaps from the point of view of each tautology being a norm for thought, we are tempted to regard it as being uniquely associated with the mind. But if it were merely true of the mind, we do not see either that it must always be true or that it need ever be true. That which is true of the mind is of course a truth, it may even be a sort of transcendental truth, but in order that it may be a truth in the sense of a tautology, it has to be true of something else as well. I shall not enter into the complexities this line of inquiry inevitably leads. I shall say bluntly that a tautology is true of Tao or to use a term more familiar to you, logos.

The significant thing about a tautology for us at present is not that it is true of Tao or logos, but that it is so without mentioning Tao or logos either as a subject or as a predicade. From the point of view of unstable object, fleeting events or contingent facts in terms of science or history, logic is indeed a subject in which we do not know what we are talking about or whether what we say is true. But ontologically we know that we are talking of Tao or logos and what we say is true of it. By asserting nothing to be a fact and entertaining everything as a possibility a tautology does manage to be non-committed in relation to history and science; but this does not mean that it is also neutral in relation to ontology. It is through saying nothing about facts that a tautology manages to say something about the ultimate reality. Therein lies the skill of the logician. What is said, however, is the barest minimum of the universe. Is it possible to have another class of stataments which assert the fullest maximum? A tautology is sometimes called a pseudo-proposition. Could we have another set of pseudo-propositions which assert everything about neither of fact? We must confess that we are bewildered by the vista. While we see that something extremely important might be done along this line, we are at a loss so far as developing the technique for making such statements is concerned. I myself do not have the ingenuity, and the only thing I can think of is to return to an inexpressible x. Drafting the inexpressible x, however, carries with it difficulties. I can not be sensed, not pointed to, not referred to time and space, nor could it be described. We arrive at it through intellectual projection. Either we grasp it or we don't. If we don't, nothing could be done about it.

If we do grasp it, we are also in difficulties. Let us give inexpressible x a proper name. We cannot think of a better name than "Stuff" in spite of the fact that it is liable to leave with us a taste of excessive stuffiness. Proper names are innocuous in the sense that they have no conceptual deducible meanings and yet if we are thoroughly acquainted with the thing named, we do acquire from some names a feeling of adequacy and propriety as compared with other names. Stuff seems to us to be an adequate name for the inexpressible x. It must be admitted that in the structure of ordinary sentences the name Stuff can only enter as a subject, not a predicate. What is even more important is that the statement expressed by these sentences are not propositions in the ordinary sense, nor are the pseudo-propositions in the sense of tautologies. Unfortunately we have to use language, and since according to Whitehead "Philosophy is to express the infinity of the universe in terms of the limitations of language", we might as well recognizine these limilations and ineffective thought our attempts are bound to be, try to transcend as much as possible these limilations. In the following sections I shall make use of both negative and positive statements in order to enable those who have already grasped Stuff to grasp it more firmly.

## IV

The expressions that are used in this section with name Stuff as the subject are not definitions, though they resemble definitions. Definitions are of terms which stand for concepts and concepts are ideal versions of universals. Stuff is not an universal. Hence the sentences in which Stuff appears as the subject are not definitions. In the sphere of expressibles we have another class of statements to introduce individuals such as in speeches and addresses. The resemblance of some sentences in this section to introductions is obvious, for the function is similar, only in the case of Stuff one can not be introduced to it as one could to a Tom or Wick or Harry. Stuff is not an individual. Though these statements are not definitions or introductions, they are yet made to enable us to grasp Stuff more firmly than we did before.

The justification for the positive statements lies in the negative ones. One previous analysis reveals that concerning any particular concrete individual thing the sum total of universal and particular propositions that can be truly asserted of "it" from the point of view of what "it" stands for leads us to an x that is inexpressible. The very way in which x is arrived at justifies a number of negative statements provided of course that the discussion in the first section is agreed to and the inexpressible x is grasped. Certain negative statements concerning Stuff are obvious. Stuff is not an universal, for if it were, it would be describable in terms of universals. Stuff is also not a particular, for if it were, it could be named by ordinary names, or pointed to, or referred to the ordered frame of time and space. It is not an individul, for if it were, it would have characteristics that would make it different and distinct from other individuals. Although each individual thing has its Stuff, Stuff that is common to all individual things is obviously not any of them. It is neither concrete nor abstract, for if it were concrete, it could be sensually experienced, and if it were abstract, it could be conceptually received. It can not be said to be either existent or nonexistent, for the former is an affirmation of a certain characteristic and the latter a denial of the same, and in either case, Stuff would have to be describable. It neither begins nor ends for if it does, it could be refered in terms of time. I shall point out later that it is the very condition for time, but for the present we needn't dwell on the point. An enormous number of such negative statements could be made. We may summarize by saying that Stuff does not belong to any universe of discourse and that is simply another way of saying that it is inexpressible. On the level of the expressibles, we are of course contradicting ourselves, but having projected ourselves beyond the realm of the expressibles, we are merely using instruments in the form of ordinary statements to enable us to grasp Stuff more firmly than before.

These negative statements enable us to pronounce some positive ones. As will be seen from the above Stuff is pure potentiality. In the sphere of expressibles, potentiality means the capacity of a thing to be something which isn't at any given moment. A has a potentiality to be B, if it can become B at $t_2$ although it isn't at $t_1$, however short or long the interval between $t_1$ and $t_2$ may be. The term does not exclude nor is it limited to values. Thus Mr A may have the potentiality for a great actor, while Mr B may merely have the potentiality of mathematician whether good or bad or indifferent. In the realm of expressibles we are inclined to say that a given A (an individual thing, let us say) has the potentiality for being B, when none of its universal or its particulars has any potentiality for any other universal or any other particular. Obviously a particular can not change for that particular which a thing changes out of merely death, and that particular which a thing changes into is merely born. If a third particular is interfered as a medium, we merely have an infinite regress with a set of particulars for which these is a series of birth and death in which none of the particulars has changed. This series of birth and death of particulars may indeed characterize the change of something that does change, but a particular by itself does not change. Neither can an universal. If in the autumn we find that some leaves have changed from being green to being red, it is obvious that the universal greenness has not changed into the universal redness. There may be what we shall later call a succession of realizations of possibilities and this succession may characterize the change of something that does change, but none of the universals in the succession has changed. Since an universal is something that is independent of time and space, it would be a contradiction to say that it changes at all.

However changes can be observed anywhere. In the world of common sense, we are justified in attributing change to the supposedly expressible things or events, states and processes. But if we proceed in the way we have been so far proceeding, we find that the expressibles can not change and that we only succeed in expressing changes by a very lumpy use of pronouns, demonstratives and proper names. Stuff can not change either. But it is responsible for all the changes. If we borrow the term potentiality from the realm of expressibles, we may say that Stuff is pure potentiality. It is Stuff underlying this table that makes it an object and not merely a collection of universals or particulars, that together with the universals and particulars make it capable of being lumpily designated by pronouns, proper names and demonstratives, and renders it capable of change inspite of the, unchanging universals and particulars. Expressibility, however, is based on separability and discreteness. Hence all that which are expressed are limited items in our total experience, they are aspects that have their own respective limitations. This wooden desk, so long as Stuff designated as the "this" is cramped in "this wooden desk", has potentiality during a certain period for certain things for example, "kindling wood", but it has no potentiality for other things, for example, a "cow". Ordinarily we say that this wooden desk can not become a cow though it may become kindling wood. What it does become is, however, not only limited, but also subject to contingencies over which, in being merely this wooden desk it has no control. But if we talk of Stuff that is not confused to this wooden desk or that red apple. We can easily see that its potentiality is all pervasive and pure. Through wearing and discarding universals and particulars, Stuff can beome anything. The richness in the multiplicity of this ever changing world reflects only to a very small degree the all pervading potentiality of Stuff, for although the latter can be easily seen to be responsible for the present, kind of world, it is yet not limited to any kind.

Stuff is also pure activity. In the sphere of the expressible, activity means such behavior on the part of the agent that influence is felt over the patient. Active, action, and actual are all related to activity. Perhaps the English term actual has been so much mixed with the term real that we lose the connection between it and action on activity. Any how I am using the word actual to mean that which is acting at present. The actual is of course indulging in activities, it is not merely active, it is also being acted upon. This brings us to the old problem of causal relations. Perhaps some readers of the preceding paragraph have felt the emergency of epistemological considerations when the idea of contingence is introduced. Epistemological considerations are unavoidable and are not limited to this preceding paragraph, but for us contingency is not merely epistemological. I hold a view which I do not propose here to elucidate or to depend. For the present I merely say that I believe in the contingency of the birth and death of particulars and in terms of activities this contingency may be expressed by saying that while universal causal relations always hold, they interfere with each other so that it is nowhere determinate as to which of them is actualized at any particular place or time. That is to say, although the universal relation A—B always holds under equal conditions, it is by no means determinate that in the sphere of particulars when "a" occurs "b" also happens for whether b happens or not depends upon conditions which are never actually equal. Evolution in the broadest sense possible never repeats itself. If it does, time has stopped during the repetition. Any how I assume the above views and assuming it I have to hold also that in the sphere of expressible particular things or events, states or processes, the activities are limited and contingent. The activities of a, b, c, d... are not pure, but the activity of Stuff underlying a, b, c, d... is pure and unconditioned.

Since we have already spoken of causal relations, we might as well make use of them further by saying that if we were speaking of universal causal relations, we can not entertain the notion of a first cause in time since universals are independent of time. Neither can we speak of a first cause in time in the sphere of particulars for unless we give up the doctrine of universal causation this would involve a beginning of the universe which is its all-comprehensiveness it can not have a begenning. In the language of cause and effects we can not speak of an uncaused cause. If now we switch to Stuff, we can easily see that there is uncompelled and unceasing activity. While we can not speak of Stuff in terms of uncaused cause we may indicate what it is like in terms of free will. The notion of free will may or may not be tenable as a philosophical doctrine to be applied to the realm of expressibles, the term free-will is not quite so open to objection as the phrase uncaused cause unless we define the former in terms of the latter. If we borrow the term free-will and strip it from its ordinary content, we may make use of it and say that in its activity Stuff is self-willed and therefore free. The impression that is meant to be conveyed is that the activity of Stuff is absolutely unhampered and purest of the pure, it is entirely for its own sake that Stuff is active and actual.

Stuff is also pure substantiality. We are accustomed to the term substance. We often say this or that substance. What is characteristic of a substance is a certain amount of stuffiness, certain rigidity, certain resistence to manipulations independent of the essence of whatever a given substance is endowed. In the sense in which we often use the term, substance is eminently describable and can also be classified into different categories. Stuff is not any of the substances, just as it is not any of expressible potentiality or activity of things or events, or states and processes. Since Stuff is pure pontentiality, it can not be limited to any specific category, since it is pure activity, it is not itself in the chain of the changes of fleeting events, unstable objects and contingent facts. But while Stuff is not itself a substance, it is that which underlies all substances, it is pure substantiality.

Without it, universals would be empty possibilities and particular would cease to be since there wouldn't be things or events. It is that which give substantiality to substances, for without it, even substance itself would be an empty possibility, definable in terms of rigidity without anything that is rigid, or in terms of resistance with nothing that resists. Perhaps the old notion of substratum as that which qualities and properties adhere may give us an idea of pure substantiality, but in so far as the notion is definable, it does not stand for an Stuff. Nor is our Stuff the lowest common denominator of all substances; we can not build a tree or pyramid in which Stuff bears the burden of anything and everything.

## V

A number of other statements could be added to the above, and while some will come later on, one will be singled out for special consideration here. In doing so, we shall expose ourselves to a barrage of arguments against our procedure, for unlike the above statements, the one we intend to single out has as its constituents terms which are ordinarily employed in an operational context. We shall say that Stuff is totally devoid of quality and absolutely constant in quantity. We shall readily agree with the view that looked upon as an ordinary proposition, the statement is meaningless, since, the term quality involves an experiential context that is here lacking, and the terms constancy and quantity call for operations which can not here be applied. It is however not the ordinary meanings that I aim at through ordinary propositions, it is rather the flavour I intend to convey through a set of extra-ordinary statements.

The first part statement really prevents us from describing Stuff in any way whatever. To describe it in any way in the ordinary sense is to attribute certain qualities, and to attribute certain qualities to Stuff is to deny its certain other qualities. To describe it in any way is to hamper it, to infringe upon its pure potentiality and activity. It is not merely that such adjectives as red or green, or square or circular, can not be applied, for obviously Stuff can not be described by any of them; but also such adjectives as real or existent can not be applied either. The term "real" can be defined, even though we may have failed in doing so, which means that the concept "reality" can be related to other concepts, and the universal corresponding to it is understandable through a combination of other universals. If Stuff were real, it would be expressible. We know that like the word "natual" the term "real" is capable of a multiplicity of meanings. I have once gathered more than twenty, and I can not claim that I have exhausted the whole list of different meanings. But each meaning is different from any other, hence each is definable, that is to say each is a concept, and therefore also an ideal version of an universal or what I shall later call a possibility. Any one who has grasped Stuff at all must be committed that it can not be said to be either an universal or a possibility. The same is true of existence, and perhaps here the point is even more easily driven home. To say that

Stuff exists is to limit it in other ways just as to say that it is real is to prevent it from being unreal and to say that it is green denies it to be red. The word "exist" as it is ordinarily used or at any rate as it is customarily used by me is narrower than the term "real". The past, the present and the future are involved in the idea "existent". Confuscius may be said to be real in some sense though he no longer exists, and the ideal of a future world state may be quite real, though it is non-existent at present. To say that Stuff exists is therefore to limit it in a large number of ways. And if you mean by existence the actual occupation of space at the present time, then to say that Stuff exists is to say that it is limited to certain space and time. Stuff can not be so limited.

Without going on further with any more specific argument, we may say again generally that no adjective can be used to describe Stuff if by doing so one means to attribute any quality to it. But you may say that Stuff must be homogeneous, because if any one grasps it at all, one is bound to admit that the Stuff in this chair and that apple is absolutely same inspite of the differences of these two objects. Quite so! Provided that home geneousness is not meant to have qualitatively predicated of Stuff. For negatively if Stuff is qualitatively homogeneous, it can not enter into the core of such diverse things as this chair or that apple, and possitively since it does enter into the core of such diverse things, it is not qualitatively homogeneous. It is only homogeneous in the sense of an absence of qualities, not in the sense of having the same qualities throughout. Obviously if it has any quality at all, it would be expressible in terms of that quality, and to borrow a word so often used in the present war, it would be "frozen" in that universal. And being "frozen" in one universal it couldn't enter into any other possibility and its potentiality and activity and substantiality wouldn't be pure. The very core of the matter is that Stuff must be absolutely free in its potentiality, activity and substantiality in order that it may be the underlying reality of such a multiplicity of things in the actual world and of the infinite richness of things in an infinity of possible worlds.

The second part of the statement is in some ways more important. Not only is Stuff devoid of quality, but it is also constant in quantity. I am aware that both these terms could have a certain redigity of meaning only if certain operations were exhibited, and where Stuff is concerned, no such operations can apply. However we have to borrow such terms to convey what is in our minds and what is intended to convey is that the total amount(if we could use the term at all)of Stuff is neither ever increased nor ever decreased. There is no old or new Stuff, no old Stuff dying or dead, nor new Stuff being born or struggling to be born. The idea or something similar to it is a very old one, we have the ancient intuition and perhaps more or less lumpy idea that nothing can not become something nor can anything become nothing. From a certain point of view, this is a very important insight, but from the point of view of certain articulateness required of ideas, it is somewhat lumpy, though immensely rich. It is not easy to assertain the sphere where it is supposed to hold. Subsequent developments of the idea made it more articulate in certain spheres, for instance, the indestructibility of matter-energy in physics. What I am concerned with here now is rather that the insight applies to Stuff. Stuff can not increase for any increment must be new and dated and then all the subsequent implications can not be denied of Stuff, and Stuff would then become expressible. The same argument applies to any decrease. If Stuff could be increased but not decreased, then there may be a time when there wasn't any Stuff, and if it could be decreased but not increased, then there may a time when there shall not be any Stuff. If increase and decrease maintain an equivalent ratio, there must be portions that are new and portions that are old, and although the quantity is constant, where does the new come from and what has become of the old are unanswerable questions. Obviously old Stuff can not become new Stuff, for in the absense of any quality, it can not be said to change and neither new nor old can be applied to it. If the new Stuff comes from anything that isn't Stuff, then new Stuff is created out of nothing, and if old Stuff disappears into something that isn't Stuff, then it is destroyed into nothing. In a word, if we speak of any increase or decrease of Stuff, we are confronted with the problem that nothing can become something and something can become nothing. It is an insight to the contrary that leads us to see the eternity of Stuff.

While we must not confuse either the phenomenal world of our common sense, or the objective world of the sciences with the ever pervading and ever underlying Stuff, we may gain an insight into the latter from our ideas concerning the former. Take the principle of the indestructibility of matter-energy. This is essentially a development from the old idea that nothing can not become something and something can not become nothing. In the world of common sense, this is probably more easily intelligible. Nothing can be created or destroyed, if we think in terms of "material" or "substance" or "matter". The watch-maker may be said to have created a watch, the hen may be said to have created an egg or a chick, but in both cases out of material they do not create. We do have the emergence of patterns some of which we know to be obeying laws while others either do not obey laws or we do not know them to be doing so; but in either case the basic material neither emerges nor ceases to be. Whether the principle could be proved or verified or met need not concern us here, it certainly succeeds in describing the natural phenomena or our experience of them. The addition of energy to matter in the more recent version of this principle in the sphere of natural sciences merely carries the analysis one step further by making matter and energy mutually transformable, the uncreatability and indestructibility of matter-energy is maintained. It is perfectly possible to discover in future something else the constancy of which may be used as the criterion for the transformations of matter into energy or vice versa. If so, the indestructibility of that thing will still be maintained, for otherwise equations of transformations would be ultimately meaningless.

When we talk of matter-energy or a third or a fourth entity in future, we are not talking of Stuff, though that which permeates and underlies it remains Stuff. In the objective world of the physical sciences, matter-energy is probably taken to be the lowest common denominator of all existents and its constancy might be utilized as the unmentioned but none the less assumed middle term in the symmetrical and transitive equations of transformations of any forms of existence. The principle of indestructibility may have this function and in the sphere of science it may be taken to be merely a methodologized principle, that is to say, that it may be justified by this function alone and not necessarily by any correspondence with reality. I do not know whether this is the case, but even if it were, it does not prevent us from seeing that this principle is more than a mere methodologized principle, that it is based on the insight that nothing can not become something and something can not become nothing. We are bound to have this insight if we were intellectually projected into the realm of Stuff. I am convinced that there is Stuff, and I claim that the conviction is based on experience and arrived at through intellectual projection. There can be no question of verification or proof for the former is confined to particulars while the latter is limited to universals, and Stuff is neither a particular nor an universal. If one grasps it, the above statements exhibit its flavour and enable him to grasp it more firmly than before; but if one doesn't grasp it, these statements do not help him in the least. They are neither propositions in the sense of tautologies. They are metaphysical statements neither proved nor disproved by history and science, nor deducible from logic and mathematics; they are negatively justified by the conviction that without them there is a desideratum in experience for which we are sensually and intellectually incapable of accounting. I am aware that this doctrine of Stuff is an old one and therefore no excitement could be attached to it, but I for one do not think that it has ever been discredited since arguments against it are in my mind irrelevant.

# Tao

## I

Let us start with abstraction. Abstraction is the segregation in thought of aspects from synthetic and concrete wholes, it is the separate distinction of inseparable or unseparated distinguishables. In 1943 you can not separate the President of the United States from the husband of Ms Roosevelt, that is to say, you can not deposit one of them in Hyde Park and leave the other in Washington. The gentleman mentioned has both these aspects, and while they are not separate and for the time being inseparable, they are yet distinquishables which could be separately distinquished. Abstraction from the concrete never cuts the concrete individual up into memerous concrete individuals, it can not, and is never intended to, its whole purpose is to enable us to think and speak of the concrete. There is no other way of dealing with concrete individual things. If you shake Mr Roosevelt's hand it is his hand that your hand is shaking, and if you embrace him, it is his body that your arms embrace. You can not come into contact with him in any concrete synthetic and all comprehensive sort of way. It is through abstraction that we are able to catch him at all in thought. The importance of abstraction is easily overlooked simply because it is done almost every minute in our lives. The moment we speak or think we are abstracting. The importance of synthesis is also easily overlooked because we are also doing it every day, but the argument in favour of it must be done without crying against abstraction, since synthesis is obviously a synthesis of the abstract.

Abstraction is done in thinking and that which is abstracted in ideas or concepts. I am using the term idea exclusively in the sense of abstract ideas. For convenience I shall confine myself to veridical ideas or concepts, excluding impossible or contradictary ideas. I shall also take concepts to be entities or items which occur in thought as units or simples rather than complexes. This does not mean that such an entity or item is itself simple apart from its occurance. "Squareness" may enter into our thought as an unit in one moment or context and disintegrates in the next moment or in a different context into propositions or associated concepts such as parallelograms, right angles, each side being equal to every other, etc. There is no ultimate simple or ultimate complex in our items of thought. But items do occur in thought as simples or units and those we call concepts provided they are not contradictory. Bearing the distinction between content and object in mind, we see that concepts are the contents in thought, not its objects. When one thinks about a square, one does have the concept square in thought, but one is not thinking of the concept "square", but of squareness, that is to say, of the object. Concepts are ideal versions of what we have hitherto called universals and what we shall later introduce as possibilities.

While based on experience, concepts need not be directly based. We can abstract from the concrete and then proceed to abstract from the abstract, hence we not only have structures of concepts but also hierarchies of concepts. There is no limilation to conception except logic, that is to say that concepts can not be contradictory. A contradictory idea that occurs as a simple item in thought is no concept at all. Experience and fact only limit the use of concepts, not their being. Concepts unsubstantiated by experience or facts can occur in thought ordinarily they don't. We can think of a "Fire eating Dragon" or "unicorn", but unless for the purpose of examples in philosophy, we generally do not think of them, that is, they do not generally occur in thought. Concepts are then neither contradictory nor true or false. If an idea is contradictory it isn't veridical, and though is may enter into our thought as a simple item or unit, it is not a concept. A concept can not be said to be true, because since it occurs as a simple, we do not assert anything by it, and the lack of an object to the content or of an universal corresponding to the concept merely renders it definitive of a null class, it doesn't make the concept false. With regard to concepts, there is only our adoption or our disuse and in this we are influenced by experience and facts. Thus the idea "Square Circle" is no concept, which the concept "Witch" though neither false nor true is hardly ever used in the present day.

Concepts are the ideal versions (versions in terms of ideas) of universals as well as possibilities. Each universal is an aspect shared by a class of objects, for example humanity which is shared by a class of bipeds, or horseness which is shared by a class of quadpeds. I am using the term universal in the positive sense, thus while existence is an universal, non-existence is not one but an infinity of universal or possibilities. This means that an universal always indicates a class of objects, and a null class is not covered by any one universal or that the very notion of any one universal involves a logical conjure of it with the universal "real". Thus if the world has never had a dragon, "Dragonness" is not an universal. Our concepts are neither limited to universals nor do they exhaust all the universals. Some of our concepts are definitive of certain null classes, they are the concepts, for which there are no corresponding universals. There are also universals which we have never conceived, idealistic arguments to the contrary notwithstanding. Thus the realm of concepts reflect past of the realm of universals. There realms merely over-lap, they do not coincide and where concepts reflect universals, they are the ideal versions of universals.

A concept that isn't a version of an universal expresses a possibility. The term possibility excludes anything contradictory, everything else is possibility. That which is unimaginable, a fantastic to the extremes in so far as it is not contradictory is a possibility. A possibility if thought of is an object of thought, not a content, hence although it may be expressed by a concept which is a content of thought, it is not a concept, since it is an object of thought. Just as there are universals which are not concerned, there are also possibilities for which there are no concepts. Although possibilities may not be conceived they are conceivable, the realm of conceivability and the realm of possibilities are coextensive for the limit to both is contradictariness. By introducing the term possibility we are able to define an universal as a realized possibility. We shall for the moment ignore the term realization which will be defined later on. An universal is real whereas a possibility qua possibility isn't. The statements in the previous paragraphs to the effect that an universal is an aspect shared by a class of objects ( or events ) or that the very notion of our one universal involves always a logical conjunction of it with the universal " real " are meant to show the reality of universals. The universal " Squareness " is real, because there are actually existing squares or in other words, there are square objects. Most of us in the level of the world of common sense would admit the reality of certain objects or events, it is they that give us the unquestioned sense of reality. That sense of reality should also be accorded to the possibilities realized through those objects and events.

But as we have pointed out in our first chapter, particular things or objects present difficulties upon analysis. There is something that changes and yet endures, something that somehow persists by piercing through combinations of universals and sets of particulars. Since universals can not change and particulars can not endure, that which changes and endures is neither universals or particulars alone nor both together. Both are aspects, it is Stuff that gives them unity and individuality. A possibility qua possibility is not real, but unless it is contradictory (in which case it is not a possibility at all) it may be real, that is to say it may be realized. What is known as the realization of possibility is merely the entrance of Stuff into that possibility. An universal is merely a Stuffed possibility. We shall not introduce here the principle of concretion and individuation. We shall assume that realization always involves concretion and individuation. Reality that is concretized and individualized is housed in sets of particulars examplying combinations of universals. What is taken to be real in common sense is on our basis simply Stuffed possibilities or universals covering concrete individuals through concretion and individuation. The difference between an universal and possibility is that the former is realized while the latter needn't be. A universal is of course also a possibility since it is a realizated possibility.

We started with abstraction and concepts. Concepts are the contents of our thought which however is not limited to its contents. When we think of squareness we are not thinking of the concept "square", not of "Squareness" which is shared by all the squares. The objects of our thought corresponding to our concepts are possibilities either realized or unrealized. Obviously our thoughts are not limited to realized possibilities or universals, we sometimes think positively of nothing or of zero or of infinity, if we know that they are mere possibilities. The fact it is through thinking of bare possibilities that we can think at all, the neglect over zero in the traditional logic has rendered it inadequate as a thinking apparatus. On the other hand, not all the universals have been conceived, unless we hold the idealistic argument to the contrary. We have to grant that at least there are phenomena in the microscopic world that one as yet unheard of. The same applies to possibilities. Thus while the realm of concepts is not a part of the realm of universals, or realized possibilities, anything that is conceived and conceivable is a possibility. The number of possibilities is bound to be infinite, since all numbers are themselves possibilities. Compared to the number of possibilities, the number of universals is very small indeed. This means that in terms of the number of possibilities, the actual is but a small fraction of the possible, or in terms of the possible worlds in the unfoldment of the universe, our present world is but a small item in the reality and a short stage in the process.

It is perhaps easier for us to be intimate with our concepts since they are the contents of our thought. If we examine our concepts we find a certain inter-relatedness that spreads into structures and ascends into hierarchies. Logic alone enables us to see that some concepts imply or are equivalent to others, while experience and science supply us with other relations. Concepts can be woven into patterns. While we do not have a huge single pattern of all our concepts, we do have little patterns along various lines of inquiry in which we happen to have interests. These patterns are partly deductive and partly inductive, and since in them the connecting links are partly true propositions, they indicate a corresponding pattern of the universals and bare possibilities. A branch of knowledge is a pattern of concepts and since it is a branch of knowledge it is also indicative of a pattern of universals and bare possibilities. At the moment we merely assert that they are patterns of universals and bare possibilities, we do not care to discuss as to what they are. In epistemology we are interested in patterns of concepts, imposed by and obtained from our experience of the pattern of universals and bare possibilities, but in logic and mathematics we are only interested in that minimum of pattern that is inescapable either from the point of view of concepts or from the point of view of universals or bare possibilities. One of these minumum patterns is what we call Form.

## II

Form is a possibility formed by the exhaustive disjunction of all possibilities. The term or phrase "all possibilities" is probably open to the kind of objections for which the theory of types is deviced. Whether the thing is adequate or not we need not concern ourselves with in the present connection, but in view of the difficulties we intend to use the term all possibililies to cover not merely the totality, but also the different hierarchies, orders or types of possibilities. The disjunction being the familiar logical disjunction renders our Form thus defined to be absolutely fluid, that is to say, Form is absolutely formless. None of the constituent possibilities is fluid no matter how broad or easy of realization it may be. Perhaps we may make use of the terms connotation and denotation and say that no matter how wide the denotation or how small the connotation of a concept may be, other than the concept Form, the possibility corresponding to the concept is never quite fluid or formless. Any constituent possibility, that is, any possibility other than Form must have at least a modicum of form, hence also a modicum of rigidity. This is equivalent to saying that it has a boundary line dividing what belongs to it from what doesn't, or in terms of analogy with space, what is inside from what is outside; and anything that does not satisfy the definition of the concept is ipso facto also outside the corresponding possibility. Any constituent possibility may admit or else reject. Even such a wide possibility as existence both admit and reject, it admit the existents and reject the non-existents. Every constituent possibility can be dichotomized into the positive and negative, but not Form. There is no boundary line to Form that divides an inside from an outside for the simple reason that there isn't any outside. Everything must be inside, and to say that anything is inside is in the context of our every day life quite meaningless. It is however not meaningless in terms of ontology and metaphysics.

It is the absolute fluidity of Form that makes it inescapable. In one of the Chinese novels we have a mythical monkey who can cover thousands of miles at a single somersault. He could easily jump out of the country, but he couldn't jump out of the Buhda's palm. The inescapability of the palm is like that of Form. It is simply is, and is so absolutely fluid that it is also inescapable. We have already spoken of the entrance of Stuff into possibilities, we have defined the realization of a possibility as the entrance of Stuff into that possibility, and we have defined an universal as a realized possibility. Form is inescapable so far as Stuff is concerned. Some of you may see at a glance the return of an ancient doctrine. The Greeks and the Europeans have been talking about form and matter and the Chinese have been talking about Li and Chi, and here we are again with Form and Stuff. It is perfectly true that we are talking essentially of the same thing, but for better or worse we are talking about it differently and it is partly at any rate the modern apparatus for thinking that is responsible for the difference. We do not think that the ancient doctrine has been disproved or useless, neither of which could be attributed to a doctrine merely on the ground that it is ancient. As far as we can see, it is the simpliest doctrine that links logic with ontology and metaphysics. Logic is essentially the exhibition of Form, metaphysics the contemplation of Stuff and ontology the Study of Tao. This however is a digression which we must not pursue in these paragraphs. Suffice is to say that Form is inescapable from the point of view of Stuff and what is probably more important the inescapability of Form imposes no limilations whatsoever on the potentiality and activity of Stuff.

We have one metaphysical principle and two metalogical

principles or two versions of one ontological principle. The one
metaphysical principle says that Stuff enters into and leaves off
from possibilities. This principle is metaphysical because it says
directly about Stuff through our contemplation of it, and it is important, because it is not only the principle of the whole process
and reality, but also that of any finite passage of time or any
change that is experienced or unexperienced. In the proceeding
chapter we have said that any statement concerning Stuff is
neither a proposition in the usual sense, nor a pseudo-proposition
in the sense of tautologies. It is incapable of formal proof or experiential verification. The former belongs to the realm of the struc-
tural content of thought and in the last analysis assumes Form,
while the latter belongs to the realm of objects and events in the
unfoldment of process and reality which in turn assumes the very
principle in question. But while it can not be proved or verified
and therefore can not be said to be true in the ordinary sense, it
yet holds metaphysically and ontologically. It holds metaphysically
because if one grasps Stuff at all, one can easily see that its pure
potentiality, activity, substantiality and its total negation of qualities must have its medium of function in terms of its entrance into
and departure from possibilities. It holds ontologically, because
once Stuff is grasped, the principle mentioned describes any form
of reality or process from the microscopic to macroscopic world. If
we do not grasp Stuff in any way, the principle is indeed unintel-
ligible, but if we succeed in grasping it, we will find it exampli-
fied in our smoking a cigarette as well as in events of

第
五
卷

astronomical propositions. Even a slight twist of one's hand is a case of Stuff entering into and leaving off from possibilities. As one smokes Stuff is Leaving the possibility "cigaretteness" and entering into the possibility "smokeness" and "ashness", etc.

The principle not merely holds, but is also of the uttermost importance. It is more important than any of the previous statements concerning Stuff, only it wasn't the time to speak of it in the last chapter. It is in fact the key principle to all assertions concerning reality. It is the basis of the principle of concretion and individuation, of time, of change, of reality and existence. It is the ultimate basis of the core of factuality. The idea is not easily conveyed, but we have to attempt to do so. Suppose you are a logician or a mathematician accustomed to structures or patterns or orders of forms, and you are convienced of their cogency or validity or truth. You may be elated over the results of your labours just as the fish-net maker may gloat over the perfection of his fish-net which can not fail to catch the fish, but just as the fish-net maker does not supply the fish and the net itself contains no fish, you may realize that no matter how facts obey your structures or patterns or orders of forms, neither they nor you supply that basis for reality, that givenness or stubbornness which is the very core of all the facts that you experience. By stubbornness or givenness I do not mean unchanging stability; if ever we were face to face with the unchanging in the concrete, as sometimes we do with the comparatively unchanging in our experience, such as being comported with the same things upon returning after a long absence, we are liable to be preyed by a sense of the unreal. Reality is shot through and through with process, and actuality or existence is but an expression of changes and activities. What is meant is rather that there is something in facts or existents or realities that resists an manipulations, that simply is, and that no matter how much we want to account for it through reasoning, we have to take it for granted. This basic stubbornnness or givenness our metaphysical principle supplies. We may not be able to do justice to the importance of this principle in a few short paragraphs, but as we proceed, its importance and significance will be more keenly felt.

One of the two versions of the ontological principle is that there can not be unstuffed Form. We have already exhibited the inescapability of Form and pointed out that this inescapability is in relation to Stuff. Stuff may enter into and depart from possibilities. With regard to Form Stuff doesn't enter and leave, it is always there. A constituent possibility of Form with a few exceptions may be empty in the sense of having no Stuff in it, if so it is not a realized possibility, that is, it is not an universal. This is so because any such possibility has a certain amount of rigidity, certain rules for admittance, hence if these rules are not satisfied, no admittance is allowed. Thus the possibility "Squareness" requires quadrangularity, the equivalence of its four sides and four angles, etc. These rules make a partition so as to result in an inside and an outside. So long as there is an inside and an outside to a possibility, Stuff may be inside or outside of that possibility. Form is not any of its constituent possibilities. Although the concept Form is definite in meaning, the meaning is yet such that the possibility corresponding to it is absolutely devoid of rigidity, and totally leading in any rules of admittance. Compare Stuff to the mythical monkey and Form to Budda's palm, you can see that Stuff can never get out of Form, because there is no boundary line and no outside. Form can not but be realized, that is, it can not but be Stuffed.

The second version is but a converse way of expressing the first: there can not be un-Formed Stuff. These two versions express one ontological principle. The same reasoning is applicable to the second version, hence it needn't be repeated. Notice however that in regard to both these versions we say there can not be instead of merely "there isn't". This brings in an element of far-reaching consequence which we have not dealt with before. Although Stuff is inexpressible and the statements concerning it are not ordinary propositions, Form is eminently expressible. We can exhibit its absolute lack of rigidity intellectually, and if one grasps Stuff, we can see quite easily that un-Stuffed Form or un-Formed Stuff are contradictories. They are nothing in the most comprehensive and deepest sense. It is here that logic, metaphysics and ontology are unified. The principles under discussion combine the results of the metaphysical contemplation of Stuff with the intellectual formulation of Form and guarantee the ultimate basis of reality so that what is logically contradictory is also ontological nothingness. These principles do not of course furnish us with one kind of world which from the point of view of what we have been discussing may be a mere contingency, a phenomenon, and at one stage of discussion, even an accident. But they do guarantee a world or a state of affairs, or a form of reality for which tautologies not merely can not be false, but also must necessarily be true.

These principles differ in that the ontological principle asserts the minimum of reality, while the metaphysical principle asserts the maximum of reality. They also differ in the way in which they are urged upon us. The discussion in the preceeding paragraph exhibits the way in which we are urged to accept the ontological principle. An analysis of Form renders it absolutely fluid and the statement that anything can escape it is easily seen to be contradictory. We may say that logically we are forced to accept the principle. Accepting it however does not enable us to say anything about the kind of world in which we happen to live, it merely enables us to accept the universe. The metaphysical principle is urged upon us through a contemplation of Stuff. The denial of this principle is clearly not a contradiction, that is to say, the principle is not logically forced upon us. And yet if one grasps Stuff at all, there is an inevitability about the principle that one can hardly fail to grasp. There is a sort of "mustness" in the inevilability which is different from necessity in logic. Voltaire was supposed to have once met a beggar who upon being asked why he begged repplied "Sir, I must live", where upon Voltaire was supposed to have said that he didn't see the necessity. There

57

was no logical necessity for the beggar to live, but non the less in his circumstance he must. Confronted with that givenness, that stubbornness, we must accept the metaphysical principle.

# III

The absolute fluidity of Form, the inevitability of the metaphysical and its necessity of the ontological principle lead us to a discussion of the apriori. Let us take first the problem from the point of view of Form and Stuff. Suppose we regard Stuff as a sort of raw material and Form as a kind of mould. There is always a question as to whether the mould fits in with the raw material. The absolute fluidity of Form makes it a remarkable mould indeed, a mould that has every shape and form in one way and no shape and form in the other way. There is no possibility that the raw material will not fit the mould. If we start from Stuff we have the same result, Stuff being totally devoid of qualities. Let us look at any constituent possibility with a few exceptions which we needn't consider at the present. Let us take up temporalness and spatiality. We take these up because they have been regarded as apriori forms of intuition through which noumena are moulded into temporal and spacial phenomena. With Stuff as the raw material and temporalness and spatiality as the mould the story is a different one. We have no logical reason whatever to guarantee that Stuff will not refuse to be moulded by temporalness and spatiality. If Stuff refuses to be so moulded, just as at present it refuses to enter into the possibility "dragonness", we simply have neither space nor time somewhat as at present we have no dragons. Having no time or space is not contradictory, though of course it is never true. Hence it is not like saying that there are no horses either, for the latter if false merely is false, and if false it can not be said to be never true. There are therefore two kinds of apriori forms, one of which is the form that can not be escaped, the whole apparatus of logic forbids its escapability and that is what Form is. The other is the form that never was or is or shall be escaped, the givenness or stubbornness of reality makes it inescapable and that is what temporalness or speciality or some other of the constituent possibilities of Form are. Let us call the first the rational apriori form, and the second the arational apriori form. Having the second implies having the first, but not vice versa. From the point of view of reasoning the former is more important, but from the point of view of experience the latter is more so.

We have already said that having un-Stuffed Form or un-Formed Stuff is a contradiction. But have we obtained anything as a result of granting that Form is always Stuffed? Yes, a form of reality or a state of affairs. Beyond that nothing is said. In this case the denial seems to mean so much and the affirmation so little. Here again we have to call our attention to the fact that fluidity and fruitfulness can not be combined. Form is inescapable because it is absolutely fluid, but the inescapability of Form or the necessary realization of it does not result in anything that is at all fruitful. If we want to know what kind of world we in fact live in even in the vaguest sense, we get no consolation whatever out of our knowledge that Form can not but be Stuffed. On the other hand the realization of spatialness and temporalness is significant, we do not know as a result that there is Grand Canyon or Niagara Falls, or the Sun and the Moon, but we do know that there is time and space together with all sorts of facts which are the results of having time and space. This is fruitful, but then we can not be logically assumed that the situation could not be otherwise. The dilemma seems to be unavoidable. If a form is unquestionably inescapable, its realization is totally devoid of fruitfulness, if the realization of a form is at all fruitful, that form can not he guaranteed to be inescapable. The rational apriori form is logically inescapable but absolutely fruitless, whereas the arational apriori form is fruitful upon realization, but is by no means inescapablle. The former gives us logical assurance for a form of reality, the latter furnishes us with the factual basis for a certain kind of world. It is the acceptance of both that we are able to account ultimately of the universe in which our kind of world must be realized in its process and reality.

Thus far we have said nothing about aprioriness. Our discussion so far assumes that an apriori form is a form that either can not but be realized or simply is always realized. We have not said anything about how epistemologically the form is arrived at. Some of you may suspect and suspect rightly that while we do believe in there being apriori forms we do not believe in there being apriori

ways in deriving or arriving at those forms; that while we do believe in have apriori knowledge, we do not believe in having
apriori ways of knowing or acquiring knowledge. We shall not digress into a discussion of epistemology, we shall merely point out
that there are apriori propositions or statements though the
methods or processes through which we arrive at or entertain or
assert them can not be said to be apriori. Concerning propositions
or statements therefore the problem of the apriori with us is one of
validity or truth or workability and not the ways by which they are
arrived at or derived. A proposition or a statement is apriori if it
is necessarily true or else must be true. There are also two kinds
of apriori propositions or statements, one kind can not but be
true, the other must be true. All tautologies are of the first kind,
the principle of induction for instance is of the second kind. Concerning tautologies nothing need be said, the principle of
induction has been dealt with elsewhere though unsatisfactorily,
but the attempt is non the less an exhibition of its apriori
character in the sense that it must be true under any circumstance
whatsoever.

The ontological principle is the first kind of apriori
statement. It can not be false in the sense that its denial is a contradiction. Our previous discussion dealt with the inescapability of
Form from the point of view of its realization and we have said
that this absolute inescapability of Form renders its realization totally insignificant or fruitless. The same is true of the ontological
principle. That it can not be false need not be discussed again,

but its unquestionable validity gets us nowhere. We merely know as result that there is eternally a form of reality which needn't be of any specific form, a state of affairs which needn't be of any specific state. An universe is indeed assured to us, but whether in it there was or is or will be one kind of world at all, we have no way of assuring us at all. The validity of the principle merely provides us with the barest minimum. It is this minimum that tautologies also assert, the minimum for which they are valid or true. Otherwise the impossibility of a tautology to be false can not philosophically be equated to its necessity for being true. Regarded in this light, the ontological principle is also significant, it does say something, though what it says does not describe our experience in this or any specific world. It asserts the barest minimum of reality, although it says nothing about what we usually call facts.

The metaphysical principle is an apriori statement of the second kind. In being arationally apriori, it is much more difficult to deal with. The rationally apriori statements succeed in being apriori by being absolutely negative about our experience or whatever contingencies there may be in our experience. It is this negativity that renders a rationally apriori statement perfectly intelligible. The metaphysical principle is not negative, its denial is not contradictory and its affirmation says everything about all possible worlds, this present one included. To deny that Stuff enters and leaves off from possibilities may be unacceptable, or contrary to our insight, but it is not contradictory so that the principle is not forced upon us by logic. If we take Stuff to be a thing or an object in the ordinary sense, we may indeed heap all sorts of contradictions upon Stuff, but we have no right so to regard it at all. If we grasp Stuff rightly, we have to grant that the metaphysical principle holds. We can not help seeing that it is pure potentiality and activity must be in terms of possibilities Stuff enters or leaves, since it is at the same time constant in quantity and totally devoid of qualities. We have to say that the principle holds, although we have no way of attributing contradictoriness to its denial. It is through metaphysical contemplation not through logical analysis that the pinciple is urged upon us.

It is one thing to say that the denial of the metaphysical principle is not contradictory and quite another thing to say that the principle says everything about the world. The former merely implies that the pinciple says something, that it is not absolutely negative, it needn't say anything about facts or experience, much less implies that it says everything about the world. Further discussion is required to elucidate the sense in which it is said that the principle says everything about the world. We are sufficiently familiar with logic to know that tautology says nothing. This does not merely mean that it does not predict what will happen in future, or unearth what has happened in the past, this means that it asserts no fact whatever. It really says nothing either about its laws which an given fact obeys, or the underlying activities of which any given fact is the phenomenal or the experiential expression. Our metaphysical principle also says nothing in the sense that with it we gain no knowledge of history or science. And yet it also says everything, not indeed about facts, but ultimately of the very core of factuality. It does so in the sense that given any fact or any item of experience or any change or any passage of nature or time, we find it to be the expression of the activity of Stuff in its entrance into and departure from possibilities. The principle is the most comprehensive way of exhibiting the essence of any thing whatever. The ontological principle says nothing about facts and the absolute mimimum about reality, the metaphysical principle says nothing about facts and the essential maximum of factuality. An ordinary tautology is necessarily true because it asserts nothing as a fact and entertains every possibility as a possibility. Our metaphysical principle must be true because it also asserts nothing as a fact but exhibits the underlying essence of any and every fact so that whatever possibility turns out to be a fact it also has that essence. If the principle asserts something to be a fact it might be false for contingencies may take place under which that something isn't a fact at all; if the principle exhibits the essence of some but not all the facts, it might be false also, contingencies may also rise under which some even most of the facts have no such essence. The combination of these two elements, namely asserting nothing as a fact and exhibiting the essence of any and every fact, is such that the metaphysical principle holds no matter what possibility turns out to be a fact. It is also apriori, though its denial is not a contradiction.

While we discuss apriori forms first, it is after all the apriori principles that are of much greater importance. In the case of

Form and the ontological principle we can hardly say which is more important or which is more fundamental, since each is directly involved with the other, the inevitability of Form is the same as the necessity of the principle. But in the case of the metaphysical principle and certain forms or possibilities such as for example spatiality or temporalness, the question of relative importance is quite different. We may feel that temporalness and spatiality must be realized and yet we may not be able to give any ground for our feeling. But if we admit the metaphysical principle, time and space can be seen to be a matter of course. We shall see this much more clearly in subsequent chapters.

## IV

It is now time to introduce Tao. Tao is simply Stuffed Form or Formed Stuff. It is therefore neither pure Form nor pure Stuff. To borrow Kantian expressions which are not strictly applicable, we may say that Tao would be empty if it were pure Form and it would be fluid if it were pure Stuff. It simply is and is so in its own right. As we shall see later on, it is the universe, but unlike the latter, it need not be spoken in terms of that totality or wholeness which is an inseparable part of our notion of the universe. The term logos might have been used originally to mean both the expression and the content of certain lines of thought, but if it were broadened to mean also the object of thought, it would be what we call Tao here. There is a passage in the *Bible* in which the English word "word" is used as a translation of the term log-os, in the Chinese version the term Tao is used and no better term could be found. Tao as it is used here however is not con-fined to the expression and content of thought, it applies also to its object. In saying that there is Tao, we are not merely talking about there being thought or thinking, but also about there being the universe.

Tao can be spoken of in at least two different ways, namely, Tao-one and Tao-infinite. The former is the Tao of the barest min-imum in connotation and the latter is the Tao with a connotation in essence of that minimum. The point might be more easily grasped if we speak of logos and let us say also of physiology. De-notatively physiology might be said to be a part of logos, while connotatively it has something in essence of bare logos. In saying something about physiology we are also saying through implication about logos, but in saying anything about logos we are not saying anything about physiology. The relation of Tao-one to Tao-infinite is similar to the relation of logos to any of the "-logics", only in the case of Tao-infinite we are not specifying which of the "-log-ics". The comparison may lead us to an idea of the all pervasive-ness of Tao: anything that is at all expressible is a part of Tao, even the expression itself since expressions belong to a sphere covered by a set of "-logics". Nothing escapes Tao. The whole universe is intelligible in terms of Tao-one and any part of it in terms of Tao-infinite.

For the moment however we shall be confined to Tao-one.

Tao-one can not be denied. The ontological principle guarantee Tao-one. To deny Tao-one is itself contradictory. Anything that is generally contradictory is the purest nothing. It is absolutely nothing. There are a number of nothings which have no purity, no absoluteness. To say that there is nothing in this room for instance does not mean that there is in it purely or absolutely nothing, it merely means either that the usual things are absent at a particular time or else that the proposition anything is there is false. Concerning this kind of nothing, there is no problem, at least not in the present connection. The problem of contradiction however may be brought up. You may say that of course there are contradictories, our history of thought is full of them. There are of course contradictory ideas in the history of human thought in the sense that they were entertained and therefore actually occurred in their process of thinking. This however means the occurance of contradictory ideas as contents of thought, not the emergence of things or objects corresponding to these ideas. Besides, contradictory ideas merely occur in thought processes, they do not function in thought structures. They may occur in your preparation of an essay, but if you are aware of them, they do not appear in the finished product. We must remember that having a contradictory idea is an event, a happening, it is not itself contradictory, and to follow the method of approach adopted here, it merely means the realization of the possibility "contradiction", it does not mean the realization of any possibility that is itself contradictory. Contradiction as an event happens every day and the occurance of a contradictory idea is merely a case in which a thinker contradicts himself. Perhaps we are beating about the bush without any clear ideas ensuing. Perhaps we better say that so far as the occurance of a contradictory idea is concerned, it is not the occurance that is contradictory, it is the idea that is so, and it is not the idea as an occurance that is contradictory, it is the idea as a part of a structure that is ruled out as invalid in content because the realization of the corresponding possibility is impossible in the unfoldment of Tao.

The procedure adopted in these pages is meant to faciletate understanding, it is not a formal procedure. Formally we should say that it is Tao-one that condemns contradictories. To say that the denial of Tao-one is contradictory means more than any ordinary statement of this kind, because the very essence of contradictoriness when pushed to the last analysis beyond logic proper is according to our way of thinking simply an affirmation of Stuff without Form or Form without Stuff. To affirm Tao-one is equivalent to ruling out contradictories. Hence in affirming Tao-one, we affirm nothing else either. The ontological principle merely affirms the barest minimum of reality, which is what we have been describing as Tao-one. As we have already pointed out, Tao-one does not imply Tao infinite. By Tao-infinite we mean the infinite possibility of specific kinds of world. Since we speak generally, we are not concerned with any determinate kind. Thus by affirming Tao-one, we are affirming incidentally the reality of our present kind of world just as by affirming logos, we are not affir-

ming a state of affairs in which physics or chemistry or history describes or explains natural phenomena. We may have Tao-one
and yet our specific kind of world needn't exist.

Suppose we describe our present kind of world in the following manner. Suppose we have the kind of world for which the following three exhaustive sets of propositions are true, that is to
say, all the true propositions are included in the following three
sets:

1. A set of universal propositions   P , Q , R , ...
2. A set of general propositions   p, q, r, ...
3. A set of particular propositions   $\phi$, $\psi$, $\theta$, ...

The sum total of these propositions jointly describe our present kind of world as well as assert the existence of this particular
world in which we happen to live. Some of the universal propositions are scientific principles or natural laws grouped under the
different categories of a whole set of "-logics". Some of the general propositions are discovered in history and the social sciences
and some of the particular propositions are found in histories and
newspaper reports. A really worth while Encyclopaedia should
cover a significant part of these propositions most of which
however are not as yet discovered by us at the present. What is
meant by saying that in affirming Tao-one, we are not asserting
the existence of our present kind of world is that while the statement "Tao-one is" or the ontological principle is true, all these
three exhaustive sets of propositions may each and every one of
them be false. This laborious process is adopted because the state

of affairs herein described is more easily conceived than imagined. It is for instance different to imagine a state of affairs in which there is no space, since imagination involves images or pictures which are concrete-like and therefore spacial. But it might be conceived. The state of affairs conceived here might very well be true and yet Tao-one is or the ontological principle holds.

We may extend the above conception. We can easily conceive the possibility that the set of universal propositions is true and yet the remaining sets are false. If so, we have one kind of world, but not this particular one, in which case, nature is as it was in terms of natural laws, but everything else is different from what it is today. It is also possible that the second and the third sets of propositions are partly true and partly false, while the first set entirely false, in which case we have this particular world in some ways but not in others and it does not belong to the kind described by the first set of propositions. We may have three sets of entirely different but true propositions in which case we have an altogether different kind of world and also a particular one different from the one we happen to have. However we may conceive, the important point remains, namely the ontological principle holds and there is Tao-one, whatever can be conceived is possible, because it is not contradictory. Only the contradictory can not be conceived hence Tao-one can not but be affirmed. Later on we shall attempt to show that all sort of possible worlds will be realized, but then that is the result of the metaphysical principle, not the ontological principle.

If we start the other way around we see possibly even more clearly the all pervasiveness of Tao-one, provided we do not forget certain implications. We are liable to forget because certain implications are tainted with false values which we don't care to keep above our level of consciousness. Thus being human and with false values attached to humanity tends to make a person to forget that he is an animal, a living being, a thing, and basically a part of Stuffed Form. Most people would be angry if they were told that they are animals, and to be told that they are things as well probably leaves them flabbergast and fills them with pity for the conspicuous lack of sanity in the one who speaks in such a fashion. And yet while a thing needn't be a person, a person is quite definitely a thing at the same time. To say that one is a psychologist teaching at such and such an university or writing or having written such and such a book gives us much more information than to say that he is a person, or an animal or a living being, and to say that he is a thing gives us very little information indeed while saying that he is a part of Formed Stuff says nothing at all. But this does not mean that the statement is false, in fact the first implies the last. The ego-centric predicament often blinds the individual to his basic identity with other individuals and the anthropocentric predicament often blinds humanity to its identity with other animals, other living beings and other things. It may be advisable to speak of universal sympathy here, but we won't do it, we are for the moment rather concerned with the all pervasiveness of Tao-one. Start from any thing whatever, and no matter how high the connotational content of the corresponding concept may be, you merely start from a part of Tao-infinite, and all the time you are within the realm of Tao-one. This applies to existent things, but also to anything imaginable or conceivable. Thus imagine or conceive yourself to be anything whatever. You can not escape your basic identity with anything else. The merest accident, the most frivolous occurance that can be conceived are but the stages in the process and items in the reality where Tao-one unfolds itself.

Thus far we have been saying that Tao can not be denied, that in affirming Tao we affirm nothing, and in affirming anything whatever, we are also affirming Tao-one. We are more concerned here with the all pervasiveness of Tao-one then with the multiplicity of Tao-infinite. We shall soon speak of the relation between these Two, but before doing so, we still have to clarify certain points concerning Tao-one. While something can be formally said of Form, and hardly anything can be formally said of Stuff, there is a sense in which nothing can be said of Tao-one and another sense in which a good deal can be said about it. It is entirety and unity nothing can be said about Tao-one since it is simply the universe. It can not be said to begin or to end, to increase or decrease, to exist or not to exist, to be real or not to be real,... In the form in which there is a subsumption of subject classes into predicate classes, no statement can be made in which Tao-one appears as a subject, and all statements are valid in which Tao-one appears as a predicate. There are of course certain difficulties in such a statement, but in these pages we overlook them. The point is of course that Tao-one can not be subsumed under anything other than itself. But while in its entirety, Tao-one is simply the eternal all pervasive unity which is but another way of saying that it is the universe, it need not be taken in its entirety. While any part or the universe is not an universe (hence the thing described by physicist and astronomers as a sphere with a radius or a diameter of so many light years is not our universe) any part of Tao-one is none-the-less Tao-one. It is this separate applicability that enables us to think of and say things about Tao-one which in its entirety and unity we can say nothing about.

# V

The ontological principle is responsible for Tao-one and the metaphysical principle for Tao-infinite. The relation between these two can be analysed into two different aspects both of which are important to our understanding of Tao. One of these is the relation of organic parts to organic wholes and the other is the relation of the inclusion of one class to another class. The class inclusion relation enables us to say that what is true of the including class is true also of the included class. A basic homogeneity is given to both the including and the included classes which may be lacking to the relation of organic parts to organic wholes. Obviously while on the one hand a brave man is a man, on the other although blood circulation is organic to human body, it is not itself a human body. Organicity involves a system of external and internal relations such that while parts may be dependent or inter-dependent upon and independent of each other, the whole is always dependent upon its parts. Given therefore the nature of parts, something is also revealed of the whole. It is thus out of the bones of the extinct animals that their bodies can be constructed. Either of these relations has its advantages and disadvantages, while a combination of both enables us to talk of Tao-one in terms of Tao-infinite, for Tao-infinite is not only included in Tao-one, but also organic to Tao-one. Perhaps a bit of imagery will help us. Tao might be likened to a piece of silk with a pattern of different but connected designs together with the woof and warf. Any part of it not only exhibits woof and warf but also a part of the pattern and design. The whole thing is so connected that if one lifts a part of it, some other parts are automatically lifted also. The piece of silk here imagined is static while Tao can be taken both in its static and dynamic aspects. Perhaps we might see in our mind's eye a picture of a running brook skimming along a slightly inclined piece of rock that isn't all smooth on the face so that a certain lacy effect is produced by the water. Every drop there is a drop of water and yet every drop also contributes to the general pattern of its face, so that if the flow is disturbed, a different pattern is produced. While a picture clarifies, it also distorts, but if we ignore the distortion, we may gain through analogy a glimpse of Tao. Tao is both a flow and a pattern, and it is neither its flow nor its pattern; it is a class of entities and events in organic unity, it could be talked about separately hence indirectly it could be talked about also jointly. From the point of view of the articulation of ideas, it is the separate applicability that renders Tao the same as and yet different from the universe.

We have already mentioned the possible equivalence of Tao to logos if by the latter we mean not only the expression and content of thought but also its object as well. The problem of non-veridical thought might be different in details, but we can easily see that even non-veridical thought with its lack of the usual object is also a part of Tao. There is certainly logos to non-veridicality. Suppose we imagine our knowledge to be almost complete in the sense that we know adequately and comprehensively almost everything there is to know. Our encyclopaedia can be roughly divided into at least two main spheres: history and science, the part that deals with parlicular occurances and the part that deals with the universal pattern. Our knowledge not only reflects Tao, but is also itself an item in the reality and a stage in the process of Tao. What is revealed through this reflection? The history part reveals process and actuality, and the science part reveals the pattern. We shall leave the former for future discussion, and concentrate on the latter. Our view is that the pattern is one of multifarious designs in the form of various "-logics" grouping different sets of natural laws interconnected with each other by natural laws, assumptions and principles of methodology. These different "-logics" as parts or designs are woven into an organic whole which is the pattern itself. A good deal might be said of the interrelations of the different "-logics". Some are more closely related than others from the point of view of intervening distance, some are on a higher plane than others from the point of view of deducibility, some are more closely knit than others from the point of view of internal organization, and some are perhaps richer than others from the point of view of content, etc. But they are connected like the cities of a country. No city is inaccessible though certain roads do not lead to certain cities. Physiology may be far distant from geology, but they are not disconnected, they may not have a direct road of communication, but by the tortuous way of biology, zoology, botany, geography, paleontology one could travel from physiology to geology and vice versa.

This pattern wouldn't be what we call logos or Tao, for taken by itself, it is empty, static and devoid of actuality, it is like a sift with nothing sifted, or window curtain that is rendered colorless by having no light going through it. We are not talking here of contrast between Stuff and Form, but of that between the actual and the hypothetical. We are speaking analytically of the universal pattern without the flow of passage of particular events and objects. Actually each is dependent upon the other. The ease of the moving picture may be drafted again for illustration. All the cross-sectional pictures do not make the moving picture, for they must come in a certain pattern as well, nor is the picture confined to the pattern for if the cross-sections were different, the whole picture would have been different. Just as it takes both pattern and cross-sections to make a moving picture, so it takes both process and pattern to constitute Tao or logos. In the last paragraph we emphasized the pattern, in the present we have to say a few words about the flow or passage of events and objects. Particular objects in so far as their particularities are concerned are the pointables, referrables or otherwise expressibles. While their particularities can not be described, they themselves can be described through the universals they examplify or the possibilities they realize. That is to say, the particular events or objects sift through and permeate the pattern like light rays that shot through the window curtains. The pattern is after all the inter-connectedness of universals with the different "-logics" as the inter connected designs. It is this flow and passage of particular events and objects that give life and actuality to the pattern and it is the pattern that gives the flow of passage its intelligibility. Tao can not be said to be rational if by it we mean something associated with conscious decisions, but it is thoroughly intelligible, because it is thoroughly according to pattern.

Given the relation of Tao-infinite to Tao-one, one can see that not only is the sum total of Tao-infinite the entirety of Tao-one, but the organicity of Tao-infinite is also the unity of Tao-one. There is an infinity to the one as well as an one to the infinity. The organicity of Tao-infinite may be discussed in terms of particular events and objects. From one way of looking at things, a particular object or event reflects the whole universe. From the point of view of epistemology I hold that particular objects and events are both internally and externally related to each other. If

77

not, knowledge would be quite impossible. But this view is not incompatible with the doctrine of organicity of particular objects and events. In the first place, internal and external relations are not always or generally symmetrical. That is to say, if x is externally related to y, y needn't be externally related to x. In the second place, there are varieties of organicity; while some demand the exercise of mutual influence of the part upon each other in terms of qualities alone, others merely demand a similar influence in terms not of qualities alone but also of relations as well. Relationally no particular object or event is independent from any other particular event or object; each is so and so because the others are or were or will be such and such. Particularity is never merely local or merely the property or the attribute of particular objects or events. If it were, it might be repeated, since it might be detached from its enviroment, and once capable of detachment, there is no reason whatever why it shouldn't be capable of repetition. But as we have already pointed out before a particular can not be repeated. That is to say, it can not be detached from its immediate enviroment, nor can its immediate enviroment be detached from its mediate enviroment. Suppose we refrain from talking about the universe, and confine ourselves to any cross-section of it which we sometimes call the world at $T_1$. The repetition of a particular in the world at $T_1$ means also the repetition of the world at $T_1$. One can easily see that the world at $T_1$ can not be repeated, either continuously or discretely. A continuous repetition of the world at $T_1$ would be a stoppage of time at $T_1$, and a discrete repetition of the world at $T_1$ would be detachment of it from its predecessors as well as its successors. This world eventually result in a repetition of the universe, and a repetition of the universe is also its denial, for an universe that can be repeated isn't the universe at all, it can not be Tao in its entirety and unity. Since a particular can not be repeated, it must reflect the whole universe, each must be because the others are or were or will be.

With the above in mind we may say something about universal sympathy. It is in terms of this doctrine of reflection that the universe is said to be in us, not merely that we are in the universe. "Heaven and earth and I myself are co-temporaneous and I am at one with myriad of other things" is a doctrine that might be interpreted along other lives, but it certainly is an off shoot of the ideas herein expounded. Mr Bertrand Russell has somewhere remarked that people hanker after eternity without desiring to be infinitely fat, that is, they want to function throughout all time without desiring to occupy all space. Esthetics undoubtedly forbids infinite fatness while economics and psychology propel people into a desire for eternity. The latter desire is less pronounced in the East, it is more or less confined to its rulers. Prosperity probably makes it more prevalent in the West. It is essentially a vulgar desire. On our basis here, if we are conscious of the fundamental oneness at which we are with the universe and everything there is in it, there is a sense in which we might be truely said to be all pervasive in space and time, only it is not a sense that gives the vulgar any satisfaction. To the philosophically minded, it is the sense that consoles, for it is the sense that gives him his universal sympathy with everything that surrounds him. To have a body that is ageless is to deprive one of the joys of change, of growth and decay. To have a spirit that is eternal is to punish him with the loneliness and solitude of the Gods. To want either or both of them is simply a hankering after priviledges which are denied to some of the rest of the existential beings, it is an attempt to preserve the egoistical status quo by exaggerating the differences and ignoring the identity. It is thus that the Greek and Hebraic tradition in the West has made human beings anthropocentric in relation to the rest of nature and ego-centric in relation to the rest of mankind. Universal sympathy is extremely unlikely if at all possible under such conditions. It is only by realizing that one is floating in on ocean of bits of Stuffed Form or Formed Stuff that universal sympathy is gained and with it also one's own all pervasiveness and one's own eternity.

Are we not going to the extreme in one direction just as the others are doing so in the other? And what are we going to do practically when for instance a mosquito bites? Kill it, if you can, but don't condemn or hate it for biting. It is the mosquito's job to bite. Don't confound the realm of qualities with the realm of values. In the democracy of existents, each has a function pertaining to the different roles that is assigned. Being a man is a job, a station if you like, but not a status; it is a charge for one to keep, not an inheritance for one to gloat over. In the unfoldment of Tao men and mosquitoes have functions assigned to their roles. The human function is the one which those objects which are human at the same time can not shirk just as the mosquito function is the one which these objects which are mosquitoish at the same time can not but perform. Once a man turns to dust, his function as man ceases and his function as dust begins. In the roles of a mosquito and a man, one bites and the other kills, in the role of physical objects, they have a physical contact in which there is transference of matter-energy with certain chemical effects. The language of biting and killing is appropriate to two objects of which one is in the role of a mosquito and the other in that of a man, it is not appropriate to either or both in their role of physical objects. We are not asking the mosquito or the man to forget respectively its mosquitoishness or his humanity, we are simply asking them to remember that they are objects at the same time, and this is not much different from asking the President of the United States or the Senator from Nevada to remember that they are also citizens of the United States.

May it not be said that our view here would impede progress? The generally accepted view in the West seems to be that progress is partly due at any rate to the conquest of nature by man and this implies the latter's assertiveness. Greek light, Hebraic sweetness, Roman law, European science and American industry would have been quite impossible if men merely tried to harmonize themselves with nature or nature's God and did nothing themselves. It is difficult to speak of progress, especially in relation to the unfoldment of Tao. Being human ourselves we naturally heap our affections on humanity, but when we come to think of it detachedly, our affection may very well be blind, there may not be any reason whatever why evolution should stop with the emergence of man. If we could be detached, we might be at a loss in trying to find any striking virtue in humanity. But even limiting ourselves to human history, what is known as progress is certainly not entirely on the credit side. And what is ever more to the point is that even taking progress to be what it is generally taken to be, our view does not impede it either. What we urge, you must remember, is not a principle guiding human conduct, it issues no injunctions against killing mosquitoes or building gigantic bridges, or investigating natural phenomena laboratories, it is a view of contemplation, of detached understanding aiming at broadening our outlook without hampering our activities. If we take it to be a sort of cosmic lassez faire imposed by man, progress in the usual sense is indeed impeded, but if we take it to be a recognition of reality and process in which whatever we do, we are functioning in the unfoldment of Tao, we needn't accomplish less as human beings, though we are bound to feel more as elements in the democracy of existents.

# Reality and Process

## I

There are four kinds of possibilities from the point of view of their realization. We shall discuss them in turn.

A possibility is necessary if it can not but be realized. It is a possibility of which the failure of realization is contradictory. Hence it is a possibility that can not but be an universal. With the previous discussion in mind we can easily show Form to be such a possibility. Although the number of such possibilities is not large, it is not confined to the single possibility Form either. Consequent upon the necessary realization of Form, the possibility realization is realized and with it also the possibility realness. Since a necessary possibility can not but be an universal, universality is also necessary. From the point of view of logic such possibilities are important in view of what has been said about tautologies. From the point of view of epistemology these possibilities are unimportant, their realization does not result in our present kind of world.

A possibility is eternally realized if it must be realized in the

senses discussed in the last chapters. The failure of the realization
of such a possibility is not contradictory, but simply never contingent. The term eternal suggests time. We should not speak of
such a possibility in terms of time, because temporalness is itself
such a possibility. But if we do speak in terms of time we can
easily see that there is one time in which these possibilities are
not realized. These possibilities owe their realization to the metaphysical principle. Their realization is not a matter for pure
reason or logic, but belongs to that givenness or stubbornness,
that core of factuality with which we are confronted in our experience and from which we are never free no matter how badly we
might want to free ourselves from it. The number of such possibilities is not large, perhaps larger than that of the first kind.
Change, temporalness and spatialness are such possibilities. We
can see here the importance of the metaphysital principle to some
extent. The necessary possibilities when realized merely give a
minimum of reality which needn't be of any specific shape or
charactar familiar to us. It is the metaphysical principle that says
that the reality thus logically forced upon us is also bound to be
changing, to be temporal and spatial, etc. As a result we have
already a kind of world which in some broad outline resembles
very much the world we live in, for not only have we change and
time, motion and space, but also a frame of reference such that
reality is disintegrated into multiplicity without chaos. The block
universe, not perhaps in the sense in which James meant, it was
never an actual state of affairs.

A possibility is contingent, if it may be realized or unrealized or once realized ceases to be realized. The realization of such a possibility is neither necessary nor obligatory and the number of such possibilities is bound to be infinite, the main bulk of constituent possibilities of Form belongs to this class. Perhaps instead of contingent possibilities we might speak of contingent realities. Most of the things with which we are faced are contingent realities. We are liable to dismiss "mere facts" with a sneer. If we are interested in universals or their inter-relatedness, the sneer may have its cause or even justification, but one is never sure that he is the one who sneers last. "Mere facts" have a givenness that is stubborn, they can not be dismissed, except by postulating a criterion of relevancy upon which they are declared to be irrelevant some what as the Fox dismissed the grapes as being sour. In either case, there is a givenness which can not be tempered with, a givenness which accrues more to the contingent realities than to the necessary realities. Since reason enables us to accept the latter, it is thus made reasonable, and since reason alone does not enable us to accept the former, all that we can do about it is to say "there it is".

Natural history informs us that a large number of plants and animals have come and gone and during their tenure of occupation or realization, if they were given the facility for imagination, they might have imagined themselves to be destined to permanence. There was a time when there were no human beings and there may be a time when there shall not be human beings. Years ago when a newspaper man upon being disturbed by Balfour's cold aloofness said that the latter seemed to be always conscious of the interglacial ages and was probably emotionally prepared to face another glacial age. It is difficult to say whether such consciousness is likely to be disturbing to human life, whether it decreases the sound and fury of the stage, but if it is also modify our view of human significance, important undoubtedly to human beings, but not applicable to the long views of evolution, it is on our basis a very healthy consciousness indeed. Nor do we have to disturb our emotional equanimity unduly. Whether or not there will be supermen to succeed us doesn't really make much difference. We have already accepted individual death, yearning towards eternity to the contrary notwithstanding. We have also learned to accept with equanimity the passing of great ages in human history. There is no reason to suppose that we need be especially disturbed by the termination of an tenure of existence at a future date. Though evolution does not repeat itself, possibilities are capable of repetitions of realizations. It is by no means impossible to have another period of human beings after we have died a few millions or a few billions of years.

What we are concerned here is however not the fate of humality, but the restatement of natural history in our own terms. When we say that Tabor-tooth tigers and Dinosaurs have come and gone, we mean here merely that in the unfoldment of Tao, there was a time when the possibilities Tabor-tooth-tigerness and Dinosaursness were realized and subsequently disrealized. In other words Stuff has entered into these possibilities and subsequently have left them. When we say that there are no dragons we mean that the possibility dragonness is not realized at the present. There is no reason to suppose that in the unfoldment of Tao there never was or never will be any dragon, for dragonness is a contingent possibility. It certainly is neither necessary nor impossible, neither eternally realized nor eternally unrealized. It is a possibility the realization of which is contingent. The same is true of humanity. Our existence is merely contingent. It is of course of the greatest importance or significance to us. But then to any class of existents whatever, the realization of the possibility corresponding to its defining concept is always important and significant. We may like to see the extermination of the ants from our point of view, but from the point of view of the ants, if they were given the faculty to reply, they would disagree with us with some degree of violence. The failure of Voltaire to appreciate the beggar's point of view is due to the former's concentration on being Voltaire, if he were more sympathetic towards the Baggar's plight, he would see that even a beggar has to live. It may be that on the basis of a certain prescribed criterion of valuation, humanity is more valuable than ants, or Voltaire more valuabe than the beggar, but valuation is prescription not description. What is prescribed as values does not always coincide with what is described as qualities and relations. Distinquish the realms and one can see clearly that the valuable needn't be the noncontingent in the unfoldment of Tao. On some criterion of values, it is the contingent that is valuable. Consider our own experiences. It is not the span of life that gives most of us satisfaction, but the significant experiences that can be crowded into it. Most people would value an hour of love or of intellectual excitement or the moment of triumphant discovery than a whole year of monotony and colorlessness. Even in more ordinary circumstances it is the anticipation of the emergent, the abandonment to the occasion, the regret over the passing and the recollection of the past that make life and living different from mere existence.

We are not here interested in the special criterion suggested above, we are concerned rather with the role played by the contingent possibilities. It is the realization of these that supplies the universe with its richness, its variety, and its colorfulness. Obviously if the necessary and the eternally realized possibilities were the only realized possibilities, the universe would have been dreary, barren and bleak and it could not have been the universe since so many possible worlds would have been excluded from it. We shall point out later that if the universe were really the all embracing entity we take it to be, then all the contingent possibilities must be realized in process. The richness, the variety and colorfulness are assured us by the metaphysical principle. While the realization of any contingent possibility is contingent, the realization of the whole class of contingent possibilities is not contingent. If the realization of the contingent possibilities were itself contingent, Stuff might stay in the necessary and eternally realized possibilities and the metaphysical principle would then be multified.

A possibility is eternally unrealized if it can be realized only when the sum total of contingent possibilities have been or are realized. Since there never was or is or will be a time when all the contingent possibilities are all realized, such a possibility is eternally unrealized. The realization of such possibilities is not impossible, for if it were, the possibility wouldn't be a possibility, it would be an impossibility. Though eternally unrealized, it is yet a possibility, that is to say, the corresponding idea to such a possibility is not a contradiction, but a genuine concept. Perhaps we have better ways of defining such possibilities, but proceeding from a discussion of contingent possibilities we find it most convenient to define such a possibility in terms of contingent possibilities. Take such a possibility as infinity. It can be easily shown to be eternally unrealized. Perhaps we better start with concept corresponding to the possibility. The idea certainly is not impossible, so far as we know it has never been proved to be contradictory. It certainly is not unreal as an idea or a concept for even those who declare it to be unreal are battling against it and do not regard themselves as battling against nothing. Some may have confused imagination with conception and regard infinity which is genuinely unimaginable to be thereby also inconceivable, but if it were really inconceivable, it should have been proved to be contradictory. But it isn't. The problem is therefore not with the concept but with the possibility. As a possibility, infinity must be admitted and yet as a possibility, it is never realized. It is this lack of realization of the possibility that makes the corresponding concept seemingly unreal.

Perhaps a reference to the doctrines of infinite divisibility will bring out the points which we are labouring under some pains to exhibit. To say that a foot of bar is infinitely divisible is really to say that it is never infinitely divided or infinitesimally is to deny that infinite dividedness is ever a fact in or on item of reality. It is because infinite dividedness is never realized that infinite divisibility is a second doctrine, and vice versa, it is because infinite divisibility is a sound doctrine that infinite dividedness is never realized. Granting the validity of the doctrine of infinite divisibility in a world in which realization takes the form of the concrete and finite and one realizes that infinite dividedness is not an item of reality, but a limit to a process, a limit which the process may approach but never reaches. If we regard the limit as being reachable, the doctrine of infinite divisibility crumbles. The very notion of infinite divisibility requires the possibility of infinite dividedness to be eternally unrealized. It can be realized only in the sense that its realization is not apriori contradictory, it isn't realized because the process of realization which is essentially a process of the realization of contingent possibilities must be complete before it is ever realized. And its process is never complete.

The first two kinds of possibilities are important because one of them guarantees us with the absolute minimum of reality while the other furnishes us with the ultimate basis of factual givenness. The second two kinds of possibilities are also important for different reasons. The realization of contingent possibililies gives us the richness, the variety and the completeness of Tao, whereas the e-ternally unrealized possibilities are useful in supplying us with the implements in the realm of thinking and thought. These possibili-ties are not so important as possibilities as they are from the point of view of their corresponding concepts. "Infinity", "nothing", "not",... are of the greatest importance not from the point of view of their being possibilities since as possibilities they are e-ternally unrealized but from the point of view of their correspond-ing concepts since these are the most important lubricant in thought processes and the most significant links in thought struc-tures. In fact, without them we can not think. Even in ordinary life we make good use of eternally unrealized possibilities such as "the future" or "tomorrow". Tomorrow as a variable never comes, but its value for Jan. 15th 1944, namely Jan. 16th, will be experienced by us in less than twenty four hours, and when we do experience it, it is of course no longer tomorrow.

# II

Reality is concrete if a plurality of possibilities are realized by one and identical Stuff. Take anything that is concrete, you will find that concreteness lies in the plurality of possibilities hav-ing one and identical Stuff. Thus, Tao is necessarily concrete be-cause on the one hand with the realization of Form, realization and reality are realized, resulting is the realization of a plurality of possibilities and on the other the Stuff that is in Form must be one and identical. Although we do not say directly that the universe is concrete, we are saying indirectly that Tao is necessarily so. We have three principles which it is our business to formulate and discuss in this section. The first one to be discussed is the principle of congruence: reality unfolds itself with congruence. The ideas of congruence is borrowed from the ordinary idea of starting from different roads and reaching without conflict the same or different destinations. Regard the different possibilities realized as the different road and the same or different realities arrived at as the destinations our principle furnishes us with a minimal character, namely concreteness. It is the principle of concretization only in the sense of the minimal content of the principle. The congruence with which possibilities are realized result in concreteness if we remember that so far as the Stuffed Form is concerned, the Stuff that is there is bound to be one and identical.

The notion of concreteness in connection with this concrete table or that concrete apple is borrowed from our notion applied to Tao. The concreteness of Tao is not open to doubt, because we have on the one hand a plurality of possibilities realized and on the other one and identical Stuff. The entirety or the sum total of anything whatever must be identical with itself, and since the Stuff in Form is all the Stuff there is, it must be identical with itself. But concerning this concrete desk or that concrete apple, the case is different. We have to be sure a plurality of possibilities realized in each case but in either of them the Stuff that realized it can only be roughly and indeterminately spoken of as one and identical. The inexpressible x in this concrete apple, the " bit " of Stuff that realizes the possibilities redness, roundness and sweetness is not the inexpressible x in that desk, the bit of Staff that realizes the possibilities rectangularity, brownness, etc. ; but beyond that our identification fails, since we can not point to the inexpressible x, we can not assert the identity of the inexpressible x with itself either in this concrete apple or in that concrete desk. The concreteness of any ordinary concrete object can not be demonstrated. It is only with rough probability of applicability that the concreteness of ordinary objects can be said to have been experienced.

Concreteness is the minimal content of the principle of congruence. As a maximum the principle is also the basis of the principle of consistency. We are familiar with the rather prosaic dictum that ideas must be consistent. Whatever consistency may mean, the dictum does not prevent the occurance of inconsistent ideas in thought processes. What it does is to invalidate the presence of inconsistent ideas in thought structures, and this presence must be invalidated because if it weren't, the structure wouldn't reflect the pattern of possible reality. The ultimate basis is that concrete reality is congruent. In the broadest sense consistency merely means the absence of contradictions, that is to say, if two or more propositions or sets of propositions are both or all false they can be also consistent, one certainly can lie consistently. Ordinarily we are liable to confine ourselves to the narrower meaning in the sense that given the truth of certain propositions the body of propositions that may be true with it are consistent with the given propositions. Here one is guided by extra logical considerations and the criterion of consistency is often very fruitful. But the fruitfulness of the criterion is obtained only on the condition that a certain givenness is given or that we do have certain non-necessary and yet true propositions. At the level of the necessary and eternal realities, the principle of congruence merely results in the concretization of reality. But given the realization of certain contingent possibilities, the principle also provides us with trends or tendencies. This merely says that if no contingent possibilities were realized, the principle of congruence is merely a principle of concretion or concretization.

Are we sure that there is to be the realization of contingent possibilities? We have already said somewhere that although the realization of this or that contingent possibility is contingent, the realization of contingent possibilities as a class is not contingent. If the ontological principle alone holds we need not have contingency, but since the metaphysical principle holds also, and we have eternally realized possibilities, contingency can not be excluded. Since time and change must be realized as a result of the metaphysical principle, contingent possibilities as a class must be realized for otherwise there wouldn't be change or time. The metaphysical principle says that Stuff enters into and leaves off from possibilities. The necessary possibilities are those in which Stuff necessarily stays, and the eternally realized possibilities are such that there is no time when they are unrealized. If those alone were the realized possibilities, Stuff can not be said to enter into or leave off from possibilities. Under such a hypothesis Stuff merely stays and the kind of world we should have would be entirely static. It is on account of the metaphysical principle that temporalness and changeability must be realized and since there is time and change, there is bound to be the realization of contingent possibilities. To say that there is bound to be the realization of contingent possibilities is to say that reality unfolds itself with contingency.

If reality merely unfolds itself with congruence we have a static though a concrete world, but since reality also unfolds itself with contingency, we have not only a concrete but also a dynamic world. Both principles together assure us of a world that is both static and dynamic, static in some respects and dynamic in others. The inevitable relativity in human experience in general and the individual or subjective preferences in particular often result in some people attaching greater reality to the dynamic while others more reality to the static. The distinction between conservatives and radicals in so far as one sees the danger of change and the other doesn't does not seem to be confined to politics; some people are perhaps more Parmenidas minded while others Heracliters minded. A different emphasis by different people is: perhaps desirable and salutary, but a sense of reality should include both the static and the dynamic. The basic core of factuality or givenness or stubborness as we have pointed out before is not attached to anything that is unchanging, nor is it uniquely associated with the ephemeral or kaleidoscopic. What is known as the nature of things gathered in our experience, no matter how prejudiced our experience may be, furnishes us with a sense of reality that appropriates a more or less adequate amount of staticity or dynamicness to various things, hence in ordinary life we have very little danger of merging the static into the dynamic or vice versa. It is only in metaphysics or in ontology that one of them is declared to be unreal because the other is some what the criterion of reality.

While on emphasis on either staticity or dynamicness may be salutary at different times, a divergence of what we conceive to be ultimately real from what is sometimes known as the apparently real is liable to be vicious. There may be causes leading up to such a divergences. It may be that ultimate reality must be eternal and the eternal is easily taken to be the unchanging; it may be that this notion of change is itself full of difficulties with which reality can not in theory be burdened; and it may also be that it is easier to turn around and regard change as the ultimate reality. But the intellectual processes leading up to the divergence is one thing and its effect is quite another. In epistemology naive realism must be criticized, but it can not be abandoned without also crumbling the very foundation of epistemology. The theory of private sense-data seems to have accumulated a wealth of detail that does credit to human ingenuity, but no matter how much theorizing we are willing to accord to this approach, we can not evolve out of these theories the common objective world so conveniently provided for us by naive realism. Once the bottom is left out, no amount of stuffing at the top will give us any solidity or security. The same may be said about theories of reality. One could be easily sympathized with or being dissatisfied with the ephemeral realities in our experience, but if we dash off at a tangent and erect a theory of reality so divergent from our experience we are bound to have the vicious result that either we feel no sense of reality in accordance with the theory propounded or by sticking to it we make ourselves unreal to our fellow men. Our notion of reality is such that on the one hand reality is static in some respects and dynamic in others, and on the other it is in essence not much different from the items presented to us in our experience. The principle of congruence supplies us with a concrete and static world, and the principle of contingency supplies us with a contingent and dynamic one. While the principles are separately stated, they do not operate separately and it is quite senseless to ask which one operated first.

The principle of contingency merely enables us to have variety. But it does not afford us economy. It is quite possible to have a series of realizations that is single file; if so, we have temporal variation or variety in succession, but no spatial richness or richness that is co-temporaneous. We may have a lumpy block of a world that changes, and yet devoid of any richness in shape or color. In order to supply us with the latter, we have to have the third principle, namely, reality unfolds itself with multiple individuality. This is a principle of economy, it assures us that the series of realizations is not in single file, but in multiple file, so that the block world is integrated into individuals capable of realizing almost all the possibilities that can be consistently realized at the same place and at the same time. If the world were one individual, only a few possibilities could be realized at any time, but since the world is integrated into a multiplicity of individuals, an enormous number of possibilities are realized. Lump the six blocks together, and you have only six sides, but break the block into six and you have thirty six sides. The number of possibilities that could be realized is enormously increased with the admission of this principle. It is on account of this principle that the realization of the contingent possibilities can come in a rush, and supplies us with a fullness that grows with the passage of time.

Although this third principle is the last mentioned, it is by no means the least important. From certain points of view it is the most fruitful. It is more than a principle of individualation or a principle of negative economy. It is also a principle of the character of series of realizations. We do not intend to make use of the terms of homogeneous heterogeneity or heterogeneous homogeneity, nor do we follow the example of the *Bible* by starting with one Adam involved with one Eve and proceeding to millions of Adams and Eves. For us the Universe has neither a beginning nor an end, it didn't start with utter simplicity nor will it end in ultimate complexity. Since there is no beginning or end, our principles are not these which began to operate in a distant past or cease to operate in distant future. But if we take any time as the "present" or as the point of reference, the principle operates and as time passes from the point onward our principle of individuation enables the world to accumulate multiplicity. Perhaps the point might be gained more easily by bearing in mind the cooperation of the principle of contingency. The more contingent possibilities are realized, the greater is also the contingency in the realization of contingent possibilities once the princple of individuation is granted. Without assuming initial poverty, richness in descriptive qualities and relations if not in prescriptive values increases in the unfoldment of Tao.

# III

With the principle of contingency, we have change. The world is an eternally changing one in some respects, that is to say, the possibility "change" is eternally realized. This is not merely implied by the principle of contingency but also by the metaphysical principie. If Stuff enters into and leaves of from possibilities there is obviously change of realizations. When it is said that "change" is eternally realized, it must be understood that change must be realized that in terms of time there was no time in which it was not realized and no time in which it will cease to be realized. The world did not start with being static and proceed to becoming dynamic. In the aspects in which the world is said to be static, it has always been and always will be, ane in the aspects in which the world is said to be dynamic, it has always been and always will be so. We have no difficulties in our every day experience. We need not for the present be concerned with abstract ideas or universals which are out of time and space. Even when we confine ourselves to the concrete items of our experience we find some of them to be comparatively permanent and others comparatively ephemeral, this indicating relative staticity and dynamicness in the objective world. We do not think that philosophers have been so unobserving as to deny change as a fact since as sentients they experience it in their everyday lives.

What seems to be the trouble lies either in the notion of change or in the reasoning associated with it. There we do have difficulties. The notion of change involves identily and difference in which there must be identity in some thing and difference in others. Either one of them is essential for obviously neither alone constitutes change without the other. If A is said to have changed into B, there must be something identical as well as something different. If there isn't something different, there isn't any change, A and B would simply different names for the same thing. If on the other hand A and B are different without any link that is identical, they are simply two entities between which there may be lapse of time but of which one can not be said to have changed into the other. The notion is obviously an abstraction from experience in which most if not all changes are partial and with partial changes the problem of identity and difference is not different in practice. Where there is a partial change, experience reveals to us certain identical aspects in the concrete together with certain different aspects. But experience is often rough and ready, it contains inferential elements which are not often well founded. Experienced differences may often be final, but experienced identity isn't. The latter as experierced is one of aspects and identity in aspects is merely an indication, not a conclusion of something else that is identical. The inference of the latter from the experienced identity in aspects may not often lead us to practical difficulties, but theoretical difficulties remain. It is of course unlikely but by no means impossible to have two different objects with identical aspects. Hence experienced identity in aspects is not a conclusive indication of basic or radical identity. If it isn't, no change need have taken place even in cases where there is partial identity and partial difference. That is to say, even when A is experientially said to have changed into B, on account of the fact that there is between them partial identity and partial difference, one is theoretically never quite sure that a change has taken place since A and B might possibly be two different entities to start with.

The criterion therefore is not identity in aspects though it involues in differnce in aspects. Identity and difference are not on the same level or applied to the same kind of entities. When we say that it is possible to have two things with identical aspects we can not possibly mean by "things" identical combinations of identical aspects, for if so, no two things could have identical aspects, since there is no sence of saying that they are "two". What then do we mean by different things or the same identical thing? Aspects can be divided into the universal and the particular. A thing can not be equivalent to a set of universals, because at any time the thing may change and a set of universals can not, though in changing something emerges from one set of universals into another set. Neither is a thing a nexus of particulars because a thing can endure while a nexus of particulars can not, though in changing something emerges from one nexus of particulars into another nexus. There must be something over and above the nexus of particulars which distinguishes it from other kinds of things. That something we have already found to be the inexpressible x or Stuff. An identical thing is not an identical set of particulars or universals, but an identical bit of Stuff. This identical bit of Stuff is what gives a thing "thisness" or "thatness", a "thisness" or "thatness" which might be pointed to through its nexus of particulars, though in being able to endure in not merely a nexus of particulars. What constitutes change in a thing is the wearing of different aspects by the identical Stuff. Any change is like the change of a man discarding his business suit and putting on his evening dress or in his forsaking his brown shoes and taking up his black ones. Nothing has been changed not even the wearer except that he has changed his clothing and his shoes. In the final analysis, it is the Stuff that is the wearer.

In experience we can never he sure of any bit of Stuff being identical. The inexpressible in anything whatever, being inexpressible, is not open to empirical distinctions or operational manipulations, strictly speaking, it is meaningless to speak of bit of Stuff, much more so to speak of them as being identical. Stuff is not divided into compartments with vacuous lines of partitions. Whatever partition there are, they are the bourdaries of events and things and are essentially aspects whether universal or particular. The only way in which we can speak of Stuff being identical is to speak of it in its entirety. Since Stuff does not increase or decrease and totally devoid of quality, it can not but be identical. The whole world at $T_m$ and the whole world at $T_n$ must be identical and yet since $T_m$ and $T_n$ are different in content, they must have different aspects. The notion of change is therefore eminently applicable to the whole world in its passage of time. The whole world is forever changing and contingent possibilities are eternally realized and disrealized in the scaffolding of space-time. It is only when we are speaking of the whole world that we have any theoretical assurance of Stuff being identical and hence it is also the whole world that we have any assurance of its having changed, or changing or going to change. It is this change which is also basically time. With regard to any other thing the notion of change is somewhat vicariously applied. The vicarious application does not land us in practical difficulties for identity in some aspects is a sort of rough and ready indication of identity of Stuff and difference in other aspects can always be empirically ascertained or inferred from an eternally changing world. When an object is said to have changed from $T_1$ to $T_2$, no matter how short the interval may be, no matter how identical all the aspects may be empirially, it is said to have done so only as an inference from the eternally changing world. When an object is said to have remained without changing, it merely means that no difference in aspects has been observed.

The theoretical difficulty in any empirical assertion of A being changed into B lies in the lack of empirical criterion of ascertaining the identity of Stuff. There is no practical difficulty if the data presented are such that there is identity in some aspects and difference in others for although the former is not a conclusive indication of identity of bit of Stuff wearing these identical aspects, yet it is almost overwhelmingly indicative of such basic identity that an assertion of change is not open to empirical doubt. This is particularly so when identical aspects far outnumber different aspects. Since theoretically anything has changed through the passage of time, any assertion of empirical change has an element of directness especially germane to an empirical context, that is to say, either a thing has been observed to be changing or evidences indicate its having changed. In the former case the change is given in the datum, in the latter case the evidence being empirical satisfies empirical requirements even though they may not satisfy theoretical criteria. All this is meant to say that in practice there isn't much difficulty. It is not meant to minimize the fact that the notion of change is borrowed from where it validly applies to where its application is often open to theoretical doubts. If we stick to the empirical world of individual objects and events and aspect the notion of change to be theoretically satisfactory when applied to each individual separately, we are confronted with the kind of difficulties, with which we started this discussion. The solution or the removal of those difficulties lies with us in assigning change property to that of the whole world and applying it derivatively to individual objects and events in experience.

When we say that the whole world is eternally changing, we mean of course the whole concrete world in the universe, not the universe itself, the unfoldment of Tao-infinite, not the being of Tao-one. There are entities in the universe that can not be said to be changing or not changing, such as for instance possibilities, universals and concepts, etc. The universe being all comprehensive and all embracing is not limited to the concrete and the concrete world in succession does not constitute the universe. We may leave out possibilities for as possibilities they are not real, although they are elements in the universe. Universals are real since they are realized possibilities, and yet they can not be said to be changing or not changing, their reality lies in the particulars subsumed under them and they are both immanent in and transcendental to particulars. The realization of a possibility is an event, so also is it dis-realization, but the possibility realized is not an event. It is possible to have a period of time in which a possibility becomes and remains an universal, if so, while the becoming and the remaining are events in history, the universal isn't. If the period of realization is ever repeated, the repetition is a different event in history from the original realization, and yet the universal is the same. A class of existents to which an universal applies are individually in history, but the universal corresponding to the concept which is the defining concept of the class in question is not in history. The rise and fall of dinosaurs is an event in history but dinosaurness isn't. While dinosaurness is an universal the proposition that the possibility dinosaurness is realized is only a particular proposition; its truth merely indicates an event having taken place or a fact having been ascertained, not an universal law. Even when we speak of individuals we have the same state of affairs. While there were only one individual Plato and only one individual Aristotle, Platonicity and Aristotelianness are universals. As universals, they are not confined to any particular place or time, they are capable of repeated realizations though it is perhaps difficult to imagine the emergence of people so exactly alike. While the individual Plato must have changed and changed continuously, Platonicity can not be said to have changed. What we have been driving at is that while the concrete world is forever changing, there are entities that can not be said to have changed or not changed.

## IV

Change brings us directly to time. In this section we shall confine ourselves to time alone, we shall discuss it in relation to space. There are a number of senses in which the terms time and space may be used and we are not here concerned with most of them. We shall use the term time to mean the flow of objects and events and space their containers. There are two aspects of the contents and scaffolding. In this section we shall pay attention chiefly to the scaffolding. Temporalness and spatiality are eternally realized possibilities. This is simply another way of saying that there is always time and space. The metaphysical principle assures us of time and with reality integrated into individuals, we are assured of space. Time can not be said to begin or to end nor can space be said to have boundaries, whether from the point of view of the scaffolding or from that of the content. Since temporalness is an eternally realized possibility, since the world does not begin to change nor does it stop changing, one could see that time neither begins nor ends. The problem of space in connection with its boundaries is somewhat different. One can perhaps easily see that as scaffolding space has no boundaries; given any starting point in space three lines in three different directions can be prolonged ad infinitum in time. If we say that any of these lines if sufficiently prolonged would return to the original point, we are not speaking of the scaffolding, but of the content and what is even more significant, we are probably speaking operationally. The operational way of speaking is inapplicable to our present sphere of discourse. Our problems are anterior to the assumptions and presuppositions of the operational view of concepts, however helpful or fruitful the latter may be as a principle of scientific methodology. The world at $T_1 - T_2$ indeed has boundaries both in time and in space for by setting limits to time one is also setting limits to space. However we are not speaking of any world at $T_m$-$T_n$, but of space and time and with the regard to the latter, not only has time no limits, but space also has no boundaries.

If we are to supply significance to a class of statements in which the notion of simultaneity is involved and the operational way of ascertaining simultaneity is not involved we have to have absolute space and time. When we say that an event happened two years ago on a star that is two light years distant from the earth, we have to grant that the time at which that event happened on that star and some time in the year before last on earth are one and identical slices of time. Unless we have identical slices of time throughout the world, we can not speak of a world at $T_m$-$T_n$, for the latter is the identification of the content of the flow with its scaffolding, the world being a convenient summary of the content and $T_m$-$T_n$ being the scaffoldirg. In fact the world at $T_m$-$T_n$ is simply $T_m$-$T_n$. If there are no identical slice of time common to all parts of the world( not the earth) the latter can not be identified with any slice. No matter how different it is to ascertain simultaneity, simultaneity has to be granted, since otherwise there would be a multiplicity of durations corresponding to the multiplicity of objects and events. In the latter case the practical difficulty of ascertaining simultaneity has become the theoretical difficulty of having no time whatever. We have to distinguish the practical difficulty of ascertaining simultaneity from the denial of simultaneity. Simultaneity must be held inspite of the fact that ascertaining it is different. If simultaneity were ruled out, not only a whole class of statements is operationally meaningless, but also theoretically in capable of having any significance. These statement are clearly significant even though it is difficult to supply them with any operational meaning.

From now on we shall take up space-time separately and each from the point of view of the scaffolding. A slice of time is a world of objects and events from the point of view of the content of time, it is also a period that can be marked off in the scaffolding. In order to have a purely theoretical and absolute scaffolding of time and space we shall introduce a few terms which stand for limits of abstraction in order to give a more precise theoretical meaning to the structure of the scaffolding. A slice of time is indeterminate from the point of view of duration, it may mean seconds or ages. We need something that is determinate and invariant. What we need is something like the familiar instant, only it is somewhat different from the usual instant. We shall use the term instant here to mean the whole of space without any temporal dimension whatever. An instant is three dimentional spatially but it does not endure. It is a temporal surface without temporal thickness. Any finite slice of time has two instants as its boundaries and an infinity of instants in between. No slice of time is the totality of time. Of the two boundary instants to a slice of time, one in the beginning of the slice and the other the end. Time neither begins nor ends, only slices of time begin or end.

We can supply finite units to any slice of time and measure its length. The world at $t_1-t_2$ is a slice of time with the operationally unascertainable $T_1 - T_2$ as the beginning and end. Hence the worlds that can be said to begin or end are such worlds, they are not the universe or the totality of Tao or reality. All the separate durations are in one slice of time or another and if their beginning or end in one individual instant, they begin or end simultaneously. Thus the period between 11 and 12 o'clock in Boston on Jan. 20th, 1994 is at least two things combined, one is a duration relative to a number of things among which the position of the Sun in Boston and the other is a slice of time that cuts across the whole universe with 11 and 12 o'clock sharp(operationally non reachable instants)as the boundaries. The latter is not relative to Boston, it is one of the values for the variable "world at $t_m$-$t_n$". Time is not merely a flow of objects and events, but also a flow scaffolded by an infinity of instants and serially ordered by them. It is in terms of this scaffolding of instants that a theoretical if not an operational meaning is given to statements which say that such and such events take place at such and such a time. It is through this scaffolding that objects and events are referred to their co-temporaneous contents in the flow of time.

An instant is an eternally unrealized possibility. It is a possibility, but it is also eternally unrealized. While we can't say that it is impossible, we are convinced that it is unreal. Nor is it unreal in the sense that at present it isn't actual or existing as for instance the possibility dragonness is. It is unreal because it is eternally unrealized. Its realization depends upon the infinite divided-ness of any slice of time which no matter how short it may be is infinitely divisible, so that there is no stage reached in which it is infinitely divided. While the possibility is eternally unrealized, the concept corresponding to it is not thereby useless. Thus 12 o' clock as an instant is never realized, but the concept is eminently useful since operations can be performed to approach it and so long as a rough meaning can be given to the concept, it can be made use of for the practical purposes of life. Neither does the unreality of the instants render the scaffolding organized or ordered by them unreal. The scaffolding is real for the slices of time bordered by these instants as well as the order in which they succeed each other are real. I do not know how the scientists will take to the doctrine herein proposed for it might very well be their exploded doctrine of absolute time. Our scaffolding here is indeed absolute, but it is also non-operational and so far as we can see all the operational objections are inapplicable. The truth of the proposition that operationally there is no absolute time does not include or imply that nonoperationally there isn't such absolute time.

Just as an instant in the whole space without temporal di-mension, so a space-time-line is the whole length of time without any spatial dimension. Just as an instant or time surface is not the usual instant, so also a space-time-line is not an Euclidean point. Euclidean space is an abstraction of space without time and con-sequently without events and objects. Its space is the space of a time surface or what we usually call space at a single instant. Like time-surface, space-time-line is also unreal. On our basis, Euclidean space is unreal since time-surface is unreal. Although it is unreal, the concept corresponding to it is yet useful, takes together time and Euclidean space form a scaffolding in which time surfaces and space-time-lines intersect. The intersection is a point-instant. A point-instant is the Euclidean point, while a space-time-line isn't. Just as time can be ordered by time-surface, so space can be ordered by space-time-lines. We have to introduce spatial lines which are space-time surfaces, spatial surfaces which are space-time volumes, spatial volumes which are hunks of space time. Space-time can be ordered by these entities into a space-time scaffolding in which reality unfolds itself. The concrete content of this unfoldment makes the scaffolding real.

The scaffolding is not something apart from the process and reality, it is so inextricably conjoined with particulars that they are identified by it. Every particular is definitely and uniquely fixed in the scaffolding, in fact, it is its position in time and location in space-time. No particular can change its position in time or its location in space-time. It can not move. Motion is only possible when we separate absolutely the temporal from the spatial aspects of things. We as enduring individuals can indeed move from A to B at $t_n$ when $t_n$ is taken as an unit of time in which our movement characterizes us, but when $t_n$ is taken to be $t_1-t_2$ with ourselves identified with the set of particulars uniquely associated with $t_1-t_2$, we can not move from A to B, since that set of particulars stays at $A_1^1$-$B_2^1$. This is the old problem of the moving arrow and the insight involved in it was grasped in China as fully as it was in the West. We are not going to digress into a discussion of the problems of motion, what we are labouring under some pains to point out is that a particular not only can not change, it also can not move and while it is born and dies in the flow of reality, it stays forever in the position and location in the scaffolding. This is at least one reason why the truth of a particular proposition is not particular in the same sense as the event asserted by the proposition. "John Lackland passed by this morning" is a fleeting event the thorough appreciation of which is attributed to Carlyle, but the historian in Carlyle is probably more interested in the truth of the proposition rather than the particular event asserted by it, for if the truth of the proposition disappears with that particular morning or with John Lackland in his particular passing by, it is doubtful whether Carlyle is sufficiently of the kind artistic temporalment as to abandon himself to the enjoyment of the particular occasion. The scaffolding of time and space is a catalogue. It has of course its shortcomings, but compared to most catologues, it does not seem to suffer more than they from excessive onesidedness. To the secret service an agent is let's say $B_{29}$ and to the librarian a book is $B_{75}M_{34}$, although as a man the former eats and drinks, loves and plays, while as a book the latter may be red or blue in its cover and in content chuck full of significant or futile ideas. The scaffolding of space-time is also one sided, but it is not more pronouncedly so than other catalogues. It is probably more indicative of the characteristics of the catalogues than more catalogues.

## V

In the previous chapter we have already spoken of the mutual interdependence of the pattern and the flow or passage of objects and events. By pattern we meant there the interrelatedness of universals. Corresponding to it is the more familiar inter relatedness of concepts. Although concepts are all related, they are yet capable of having arranged into groups. A science in the broadest sense—that is to say, not confined to the physical sciences though the meaning of the term science is borrowed from them—is a body of knowledge having for its object the interrelatedness of possibilities and universals and for its content the interrelatedness of concepts. We shall not digress into a discussion of epistemology here, what we want is to talk about interrelatedness of possibilities and universals through the interrelatedness of concepts. Euclidean geometry is from the point of view of its contents a pattern of interrelated concepts, so also is physics. Since the content is one of the interrelatedness of concepts, scientific knowledge is a knowledge of universals and possibilities. Since concepts are ideal versions of possibilities and universals the interrelatedness of the former is also an interrelatedness of the latter. All the " -logics" have for its content an interrelatedness of concepts corresponding to the interrelatedness of universals and possibilities. Hence the sum total of "-logics" reflect the pattern in which reality unfolds itself. At any particular time the pattern is never complete since the process of realization will never end. This means also that there is no day in which scientific knowledge is complete or scientific research will come to an end.

The term natural law is sometimes used to mean the object, sometimes to mean the content and in extreme cases even the expression of the content of scientific knowledge. We shall ignore the last, for taken in this sense, the English and Chinese versions of the law of gravitation would be two or two sets of natural laws. The term is however often used to mean the content of scientific knowledge. When it is said that natural laws have changed from time to time, we have very likely a case in which the term is used to mean the content of scientific thought for in the history of scientific thought scientists do give up certain concepts and adopt certain others, and in so far as the term is used in this sense, and change means the rejection of one set and the adoption of another set of ideas, natural laws do change. We are using the term natural law here to mean the object of scientific knowledge. If so, it is simply another name for the interrelated universals and possibilities. Since the interrelatedness is itself an universal or a possibility it can not change. The term natural does not exclude men and the term law is here temporarily restricted to the sense of justice. A natural law simply is, and by saying that it simply is, we also mean that it must be obeyed in the sense that other things being equal it has no exceptions to the rule.

When we say that the process of reality flows in accordance with pattern, we mean that objects and events obey natural laws, while natural laws are universal, they are not apriori either in the sense that they can not but be so, or in the sense that they must be so in any circumstances. They are aposteriori in the sense that they have to be discovered and verified. Each and every one of them simply is. Taken as a totality, there is indeed a mustness about natural laws so that given a certain number of them, others may be inferred, and the more that is given, the more can be inferred. But taken separately each simply is. A natural law may take the form of a statical summary, even when it does so, it has no exceptions. In any given stance however, a natural law may not be realized, for the realization of a given natural law is contingent although the realization of some in the totality of natural laws isn't contingent. We must not take the contingent realization of a natural law as a reason for granting exceptions to the rule. In the case of a person having had a fatal dose of poison without resulting in death, it is the failure of one natural law to realize and the success of another one to do so. Natural laws are universal aspects the realization of which depends upon the presence of equal conditions summarized by the phrase "other things being equal". Since conditions are never quite equal, there never any telling as to which of the natural laws is to be realized at any particular moment. Here again we have to emphasize the distinction between natural laws taken as a whole and each and every one of them taken separately. We have already mentioned that the realization of contingent possibilities as a class is not contingent, although the realization of any one contingent possibility is contingent. The same is true of natural laws. Only in this connection we have to put the matter the other way around. Although the realization of natural laws taken together is not contingent, the realization of any one of them is. Where a natural law fails to realize because the conditions are unequal, it does not mean the presence of exceptions, for there are exceptions to a rule only where the rule isn't followed under equal conditions.

There is a good deal of talk about the conquest of nature and there is a sense in which this may be correctly said. If we mean by it that we are not able to bring about an actualization of a series of objects and events favorable to ourselves through the operation of certain natural laws where others might have operated, we may correctly say that we have conquered nature to a much greater extent than we ever did before. But if we mean by the conquest of nature the ability to dispense with natural laws or to disobey them we are very likely talking non-sense. The operation of natural laws has never been suspended and it is not more suspended today than it ever was before. The Boulder Dam does not dam nature or natural laws, it merely enables us to encourage the operation of certain natural laws at the expense of certain others. The significant thing for human beings is rather that the operation of natural laws taken as a disjunctive whole is inescapable, while taken separately each can be dodged. It can be dodged however only through the operation of other natural laws. Clearly in this case one can not say that natural laws have exceptions. Quinine cures malaria not by suspension of natural laws, it is rather the operation of one to off set the operation of another that undesirable effects are avoided. The ability to do so depends upon our theoretical knowledge, our practical ingenuity as well as the capacity to maintain more or less equal conditions. The hospital is an effort to maintain more or less equal conditions so that certain natural laws can operate towards certain desired efforts and the laboratory is an attempt to maintain more or less equal conditions so that certain natural laws can operate so that certain desired discoveries can be made. If natural laws have exceptions, our world would be a chaos instead of a cosmos.

Concrete reality then unfolds itself in accordance with the pattern of natural laws. This means that reality is thoroughly intelligible. By intelligible we do not mean rational on the one hand, or predicable on the other. Rationality involves adopting adequate means towards an end as well as avoiding anything that does not contribute towards the end. If a person is rational he does certain things and avoids certain others. Reality in its unfoldment does not seem to adopt certain things and avoid certain others even though an end can be attributed to it. Predicability involves such a connection between the past and the future that given the past, the future though unactualized is yet given in some sense also. While we do not say the reality in process is rationed, we do not say that it is irrationed either. It is predictable in some ways and unpredictable in others. The emergence of particulars is unpredictable, while the realization of possibilities may be predicted some times with very high degrees of probability. Intelligibility is different, it is understandability if any body is given the capacity to understand. It involves the explanation of the present in terms of the past as well as of the actual in terms of the universal and the possible. It involves on the part of the person who understands the ability to answer the questions of what, how, why or when concerning the actual. For the present we shall not touch at all understanding in the sense of answering the question how the actual has come to be for this is a question of history and is therefore outside the subject matter of the present section. If now we confine ourselves to the kind of understanding which involves the ability to answer questions as to how or why or what the actual is cross-sectionally, not historically, we are speaking of understanding in terms of abstract concepts and their interrelatedness. This is another way of saying that when we do understand, we are able to exhibit the natural laws which the actual obeys. Hence when we say that concrete reality unfolds itself in accordance with pattern we are also saying that it is thoroughly intelligible or understandable.

The pattern in which reality unfolds itself is the pattern of the interrelatedness of possibilities and universals, and this in turn is the object of all the "-logics" taken as the content of scientific knowledge. There are a number of questions from the point of view of the different sciences as well as their inter-relation.

Each science is from the point of view of contents a group of interrelated concepts. Some of these groups give us certain indications of the nature of their interrelatedness. Physics seems to be capable of being organized mathematically and almost deductively though the time to organize it deductively may not yet be ripe. With further advance in physics it might be possible to start with certain fundamental principles from which the whole body of physics can be deduced. If so, this group of concepts can become a deductive system. Are the other branches of concepts like physics? Then again there is old question of the interrelatedness of the different group of concepts. Is it possible in future to have an encyclopaedia as systematic and deductive as *Principia Mathematica* so that starting with certain sciences others can be deduced? Some years ago there was the question as to whether biology could be deduced from physics. Although the problem has been laid aside or dissolved for a number of years, it does not seem to have been solved, and with further advance in thought, it may be brought forth again. What the answers to these questions are we do not know, but whatever they are, they reflect the interrelatedness of possibilities and universals. The scientific answers to scientific questions reveal the pattern in accordance with which concrete reality unfolds itself. The object of scientific knowledge is not something apart from reality, it is not its "phenomena" or "appearance" and still it is the universal aspects of reality, it is not something from which reality differs.

# VI

In this section we shall take up particulars and individual objects or events. Particulars are distinquished from particular or individual objects or events in that the former are an aspect and the latter are concrete wholes, the former can be pointed to, named or referred to, while strictly speaking the latter can not be expressed since they house or contain the inexpressible x. We shall take up the particulars first. As we have already said a particular is different from an universal only in that it is a particular, it remains an aspect. By itself it is as "bodiless" as an universal. An aspect is particular when it is uniquely a certain position in time and location in space. A set or a nexus of particulars is itself a particular, so also is a series. That is to say, taken as a whole it is also uniquely its position in time and location in space. The composition of a set or a nexus or a series of particulars lies therefore in the scaffolding of space-time, not in the pattern of universals which we discussed in the last section. Since a set or a nexus or a series of particulars is itself a particular, it would be simpler for us to speak merely of particulars. A particular does not endure in time, since it does not persist beyond the period of time for which it is a particular into another period for which it isn't a particular. A particular is finite, that is to say, there is no particular that occupies a point-instant, nor any that occupies the whole of space-time. A particular can not change since there is no difference in one particular, nor any identity in two particular. Since it can not change, it can not move either. Sometimes we say for instance that this glass has a particular shade of blue, since the glass has been here for a few months and been moved from one place to another, the particular shade of blue might be supposed to have changed and moved. But if we take the whole life of the glass in question to be the period for which the shade of blueness is a particular, this single particular has neither changed nor moved. In this case we are simply taking the whole period as a simple unit of time during which there may be a succession of other particulars but obviously no change of that single particular, since that unit of time does not succeed itself. Similarly its location in space. Each particular we must remember is both a particular and a set or nexus or a series of particulars. The particular shade of blueness for the whole life of the glass is one particular in one sense, and a set or a nexus or a series of particulars in another sense in which there may be darker shades as distinquished from the lighter shades of blue none of which has changed or moved. No particular is so simple as to cease to be a set or nexus or a series of particulars, or so complex as to cease to be a single particular. There is no ultimate simplicity or complexity to a particular.

Conversely a given position in time at a given location in space is the particular there is at that position and location in the sense that it can not be anywhere else. For the moment let us separate conceptually the scaffolding from the particulars that occupy it. Particulars are aspects and as such they act and react upon each other in accordance with natural laws. Each is in a complex of internal relations other than the external relations of time and space. Since a particular can not change or move or persist beyond its time it can hardly be said to <u>have</u> such and such, it can only be said to be such and such. With regard to an individual object, we may say that under such and such influence it has changed, but with regard to any particular we can only say that under such and such influence it ceases to be. The influence mentioned is either the operation of natural laws or the co-temporalness or co-spatiality of other particulars. A particular is not merely a relational property of internal relations but also a relational property of external relations. Change the position of the ink bottle on this desk, you have a different set of particulars. To borrow a term often used in political science each particular is a status quo. Change the status in any way, you have also myriads of death and birth of myriads of particulars. We are trying here to exhibit a certain kind of organicity of particulars in which any change in reality whatsoever brings not merely changes of objects and events, but also births and deaths of particulars. It isn't that a particular has gone through certain changes and to the presence of other particulars, it is rather that some die and others are born, the moment other particulars are introduced. That is to say, with regard to particulars, each is because the others are. This organicity is not limited to the particulars as such, for since each particular is its position and location in space-time, all the positions and locations conceptually separated from the particulars have the same organicity. Thus is the flow or passage of time we are not merely confronted with different sets of particulars we are also passing through different time-surfaces and occupying different space-time-lines. When it is said that a person is killed in New York City on Nov. 3rd. 1943, the statement sounds extremely simple, but the particular way in which that event took place is so complicated as to baffle any kind of adequate treatment on our part and that is part of the reason that we summarize the whole situation by using the phrase "in New York City on Nov 3rd. 1943". The reason why we can do so is that the organicity of particulars can be conceptually separated from the organicity of spatial and temporal positions. In practice they can not be separated. The police may reenact the event but what is reenact is not the original event.

Let us next take up individual objects and events. They are distinguished from particulars in that they are concrete wholes not aspects, and they house or contain the inexpressible x which we call Stuff. We have already said that in practice we identify an individual object or event with a set of particulars at any particular place and time. This identification is theoretically unsound. None of Hume's arguments is conclusive in establishing identity. But practically we do not have much difficulty. If we ignore the theoretical difficulties for the moment and follow the practice, we can easily see that through the identification of particulars with the scaffolding of space-time, the individual objects and events are also catalogued in it. These are the actualities that form the content of concrete reality in process, they are the things that sift through the pattern, the sun light that flashes through the window curtains. Concrete reality therefore not merely proceeds in accordance with pattern but also fills the scaffolding of spacetime with individual objects and events. The latter not only realize possibilities, but also take place at certain times and in certain spaces. They can be understood in terms of the universals they realized and assertained in terms of their position in time and their location in space. While science discovers or tries to discover the patten or the natural laws the objects and events obey, history ascertains or tries to ascertain the facts about the objects and events, namely their qualities and relations in terms of their temporal and spatial relations with other objects and events. We are here using the term scientific knowledge to mean horizonal knowledge of universal patterns, and the term historical knowledge to mean vertical knowledge of particular or general organicness. We have said something about the term "general" previously. Compare the proposition "Red Indians were in America before 1492" with the proposition "Everything heavier than air falls down in air when unsupported". The former is only general, whereas the latter is universal. History deals not only with the particular, but also with the general.

The use of terms here is sufficiently novel to merit a few words of clarification. While all branches of knowledge are involved or concerned with true propositions not all of them are interested in their discovery. Some of them are disciplines for conduct, others for service, while still others for the expression of creative impulses. Of the branches of knowledge interested in the discovery of truths, science aims at the universal, history aims at the particular and general. Obviously this distinction has little to do with books or persons. An Encyclopaedia is all of the branches of knowledge squeezed into a book and a Liebuity is a participant in a number of them. There is a history of science, it is history not science, there may be a science to history, if so, it is science not history. A scientist may be at the same time a historian, but in the capacity of a historian, he is interested in particular or general truths. A historian may be at the same time a scientist, but in his capacity as a scientist, he is interested in universal truths. What are known as social sciences now seem to be sciences in name, not sciences in fact, at least they do not seem to have become sciences yet. It seems that they have discovered no universal truth and as yet have developed no technique for discovering universal truth. Almost all of them are mixed branches of knowledge and a large part of their component is history, only what is discovered seems to be mostly general truths. We are using the term history to mean those branches of knowledge which ascertain or try to ascertain the particular and general truths. Their object is the interrelatedness of qualities and relations in terms of the scaffolding of spacetime.

What have we obtained so far? Our principle of congruence gave us a concrete world which can not be denied, no matter how skeptical one is in doing so or in trying to do so. The principles of contingency and economy supply us with a reality in process a changing temporal and spatial world diversified into individual objects and events which realize universals through the births and deaths of particulars and which are catalogued by the scaffolding of space-time. In broad outline we have essentially the world we experience. We do not bifurcate reality into the phenomenal and nonmenal or the apparent and real. While we are here not dealing with epistemology, we may tarry a bit just to say that although we admit a certain relativity of the sensed to the different classes of the sentients in terms of particulars, we do not admit any relativity of the known or the knowable to the classes of sentients as knowers in terms of the universals. That which is red is relative to men, dogs, horses, monkeys,... as different classes of sentients from the point of view of the particular that is sensed, but redness as an universal, the object of knowledge instead of sensation is not relative to the different classes of sentients as knowers. We are here speaking in terms of universals even when the subject matter of our discussion happens to be particulars. In terms of universals the world supplied by the three principles is essentially the world of our experience. There are different realities but there are neither higher or lower, nor deeper or shallower realities. There are realities for which different values might be prescribed and while as values there are different gradations, as realities none is more valuably real than any other.

The emergence or the evolution of human beings is neither

accidental nor final. It is the recognition of these that gives us our essential dignity. Just as individual human beings are stations in human life, so also is humanity a station in the unfoldment of Tao. We subscribe to some of the views expressed in Russell's *A Free Man's Worship*. The span of human life may be very long for us, but the day will inevitably come when human life itself will be just a short period in the past, a short chapter in the unfoldment of Tao. Whether after that the world turns to be inert matter or supermen succeed us seems to be quite immaterial. Although we are not final, we are not accidental either. The universe wouldn't be complete if the kind of entities that human beings are were not in it at sometime or other. During the span of human life those who are human have to try to behave as human beings, they have to struggle along to perform the function or the role expected of them, to fulfill as much as they can or to approach as near as they can to the most comprehensive and the most essential realization of humanity. None of the Golden Ages would be more valuable if they persisted, and if any persisted till eternity, it probably wouldn't be valuable at all. The destination is not more valuable than the transit, nor is the end more important than the means. It is only when the job is done in the transit that the destination becomes more valuable. Human life as a whole is like individual life, it is not the pompous funeral that gives an individual life its dignity, it is rather the way one lives one's life that makes him dignified.

# Time and Actuality

## I

The last chapter has furnished us with a world of objects changing in accordance with pattern and catalogued in the scaffolding of space-time. In terms of the pattern universals are realized and disrealized, and in terms of the scaffolding of space-time particulars appear and disappear. For each particular that appears there is an universal covering it, but since there may be a multiplicity of particulars to one universal, there is a richness to the particulars, which is denied to universals. Hence although reality unfolds itself in accordance with patterns, it has a wealth of particulars in the scaffolding of space-time that is not found in the pattern itself. Thus far we have spoken of reality in its static mood, even when we speak of the changing world or of reality in process we have restricted ourselves to changed states or stations of reality, not change or process itself. In neglecting the dynamic mood of reality. We have also neglected the acting and the acted, or in a word, the actual. We are using the term actual here to include the notion of the present. The actual is not merely reality, it is also the present reality. Composed to its theoretical version the actual is by far the richer. Let us call the appearance and disappearance of the particulars the drift. Perhaps we can approach the problem of the actual through the drift of reality more easily than through its pattern. It is through the drift of reality that objects and events act upon each other, and although when they so act upon each other in accordance with the pattern it is not the pattern that is actual. The drift is in accordance with the pattern, it obeys natural laws, but while what is obeyed or realized is a natural law or a group of natural laws, that which is there and does the obeying isn't a natural law at all, it is what we usually call fact or facts. The world is like a game of chess, and yet with all the rules of the game and the presence of pawns, the knights, the bishops and kings, a game need not actually be played, though if it were played, it obeys the rules. The question is what is there that is actual.

Ordinarily we attribute this activity to objects and events We experience the burning of the red hot coal or the scalding of the boiling water, we conclude that something there is being acted upon while the coal and the water are active. Objects change and move, events take place, and so long as it is convenient for us to identify objects and events with their nexus of particulars or sets of universals which clothe them, we might as well do so. In pratical life there is hardly any inconvenience. Theoretically there is a good deal. While objects do change and move, the nexus of particulars neither changes nor moves. The same is true of universals.

It is easy to see that other universals aside, the universal change itself doesn't change, nor does motion itself move. If objects were identified with certain nexus of particulars or certain sets of universals, they can not change or move. If they can neither change nor move, how could they act and be acted upon? The only thing that enables an object to change or move is the Stuff that is housed in it. Basically therefore it is also Stuff that is active. It may have to have the help of the nexus of particulars, or the sets of universals, just as a wearer has to make use of his clothes in order to change his appearance, but it is the Stuff or the wearer that does the changing or is active. Its activity is expressed through the entrance into and departure from possibilities.

There are two ways of entrance or departure, voluntary or involantary, unconditioned or conditioned, free or compelled. None of these terms is adequate, but the idea may be smuggled across through any pair of them. When Stuff is about to enter into or leave, or on the point of entering into or leaving a possibility we call it an occasion or Chi( 几 ). We are using the term in such a way as to rule out on the one hand what we sometimes call a "change of mind" and on the other what ever determination or purpose that may enter into the activity. We are trying to make the term as casual and factual as we can. An occasion is no more than any thing being what it has come to be, it simply becomes or is. It is not casual, nor is it purposive. It may result in the realization of a possibility that is previously unrealized, or the disrealization of a possibility that is previously realized, in which case it is an occasion concerning universals as well as particulars. The appearance and disappearance of dinosaurs in natural history belong to this category. Occasion may also result merely in the appearance or disappearance of particulars in which case it is an occasion concerning particulars alone. Thus the disappearance of the green of yesterday and the appearance of the red of today in the history of an apple belong to the second category. Since all occasions concerns the appearance or disappearance of particulars, it is with the second category that we are more con-cerned here.

An occasion is not an object or an event, it is not an univer-val, neither is it a particular. An occasion is not an object, since it is an activity, and while objects are active, they are not activi-ties. Although it is an activity, it is not an event. In the last anal-ysis, events are entrance into or departure of Stuff from possibili-ties. Events may be comparatively simple or comparatively complex, in which case, you have either simple combinations of entrances or departures or else comparatively complex combinations of entrances or departures. An occasion is not an entrance into or departure of Stuff from possibilities, it is that state in which either is about to or on the point of taking place. If one watches the Leaning Tower without any knowledge of the fact that it has stood for centuries, one may have a sense of something impending, somthing about to happen or on the point of happening that is distinct from the sense of the happening of that something when it does happen. Only in the case of our present notion of occasion, it is always accompanied by entrance into and departure of Stuff from possibilities, since we have ruled out any "change of mind". That an occasion is not itself an universal need not be dwelt upon at all. It is not a particular either. A particular is an aspect, it is like an universal in being an aspect, its expression is adjectival or adverbial, it adheres to objects and events. While an occasion is not an aspect, and it can not be said to adhere to objects and events. Perhaps what is even more important is that a particular is what is catalogued in the scaffolding of space and time, it is of the flotsam and jetsam of the flow of time, not the flow itself; whereas as we shall see in a few paragraphs hence occasions are a part of the flow itself.

The change or motion of an object is always accompanied by its occasion in so far as it is occasioned. No change or motion takes place before the appropriate occasion, not after it. The former is obvious, since before Stuff can enter into or depart from a possibility, it must have had that state of being on the point of entering into or departing from a possibility. It is more difficult to see why change or motion doesn't take place after the appropriate occasion. Our terms "about to" and "on the point of" are inadequate, they suggest a temporal sequence of purpose precedent to action or of action subsequent to purpose. What we need are terms that do not suggest this temporal sequence and we do not know of any such terms. It is here that we need the term "appropriate" to introduce the idea that given any change or motion that is not preordained, there is an appropriate occasion. A change or motion can not take place after its own appropriate occasion simply because if it did, it might be detached from its own appropriate occasion, it might then be without its own occasion or occasioned by something that isn't its own appropriate occasion. What is urged is that there is a one-one correspondence between occasions on the one hand and changes or motions on the other so that for each motion or change that is occasioned, there is an appropriate occasioning and no change or motion that is occasioned is either before or after its appropriate occasion. Just as the world is eternally changing, Stuff is eternally occasioning. There is no temporal sequence between changes and motions on the one hand and their appropriate occasion on the other.

Neither is the occasion the purpose of its appropriate change or motion. No purpose is implied in the notion of occasion. Occasions are random efforts of Stuff. Neither are they caused. They certainly are not caused in the sense that they are inferable from previous occasions in accordance with causal laws. If we take the world at $T_1$ and the world at $T_2$, no matter how short the interval may be, we can easily see that the first does not cause the second. There is no caused law in terms of which these worlds could be subsumed and their relation inferred. Besides both are wholes hence neither happens in a background for which the problem of similarity arises, simply because there is no background whatsoever. Hence the occasion appropriate to the world at $T_1$ does not cause the occasion appropriate to the world at $T_2$. An event A in the world at $T_1$ and an event B in the world at $T_2$

may be causally related, if so, the occasion favours the realization of a certain causal law and not certain others. We merely say that the occasion favours the realization of a certain causal law, we do not say that the occasion appropriate to A causes the occasion appropriate to B. As occasions go, B need never be occasioned. That it does happen under hypothesis merely indicates that it favours the realization of a certain causal law. The causal relation that is appropriate to events is not appropriate to occasions. In terms of causal relations, an occasion is uncaused. If it be said that is caused by Stuff, we are simply asserting that in so far as anything else is concerned, it is uncaused. And to say that Stuff causes its own occasion is to say nothing at all.

Since an occasion is neither caused nor is it purposive, it can not be known before hand. So far as occasions are concerned, the world is free. It is free not merely in the sense that our knowledge is not comprehensive enough or detailed enough to predict beforehand what is going to happen, but free in the sense that the world is fundamentally undetermined beforehand so far as occasions are concerned. This has nothing to do with Heisenberg, nor is it a denial of the option of natural laws or causal relations in the world of objects and events. Objects and events must obey natural laws and given the appropriate similarity of conditions obtaining at any time and place, the realization of some law might even be predicted with such an overwhelming degree of probability as to make it approach to certainty. But as to which of the laws is to be realized there is no predetermination so far as occasions are concerned. The certainty of prediction may be approached but it can not be reached. We must not confuse occasions with the operation of natural laws. The operation of natural laws is indeed obligatory, but the operation of any one natural law at a certain time and place is not itself under the operation of natural laws. If I am hungry, I am bound to eat, but I am not bound to eat at 11 : 58. If you say that the operation of other laws result in my eating at 11 : 58, you are not taking any one of them separately and are assuming at the same time that the actual conditions are such as to favour the operation of some of them so as to result in my eating at 11 : 58. The latter is begging the question from the point of view of occasions since from that point of view the similar conditions given in the argument needn't be given at all, and are only given because they are occasioned.

We have thus far treated Chi or occasion from the point of view of Stuff or its activity. Neither Stuff nor its activity is directly experienced by us, and the notion treated in terms of either is liable to be unfamiliar. Fortunately we needn't restrict ourselves to this way of speaking. We have already spoken of an occasion as being appropriate to a changing individual or a moving object. If we take the point of view of the individual object, we find the occasion appropriate to it to be essentially what we sometimes call luck. The notion of luck implies subjectivity and since we take point of view of the individual object to which the occasion is appropriate, we have the subjectivity of the individual object. In the preceding paragraphs we have no such subjectivity and we can speak of occasions only in terms of Stuff and its activity. By bringing in this subjectivity we can easily see that occasion is transformed into luck. The notion of luck is essentially that of the occasion, it contains that element of "needn't be", but simply "is". To some individual object, it also contains the element of good or bad, favorable or unfavorable, but for the present, we needn't dwelt on that.

## II

Unlike Chī or occasion, Shū or pre-ordination is when Stuff shall enter into or depart from possibilities. As we have already said, the entrance into and the departure from possibilities may be voluntary or involuntary, unconditioned or conditioned, free or compelled, and we have already pointed out that these are inadequate terms. They are especially so in relation to Shū or pre-ordination. We use the term "shall" to mean free and yet decided. The word "will" might be used, but in order to avoid the whole doctrince of free will, we prefer something that is not quite so rich in its implications. What is intended to convey is that on the one hand Stuff is free to enter into and to depart from a possibility and yet on the other it has decided to enter into and depart from one rather than any other possibility. It is free in the sense that it is not determined by anything else, and decided in the sense that it is not casual; that is to say, it is not compelled, but compelling. The flavour of decision herein attributed to pre-ordination furnishes us with the sense that whether a certain course is wise or not, it is yet to be pursued rather than merely entertained or considered. Since an enormous amount of decisions are made as practical measures without conviction or faith or previous knowledge of their consequences, the flavour of decision need not contain the complicated notions which the terms "will to believe" or "will to live" often imply. We may also start from the other way around by considering pre-ordination from the point of view of the changing or moving objects. To them pre-ordination is something that can not be helped, it just will happen, and the psychological state to receive it is either bland acceptance as if it is properly due when it is favorable or indifference, or resignation when it is unfavorable or even disastrous. While an occasion is something that simply is actually, pre-ordination is something that actually can not keep being.

The above attempt at a clarification of the notion of pre-ordination may enable us to distinguish it from other things and these distinctions again may clarify the notion. Like an occasion, pre-ordination is not an object or event or an universal or particular. We need not go into these again since the distinction between these and occasion holds equally between them and pre-ordination. What it might be confused with more than anything else perhaps is the effect of the operation of a natural law. If A—B is a natural law and "a" happens at $t_1$ and let's say "b" happens at $t_2$, the pre-ordination appropriate to "b" $t_2$ may be said to be merely the effect of the operation of the law A—B. The event "b" $t_2$ is the effect of the natural law. It is the effect of the operation of A—B with the help of the appropriate background S in which A—B operates. But if we left ourselves out of the activities, that is to say, if we do not let our ideas be bound by them, we see no reason why S should be realized so that A—B operates instead of let us say A—C another law which might operate under a set of conditions different from S. Hence although the event "b" $t_2$ is the effect of the operation of a certain naturall law under the given circumstances, the pre-ordination appropriate to b $t_2$ is not, since it is a part of the pre-ordinations or occasions responsible for those circumstances as well. The effect of a natural law requires something given, whereas pre-ordination requires nothing given and is responsible for the given. Every move on the chess board obeys rules, but that any one move should be actually made is not a question of rules, it is either casually made or made with decision. With regard to every event there is an element that is casual or else an element that savors of decision. We call the former Chī or occasion, and the latter Shū or pre-ordination. It is these elements that chose the possibilities to be actualized at a certain time and place. If natural laws themselves chose the actual, civilization would have been impossible, and it would have been impossible, if natural laws were not operative. Civilization requires a certain maneuverability of the given so that natural laws can operate towards the achievement of the end desired.

We have already said that the actualities are realities, but they are not co-extensive with realities, since some realities can be said to be non-actual. Confuscius is in some sense real though he is no longer actual. Some astronomical realities are actual while others are not. The actual is always the existent, it has the element of now, and if we are talking of local actualities, it has the additional element of the here as well. The actual is that which is acting. Taking any slice of time as the present, there is a whole world that is actual, a world of objects and events that act and react upon each other. Since activity is not itself an object or an event it can only work through the actualities as its medium or through the objects and events as its instrument. Objects and events can not however function as instruments through their universals or particulars, since the former can not be said to be here and now, while the latter is being so uniquely here and now can neither move or change. Basically activity is that of Stuff and Stuff is active in two ways, either through occasions or through pre-ordinations. When it is said in the last paragraph that it is these activities that chose the actualities we also mean that it is they that chose what universals are to be realized and what particulars are to appear at the present. Like all realities actualities obey natural laws, but which of the laws is to be obeyed is not itself the operation of a natural law. Hence while actualities obey natural laws, their being actual is not the effect of the operation of a natural law. This may at least be one sense in which we sometimes say that while we can describe nature we cannot explain it.

Perhaps we can make use of the difference between implication and inference to make the above point clearer. Implication is expressed by a series of if-then statements in which whether the implican or the implicate is separately true or not is irrelevant. But if any inference is to be drawn some implican has to be asserted to be true. The truth of the implican is not supplied by the implications, it is drawn elsewhere. Natural laws are knitted into a pattern very much like the interrelatedness of propositions connected by if-then relations. Any genuine universal proposition is expressed in the form of an if-then sentence. The presence of the actual is like the truth of the second premise to a traditional hypothetical argument, if it is not given in the manner of the truth of the second premise being asserted, no conclusion can be drawn hence no inference made. Just as a whole set of hypothetical major premises do not yield a conclusion, so the whole set of natural laws do not allow us to infer what actuality is any particular time or place. The actual obeys the natural laws in the sense that with the truth of the second premise given, the conclusion is inevitably arrived at, it is not determined by natural laws in the sense that the truth of the second premise is not contained in the natural laws themselves, the actual can only be inferred from the natural laws with the actual given. This is the fundamental stubbornness we find in facts. So far as occasions and pre-ordinations are concerned, we are faced with the purely given. We can not do anything with it other than to accept it, and therein lies the stubbornness of the given. When it is said that we may explain facts, but we can not explain them away, part of what is meant may very well be that feeling of stubbornness involved in actualizations that obey natural laws and are yet not dictated by any of them, that are no more intelligible than any other possible alternatives and that no matter how intelligible the other alternatives may be they are yet not actual here and now.

Unlike occasions pre-ordinations can be known before hand. They are known partly through the operation of natural laws, and partly through the actualization of the background favorable for the operation of certain natural law against certain others. They may not as matter of fact be predicted, but they are predictable. The reading of actuality may mislead us, and the reasoning may be faulty, but otherwise pre-ordinations may be predicted with some degree of accuracy. The usual inference from cause to effect is both a reading of the actual in terms of causal relations and a prediction of pre-ordinations. Rules may be adopted for doing so and the prevailing theory of relativity helps us to correlate time and space in such away that given the time interval certain space distances become irrelevant and vice versa. Calculation fails more and more in proportion to the increase of time or space intervals between events. Hence prediction is more or less limited to localities under certain limited time intervals. The point to be emphasized here however is that prediction is not merely based on what we call usually the operation of natural laws, it is also a prediction of pre-ordinations through the reading of the actual.

There is a drift as well as a pattern in the actual, and the drift of the actual indicates pre-ordinations if correctly gauged. We are here essentially advocating the common sense view that in order to be able to know the future to any extent we have to know the past and the present. Only in our language we say that the actual indicates pre-ordinations. In order to pre-dict pre-ordinations we have to know natural laws as well, but knowing them is not sufficient. Here again we may return to a point already mentioned, reality proceeds in accordance with pattern, but it is not propelled by pattern; it is post facts intelligible, but not anti facts rational. Besides pre-ordinations there are occasions as well. The sum total of circumstances relevant to a given locality together with the operation of certain laws toward which these circumstances are favourable indicate pre-ordinations relevant to that locality.

To the individual object or event, the pre-ordination appropriate to it is its fate. We have already pointed out that the occasion appropriate to an individual is its luck. Just as an occasion is different from pre-ordination, so luck is different from fate. One difference is felt by the kind of individual, who are endowed with feeling and intelligence. Though related and relevant to the individual alike, luck is external while fate is internal to the individual. An individual without his luck remains that individual whereas an individual without his fate may often be not quite that individual. Luck is what happens to an individual whereas fate is what is bound to happen to an individual, it is a part of his character that actuates his fate. Fighting against one's luck is some-times rediculous sometimes comical, since one is often outside the conflict as a spectator, but fighting against one's fate is always a tragedy since one is always fighting against one's self. Luck is what needn't be but somehow is, whereas fate is always bound to be. Just as luck may be good or bad, so also fate, but we shall not dwell on these aspects. We have been talking of the kind of individuals endowed with feeling and intelligence so as to bring out the difference of feeling attached to luck and fate, but the more general way of speaking is not to limit ourselves to these individuals. We have seen the change or motion that is occasioned does not come before or after its appropriate occasion, we may say that no change or motion that is pre-ordained can es-cape its pre-ordination. This is another way of saying that no indi-vidual whether endowed with intelligence and feeling or not can escape its fate whether it is good or bad.

## III

We have already said that the metaphysical principle has provided us with time. This is perfectly true. Time is however quite complex, and although we shall leave a number of senses untouched, we still have to admit a number of senses in order to do whatever minimal justice there may be to the subject. We have already distinguished the content of time from its scaffolding. Al-though analogies are misleading we might indulge in them to some extent in order to smuggle certain ideas across. Time may be likened to the railroad together with the running train. The road bed together with milestones is like the scaffolding and the train together with whatever there is in it is some what like the content. The scaffolding of time is static if one views it from the outside, its Januaries or Februaries are like the milestones of the road bed. It becomes dynamic only when viewed from the content of time just as the milestones on the road bed run away from us when we are on the train that runs over the road bed. But the content has also two elements, the flow and what is carried in the flow just as the running train consists of running on the one hand and on the other the train and everything that is carried in it. Analogies should not be pushed too far or else dissimilarities will spoil the picture, and ideas other than those that are meant to be conveyed may be brought alone to confuse the issue. Don't think of the train that goes back and forth or the bare track with no running train on it. Time is a one way traffic.

The content of time then consists of the pure flow and the flotsam or jetsam in it. The former is the series of occasions and pre-ordinations and the latter is the sum total factualities. The content is always in the present and the flow is irreversable. Such terms as "about to", "on the point of", "shall" used in our discussion of occasions and pre-ordinations are inadequate in some significant senses, but they have the virtue of indicating genuine becoming instead of that which becomes or that which has come to be. The actualities are the realizations or disrealizations of universals, the appearance or disappearance of particulars in the history of objects or events. The time-content is a flow of occasions and pre-ordinations loaded with actualities, it is same old reality in process viewed from the actual and the present, it is congruent, contingent, economical, as well as in accordance with pattern and eternally drifting into a wealth of co-temporal and co-spatial nexus of particulars. This is the content of time as distinguished from its scaffolding. Since there are occasions and pre-ordinations to the flow, there are also luck and fate. Quite apart from intelligence and feeling, there is relativity and subjectivity among objects and events in their relations to each other. A landslide brings a change of course to a stream, let us say. In actuality, it is more relevant to some one mountain or hill as well as to some one stream. So also are occasions and pre-ordinations. They are more relevant to some than to others and in that relevancy we have to distinguish congeniality or uncongeniality. The occasion or pre-ordination appropriate to the landslide in uncongenial to the mountain or hill from the point of view of that mountain's or that hill's continued and comparatively unchanged existence and it may be congenial to a number of other things in the sense that it favoured their continued existence such as flowers and trees that were formerly too shaded and are now directly under the sun. While actualities are congruent, the interrelations of the different items in them are not all congenial or uncongenial.

We shall cease to speak in terms of occasions and pre-ordinations and for convenience sake we shall only speak of time under the proviso that it means the content and the flow as distinguished from the scaffolding. In terms of congenialities or uncongenialities, time retains certain items of what is carried and throws overboard certain others. That is to say, some survive and others perish. In between there are all sorts of degrees of changes varying from those that are extremely slight to these that are quite radical and all, including survival and perishing, are indicated through the appearance or disappearance of particulars. The perishing or survival is often predicated of individual objects, for example: "As a result of the landslide, a certain mountain or hill disappeared". That mountain is regarded as an individual object and so regarded it means more than a particular, but while it is more than a particular, its disappearance is none the less also the disappearance of a particular. The change of an individual object is usually expressed in terms of the appearance and disappearance of particulars, for example: "The apply which was green yesterday is now entirely red." Here we regard the apple as the individual object, green or red as the particular that disappears or appears. In terms of perishing and survival, however, we may just as well say that the apple survived while the green object perished. At any rate as time flows, particulars appear and disappear and individuals survive or perish. Survival and perishing may appear in two ways, in one of them it is merely the individual that survives or perishes, while in the other the species to which the individuals belong also survives or perishes. In the latter case we have the appearance and disappearance of species

147

of the kind that happens in natural history. Distinguishing an object or an event from its environment we can easily see that time brings forth relative to each object or event an environment with some elements that are congenial and others that are not. This is merely another way of saying that actualities act and react on each other in a way favourable to some and unfavourable to others. Some survive and others perish, some are the cargos of time while others are its flotsam and jetsam.

This notion of time is not contrary to certain significant usages in ordinary life. When it is said that the time has come to talk of many things, it does not mean that it is now twelve o'clock or March 15$^{th}$ 1944. It means that certain potentialities of the kind described are about to be actual in an errivonment in which the given actualities point to their immediate actualization. Whether the "time" has come to talk of cabbages and kings, or to leave your host and go home, or to start a revolution or merely to smoke a pipe, what is meant is that the flow of time will carry with it the actualization of the potentialities described by these phrases. Then again we sometimes speak of a good time or a bad time. It is not the scaffolding that is meant and although it is not the pure flow that is meant either, it is yet the flow together with what is carried in it. When we say that "in 'times' like those when we are fighting for our very lives, we should not expect to eat as well as we did ordinarily", or "if we read the signs of the 'time' correctly, we...", we are talking of the flow of time together with some of the actualities in it. Something in time is said to be good or bad, or else it is such that certain behavior which might be described as moral or intelligent is called for, or yet it is such that relative to certain measures should be adopted. There is in time a sort of internecine relationship between actualities in which there is subjectivity relative to certain things and objectivity relative to certain other things, so that there is also a conglomeration or convergence of congenialities and uncongenialities. When uncongenialities cut balance than congenialities for an individual, for that individual the time is about over. When a man declares that his time is over, it does not mean any stoppage of the flow of time, it means that he is about to be jettisoned out of the actualities into the limbo of the past.

Time then is essentially an evolutionary process. It is the basic element in what we call in these papes reality in process. It is that flow in which all things change, some survive, others perish, and all the changes take place in terms of particulars that appear or disappear or else of possibilities realized or universals disrealized. We are here merely describing time as evolution, not propounding any specific theory of evolution, or tracing its history. As to what survive, or what they survive from, or whether in the process there is progress or not, or if there were, what is the criterion, etc. are not questions with which we are here concerned. Nor do we start with certain remote ages, for no matter how remote they may be, they can not be as remote as the beginning of time since for us time has no beginning. Whatever age natural history choses for its starting point of its subject matter, there was time before that age and therefore also evolution. It does not stop with the emergence of men, nor with the arrival of the $20^{th}$ century. What we are talking now is not a segment of time nor is our actuality confined to the surface of the earth. Since we are essentially talking of reality in process, we are also talking of the unfoldment of Tao. To indicate that time is an evolutionary process is also to say that there is evolution going on in Tao's unfoldment. We may as well say that all the contingent possibilities will be realized in the evolution and this is simply another way of saying that time is endless.

Time as evolution is an infinite process in which all sorts of things imaginable and conceivable will happen. Whatever is imaginable or conceivable is a possibility and unless it is an eternally unrealizable possibility, it will be realized, and unless it is a necessary or an eternally realized possibility, it will be realized in time. This statement is very likely staggering to some, it certainly sounds incredible. Let us try to make it clear by ruling out that it does not mean and finding out that which it does mean. One thing it does not mean is that all sorts of imaginable or conceivable will happen in what we sometimes call "this world". Whatever this world may mean, it is a slice of time from $t_n$ to $t_m$. Whether we speak of geological ages or astronomical ages, or merely in terms of historical ages or even generations, we are merely assigning values to n and m. If their difference is large, we have a long slice of time and if it is small, we have a short one. In any case what we are really talking about when we talk about this world is merely the sum total of actualities of a slice or a period of time and in that world or during that slice of time, some things happen and others don't. But even in such a world lots of imaginable and conceivable things have happened which we have not imagined or conceived and although lots of things may happen in any such world, we can not say something imagined or conceived, let us say x, will happen, because $t_m$ may come before x happens no matter how distant $t_m$ may be from the time x is imagined or conceived. There is no obligation on this part of $t_m$ to postpone its arrival until x happens. When we say ordinarily that certain things will happen or not, we have surreptitiously or unconsciously set limits to time in which it is expected to happen or not be happen. When universal peace is said to be possible or impossible, a certain time limit is brought along with the question or statement. It is doubtful whether most people world be interested in world peace if it comes in ten thousand years. One should not be surprised if the assumed limit of time for most people interested to universal peace is the peace immediately after the present war.

If no time limit is set, the problem is quite different. Anything possible(other than the eternally unrealizable possibilities) will be realized in infinite time, because so long as it is not realized, time simply flows merrily on without limit, it is only when the possibility is realized that a limit to time is set, namely, the time of the realization of the possibility in question. It was, I think, Eddington who suggested that given infinite time a monkey will be able to type out mechanically without knowing what he is doing, let's say Keats' *Ode to the Grecian Urn*, provided he does not repeat himself. This may not be accomplished in billions and billions of years, but it will be accomplished in infinite time, because if it weren't accomplished in any finite period of time, typing goes on endlessly, the only limit set is the typing of the *Ode*. The same thing is true of the realization of any possibility that is not itself eternally unrealizable. The statement that such a possibility will be realized in infinite time does not mean much practically or positively, since it includes the possibility that the said possibility in question may not be realized in any finite time. It may not be realized that is to say in $t_n$—$t_m$ no matter how large the difference between m and n is, provided it is finite. To people speaking in the context of ordinary life, this means that some possibilities simply won't be realized. The statement that all imaginable and conceivable things will be realized in infinite time carries with it a number of assumptions, one of which is that reality like history does not repeat itself, or that if it does give the impression of doing so, it does so with a slight similarity of pattern and not identity in drift. Most likely there are other assumptions, but we shall not try to enumerate them here. Time is an infinite flow, that is, it flows ad infinitum partly because the universe is taken to be infinitely rich in variety and more things happen in it than we can ever imagine or conceive.

# IV

With the above in mind we can see that in the unfoldment of Tao or in reality and process, an infinity of things have happened and an infinity of things will yet happen unless it is something that is impossible, or if possible, eternally unrealizable. Speaking from the point of view of some slice of time as the present, anything will be realized in infinite time. We can not say when certain things will happen, but that they will happen sometime or other does not seem to be open to doubt. The attitude here taken needs a bit of further clarification from another angle. We do not attribute the existence of things or the emergence of actualities to the propulsion of any transcendental reason, or the will of a transcendental God, or the fulfilment of a transcendental purpose. Since Tao is co-extensive with the universe, there can not be anything transcendental to Tao or to its unfoldment, if there is, it is something that is a part of Tao, or something that functions in the unfoldment of Tao and if it is transcendental it is so only to some of things in reality or process. Since all sorts of things happen in the unfoldment of Tao, all sorts of values will emerge in it. In this section we shall deal with the emergence of purpose and mind. It can be easily seen that Tao is neither purposive or non-purposive, neither knowing or conceiving nor not knowing or not conceiving. But since purpose may emerge in the unfoldment of Tao in so far as it emerges the unfoldment in which it emerges becomes partly purposive. The same is true of the emergance of the mind. Tao unfolds itself through the vehicle of the actualities. Nothing can be predicated of Tao-one, while all that can be predicated of the actualities separately is but a functioning of Tao-infinite. If Tao can not be said to be purposeful itself, it must be admitted at the same time that it can not but have purposefulness in the unfoldment.

"Purpose" is most generally used to mean desire or need together with the adoption of means toward its satisfaction. In some of the ways in which the term is used it involves consciousness, but since we shall discuss the emergence of mind separately, we might as well rule out consciousness as one of the ingredients. We shall limit the term purpose to mean certain ends to be achieved by certain means whether the latter is consciously adopted or not. In this sense, the ends are purposes and the means are the purposive or purposeful action or activities. Thus the bending of the stalk of a sun flower toward the Sun is purposeful, because it can be said to be indulged in to achieve an end, namely, the facing of the flower toward the Sun. The emergence of purpose brings with it the emergence of the individual capable of purpose as well as of purposive act. These belong to the realm of objects and events. They are different from other objects only through having purpose so far as our discussion is concerned. Purposes involving needs may be considered to be comparatively primitive while these involving policies complex. It is possible to have a gradation of purposes from the comparatively simple to the comparatively complex, but even so it does not mean that evolution proceeds in accordance with that gradation. While a theory of progress may be maintained in relation to specific aspects within certain areas and for a period of time in the scaffolding of space and time, it can hardly be maintained universally. A criterion of value may be adopted upon which values may be assigned to purposes and it is possible to have a gradation of values from the almost valuable to the enimently valuable. Here again we may note that while a progressive growth in valuation may take place in limited spheres, an universal theory of an all pervading growth can hardly be maintained. The adequacy of means to end may be compared and a scale of adequacy might be urged, but again while adequacy might be gained from the point of view of certain aspects at the expense perpaps of certain other aspects, an universal increase in adequacy along all lines can hardly be read into the evolutionary process of time.

That purpose will emerge in time, we have a doubt after what has been said about time has been made clear. Purposiveness is a possibility, the corresponding concept of which is not contradictory, nor is it such that it is eternally unrealizable. Hence it is a contingent possibility. The realization is contingent from the point of view of any particular time or place, it is not contingent in the sense that it may never be realized. In one way of speaking there is no contingent possibility that will be realized, that is why we say that the sum total of contingent possibilities will be realized as time flows into infinity. The emergence of purpose is dependable, but as to when it is to emerge is quite a different question, and one in which we are not interested, it being a question of history. That there is purpose now is merely a question of fact. Nor are we interested in how long purposiveness stays. There is no reason why it should not stay for a long time, neither is there any why it should stop rather abruptly. There has been ages of inert matters in the past, and there is no reason why it shouldn't be any in future. It must be understood that we are talking factuatizations and actualities of the stations of process separately, not of the unfoldment of Tao as a whole. The latter can hardly be said to be purposive or nonpurposive, it may be said to be neither or both. When the actualities cease to include purposive individuals, it does not mean that the whole unfoldment of Tao ceases to be purposive just as when glacial ages of inert matter returns, the whole unfoldment of Tao does not thereby become inert. The emergence of purpose affects the interrelations of the actualities, it disturbs the congenialities or uncongenialities of the entities in the actual, it does not modify the unfoldment of Tao itself.

With the emergence of purpose something most significent happened. There is a minimal bifurcation of reality, a faint separation of the self from the others, or a slight demarcation of the inside from the outside. The whole world of reality actualized at any particular time and place is no longer quite lumpy with the emergence of purpose, some of the items in the actualities set themselves apart, not indeed in the sense of taking themselves out of time and space, but in the sense of introducing subjectivity. Since we are not associating purpose with mind, or consciousness, the bifurcation is not conscious and therefore not pronounced, at least not so pronounced as when purposes is aided by mind. But bifurcation is there just the same. The adoption of means towards ends whether conscious or not means that ends would not be accomplished if means were not adopted, hence it means a modification of that part of reality that is other, but not self, or that is outside, but not inside, or that is object but not the subject. The capacity to adopt means to ends is often accompanied by the capacity to avoid what is harmful. The objectified reality is modified in any case in the direction of what the subjectified reality wants or needs we should not discuss the success or failure in these modifications of the objectified reality. We want to point out rather that no matter how much or how little modifications there may be, it is only the objectified reality that is modified, reality in the sense of the non-bifurcated totality remains unmodified, it is what it is in the sense that whatever inovations there are they are what occasions and pre-ordinations have actualized them to be.

The term is used in a large number of sense and elaborate theories may be proposed for any of them. We shall use the term here to mean the capacity to abstract, to symbolize and to apply the abstract or symbolic to various data (that of sense included). If one has such capacity, one has a mind. It is something that may or may not function, but if or when it does, its function is entirely intellectual, and it is so quite irrespective of degrees of intellectuality. In this sense a number of animals seems to be endowed with minds since their capacity to symbolize and abstract is undoubted as they do apply the abstract and symbolic to their data. The emergence of mind like the emergence of purpose can be counted on. Again it is not a question of when it does appear. If the world is capable of waiting, it might have waited for ages and ages for the appearance of mind, and it might have waited in vain in all those ages. That we have it now is essentialy a point of historical interest quite devoid of philosophical significance. It may also disappear all together or disappear only to appear again under quite different conditions, that is to say, in a context of actualities different from these that are actual here and now. There is no worry that the world will always be without minds, neither is there any that it will always be burdened with minds. Although needs and desires need not be associated with mind, minds are associated with needs or desires. Thinking involves the urge to do so, and knowing involves the desire or need for knowing. Even knowing for knowing's sake is merely a case where knowing is itself and end. While mind is active, its activity is not itself directed towards the modification of the objectified reality. What is aimed at is rather what we call understanding of the objectified world. A thorough knowledge of that world leaves it as it was or is or is going to be, that is, it leaves it unmodified. The emergence of the mind also bifurcates reality but while the emergence bifurcates it into the agent and patient, the emergence of

mind bifurcates it into the known object and the knowing subject.
The emergence of purpose and that of mind are both significent, each in its own way. But when they are combined, that is,
when individuals emerge endowed with purpose as well as with
mind, the interrelations of actualities in terms of their congenialities or uncongenialities are enormously changed. Purpose without
mind is sometimes effective sometimes ineffective and must of necessity be limited to purposive activities of limited scope. Mind
without purpose (other than purely cognitive) merely distinguishes
the knowing from the known, by itself it results in no
modification of the known in any way. But when these are combined, the adequacy and the scope of the means adopted towards
the ends are both increased by the help of mind, purpose
becomes comprehensive, complex and effective. With mind and
knowledge it is possible to have a series of ends and means such
that the end may be the means to other ends and the means may
be the end to other means. The longer the series of means, the
more far-removed and complex the end, and the more likely also
it is to mistake the intermediat means to be themselves the ends.
The link of the means to each other may be based on knowledge,
or on what is believed to be knowledge or on what is imagined to
be knowledge without its being so, hence the adequacy of means
towards ends may not be uniformly increased, but the scope is
bound to be enlarged when purpose is combined with mind.
Values may come in to complicate the issue. Upon some criterion
of valuation, the end may be eminently valuable while the means

might be condemned. Moral problems or issus there may ever be, if mind were not joined with purpose. If there ever was any original sin, it was the alliance of mind with purpose, but then it was through their alliance that both virture and vice are realized. Enormous number of other things emerge with the combined emergence of mind and purpose culture is born, artifacts are created, politics, ethics and various sciences make realities more complicated than ever before. But we shall not dwell on any of these, important as they are from the point of view of the growth of civilization. From the point of view of time as an infinite evolutionary process, there is no reason why civilization should endure. Quite a different kind of world, or a different kind of civilization may be actualized through future occasions and pre-ordination.

What we want to emphasize is rather that reality is more dichotomized with the combined emergence of purpose and mind than by either of them alone. Let us call the bifurcated realities the object and the subject realities. It is easy to have the agent and patient relation of these two realities exaggerated. Mind and knowledge enable the subject-reality to be much more of an agent than purpose alone does, hence the object-reality becomes also much more of a patient. On the part of agent, it is easy to feel or to be emotionally turned to the feeling that almost anything could be done to the patient in the direction of transforming it to suit the desires or needs of the agent. In doing so, the agent or the subject-reality is lifted out of the world of existents or actualities or realities, it becomes their ruler and a despotic one at that. A good deal can be said for the ascendancy of mind and purpose. An enormous amount of modification of object-reality may have been accomplished, an enormous number of artifacts may have been created, values relative to the purpose of the subject-reality may be assigned to their modification, creative progress might be maintained and satisfactions might be felt in various lines of endeavor. But the demarcation between object and subject realities becomes more pronounced, their separation becomes further and further apart and a sort of bloated self importance of the agent may easily become the result. It is also easy to feel that in modifying the object reality, the subject reality is also modifying the whole reality in process or the unfoldment of Tao. The latter is not the case. Mind and purpose are possibilities, they themselves are actualized through occasions and pre-ordinations and what ever modification or creation there may be as a result of the emergence of mind and purpose are also actualized by occasions and pre-ordinations and the whole subject reality is not any exception. The unfoldment of Tao is just as responsible for the modification of the object reality as the subject reality, since it is responsible for the latter as well.

# V

It is about time to say something about human beings in this connection. Up to the present they are the most effective combinations of purpose and mind, if we speak from the point of view of that slice of time that is packed with what we now call natural history. There may have been more effective combinations before and there may yet be afterword, but if we take the present with the not too distant past and future in mind, men are certainly the actualities of destiny. The emergence of humanity is neither accidental nor final, if it is only at all accidental, it is only so in taking place in this particular slice of time, that is to say, in being occasioned or ordained as it has been or is. Humanity is bound to emerge in time, because it is a possibility that is contingent. On our classification of possibilities, it does not belong to any other category. Obviously it is not necessary, nor is it eternally realized nor eternally unrealizable. Since it is a contingent possibility, its realization will come in time. Its emergence need not be heralded with exaggerated glory, nor should its tenure of existance be falsely credited with finality. Compared to other contemporary actualities, or compared to other periods of actualizations in the known span of natural history, human beings and the period in which they function may indeed be glorious. But no matter how glorious human beings may be in comparison with other contemporary species, they are also dependent upon the cooperation of other species, and no matter how glorious the period in which they function may be, it is one station in the unfoldment of Tao and requires other periods to bring it to a focus. There is a sort of mutual dependence or mutual infiltration of being that is easily neglected through our necessity for economy in thought and action. For practical purposes it is necessary to single out our species from the cumulative effects of other contemporary species as it is to single out any one person from the complex effects of his environment. If we bear in mind, however, this muturel infiltraction of being (mentioned already in chapter II), we are not likely to be excessively modest or excessively boastful.

Human beings are of course immensly important to themselves. To a human being, his desires his needs, his hopes, his whims and what not are all important, they only differ so in degrees that some of them are unimportant compared with others. So also is the satisfaction of these. His mind alone is capable of making him filled with pride. What is more important in this connection is that with the help of the propelling force of his purpose, his mind gives him his power. No species ruled the world with greater power or more efficiency than the human species. Whether the rule has been benevolent or not, there is as yet no prospect of a revolution in sight, and even if the rule were resulted, no species is as yet powerful enough to effect an overturn of human power. With medicine and doctors as the police, germs and diseases are mere thieves and thugs who disturb the peace occasionally but are not likely to be powerful enough to effect a revolution against the human species. Like all rulers human species face more difficuties from within. There is internal strife, there is greediness, desires seem to run rampant, luxuries continue to become needs; society may become so integrated and so differentiated that individual may cease to be and different social or economic strata may become almost like different species. These difficulties may be overcome and a long period of benevolent and despotic rule may take place. From the point of view of the human species, nothing is more desirable. Since the underlings that we are not in the habit of looking ahead in terms of millions or billions of years, the complacency of human beings due to their achievements is perhaps securable. Power is liable to intoxicate its prossessor into complacency.

There is however a question of value which may fill human beings with diffidence. With regard to value there is of course a choice of criteria. A number of criteria may be adopted so as to fill human beings with pride. On the adoption of a certain criterion, Indian philosophy is to be prefered to the Greek, but if another criterion is adopted, the Greek intellect is the more valuable. Between Chinese social control and Roman law, we also have a question of the choice of the criteria of values. While granting that a number of criteria might be adopted so as to fill human beings with pride, others might also be selected as to fill them with diffidence and trepidation. On the basis of nicety of instinct, we probably suffer from a comparison with other species, we may prefer to have penguins rather than monkeys as our near relatives. It may have been Rousseau who said that an intelligent being is a depraved animal; On the basis of the cooperation of physical faculties we suffer in comparition with tigers, leopards and even our ancestors the primitive men. In certain ways we can hardly be said to be more moral than certain animals. We are not

likely ever to attain to the functional beauty of an eagle or the visual beauty of a puesant. From the point of view of instinctive lik-
ability, few of us are comparable to the frauk and eager airdale.
Like individuals, human species are burdened with its strength,
for like individual strength, its strength is also its weakness.
Mind is probably the strongest asset of the human species and yet
it is through having that remarkable mind that human beings are
sometimes made more calculatingly immoral, more disgustingly
depraved, more painfully and falsely miserable, more unnecessarily and cruelly at war with themselves than any other species. On
the basic of values where is no conclusive reason why human
species should survive. Fortunately or unfortunately survival does
depend not upon prescriptive values.

Human beings may claim that they are not merely important
to themselves. With reality dichotomized into the subject and object, there is not merely a question of the subject reality, but
also that of the object-reality. Compare the difference of the
object reality before and after the emergence of man, It is such a
difference as to bad men that they have conquered nature. In a
large number of ways, this might be truely said. The face of the
earth is certainly changed by men, and one might say that were it
not for the emergence of men, it would not have changed in that
way it did. A considerable part of the object reality might be described as the creations or artifacts created by men. They are the
traces of what we call civilization and depend for their
preservation and mainteinance upon the emergence and continua-

tion of the human species. Nor is the human achievement limited to creations, it is even extended into spheres in which it might be said to have changed the course of evolution. Left to itself, the ginkgo might never have survived to their day, and the fate of dogs, horses and cats is certainly questionable if left to themselves. In the language of these pages, certain possibilities which might not have been realized without men are now realized with the emergence of men, certain others which might have been dis-realized are now continually realized, while still others which might have been rampant are now disrealized simply because they are harmful to men. Whether more are distroyed than preserved or vice versa, it is of course different to say, but changes in object reality seem to have been expedited considerably through the emergence of human beings who arc therefore of significance not merely to themselves.

There is however a significant sense in which we can say that nature has never been conquered. Certainly no natural law has ever been suspended merely for human benefit and at human will. What is accomplished is the acquirement of capacity to make use of the operation of certain natual laws to prevent the operation of certain others so that the state of affairs desired by human beings may be realized. The pattern in accordance with which reality proceeds is not changed by men. Even without men some natural laws operate in such a way that the operation of other natural laws is prevented. The only difference is that the re-sultant state of affairs in the one case is desired by men whereas in the other it may have never been desired by any species. While certain changes which have taken place in object reality are due to the emergence of men, these same changes considered from the point of view of the unbifurcated reality can not be similarly charged to the emergence of men. Object reality is something set about from subject reality only when reality is bifurcated, but when it is not bifurcated, there is no such thing as object or subject reality. Whatever changes that take place are merely changes that do take place, not such that from a subjective point of view their having taken place could be attributed to the activity of the subject reality. For the unbifurcated reality, any change is change of its own accond. Once we think of the unbifurcated reality, we think also of its organic unity and that unity consists partly of an infiltration of being such that human beings are as much soaked and shot through and through with there contempraneous objects and events as they are shot through and soaked with things human. There is a nutural interdependence of all actualities and with out a subjectivity of view points no one is more responsible for the process of reality than any other. The actual is what is brought along in the pure flow of time and if human beings function in it, they like everything else in it are occasioned and pre-ordained in the unfoldment of Tao.

We have said repeatedly that human beings will disappear. They may do so either in the way of abrupt termination or in the way of gradually changing into other species. We are accustomed to saying that nothing is final with however an emotional reservation that we ourselves are the exceptions. There is no reason why we should be the exceptions in the sense of a sort of crowning glory in the pure flow of time. We may imagine ourselves to be valuable cargo, and we may actually be that, but the time will come when we will be stored up in the oblivion of the past. As individual we come and go, and whether we come from and go to dust or not, no difference is made to the coming and going. The same should be of the species. It is only as Stuffed Form or Formed Stuff that we are immutable, as human beings we are as much in the whirlpool of change as anything else in the reality of process or in the process of reality. We may of course survive so very very long that even for millions of years we are assured of our tenure of existence or actualization, but the all comprehensive universe which has tolerated us for so long will not tolerate us ad infinitum. What will succeed us can hardly be predicted. While we may say something on the basis of pre-ordinations we can not say anything on the basis of occasions. That we are bound to go is however not open to doubt.

The usual objection is that with such a view human beings are bound to become phlegmatic, lethargic and fatalistic and that in the apathy that ensues while whatever that is "bad" may be avoided, whether that is "good" won't be accomplished either. Civilization wouldn't have advanced to the present stage, it may be said, if such ideas as there were entertained by men, and if we are to entertain them now, civilization will remain, stagnant and futile. There may be danger from those who not merely crave for eternity but also make it the condition of their continual existence. Most people would not be affected in any undesirable way. Life after all consists of activities and no one commits suicide merely because life is to be followed by death. Consciouness of death has never prevented any one from enjoying the present, or creating forms of beauty, or working towards a more desirable future or seeking for truth or thinking about the ultimate. If sometimes we drink because tomorrow we die, we sometimes also work for the same reason. It may even be argued the other way around and say that we are destined to eternity we won't do a thing today since there is always a tomorrow. Neither can be urged and accepted since life is actual and active, the essence of any form of living is to function in the role that is given or assigned. A living man is the functioning or actuating towards the essence of man just as a living. Aristotle is a functioning or actuating towards Aristotelianness.

# Nature and Man

## I

There is a doctrine in Chinese philosophy which may be summarized as that of the unification of nature and man. It is a doctrine that is perhaps more emphasized in some philosophies than in others, but it is not merely a technical idea, being entertained as well by the average educated man. It is a complicated pattern of ideas and we do not intend to deal with it in the manner of systemative exposition, nor do we claim that what we say here represents exactly the doctrine actually held by any thinker or any school of thinkers in the past. What is intended in those pages is rather to present some similar idea in terms more or less of our present day language through reasoning that is somewhat indicated by the previous chapters. It is not our purpose here to introduce a historical doctrine in its historical perspective, to trace its origin or to delineate its development, neither do we intend to present the cause of its development in terms of the physical evironment of its propounders.

It is perfectly likely that some such doctrine as we are

dealing with here is peculiarly wedded to an agricultural society or civilization in which technical knowledge hasn't advanced enough to afford people with the idea of their power over nature which their consciousness of their dependence upon their environment has sufficently developed so as to give them instead the idea of the power of nature over man. Perhaps a more nomadic life in which hunting predominates brings out much more the idea of the importance of individual initiative, since the success of hunting depend much more upon the capacity to perceive what is coming, to gauge the chances accurately, to seize the moment of decision and to act accordingly with adequacy and courage. With the idea of the importance of individual initiative firmly established, the idea of the power of man over nature is much more likely to follow than it is in a civilization in which people follow seasonal changes, watch the weather passively and are entirely helpless in the face of floods and draughts. The kind of civilization which China has had for thousands of years may have been responsible for the doctrine of the unification of nature and man. Sample and Huntington may be able to account for the emergence of this doctrine in ways similar to what they have done concerning a number of other ideas. This may very well be true, but if it is, it is a historical truth, not a philosophical doctrine.

How ideas come to be is quite different from what they are. For all we know, Euclid might have been a psycho-analytic case; he might have had an obsession with figures traceable to a psychosis for which his child-hood experiences were responsible; but even so, his obsession is not a part of his geometry; and while it is relevant to the historian, it's irrelevant to the geometer. It has become somewhat fashionable to speak of the falling apple in connection with Newton; the story is interesting, and may even be instructive; but it is not a part of physics. Give the history of law an idea has come to be, we have yet to face the problem as to what it is. Quite a large number of ways of dealing with it remains. There is for instance a question of its truth or falsehood, its consistency or inconsistency, or its tenability when no decision can be arrived at concerning its truth or falsehood, or else its fruitfulness or wisdom when judged in terms of what consequences there may be when the idea is seriously entertained. The doctrine of the unification of nature and man may owe its historical origin from the kind of civilization China has always had for ages, it is none the less a pattern of ideas which should be examined in some of the ways mentioned. It is besides an ideal to which a large number of people are emotionally attached, and whether or not it is otherwise acceptable, it is as such a part of the fund of beliefs and main springs of life of a section of mankind.

We should distinguish knowledge from belief. Human actions up to the present are not always guided by knowledge. On the one hand, we may say that our knowledge is as yet limited; we are ignorant of so many things that even if we do want to be guided by knowledge we have not sufficient knowledge to guide us. On the other hand, even if we have sufficient knowledge to guide us we are not always so guided. In some cases, there is a willful persistance in what we do, in others, a tendency to follow the line of best resistance; and in extreme cases, there may even be an indulgence in action or behavior in defiance of what knowledge foresee to be the consequence. Perhaps our actions should be guided by knowledge, even though they often are not. From the point of view of the efficiency in obtaining the kind of result desired, there is no question at all; knowledge should guide our actions and behavior. On some other criterion, the question is not so simple. As a matter of fact we are guided by habits, by custom, by law and in the mental basis of our actions we are as much guided by beliefs as by knowledge. Knowledge is of course accompanied by beliefs, but belief is not always accompanied by knowledge or even based on it; and what is more significant, the efficaciousness of belief does not suffer even through it is not accompanied by or based on knowledge. Everyone of us has a fund of such beliefs, and excluding an idea from the sphere of knowlege does not mean excluding it from the sphere of beliefs. Even if the doctrine of the unification of nature and man should be rejected as knowledge, it may yet be accepted as belief, and even though the question of truth and falsehood is to be ruled out, the question of fruitfulness and wisdom remains.

I am not a student of Chinese philosophy or history, and so far as ideas are concerned, I'm interested only in their cross-sectional pattern not in their historial development. I'm emotionally somewhat attuned to the feelling or flavour of Chinese philosophy and frankly partial to the ideas soon to be presented. In the previous chapters we have said that in the unfoldment of Tao, human beings are bound to appear, their emergence is neither accidental nor final, and while their tenure of existence is limited, their essence requires a function that is both earnest and real. So long as they function in actualily, they have to function in what we call the democracy of co-existents. For as we individully have to get along with our neighbours, human beings have to get along with their coexistents. Intellectually there is a question as to what attitude to take on the part of human beings and emotionally there is a question of harmony between what we have been discribing as the subject and object realities. Here we must introduce the term t'ien. We have conveniently but inadequately called the doctrine the unification of nature and man. "Nature" is not a synonym of "t'ien". If we speak analytically, it is a bad policy to use the term "nature", for it is obviously capable of many and diverse meanings. But it has the closest flavour to the term "t'ien" which is itself ambiguous. The latter may be combined with different terms to mean entirely different things, and what appears in the doctrine of the unification of t'ien and man, it expresses more than the term "nature" expresses in English. Perhaps the phrase nature and nature's God is more nearly equivalent to t'ien than any other term or phrase, if we bear in mind that the God mentioned is not the Christian God. We shall use the term "mere nature" to mean dichotomized nature which falls into the realm of the subject or object and reserve the term "nature" to mean both nature and nature's God.

The difference between nature and mere nature is that with the former men are subsumed under it, while with the latter either men are excluded from it or it is set apart from men. No matter how the deity part of nature is conceived whether Christian or not, it permeates both men and mere object nature, it enables men to be conscious that they have a nature of their own and that mere human nature is part of nature just as mere object nature is. The significance to be emphasized in the case of nature is located not in the concrete and discrete things, but rather in the inter-related pattern in which men can hardly set themselves apart. Conceive nature to be not merely nature but also nature's God, natural law is no longer merely the invariant relation which holds between bits of matter or describes the change and motion of discrete objects or things, but also laws of conduct so far as purposive and conscious human beings are concerned. The law of nature includes not merely jus natural but also lex naturalis, provided we do not attribute the imperative element to the will of a God who assumes the human form. Inanimate objects merely obey invariant relations, they are neither blessed nor cursed with purpose or knowledge to land them in inextricable difficulties, their virtues being merely their qualities are not their vices, nor is their strength their weakness. The strength of a tree that shoots into the sky is not the weakness of its being torn by the wind; in either case, it merely obeys invariant relations; but bless that tree or curse it with knowledge and purpose, a number of if-then propositions may be entertained informing the tree that if it doesn't aim too high, it won't be torn up; that if it doesn't want to be torn up, it had better not shoot to high; that if it cannot resist the temptation of shooting above the shoulder of other trees, it must be prepared to be torn up by the winds, etc. In the latter case the tree would beg in to have spiritural struggle, and like Hamlet, it would be tormented by the question to shoot high or not to shoot high; and what is even more to our point, a single invariant relation invokes precepts and rules on the one hand and invokes wisdom of choice on the other. Natural law so interpreted if not richer than the traditional jus naturale is the modern invariant relations.

## II

But why unify nature with men? Are they not already unified? If they can be unified, why aren't they? If they can not be unified, why advocate their unification? What is meant by unification any how? We must present the problem of disunification. We have already pointed out that with the emergence of purpose and knowledge, reality is dichotomized into subject and object realities. Since human beings are endowed with both purpose and knowledge, they not only demand modifications of object reality, but also know to an increasing extent how these are to be brought about. Object reality often resists these modifications and it succeeds or fails in accordance with the power the subject reality wields, and his power is proportionate to his knowledge. What we call mere object nature is what we have been calling object reality, and what we have been calling subject reality, we now limit to mere human nature. There wouldn't be resistance on the part of mere object nature if there weren't purposive men, for the reality wouldn't have been dichotomized. Once reality is dichotomized struggle and resistance are inevitable. So far as mere object nature is concerned, the issue seems to be more or less decided, the victory so far belongs to man. From some other point of view to be later presented, the result is not quite so conclusive, it may even turn out that the victor is also the vanquished.

There is of course a good deal to be said on behalf of the plight of man. They acquire purpose and knowledge after they are conceived or born, none of them becomes a human being with his own consent, and yet being assigned the human role, he has to function as a human being. He has to exist, to eat, to propagate, and to be clothed. There are basic desires and needs, and their satisfaction is not always easy, for obstacles there are and often are such that they can not be overcome. He has to struggle for his existence, to gain power over his adversaries. He has to gain knowledge and with its power in order to exist and he has to exist in order to fulfil the function required of him. Whether conscious of it or not, his own mere nature, the mere nature of being human, drives him towards the acquision of power. He can not very well renounce his desire to push forward without also curtailing the mere nature of his own being. However different he may be from the other animals or objects, he is not different from them so far as the fact that his existence is shaped by his essence is concerned; he has to be human just as a log has to be loggish or a horse to be horsy. But whereas a stone does not require any effort to be strong or to achieve stoniness, it is also the essence of human beings to make efforts, since he is endowed with purpose and knowledge. He is bound to modify mere object nature to suit his needs or desires and to adopt means towards achieving end. Here again he can hardly help this any more than a horse can escape being horsy or a piece of stone from stoniness. In his efforts, he is all too human. Being human means in the language of preceding chapters merely fulfilling the essence of humanity or realizing the possibility Humanness. So far as the struggle for existence is concerned, being human is also being merely natural.

But the combination of purpose and knowledge affords human beings power and while power needn't be dangerous, it often is. It breeds the desire for greater power and instead of being merely a means to an end, it has the tendency to become itself an end. The struggle for existence may turn into a struggle for power. As means, power is limited, it ceases to function when the end is achieved. If stamps are used for letters, we need only as many stamps as the letters require; if money is needed to maintain a certain standard of living we need only the amount required for the maintainance of the standard. But if stamps and money are collected for their own sake, there is no limit to their collection.

The same is true of power. With the accumulation of power, there is also an expansion of desires along lines that may never have been dreamed of before, and for beyond the requirement for existence. With mere human nature driving, there is no guarantee how the power is to be used. It may be used against obstacles in mere object nature or it may be used against fellow human beings, or it may even be used against oneself. One is liable to agree with Rousseau that man is everywhere in chains whether or not than ever was once a state of nature in which he was free. Knowledge by itself is harmonious, but purposes often conflict with one an other not merely between states or races or different men but also in single individual himself. An individual with conflicting purposes is the enclosed battle ground for spiritual struggle, and although stone wells do not make a prison, nor mere object nature any obstacle to his yearnings, he is yet his own prisoner. The more power one acquires, the more one may be enslaved.

We have already pointed out that with the aid of knowledge purpose may become extremely complicated. There may be a chain of means to ends such that some ends are means to other end and some means end to other means. If one tarries in this chain, one is liable to take means for end. And value may come in to complicate the issue. The question of the justification of means by end may be raised and if one tarries with certain means so long that the ends are lost sight of, the means which was formerly justified by the ends is no longer so when the end is no longer in view. If the ends are not supposed to justify the means, then no matter how far removed the ends may be, whether or not they are lost sight of, they do not affect the means, since the latter will have to be justified on their own ground. But then the power to achieve ends is greatly diminished. Secondly, the longer the chain of means to ends, the more conflict of ends there is likely to be. Conflict with mere object nature is a straight forward issue, one could march into it with a stout heat, conflict with other human beings is liable to be accompanied by misgivings, and conflict with one's self may result in tragidies, since it is here that one's strength is also one's weakness, one's victory also one's defeat, and where a person is himself a house divided, nothing can possibly console. In the third place, with the aid of knowledge, purposes multify, desires increase. Some desires are transformed into needs while whims are changed into desires. The transformation may be highly satisfying, though it need not be so. But whether it is so or not, something is lost in the process. What was once only a whim or a wish or a hope with the softness, the lightness and the poetic quality that accompany it, is transformed into desires and needs with all the grossness and coarseness that a company the will to achieve. If we ever gain the capacity to have picnics on the moon, it will be welcome by some element in us and resulted by others for the whimsical wish of enjoying solitude on the moon is transformed into a gross desire resulting in a struggle for tickets and jostling at the gang plank with perhaps a notion as clear and distinct as Cartesian ideas that no solitude is to be had even on the moon.

But perhaps the most important result of increased desires is that we are more enslaved by them. With the increased facility to satisfy, desires tend to increase in a geometrical ratio. In simple and naive desires we may not feel enslaved for the end is in view and the means direct. If we merely walk down a few steps to a brook for a drink, we won't feel that our drink or the few steps we have to walk encroaches upon our freedom. But if we have to do it scores of times in order to carry water for different families so as to support our own, we are liable to feel that walking up and down these steps interferes with our conversation or quiet afternoon at the tea house. Where the end is not a sensed or felt need of the present, even a simple desire may give rise to a feeling of enslavement. Imagine the enormous number of desires that accompany modern civilization, and the long chain of means to ends they involve! One can not help feeling that a man is like a silk-worm that spins a cocoon to enslave itself. While on the one hand we have to admit that the scope of human activities is greatly increased, things that formerly were incapable of accomplishment are now easily done, on the other, desires and needs also multify so that one is drived and enslaved by them more than ever before. It may be poetic sublimation to proclaim that an "iron master" drives us; obviously it can not, unless human beings drive themselves. One may revolt against being driven by others, but when one drives one's self, there is no possibility of redress. The chance of self enslavement is greatly increased by the increased power over object nature and fellow human beings. Whether there is any struggle against the domination of desires or not depends upon the individual, but even when there is any struggle, one can not help feeling that one is not chained. The question is do we conquer mere object nature to make ourselves slaves? Does the greater freedom to do things compensate for the greater enslavement of and by ourselves?

There is then a problem that is essentially human. Somethings might be done through social economic and political measures. To start with, however, a choice is involved. The great society may be organized for power or for happiness. By happiness we mean the synthetic harmony of the different ingredients in the make up of a man. It is not to be confused with pleasure which may be unhappily enjoyed or with the mere satisfaction of desires which may be such as to disturb harmony. If the great society is to be organized merely for power, whether military or industrial, the above problem can hardly be solved. If the great society is to be organized for happiness, individuals will have to cooperate in making positive efforts towards their own salvation. The great society can merely provide for the conditions, under which individuals may rescue themselves, but in the last analysis they will have to do their own rescuing. Formerly it was religion that performed the task of individual salvation, but religion seems to have lost a good deal of its former effectiveness, and since what is relevant to our problem is only that part of religion that deals with the human, we may set formal religion aside in our present discussion. Even the relevant part has to be taught to the individual, to be experienced, meditated and divined by him. The problem is not merely human but also individual.

# III

We shall use a term in the following paragraphs to mean something more than the dictionary allows. The word vista according to Webster means "firstly a view or prospect commonly through or along an avenue as between rows of trees, or secondly a mental view or prospect extending over a series of events". We shall keep the view or prospect part of the meaning and discard the tree or the event part. We are not interested in what is seen or heard but in the significances gathered from experience. It may be that the kind of significances gathered depends upon individual characteristics as well as their relation to their environment; and there may in turn be due to mere subject nature or nurture; but whether this is so or not, we need not try to ascertain, since we are here only interested in the kind of significances gathered. What is known to any individual as the meaning of life is on our account the total amount of significance, gathered and organized into a pattern, it is not merely the conceptual meaning of the term life, nor the emotional content of living, nor the flavour with which one's life is lived; it is all things combined with something in addition, something that motivates or guides or directs the basic promptings of one's heart. In fact the usual word to discribe it is philosophy in the sense in which one often says that everyone has his own philosophy; but in order to preserve the term for the formal and conceptual approach to fundamental problems as it is now used in colleges and universities, we call the pattern of significances one's vista.

We have already said that either mere subject nature or nurture or both may be responsible for the kind of vista one entertaines. It may be that a certain minimal instinctive endowment is neglected in order that certain vista may be attainable. It is t'ain however that nurture has to assert its effects even though the required instinctive endowment is given. The statement that every body can be a sage means to assert also the importance of nurture. Even if some vistas are born, others are achieved. The acheivement of some vistas must be accompanied by conscious and strenuous efforts and these may fail, if they are misdirected. It is with views and prospects that we are concerned, not acts or instincts or impulses. If our efforts are directed towards the stoppage of certain propensities that are about to be actualized, the suppression of certain instincts which struggle for expression, or the frustraction of certain impulses which have already manifested themselves, our efforts are liable to be misdirected, and instead of gaining vistas, we may become psycho-analytic cases. But if our efforts directed towards working out a view and maintaining it, we may succeed in allowing certain instincts to function without others manifesting themselves, in encouraging certain feelings to be entertained so that others won't emerge, or certain acts to take place so that others may be nipped in the bud. In the simplest language possible, we may live as every other person in the world of facts and yet so lifted out of it that our world of significance is quite different from many of our contemporaries. One's problem in gaining vista is not to change the object or the man, it is rather to fulfil as much as possible the man in the animal or object. It is only the vulgars who erect idols of worship or expect the coming of superman to solve essentially human and even somewhat earthy problems.

There are probably large varieties of different vistas. If one thinks of the different "philosophies" of different man, how various and multitudnious they are, one has a rough idea of how many combinations and permutations there are to vistas. We are however only interested in three main and somewhat platonic types; the naive, the heroic and the sagely. These terms discribe vistas, not a person's occupation, or character, or capacity, or mere ideas. Obviously a great scientist or musician may have a heroic vista although his interest in science is single tracked or his interest in music purely emotional expression. When it is said that great men are basically simple, it is probably not meant to convey that they are simple in the various ways in which they are great, more likely it is meant that inspite of their greatness or even responsible for it there is a simplicity of vista. A hero in war may be a man of naive vista, his heroism may consist of bagging as many enemies as he can while his vista is naive. It is probable and even likely that a man with a naive vista is a naive man in many ways, and a man with a heroic vista a hero in the eyes of his contemporaries. None the less a distinction should be made. Whether Plato's "Artisans" warriors and statesman who are supposed to enbody the respective vistas of industry, honour and wisdom are meant to discribe vistas or not, our terms here are not meant to discribe social strata or individual virtures. If vistas are the products or the corresponding virtures of professions or stations in life, one can hardly live oneself out of the world of facts in which one happens or choses to function.

A naive vista is one in which the dichotomy or bifurcation of reality as well as that of self and others is reduced to a minimum. It is such that a person who achieves it is free from ego-centric predicament. While it is perfectly true a child can not be said to have a vista since he has gathered no significances, it is now the less profitable to compare the child-like quality in his behavior with the attitude of a sophisticated man. A child enjoys a certain harmony with his environment. He is not likely to revolt against his environment or to want to conquer it. If he is frustrated, he probably cries whole heartedly, and if immediately he is moved to laughter, he does not hesitate to do so. He is not affected by any desire for consistency of behavior, neither is he possessed by spiritual struggle. The child-like qualities of his behavior may be achieved by a man with a vista. A man with a naive vista is one who has achieved this child like simplicity, it is not the simplicity of a simpleton or a dullard. It consists of being humble, of entertaining desires without being enslaved by them, of having a certain consciousness of self without ego-centricity, so that one is neither unduly elated by success or unduly humiliated by failure. He is not likely given to comparisons with other men. Whether he is dull, devoid of talent, or lacking in social grace, or else sparklingly witty, extraordinarily talented, or intensely intellectual, he accepts himself; he accepts himself as being merely given and fulfils his function in life with equanimity in either case. So far as he himself is concerned, he is merely conscious of a charge to keep what he is, and so far as his environment and fellow human beings are concered, he demands so little of them that he is not likely to be obstructed by them. He is not estranged by them. The vista enables him to achieve what is often called peace of mind.

A heroic vista is one in which dichotomy of reality is almost at a maximum. Again it is the vista that is heroic, not necessarily the person. The heroic vista has large number of varieties and is also permeated with more psychological complications than any other vista. There may be anthropocentric heroism. One may be fired with the idea of the conquest of mere object nature by man and emotionally propelled towards its achievement. Here the dichotomy is between mere object nature and man and the obsession is with the conquest of the formers. So far as the mere object nature is concerned, the victory thus far belongs to man; but so far as mere human nature is concerned, the issue is as yet uncertain, it is quite likely that the victor may turn out to be himself equally: the defeated. There seems to be on the one hand an intrinsic unwillingness to deal with men, to solve their problems, and on the other to whip them into a concerted action towards the conquest of mere object nature just as a nation harrowed by internal dissention often seeks unification through external aggression. But just as external aggression does not solve the problem of the internal dissention of a nation, so the conquest of mere object nature does not solve the intrinsic problems of man. Proplems may be ignored for a time, they may even be temporarily dissolved, but emerge they will, and when they do, they are likely to do so with a vengeance. Human desires may become rampant for which the conquest of mere object nature is not a solution, but instead an aggravation. To use a phrase so often employed in military strategy, the initiative may be lost; human beings may be driven not merely by the mere object nature they have conquered, but also by their own mere nature which they have ignored.

There may be ego-centric heroism. Here the line of demarcation is drawn between the human environment and the ego. External achievement is again the predominant element, only it is not aimed at the conquest of mere object nature, instead it is directed towards the human environment. Satisfaction is derived from making or imagining the individual ego, the victor over circumstances that are chiefly human. Such doctrines as "Whenever there is a will, there is a way", or "one is the sum total of what one has achieved", or "with concentration and effort one always succeeds" are expressive of their brand of heroic vista. One may be the most un-heroic sort of person and yet believes that it is only through the conquest of one's human environment that one finds one's individual realization. The heroic vista is not limited to an individual society, but it is there that the single-tracked heroism is most predominant. The multitudinous and yet definitely channeled opportunities enable a person to identify his personal worth with his success or failure in a single line of ambition or achievement. The qualities required for success and quickness of perception, facility for projects, capacity for seizing opportunities and ruthlessness in carrying out one's projects; and although the resultant effects of success may sometimes be sound and fury devoid of deep human significance, yet since nothing succeeds like success, one is likely to make heros out of ruthless, capable and successful men. And in an important sense they are heros. Most of the great statesmen, soldiers, or industralists or even some of the religious leaders were men with heroic vistas. Civilization might have been a static affair, if those weren't a galaxy of such men. They are necessary to civilization, more especially perhaps to its environment, but they are not sufficient; they are victors in wars, not preservers of peace, and so far as their vista is concerned, the significance gathered are partial to one aspect of the essence of being human.

# IV

The sagely vista is somewhat like the naive except that its apperant naivete is arrived at through advanced meditation and contemplation. The behavior of a man with a sagely vista may appears naive as a man with a naive vista, but the discipline behind it is based upon meditation that transcend the human function with the result that one is not merely free from ego-centricity but also of anthropocentriely. It is not necessary here to dwell at length the idea that among human beings in the concrete each is because the others are. It is only in the abstract that individuals are independent of each other. The question as to what Aristotle might have been if he were in ancient China for instance is a speculation concerning Aristotelianness; the actual and concrete Aristotle was, because his local contemporaries were. We are not talking of the dependence of each other for certain purposes such as security, protection, food and employment, etc., we are rather speaking of the very core of each individual character. We are all of us in varying degrees Laured and Hardies, or Matt and Jeffs, or Berger and Mcarthers, or even Siomee twins. The more intimate the relation between individuals, the more each is integrated with the other, and the more one projects oneself into the other, the more one is because the others are. There is in the concrete a mutual permeation or infiltration of individual characters and once this is realized, there is a democracy of giants and pygmies since each wouldn't be if the others weren't so that both the strong and the weak suffer the same fate or inherit the same world. Individual differences there are and must be, and while for certain purposes, they are usefully accentuated through labels and abstractions, they shouldn't be emphasized to the extent as to obscure the mutual interpenetration of individuals in actual and concrete life.

Since the very being of each is soaked through and through with the very being of his intimate contemporaries, where is the line that divides people into selves? To be sure, physiologically each one of us is an unit, but then to single out the physiological aspect is surely an abstraction. Certainly some of us have mental qualities that are not shared by many others, and whether we call them extra-ordinary or remarkable or peculiar, they are at any rate distinct; but surely this is description if not valuation, and to describe is after all to abstract. Can we distinguish a man's qualities from these of his forefathers and of his contempararies or determine what portion of them is due to history, to the cultural environment and to the zeitgeist? If we can not so distinguish or determine, one's mind is a jumble, a complex, or a welter of multituding ingredients and no longer an individual. If we can so distinguish and determine, there is either a residue which is hardly the whole individual, or else there is nothing left so that the concrete individual has evaporated. It may be said that each individual has a soul distinct from the soul of any other individual. Whether this is true or not, we need not ascertain, for unless we think of souls as being windowless or else in vacuum, we can hardly end the problem of their interpenetration. The crux of the whole matter is that what is known as the individuel is itself an abstraction; in the concrete it is a mobile area of accentuation where an enormous number of events take place in action and reaction. A mind that is aware of this universal penetration is bound to entertain a vista that transends individual differences and while admitting them intelletually, a mind so lifted out of itself in such awareness refuses to have any emotional vested interest in any single self.

This mutual inter-penetration is not limited to human beings. Each particular object reflects the whole particular world to which it belongs in the sense that each is because the others are. Such particular object is related to every other particular object in different ways and while some of these relations are internal and others external, the qualities and relational properties of any single object depend upon the qualities and relational properties of every other particular object. So far as the particularity is concerned no object can change or move; the particular stays put. What is repeatable elsewhere and at different times in any particular object is either the set of universals realized by the object or else its own illusive identity. we are so accustomed to abstraction that it is difficult for us to reason or even to talk about the particular. Take the desk on which I now write. We are accustomed to thinking that it could be moved; we may indeed say that as a matter of fact it was moved only yesterday. It could be moved as an enduring object, but so far as its particularity is concerned, we insist that the term "this desk" covers a series of particulars first at a certain original position, then in transit and finally in a new locality, and none of the particulars has either changed or moved. To say that an object has changed either its qualities or its location is merely to affirm either that it has gone through a set of different and dissimilar particulars or that its internal and external relations with other particular objects are no longer the same as before. In either case, the pattern of the whole world in its particularity is also different.

There are other ways in which a particular object reflets the world particular world, but we shall not dwell on them. What we must not forget is that a man is also an animal and an object. It is perfectly true that one is different from some objects in being an animal, and from some animals in being a man, and from the man in being oneself, but if one realizes that what is known as oneself is permeated with other men as well as other animals and objects, one can hardly be much excited about being a particular self. The realization enables him to feel at one with the world and every thing in it. He acquires universal sympathy. He does not despise other objects for he is himself one of them, and in a democracy of existents, he gives as much as he takes. He does not frown upon other animals for like him they are merely functioning in accordance with their respective essences; and he doesn't condemn certain animalistic proclivities in himself since being a man does not release him from the function of realizing the essence of an animal. While a number of senses might be urged in which the man in him may be regarded as being better or worse than other objects or animals in the concrete flow of life, or in the actual passage of time he is merely different from the others just as they are different from each other among themselves. The humanity in a person gives him the most serious of problems for it is the capacity of a human being that his relations with others of his species are most complicated; there he is liable to enjoy the keenest pleasure or else suffer the most poignant pain. If he is incapable of either, it must be due to a certain lumpiness in himself, and the uttermost he could achieve is the naive vista. If he is capable of both, he must be a keen as well as a passionate man; either blind passion spells his doom, or sublimated and wisely directed passion guides him towards salvation. If one struggles against one's own passions, one is a cornered animal, an imprisoned man, immersed in a maze of conflicting emotions from which one can hardly extricate oneself. One must have significant knowledge and relevant wisdom in order to cope with the problem; and the man with the sagely vista does not solve the problem in the usual sense, for him the problem is dissolved so that it is no longer there to plague him.

Perhaps the most unselfish at all emotions is sympathy. In its pure sincerity, it is obviously selfless. With the realization that one is permeated with the qualities and relations of one's co-existents, one is capable of universal sympathy in all its sincerity and purity. In ceasing to be anthropocentric one may also cease to be ego-centric. Once free of ego-centricity, one is no longer plagued by the problem of self-enslavement. It is the vested interest in a person that makes him the slave of his own desires, and it is his desires that disturb the peaceful relation between him and other men. It is also his desires that render him struggling within himself. Desires however are burdened in themselves only when they breed other desires that strive for satisfaction with equal persistency. Once they are given the chance of island hopping, there is no way of preventing them from hopping on ad infinitum. Nor is the problem one of curbing one's desires. The only way to do is to know one's destiny, to be at peace with one's station in life in a much more comprehensive than the merely social or political sense. Obviously some desires will have to be satisfied, but if in satisfying or trying to satisfy them, one is at peace with one's destiny, one is reconciled with one's limitations. Whatever destiny or station that is given, it is for him a charge to keep, a function to fulfill in the democracy of mutually dependent co-existents. He admits neither self satisfaction, nor self deprecation. He does not struggle against what is within his function, nor does he crave for what is beyond it. Since he is a man, he has to realize the essense of his being, and whatever is given him in addition as a separate self he accepts with as much good race as he accepts his humanity. What is needed is not saintliness which involves being Godly and therefore other than man, but sagacity which involves the transcendence of the mere nature in man so as to approach that nature in man which is also t'ien. The latter is within the possible reach of any man. Once it is reached, one may be in vista different from most men and yet in every other aspect the same as any Jorn Dick or Harry. In him object nature and subject nature are unified and in the unification there is harmony.

It must be emphasized that we are talking of vistas, not classes of men. We do not urge upon the creation of a class of sages any more than the institution of a class of heros. In our present day society, there is so much differentiation and integration of function that people can hardly be stratified into any simple hierarchy of classes. There is no reason why a paddle or shoe-maker or a lawyer or a docter shouldn't be a man with the sagely vista. A man with such a vista is equally at home with shoe-making as with statecraft, for in either of them he is fulfilling the function that is given, that contributes to the pattern of the particular world in which he lives and in making such a contribution he allows no distinction between the humble and pretentious. Nor is there any particular profession that is never suited to the achievement of the sagely vista, everybody is capable of it. Of course not everybody will succeed. The important problem is not so much as to make everybody a sage or to lead or to encourage them to entertain it as an ideal. With this ideal in mind, one is not likely, to mistake power, knowledge, wealth, etc., for human wisdom; useful as these are for certain specific purposes, it is yet the latter that enables a person to live a life that leads to social harmony and individual peace of mind. Take knowledge for instance. It has become objective, reliable and eminently useful for the maintainance and improvement of the conditions of life; but it has not been equally successful in supplying human beings with such wisdom as to direct the kind of life to be lived. The advance in knowledge has thus for resulted in the heroic and tragic enslavement to one's desires, whether good or bad or indifferent, and knowledge itself has become so neutral that saints and devils could make use of it alike. And power and wealth do not face any better. The fundamental problem of today may be one of social legislation or economic rearrangement so as to better the conditions of life, but that of tomorrow is bound to be one of individual salvations so as to improve the quality of living. What is needed is not a class of sages, but a section of people in different functions achieving the sagely vista. Socially as well as individually the trouble is not with our stars but with ourselves, and to prevent the social organism from being dominated by the heroic vista which is going to sweep the world, it is necessary to permeate it with the sagely vista.

# V

The West seems to have been dominated with the heroic vista. While it is occasionally asserted that the meek shall inherit the world, the predominant attitude is one of self-assertiveness, of striving towards the satisfaction of desires and of identifying it with the pursuit of happiness. The resultant social organization is one of power and achievement. Achievements alone stagger our imagination, their number is tremendous, their scope exceedingly wide and their significance far reaching. They are in fact such that in the West one lives almost in a created environment of artifacts. New York City is a crowning glory of human achievement; subjective nature seems to have dominated to such as extent that object nature is almost missing. And the power of knowledge of industry and of social organization is even more terrifying. While its constructive side is expressed in achievements, its destructive side is expressed in the tottering effect or civilization by the present global war. Civilization in the past may have been wiped out by glaciers, by floods, be earth quakes or landslides, or by desiccation and decay, but they are not likely to be wiped out through any such agency in the near future; if their destruction ever takes place, it is likely to be effected through human beings themselves. Progressives everywhere are looking forward towards an individual organizition for security, some are even planning and working for a world state. This is indeed as it should be. There is however no assurance that the world state will soon emerge, and even when it does, there is no assurance that there won't be any civil war or that the future civil war will be less destructive than the present international wars. There seems to be an attempt to externalize human problems, to solve them with a sort of intellectual legerdemain; the attempt is probably based upon our reluctance to look at problems from the angle of the human material. Terrifying as the power over us is, it is yet wielded by human beings, and how it is to be used depends ultimately upon the kind of persons we are going to be. We can not externalize our problems for we are ourselves a part of them.

That the West has been dominated by the heroic vista does not seem to be open to doubt. The ideological evidence seems to be overwhelming. The doctrine that man is the measure of all things, that the essence of a thing is our perception of it, that understanding makes nature are all offshoots of a basic anthropocentricity which one accepts almost as a matter of course. Even the *Bible* is not free from it. Without anthropocentricity and even egocentricity who would believe that God created man according to his own image, or want Him to do so? If we really had a lively sense of humility we certainly would not want to humiliate Him with our own image, the image of underlings that we are and underlings that we will continue to be. It seems safe to conclude that not only in Hellenic light but also in Hebraic sweetness there is a strain of human assertiveness, of pride in being what we are, of deep seated belief in ourselves as the salt of the earth. The role of human beings is so glorified that one seems to be eternally smiling with an almost militant satisfaction over one's biological heritage. Social variaties there certainly are and cases of extraneous dissatisfaction with oneself are occasionally found. But even in self mortification and self torture there is no real sense of anthropocentric humility, what is motivating behind it is likely to be a militant desire to be other than oneself. The normal person is one who is anthropocentric if not egocentric and his normal attitude is to regard object nature either as an enemy to be conquered or as plastic material to be shaped according to his desires. In doing so, he may succumb to the mere nature in man. He may proceed to "construct" objective nature in philosophy and try so "conquer" it with all the sources at his command. He may become a conquering hero in one sense, but if he succumbs

199

to the mere nature in man, he is also the vanquished in another and probably more significant sense.

That the heroic vista has advantages is not open to doubt. That it has worked wonders in the way of achievements has been mentioned earlier. There certainly should be more of it in the Far East. But in order that the advantages of such a vista should be unaltered, it has to be tempered with the basic humanness of the sagely vista. The so called conquest of nature would be saluted if it did not result in the greater enslavement of human beings by themselves. In a sense objective nature has never been conquered, no " natural law" has ever been suspended or nullified for human benefit and merely at human will; what has been done is to bring about a state of affairs such that certain natural laws opperate against certain others so that the result desired by human beings are realized. Human beings play one part of object nature against some other part in order to satisfy their desires. Since desires breed other desires, the more nature is " conquered " the more rampant our desires also become. Achievements succeed achievements and power generates power. We may of course say that there is a good and bad or a constructive and distructive side to the "conquest" of object nature; but while some useful purpose is undoubtedly served in looking at the problem in this eclectic sort of way, a more important truth is likely to be ignored. The root of the problem is the same, achievement and power are but different expressions of the same impulse, and if one hankers after the constructive, one also brings with it latent destructions. The heroic vista regards the will to achieve as given and final and unless, this will is itself tempered by the sagely vista at the source there is no assurance that it won't destroy humanity through that chain of desires and satisfactions.

The East certainly has not solved the problem of human misery and the West may not have solved the problem of human happiness. Once the Indian of the Pacific is crossed in different directions, human misery is probably agonizing to the Western traveller. Life there still depends upon climate; upon recurring floods and draughts as it did ages ago. Live and let live seems to go hand in hand with die and let die. Life is not valueless, for even with the humble, a good deal of fuss is individually made over birth, but it may indeed be said to be cheap for even death on a large scale does not give rise to much social and political concern. Between birth without one's consent and death not always against one's will, life is a stolid and squalid affair following the line of least resistence to what fate dictates. And yet incredible as it may seem, in the midth of all this misery happiness is not necessarily absent. There is little regret or resentment; seldom is there anguish or agony, since there is little desire to be other than oneself; hardly ever is there tragedy, for tragedy involves such a war of passions as to render the possessor of them always the vanquished no matter which side wins, and contrary to popular belief, such a war is on the whole alien to the oriantal. The heroic vista is not absent in the East, but in the anthropocentric form it is so seldom entertained as to be of no practical significance. Objective nature still overwhelms mere man. It is this fact in the East that impresses upon the Western mind with greater force than anything else. Undoubtedly more anthropocentric heroism should be encouraged, greater efforts should be made towards the "conquest of nature", undoubtedly also a higher standard of living should be the aim of every man, but it must be understood that these things would be a blessing only if in having them accomplished certain naivete or sagaciousness is not lost together with its natural naturalness or contented contentedness.

The Western civitization will sweep over the whole world, perhaps for its own excellence, but also for its power. Once given a start, it rolls on of its own momentum crushing any and every obstacle in its path. It has obvious virtures; it raises the standard of living to a previously undreamed level, it insures a condition of life that is almost free from natural calamities, and while miseries due to human management have not been eradicated, they will undoubtedly diminish as improvements are made in social and political reorganization. For the achievements, the oriental has nothing but admiration; he may feel wonderment and awe for the speed and efficiency with which the world becomes transformed; but so far as the destination is concerned, he might yet have his misgivings. Is there any guarantee that the whole civilization wouldn't be something like getting all dressed up with no place to go, or making elaborate preparations for a journey that doesn't take place? If happiness is to be identified with the mere satisfaction of desires, it is doubtful whether any one in the brand new world will be happier than the early Greeks or Chinese or the Elizabethan Englishmen. Happiness is both harmony within and the ability to get along without, the latter is an asset only when it contributes to the former. But if the heroic vista is allowed to dominate our thought and behavior, with all its pungency, all its vigour and nigour, it may drive people into a beehive of activity so that each is stressed, strained and torn between numerous and ever increasing desires with the net result that the absense of misery does not mean the presence of happiness. What is needed in the West is greater sageciousness, admitting only that kind of assertiveness that is neither anthropocentric nor egocentric, an assertiveness that is consonant with human dignity and yet does not give rise to false human pride. The belief in democracy, the conception of human worth, the striving towards an equalization of the conditions of life should be accompanied by the realization that man can not set himself apart from mere object nature and lord over it, for in doing so he is merely giving aid and comfort to the mere nature in him which he must transcend in order to save himself.

# The Political Theory of
# Thomas Hill Green

本文是作者 1920 年在美国哥伦比亚大学政治学系的博士论文。

——编者注

# Preface

Shrouded in mysticism, the idealist political philosophy seems to be as far removed from practical politics as the Einstein formula is from everyday engineering; but far removed as it may seem, it was and yet remains an influence to be reckoned with. It is on this ground that this monograph is justified, and readers, if any, are requested not to regard it as unnecessary exertion in a mental gymnasium.

Errors and inaccuracies there may be. Writing in a language that is not his mother tongue, the author is confronted with difficulties which only those who have struggled hard to express themselves in distant lands can adequately appreciate. Fortunately he has enlisted the aid of a number of his friends. To them he is grateful. He is thankful to the Professors whose lectures he attended. Finally, he is at a loss to express adequately his indebtedness to Professor Dunning, whose suggestions and criticisms have been at all stages helpful; but then, consistent with "oriental inscrutability", silence probably speaks with better eloquence than words.

Y. L. Chin.

New York City, September, 1920.

# Introduction

"For thirty years and more," said Prof. Hobhouse in his *Democracy and Reaction*, "English thought has been subject, not for the first time in its modern history, to powerful influences from abroad. The Rhine has flowed into the Thames, at any rate into those upper reaches of the Thames, known locally as the Isis, and from the Isis the stream of German Idealism has been diffused over the academical world of Great Britain."[1]

Briefly stated, the German political philosophy, according to Prof. Hobhouse, consists of three fundamental conceptions.[2] The first is that Will is free; that it is self determined; and that individuality or true freedom lies in conformity with our real will, which is different from the will we manifest as private individuals. The second is that our real will is identical with the general will, which is best, if not completely, expressed in the social fabric. The third is that the state is the embodiment of the general will, giving it "vitality", "expression" and "coherence". The state is

---

[1]   Hobhouse, *Democracy and Reaction*. p. 77.
[2]   Hobhouse, *The Metaphysical Theory of the State*.

the common self in which the individual self is absorbed. It is the fountain of authority. It is the realization of our moral ideal. It is an end in itself. Thus German idealism becomes political absolutism.

One of the scholars formerly credited with and now blamed for the introduction of German political thought into England is Thomas Hill Green. He was born April 7, 1836, at Birkin in the West Riding of Yorkshire, the son of a local rector. He went to school at Rugby and in October, 1855, he entered Balliol College, Oxford. In 1860, he was employed to lecture on history, "and in November of that year he achieved his youthful ambition by being elected a fellow of the College"①. From 1860 till his death in 1882, he taught at Oxford and was active in local politics, being elected in 1876 to the Oxford town council. He was the first college tutor to enter public service of that sort.②He was interested in education and temperance. In 1878 he was appointed to the Whyte's professorship of moral philosophy, a position which many had long considered his due. He died March 26, 1882.

We are indebted to Mr. R. L. Nettleship for the publication of Green's works, which are contained in three volumes. The first and second volumes are philosophical and the third miscellaneous. Green's political theory is practically embodied in

---

① *Works*, Vol. III. Memoir XVII.
② *Works*. Vol. III. Memoir CXIX.

his Lectures on the *Principles of Political Obligation* delivered in 1879 and 1880. They are reprinted from the second volume of the *Works* and now appear in a separate volume for the convenience of the readers. His *Prolegomena to Ethics* contains the substance of a series of lectures on philosophy, embodying the metaphysical and ethical background of his political thought. It was published posthumously and not included in the *Works*. His lectures on Good Will, on The English Commonwealth and on Liberal Legislation and Freedom of Contract contribute directly to the understanding of his political theory.

In order, however, to give a clear view of his theory, it is necessary to present a general review of the intellectual tendencies of his time. A man of Green's type could not be easily satisfied with the traditional and the then existing English political and social philosophy. To him at least that philosophy lacked an adequate notion of the individual man. It more often considered man as a passive recipient of external stimuli than as an originator of various phases of human activities. To appreciate this let us trace the course of English speculation from Thomas Hobbes to the present time.

Hobbes(1588—1679), it will be remembered, was frankly materialistic.[1]He explained the acquisition of knowledge by the operation of the senses and attributed human passions and emo-

---

①   Dunning, *A History of Political Theories*. Vol. 2, p. 266.

tions to the antithesis of appetite and aversion.①In political theory, his conception of sovereign power was somewhat too absolute and his picture of the state of nature was altogether too gloomy. In this respect, Locke ( 1632—1704 ) was happier. His state of nature was by no means lawless. Intensely sympathetic with the revolution, he argued for popular sovereignty. Governmental power was to him always in the nature of fiduciary trust, hence he made it ultimately responsible to the people.②In his theory of knowledge he was essentially a sensationalist. His enthusiasm in combatting the theory of innate ideas carried him far into the precarious position of championing the doctrine of Tabula Rasa.③ Baldly stated, mind was to him but a blank and ideas were merely sensations "continued to the brain". That the doctrine was futile to the theologians need not be dwelt on at any length. Berkeley ( 1685—1753 ) inspired by theological idealism, struggled hard to overturn the Lockian premise, but his efforts seemed to have only resulted in the more cogent empiricism of David Hume ( 1711—1776 ). While in political theory the latter inflicted a fatal blow to the conception of social contract④, in ethics he prepared the way for Jeremy Bentham. His belief that utility was the determining motive in all phases of human conduct was strictly utilitarian and his conception of human nature as es-

---

① Hobbes, *Leviathan.* chap. 6.
② Locke, *Two Treatises of Government.*
③ Locke, *Essays on Human Understanding.*
④ Hume, *Essays, Moral, Political and Literary.* Vol. I, p. 443.

sentially knavish①was not different from that of Thomas Hobbes.

In the meantime the political doctrines promulgated by Locke were spread broadcast. In America the conception of natural rights and the idea of popular sovereignty found their way into legal documents.② While party differences soon appeared there was really no disagreement as to the fundamental principle. In France rightly or wrongly Montesquieu ( 1689—1755 ) admired the English political system of his time. Through him the doctrine of checks and balances became a political dogma for it was believed that only through that system could liberty be made secure.③At the same time Physiocrats were formulating their dogma of laisser-faire, and Jean Jacques Rousseau ( 1712—1778 ) paved the way for the principles of 1789. It was the former who started the study of economics, it was the latter who popularized the social contract.④His state of nature was one of isolation. His conception of a general will as the principle of sovereign action was revolutionary to the traditional line of thought, but his insistence that government should be based on the strict consent of the governed contained the same difficulty inherent in that theory. Though they—Rousseau and the Physiocrats—ran into different lines of thought, it may be safely said that they started from the

---

① Dunning, *A History of Political Theories.* Vol. 2, p. 383.

② Virginia Constitution of 1776 and Declaration of Independence.

③ Montesquieu, *Spirit of the Laws.* Book XI, Sec. 5.

④ Rousseau's influence on French Revolution, claimed by Janet, denied by Jellinek.

same principle. In England Adam Smith ( 1723—1790 ) , with a full load of physiocratic tendencies, came forth with a comprehensive system of political economy. At a time when the Industrial Revolution was making its initial progress, the Scotch moral philosopher could not be deprived of a large following. Where, however, the master was cautious, the disciples became positive and certain. Precepts became dogmas. Social relationships became economic laws. There soon came into prominence a group of men known as Classical Economists. Whatever their differences, whether the pessimism of Malthus ( 1766— 1834 ) , or the hardheadedness of Ricardo ( 1772—1823 ) or the rigidity of Senior ( 1790—1864 ) and M' Culloch ( 1789—1864 ) , they were all worshippers of what was then believed to be nature and natural taws. Human beings were primarily economic and economic laws were generally conceded as immutable.

In the field of law Blackstone ( 1723—1780 ) came out with his *Commentaries*. With an interest in history as intense as his, he could not regard with favor the conception of social contract. In fact, according to him, people kept together because of their sense of fear and helplessness. It was, however, in the rigid conception of sovereignty that he exercised the greatest influence. His analysis of law presupposed a political Superior and sovereignty came to be known as "supreme, irresistible, absolute and uncontrolled power". His *Commentaries* called Bentham's genius into play. With Bentham ( 1748—1832 ) and his disciples Utilitarianism came into prominence. Human motives and activities were according to them reducible into pleasure. That which produced pleasure was considered good and desirable, and that which produced pain, bad and to be avoided. Carried to the political field the slogan became "the greatest happiness for the greatest number". Government existed because people on the whole were happier than without it.① Law to Bentham was an expression of will in the form of a command. The conception of rights was unmeaning if not accompanied by a conception of duty. Rights and duties were interdependent. Legal rights and duties were not predicable of the sovereign, but moral rights and duties were. The power of the sovereign was finally based on the ability to cause the greatest happiness to the greatest number. The influence of the Utilitarians was readily felt, for even if nobody knew exactly what happiness was, every one could figure out for himself as to who really constituted the greatest number.

From the above review, it is easy to understand why Green is not in sympathy with the traditional political and social philosophy. Basically it is either materialistic or at best empirical, but Green is an idealist. Both Hobbes and Locke believed in the conception of a social contract, but to Green such a contract is both historically and logically impossible. The Utilitarians characterized human effort as pleasure seeking, but to Green pleasure is never the propelling force. The Economists created the fiction of an economic man, but to Green to believe in an

---

① Bentham, *Fragment on Government.*

economic man is to subject freedom to necessity.

John Stuart Mill ( 1806—1873 ) was somewhat of a puzzle. Indeed, it could be said of him as of the *Bible*, that saints and devils would make use of him alike. Known as a bourgeois economist, he was claimed by some to have died a socialist.①Starting as a Benthamite, he ended merely a nominal Utilitarian. Arguing for individualism, he was yet free from anarchistic tendencies. His essay *on Liberty* was a departure from the traditional point of view. In the words of Mr. Barker, it "gave a deeper and a more spiritual interpretation to the conception of liberty. From a conception of liberty as external freedom of action necessary for the discovery and pursuit of his material interests by each individual. Mill rose to the conception of liberty as free play for that spiritual originality with all its results in individual vigour and manifold diversity...In a similar way, in his *Essay on Representative Government* he spiritualized the Benthamite defense of democracy." ②

The period starting from 1848 to the late seventies was as diverse as Mill's intellectual personality. Enormous progress was made in all aspects of social science. Let us note the tendencies in Political Economy, Jurisprudence, History, Sociology and even in Biology in so far as they bear on political theory.

In Political Economy the theories of the Classical Economists still dominated the field. In their interpretation and

---

① Barker, *Political Thought from Spencer to To-day.* p. 213. "Pease, History of the Fabian Society". p. 259.

② Barker, *Political Thought from Spencer to To-day.*

formulation of economic laws, they in effect became the defenders of the then existing order. While foreign influence, whether the Nationalist Protectionism of Frederick List, or the International Socialism of Karl Marx ( 1818—1883 ), or the Communistic Utopianism of the early French writers, was not yet much felt in England, a somewhat disconcerting doctrine appeared on the horizon. Robert Owen's schemes failed in practise but his ideas succeeded in directing thought to a new direction. In the sphere of theory the Ricardian Socialist①failed to see any particular glory in the existing system of distribution of wealth. In the sphere of practical politics while there were no national workshops in London as there were in Paris in 1848, different attempts at economic and social reform were not totally lacking. While Cobden ( 1804—1865 ) and Bright ( 1811—1889 ), specifically aiming at the corn laws, preached for *laisser-faire*, Maurice ( 1805—1872 ) and Kingsley ( 1819—1875 ), moved by the prevailing misery, prayed for a more genuine cooperative effort.②When Henry George ( 1839—1897 ) published his *Progress and Poverty* in 1879 economic thought had already entered a new era.

In Jurisprudence the analytical school had its exponent in the person of John Austin ( 1790—1859 ). To him state was chiefly based upon force, and obedience was essentially a matter

---

① Lowenthal, *Ricardian Socialists.*
② Woodworth, *Christian Socialism in England.*

of fear. His theory of sovereignty, no matter how concisely stated, would involve a description rather than a definition. It involved firstly a determinate superior not in the habit of rendering obedience to a like superior, and secondly it involved a given society with its bulk of people habitually obedient to that determinate superior. "Positive law" was distinguished from positive morality. "Since" positive law "was primarily considered as a command from a superior, it followed that the sovereign was above legal rights and duties. On the other hand, Sir Henry Maine ( 1822—1888 ), dissatisfied with the analytical school, traveled far into antiquity and on his return trip sought to stem the rising tide of popular government.①The doctrines of Rousseau as well as those of the Benthamites were equally distasteful to him. With his immense intellectual power he sought to destroy both by a single blow, but in doing so he probably became more pessimistic than intended. Mr. Barker thinks that being a lawyer, Maine shared the conservatism of his profession, ② while Professor Giddings suggests that in his thoroughgoing study of early institutions he neglected the psychology of modern men.③

The historical method in the study of law in Germany as well as in England necessarily affected history proper, especially so when the idea of evolution began to be popular among the intellectual luminaries. The idea of evolution was claimed to be histor-

---

① Maine, *Popular Government.*
② Barker, *Political Thought From Spencer to To-day.* p. 168.
③ Giddings, *Democracy and Empire.* p. 181 Footnote.

ical method applied to the facts of nature and historical method was regarded as the idea of evolution applied to the development of human institutions. The roots of the present were believed to have been planted deep in the past. Hence antiquarian spirits of all sorts began their mental excursions into the back forests of Germany in order to explain the then existing political and social facts. Nor in historical interpretation was innovation lacking. The traditional method of a chronological enumeration of events was not entirely satisfactory. Neither was a teleological interpretation quite in keeping with the spirit of the times. Though the doctrine of economic determinism①of Karl Marx was not yet in vogue, Henry Thomas Buckle had already made an ambitious attempt②in a similar direction in 1857. While his particular work was not as successful as expected, it did stimulate further attempt by the younger generation.

From across the channel came the gospel of positivism and the worship of Humanity. A priori or metaphysical speculation was not believed to be capable of leading us anywhere, hence knowledge must be generated from the accumulated data of experience. From the conception of man as an independent atomic unit, there seemed to be an attempt to return to the Aristotelian dictum that man is by nature social. But in general outline, it looked as if traditional empiricism acquired a new garb and with

---

① *Communist Manifesto*, 1848.
② Buckle, *History of Civilization in England.*

218

it attracted wide attention. It made immense appeal to J. S. Mill and spurred Frederic Harrison ( 1831—    ) to a consideration of "Order and Progress." Comte was further regarded as the forerunner of the science of sociology. While America was and probably is the fertile home for this particular branch of science, England should see no cause for envy. Walter Bagehot ( 1826—1877 ) may not be classed as a formal sociologist, but he cherished genuine hope for political regeneration in the sociological process of imitation. His *English Constitution* was for quite a period the last word on that subject, and his *Physics and Politics* broke away at least in method from the more formal and legalistic writers. Herbert Spencer incorporated Sociology into his Synthetic Philosophy and produced the belated argument for laisser-faire embodied in his *Man versus State.*

There was enormous progress in the study of natural sciences after Darwin ( 1809—1882 ) came out with the results of his observation. It stimulated the study of animal organism and its adaptation. By analogy the study was gradually extended to the so-called social organism. Just as animal organisms have blood vessels and arteries, so also social organisms were believed to have the same. Just as animal organisms struggle for existence, so also social organisms were believed to be engaged in a similar struggle. The fit was believed to survive, but, as Prof. Huxley has pointed out, [1]

① Huxley, "The Struggle for Existence" in *Nineteenth Century*, for Feb., 1888, p. 165.

the fit was not necessarily the better, much less the best. This theory of social organism was not new but it was very much enriched in content, and received a different interpretation. In the hands of Plato it had served one purpose. In the hands of the Germans it served another. But under the leadership of Herbert Spencer it has become somewhat fatalistic, for while on the one hand it has led to a declaration of independence for matter in philosophy, ① on the other it has turned to be an argument for individualistic anarchism in politics.

In spite of previous statements, it may still be asked what is the exact connection between these sciences and political theory. We need bear in mind that political theory is not confined to articles and sections of this or that law. Nor is it limited to constitutions and governments, nor yet to conventions and customs. If it deals with men in society, it also has to deal with men as individuals. If it deals with the aims of political societies it also has to ascertain the vocation of the individual man. What, then, is the conception of man back of these sciences just enumerated? According to the classical economists man is an economic being. According to the utilitarians he is a pleasure seeker. From the point of view of the naturalist he is primarily an animal organism, and from the point of view of economic interpretation of history he is essentially a passive recipient of external forces. Historians tell him how he has come to be and the lawyers describe his legal

---

① *Works of T. H. Green.* Vol. I.

status. In fact every writer as well as every school of political thought, as Mr. Wallas has pointed out, ① has his or its own conception of human nature, and that conception is generally based on an abstract being who does not exist. Probably there is truth in every one of them. More likely there is exaggeration in all. Anyway, they seemed to Green to be one-sided and therefore inadequate conceptions upon which to build a comprehensive political philosophy. Political philosophy can not be satisfactory when it is built on inadequate conceptions. If it is unsatisfactory, it needs revision, but it can not be thoroughly revised unless for that purpose you also build a solid foundation. This, then, is the problem which Green took for himself to solve in his Ethics. His political theory built upon his ethics was embodied in his *Principles of Political Obligation*. With him ethics and politics can not be studied apart. Being a thorough-going idealist he revolted against empiricism. Believing in the moral vocation of man as differentiating him from mere animal organisms, he assumed the responsibility to emancipate English political theories from the domination of their naturalistic tendencies.

---

① Wallas, *Human Nature in Politics.* p. 12.

# Chapter I  The Metaphysical and Ethical Background

Green argues from the existence of nature to the possibility of knowledge and finally to the existence of an Eternal Consciousness. For our present purpose, since we are primarily concerned with the results of his speculation, we might as well start with his Eternal Consciousness without repeating the elaborate process of deduction.

According to him, there is for us and this world a supreme being or existence or God or whatever name you may give it, which is an Eternal, Unifying and Unconditioned Consciousness. It is not in time because it is the condition of there being time.[1] Neither is it in space because it is the condition of there being space. It never began nor will it ever end, because it is that by virtue of which there can be either a beginning or an end. There is no doubt that, according to Green, it is God; but whether or not it assumes the form of human personality he does not expressly affirm. We are told, however, that being divine it has

---

[1]  *Prolegomena to Ethics.* p. 59.

the attributes of divinity. It is complete and perfect. That which pertains to others gradually becomes, but it eternally is. It reveals itself in two different ways.[1]On the one hand, it reproduces itself in the subjective units which we call men, and on the other it is responsible for the single unalterable system of relations which we understand to be nature. In the one direction, because man is a subjective unit of consciousness, a reproduction of the Eternal Consciousness, he is also divine; and in the other because nature is thus constituted as a single unalterable system of relations which implies spirituality, it is on that account not merely natural. The Eternal Consciousness, while branching into these two directions, is none the less the source of both and therefore transcends them. It is at once responsible for what is called the spiritual principle in nature as well as the spiritual principle in knowledge—spiritual not in the sense of being mysterious but as opposed to phenomenal, that is, opposed to natural.

It has been shown in the introduction that the predominant influence in the intellectual world of Green's time was naturalism. Naturalism implies a study and knowledge of nature and its application to man. Green has no quarrel with the content or the usefulness of that knowledge, but he denies that that knowledge explains its own possibility. To state it baldly, a knowledge of nature does not explain the nature of knowledge. Probably the phrase "nature of knowledge" is one which Green would not employ himself, but

---

[1]  *Prolegomena to Ethics.* p. 37.

for our present purpose it serves our convenience without getting us into trouble. To Green, then, the fundamental question is: how is knowledge possible? The answer to this question is supplied by what he calls the spiritual principle in knowledge.

Let us first find out what nature means. To Green it means objects of possible experience, related events, the connected order of knowable facts or phenomena.①Knowledge implies that which knows and that which is known. The fact that nature in its mani foldness is or can be known implies a synthetic unifying principle that knows or is capable of knowing. In Green's words: "Nature implies something other than itself as the condition of its being what it is."②Since that something is other than nature, it does not exist as a part of nature. It is neither in time nor in space. It is a self-distinguishing Consciousness.

This consciousness is the agency through which there is for us a possible objective world. But it may be argued that mental actions are materially conditioned. That, however, may very well be so without making consciousness the result of material conditions, since those very conditions imply a consciousness which renders them in anyway comprehensible. It is also necessary to avoid a dualistic conception from which even Kant was not free.

"Macht zwar der Verstand die Natur, aber er schafft sie

---

① *Prolegomena.* p. 58. Hereafter the word "nature" or "natural" will be used only in this sense, and the word "phenomena" not limited to the Kantian sense.

② *Prolegomena.* p. 58.

nicht." By this Kant means that understanding makes nature, but out of material which it does not make. It implies a dualistic existence of a single reality. With Locke there is in existence an objective world side by side with what is called the work of our mind. The former is real, the latter is denied reality. Reality is attained only when what is conceived in the mind corresponds to the objective world. To Green this is entirely unmeaning, since it is only through our consciousness that it is possible for us to have an objective world at all. Reality is therefore not apart from consciousness. Since nature is an order of related objects or facts or events, reality is but the unalterableness①of a certain relationship presented to consciousness. Since relating is a matter of consciousness and therefore not merely natural, reality in the sense already defined can not be merely objective.

There is always the tendency, Green asserts, to treat the knowledge of nature as itself the result of natural processes. It is said that knowledge can not but proceed from experience and experience can only be deduced from objective reality. That in a sense there is truth in this statement Green does not deny; but he holds that we must accept it with reserve, for much, of course, depends upon the meaning of the word experience. If it means chemical or physical effects upon our physical organism, it may continue for any length of time without our knowledge of it; but the kind of experience we are supposed to derive knowledge from

---

① *Prolegomena.* p. 17.

is an altogether different thing. The latter is the experience of matters of fact "recognised as such."[1]Therefore there must he something that does the recognising. In other words, there must be consciousness, and a consciousness of matters of fact thus experienced can not be itself the result of those facts. Neither can a consciousness of experience be the result of that experience; for that experience can not be such if not recognized as such by consciousness. Then there is again the argument that consciousness is derived from previous events. This contention involves the supposition that "the primary consciousness of events results from a series of events of which there is no consciousness"[2]. This seems to be merely an attempt to postpone the difficulty, and as such is quite unmeaning; for events of which there is no consciousness can not be events within our experience and therefore can not be the source of our knowledge. From the argument above presented it appears to Green that knowledge is not a result of nature. Neither is it merely a result of experience. It implies a synthetic unifying principle which is the spiritual principle in knowledge.

But if it is by virtue of a consciousness that there is for us an objective world, does it not follow that the objective world is dependent upon our consciousness? Does it not further lead to the untenable conception that consciousness can create objects at will? And since human beings differ and thinking becomes diver-

---

① *Prolegomena*. p. 20.
② *Prolegomena*. p. 22.

gent, what is the basis of reality which, though it is an unalter-ableness of a system of relations, may be so to one without being so to an other? In order that we may be able to answer these questions, let us first examine roughly with Green the nature of nature.

Nature is, as has been pointed out, the connected order of knowable facts, or related events, or objects of possible experience or phenomena. Objects are always related. They are related in identity and probably in half a dozen other ways. If they are not otherwise related, they are related in difference. An unrelated object does not exist. Reality from our definition involves a system of relations. But when we speak of a system of relations we ought to be aware of its implication. It is to us such a familiar fact that we are apt to forget that it involves all the mystery, if it be a mystery, of many in one. Whether we say that a related thing is one in itself, manifold in respect of its relations, or that there is one relation between manifold things, we are equally affirming the unity of the manifold. Abstract the many relations from the one thing and there is nothing. They being the many determine or constitute its definite unity. It is not the case that it first exists in its unity and then is brought under various relations. Without the relations it would not exist at all. In like manner, the one re-lation is a unity of the many things. They, in their manifold be-ing, make the one relation. If these relations really exist, there is a real unity of the manifold, a real multiplicity of that which is one. But a plurality of things cannot of themselves unite in one relation, nor can a single thing of itself bring itself into a multitude of relations." ① There must, therefore, be something, other than the manifold objects, which does the relating and combining without effacing their individuality.

This unifying and combining principle on behalf of our intelligence we have already identified in our consideration of knowledge. In that case it is the spiritual principle in knowledge. According to Green, "the same or an analogous action is necessary to account for any relation whatever.... Either, then, we must deny the reality of relations altogether and treat them as fictions of our combining intelligence, or we must hold that, being the product of our combining intelligence, they are yet 'empirically real' on the ground that our intelligence is a factor in the reality of experience; or if we suppose them to be real otherwise than merely for us, otherwise than in the 'cosmos of our experience', we must recognise as the condition of this reality the action of some unifying principle analogous to that of our understanding." ②

It is evident that there must he not only a synthetic unifying principle in our knowledge of uniform relations between phenomena, but also a similar principle that accounts for there being such uniform relations at all. There are two principles, and the question that naturally arises is: how are they to be harmonized in order that there may be a single reality? From our conception

---

① *Prolegomena.* p. 33.
② *Prolegomena.* p. 34.

of Eternal Consciousness, it can be easily seen that the source of the system of relations in nature and the source of our knowledge of it are one and the same. The question, how does the order of nature harmonize with our conception of it, is answered by our recognition of the fact that our understanding of an order of nature and the relations that, constitute that order have a common spiritual source, namely, Eternal Consciousness.

Fully convinced of the futility of a dualistic conception of nature and knowledge, Green concludes that the true account to be given is that "the concrete whole, which may be described indifferently as eternal intelligence realised in the related facts of the world, or as a system of related facts rendered possible by such an intelligence, partially and gradually reproduces itself in us, communicating piecemeal, but in inseparable correlation, understanding and the facts understood, experience and the experienced world."①There is, in other words, a unity of nature and knowledge in Eternal Consciousness. In such a conception, there can not be any antagonism between appearance and reality, or between the work of mind and the facts of nature. The difficult problem of reality is for Green thus solved.

We have considered nature and knowledge as each having a spiritual principle and both having unity in Eternal Consciousness. We have yet to examine the bridge between the two in the actual process of acquiring knowledge. We need not go

---

① *Prolegomena.* p. 41.

into the details of the philosophical commonplaces, such as sensation, conception and perception. Being an idealist, Green necessarily discards the sensationalist point of view. Though he believes in the possibility of a priori conceptions, he concedes that knowledge may and generally does involve sensation. But it must be understood that mere sensation does not constitute knowledge. Knowledge, if it involves sensation, involves it as comprehended by consciousness. Only when consciousness is called into play can there be perception or knowledge.

It may be objected that under this doctrine we can make objects at will. But Green says that we can not make objects at will just as we can not make consciousness at will.[1] Again it may be said that our perceiving consciousness varies from time to time. It seems to be so in the process of our knowing, and our learning to know this world. That is explained by Green as a process through which our animal organism, which has a history in time, is gradually being made a vehicle of the Eternal Consciousness, which has no history and is not in time. Our consciousness may be viewed in two ways. It may "be either a function of the animal organism, which is being gradually and with interruptions made a vehicle of Eternal Consciousness; or that Eternal Consciousness itself, as making the animal organism its vehicle and subject to certain limitations in doing so, but retaining its essential characteristics as independent of time, as determinant of becoming,

---

[1]  *Prolegomena.* p. 74.

*which has not and does not itself become.* ①The consciousness that varies from time to time is the consciousness in the former sense. The consciousness in virtue of which there can be either nature or knowledge is the consciousness in the latter sense. The above conception does not mean that there is double consciousness in men, but it does mean that the one individual reality of our consciousness can not be comprehended in a single conception. ②

We may profitably illustrate the whole process of our knowledge by the example Green furnishes out of our reading. " In reading the sentence we see the words successively, we attend them successively, we recall their meaning successively. But throughout their succession there must be present continuously the consciousness that the sentence has a meaning as a whole: otherwise the successive vision, attention and recollection would not end in a comprehension of what the meaning is. This consciousness operates in them, rendering them what they are as organic to the intelligent reading of the sentence. And when the reading is over, the consciousness that the sentence has a meaning has become a consciousness of what in particular the meaning is, a consciousness in which the successive results of the mental operations involved in the reading are held together, without succession, as a connected whole. The reader has, then,

---

① *Prolegomena.* p. 78.
② *Prolegomena.* p. 78.

so far as that sentence is concerned, made the mind of the writer his own. The thought which was the writer's when he composed the sentence, has so determined, has so used as organs, the successive operations of the sense and soul of the reader, as to reproduce in him through them; and the first stage in this reproduction, the condition under which alone the processes mentioned contribute to it, is the conviction on the reader's part that the sentence is a connected whole, that it has a meaning which may be understood." [1]The world has its author, nature is his book, man is the reader and reading is knowing. The above may be a crude illustration in philosophy, but it is one that renders clear the acquisition of human knowledge.

That knowledge is empirically conditioned is not open to doubt in Green's mind. He says in one place that the fact that there is a real external world of which through feeling we have a determinate experience, and that in this experience all our knowledge of nature is implicit, is one which no philosophy disputes.[2]That is to say, consciousness would not be what at any time it is but for a series of events sensible or related to sensibility. On the other hand, man would not be the same subject of intelligent experience if not for the self-realization or reproduction in himself of an Eternal Consciousness which is the condition of there being experience. In virtue of his knowing character in the

---

①    *Prolegomena.* p. 81.

②    *Works of T. H. Green.* Vol. I, p. 376.

latter sense, man may be said to enjoy freedom in intelligence. In Green's words he is a "free cause." The word "cause" is not used in the ordinary sense of a necessary antecedent to a given effect; for then it also implies conditions precedent to that antecedent. Cause and effect in the world of phenomena represent a kind of relationship, with one determining the other and itself determined by still other causes. Freedom is not involved in the determination of one natural event by another or of one phenomenon by another phenomenon.①Such determination is in two senses unrelated to freedom: first, it does not imply in either the cause or the caused a consciousness of self both as a subject and as an object; and second, it is a determination in which things external to each other form that particular relationship which we call cause and effect.

If we transfer the term "cause" from the above sense to apply to the relation between the world and the agent implied in its existence, we shall find that "free cause" means the determination of man to action by himself. Man is really only free when he acts under the idea that he himself determines himself or his action. The man whom we contemplate from the point of view in which he appears as subject to the laws of nature, as part and parcel of nature, is not a real man.②Real or not, it may be objected that man's attainment of knowledge is conditioned on

---

① *Works of T. H. Green.* Vol. I, p. 109.
② *Works of T. H. Green.* Vol. I, p. 108.

processes in time and on the performance of strictly natural functions. If these processes and functions are so essential to him, how can it be said that a man thus conditioned is not a part of nature but is himself free? The fact that consciousness realizes and reproduces itself in an animal organism does not render a man a mere animal, any more than the fact that animals employ mechanical structures for their movements make the animals mere machines.[1]Man is conscious of himself. He consciously distinguishes himself from his relations. He is conscious of his being a unit, a subject and an object at the same time. Now this self distinction of himself as a manifestation of consciousness is not a process in time, for it is that by virtue of which there can be time. By virtue of his self distinction, he exerts himself freely in activities which are not in time and are not linked in the chain of natural events. His activities are self originated. There is no incompatibility between this principle and the physical processes of brain and nerve which are necessary to human activity. These processes do not make up the knowing and self distinguishing man, and it is, after all, the knowing and self distinguishing man who is a "free cause" in intelligence.

The above paragraphs aim to show that according to Green there is an Eternal Consciousness and that Consciousness reveals itself in two ways: first, in what is called the spiritual principle in nature; and second, in what is similarly styled the spiritual

---

① *Prolegomena.* p. 89.

principle in knowledge.

The former becomes the knowable nature. The latter becomes the knowing man. His freedom, as we have seen, is established and his spirituality proven. But we have not yet dealt with man other than as a knowing being. We do not yet know his moral capacities. Morality consists in the disinterested performance of selfimposed duties.①Moral actions involve willing and the objects willed. It is therefore necessary in the following paragraphs to dwell on the nature of will and the considerations it involves. It is also necessary to examine into the character of the objects willed and its bearing to the persons other than those who do the willing. In the previous paragraphs we were speculating in the world of knowledge, but in the following paragraphs we shall be speculating in the sphere of morality. In the former the purpose is to explain the human effort to know that which is knowable and in the latter the purpose will be to account for the attempt to achieve that which is desired. In other words, to make the contrast more striking even at the risk of being misunderstood, the former is to reduce that which is real to ideal and the latter will be to render that which is ideal also real.

Leaving the world of knowledge we now proceed to the world of practise, bearing in mind that by practise is meant giving reality to conceived object.②We have shown that the process of

---

① *Principles of Political Obligation.* p. 40.
② *Works of T. H. Green.* Vol. II, p. 117.

knowledge is not natural, we shall now try to demonstrate that moral action is not natural either. Since all actions involve willing, it is only logical for us first to define its character and then to find out what it invariably involves. "Will is the capacity in a man of being determined to action by the idea of a possible satisfaction of himself. An act of will is an action so determined."①Will always involves motive, for there is no unmotivated will.② And motive involves wants and desires which may be, and often are, of animal origin. But on the other hand, it involves not only those wants and desires but also a presentation of them to a self-distinguishing consciousness. A desire is not a motive unless it is presented to consciousness and recognised as such and also as a possible source of satisfaction of one's self. Furthermore, it always involves an idea of good—whatever that may be—in that satisfaction. This idea of good is what gives rise to moral action. It involves a self-reflection and it also involves a judgment. Such reflection and judgment may require constant reference to "customary expressions of moral consciousness" and to "institutions embodying ideals of permanent good". But in the interpretation of these expressions and institutions, reflection and judgment are after all the ultimate determining factors. Motive thus considered involves animal objects, desires or sensible phenomena, but is not itself animal or phenomenal. Just as understanding involves

---

① *Principles of Political Obligation.* p. 31.
② *Principles of Political Obligation.* p. 13.

nature that is in time but is itself not in time, so also motive involves objects that are animal and therefore in time but is itself neither animal nor in time. Just as there is freedom in intelligence so also there is freedom in will. In both cases the self-determining and self-distinguishing consciousness is at work.

Will is necessarily influenced by our desire and intellect. In order therefore to understand the character of our will, we have to examine it in relation to both desire and intellect and their interrelation. Ordinarily when we speak of desire we do not differentiate mere animal desire from the desire that is identified by a self-determining consciousness. The former has no moral character because, itself apart from and unidentified by consciousness, it is merely physically determined. Mere animal desires are, however, of a very limited range. Most desires are not dependent upon animal susceptibility, ① and even if so dependent are themselves transformed by a new element derived from the action of a self-determining consciousness. There is sometimes a state of mind in which many desires conflict and it is said that the strongest desire emerges victorious and hence becomes our will. This, however, does not meet Green's approval. To him will is not desire, whether strong or not. If the word desire is to be persistently used to cover the meaning of both will and animal wants, we need bear in mind that it does not mean the same thing. The desires that are yet conflicting are desires

___

① *Prolegomena.* p. 141.

that are not identified by self-consciousness as possible sources of satisfaction out of which good may be derived, while the desire that is so identified by a self-consciousness is already different from those that are conflicting, that is, it is already a motive. In the one case man is acting himself in acting upon a desire that is identified by himself, but in the other the desires exert an influence on him when he is yet undecided. There is no moral significance in the latter but there is in the former.

Let us next turn to the relation between desire and intellect. Is there any unity between the two or are they diametrically opposed to each other? Unity is easily seen at the source, for "the real agent called Desire is the man or subject or self as desiring: the real agent called Intellect is the man as understanding, as perceiving and conceiving: and the man that desires is identical with the man that understands."①The problem is, however, that to desire is plainly not the same as to understand, and the two things can not be satisfactorily explained merely by their relation to the identical source. Green's explanation②is that both desire and intellect involve the consciousness of self and of a world as opposed to it and the effort to overcome this opposition. Desire strives to overcome this opposition by giving or trying to give reality to an object which when first desired is only ideal. Intellect strives to overcome the opposition by rendering or trying to render

---

① *Prolegomena.* p. 146.
② *Prolegomena.* p. 147.

ideality or intelligibility to an object which when first presented is only sensible. Furthermore, "the exercise of the one is always a necessary accompaniment of the other. In all exercise of understanding desire is at work." ①And vice versa. "No man learns to know anything without desiring to know it." ②Conversely no one really desires anything without intelligently calculating the possibilities of its realisation. Thus it will be seen that desire and intellect are interwoven, and after all they are different manifestations of the same self-consciousness. They are not separate powers of which one can be exercised without the other. The act of thinking involves the act of desiring and the act of desiring involves the act of thinking. Therefore there is a unity inherent in the actions of both besides the identity of source from which these actions necessarily spring.

It remains necessary for us to examine the relationship between will and intellect. It has sometimes been urged that willing and thinking are opposite to each other. It has also been said that mere thinking is not willing or that willing is more than thinking. The latter implies that a complementary element needs be added in order to make thinking equal to willing. That is, "if we say, for example, that the act of willing to pay a debt is more than mere thinking" of paying it: what we mean is that "the mere thinking about paying the debt falls short of willing to pay it."

---

①    *Prolegomena*. p. 151.
②    *Prolegomena*. p. 151.

This depends upon the meaning of the term thinking. Evidently it is not the kind of thinking that involves a consciousness of "self and the world as mutually determined, of an object present to the self in a desire felt by it, but awaiting realisation in the world."① Such thinking is always present in willing. A thoughtless will in the above sense is not a will at all. Furthermore, the object willed is the realisation of an idea. It may be an idea of good, or of self-satisfaction or of a dozen other things, but it is none the less an idea. The object of will is also an object of thought.②In this sense, therefore, thinking is willing. It is not merely a part of us. It is not merely an element in willing. Nor is there any element or factor in willing that is separate. and separable from thought. That is, will does not consist of different elements of which thinking is one and has a compartment of its own altogether separate from that of the others. Such a conclusion is inevitable, as will be seen from our discussion of desire and intellect, knowledge and nature and the synthetic unifying principle of human consciousness.

However, this separate discussion of desire, intellect and will may leave the impression that they are independent elements that make up a given action by man. This is, of course, far from being the opinion of the author himself. He does not, for a moment, think of will as consisting of desire in addition to, and

---

① *Prolegomena.* p. 170.
② *Prolegomena.* p. 171.

therefore apart from, intellect; for "desire of the kind that enters into willing involves thought; and thought of the kind that enters into willing involves desire."①Each is not without the other. In fact, there is unity in all. According to Green, "will is equally and indistinguishably desire and thought.... If so, it must be a mistake to regard will as a faculty which a man possesses along with other faculties and which has the singular privilege of acting independently of other faculties, so that, given a man's character as it at any time results from the direction taken by those other faculties, the will remains something apart which may issue in action different from that prompted by the character. The will is the man. Any act of the will is the expression of the man as he at the time is."②All the time that he so wills, he may feel, think and desire one hundred and one things, but after all, "it is only the feeling, thought and desire represented by the act of the will that the man recognises as for the time himself."

When Green speaks of self, he means by it the unit in which the Eternal Consciousness reproduces itself. It is "the only thing or a form of the only thing that is real in its own right: the only thing of which the reality is not relative or derived."③That thus conceived the socalled self becomes somewhat mysterious, Green concedes, if by saying mysterious is meant the inability to explain the question why. But then it is no more so than the very

① *Prolegomena*. p. 171.
② *Prolegomena*. p. 173.
③ *Prolegomena*. p. 113.

241

existence of the world. Nor is it in any way abstract; for just as desires, feelings and thoughts would not be what they are if not related to a subject which distinguishes itself from each and all of them, so this subject would not be what it is, if it were not related to the particular desires, feelings and thoughts which it thus distinguishes from and presents to itself.① In other words, this conception of self as uniting these desires, feelings and thoughts can not be regarded as too abstract. It expresses itself through them when at any particular time it identifies itself with any of them.

Human will may be either good or bad. Since good and bad are relative terms, a discussion of the one will reveal the nature of the other. What, we may ask, does good will consist of? According to Green, who agrees in the main with Kant, good will consists chiefly of determination by "practical reason" to an action involving an object which is capable of an unity in one's self and others. What is "practical reason"? Practical means that which pertains to giving reality to conceived objects. And "practical reason" Green defines as "a consciousness of a possibility of a perfection to be realised in and by the subject of consciousness"②. Willing involves a subject, as has been explained at length, but in this case, in the case of good will, it involves also an object that originates in reason.③ This object does not originate

---

① *Prolegomena*. p. 113.
② *Principles of Political Obligation*. p. 20.
③ *Works of T. H. Green*. Vol. II, p. 110.

in desire, for it is "desirable before it is desired and it is coming to be desired because it has been previously recognised as desirable" ①. There is, then, a quality of unconditionalness of this object. Green is careful to point out that the object of will is not ordinarily, and to use his own words, does not generally coincide with, the object of reason. But like a good philosopher he is far from being hopeless, for the object of will is "intrinsically or potentially and tends to be actually the same as that of reason" ②.

Good will, in order to be directed to a common object, also involves an idea of an unity of one's self and others. This point can be made clear by Green's discussion of common good and pleasure seeking. His writings are so full of attacks on Hedonism and Utilitarianism that it is hard to single out any particular one for quotation. In the following passage his expressions are quite emphatic and almost vehement. To seek pleasure is to direct one's "dominant interest to an object private to himself, a good in which others can not share. The character of a pleasure seeker is necessarily selfish in this sense.... That the pleasure seeker lives for an object private to himself may seem inconsistent with the fact that we share each other's pleasure, but it is not so. When a man is said to share another's pleasure, what is meant is that having desired the same object with the other, he is equally pleased with its attainment; or that, the pleasure of the other

---

① *Works of T. H. Green.* Vol. II, p. 111.
② *Principles of Political Obligation.* p. 21.

having been his object, he is satisfied when that object is obtained when the other is pleased. In each case the pleasure is private to the person enjoying it, and so it must be even when it is incidental to the attainment of an object which is really common. It is only because we confuse the pursuit of a common object, that is, of a good by which others than the pursuer will be the better, with the pursuit of pleasure which will ensue when the object is attained, and thus regard those as pleasure seekers who are not really so, that we come to imagine there can be pleasure seekers who are not selfish, not living for an object purely private to themselves." ① Pleasure, then, is not necessarily good. It may be incidental to the realization of an object considered good, but it is not itself the object.

The above account serves to point out that pleasure seeking is not willing a common good, but it does not exactly tell what that common good is. In order to know what common good is, we have to know what good is. Good, if it is to be true at all, is that which satisfies the desire of the moral agent; and a moral agent is defined as one who is disinterestedly performing self-imposed duties. But according to Green, just what is the nature of good can not be exactly ascertained. We may, however, form a general idea about it. As has been pointed out earlier. The Eternal Consciousness reproduces itself in human beings. "In virtue of this principle in him, man has definite capabilities, the realisation of

---

① *Works of T. H. Green.* Vol. II, p. 144.

which, since in it alone he can satisfy himself, forms his true good. They are not realised, however, in any life that can be observed, in any life that has been or is or that can be lived by man as we know him; and for this reason we cannot say with any adequacy what the capabilities are. Yet because man's spiritual endowment is the consciousness of having it, the idea of his having such capabilities and of a possible better state of himself consisting of their further realisation is the moving influence in him.... As his true good is or would be their complete realisation, so his goodness is proportionate to his habitual responsiveness to the idea of there being such a true good in the various forms of recognized duty and beneficent work in which that idea has so far taken shape among men. In other words, it consists in the direction of the will to the objects determined for it by this idea, as operative in the person willing, which direction of the will we may, upon the ground stated, fitly call its determination by reason."[1] And reason is defined as the capacity on the part of the self-conscious subject to conceive a possibility of perfection of himself as an end to be attained by action.

The above, then, is the conception of a true good. That it is somewhat dogmatic, Green expressly admits.[2] That it fails to offer a sure guide seems to be unavoidable; for if we know definitely what those capacities are we shall be more than human be-

---

(1) *Prolegomena*. pp. 206-207.
(2) *Prolegomena*. p. 206.

ings, we shall be God. But it is this idea of a true good that makes possible the idea of a common good. In fact the latter is inherent in the former. The idea of the absolutely desirable arises out of man's consciousness of himself as an end to himself. Now this self is neither abstract nor empty. He is bound up with interests in common with others. One can not contemplate himself in a better state without contemplating others, not merely as a means to that better state but as sharing it with him. In other words there is a consciousness of kind. Satisfaction of one's self should include satisfaction of others. Well being, in order to be permanent, must be one in which self and others are included. In fact individuals and society are mutually interdependent. While "the life of the nation has no real existence except as the life of the individuals composing the nation"①, individuals could not be what they are independent of their existence in a nation.

Green's discussion of the development of personality reveals further the interdependence of individuals and society. Human society to him presupposes persons in capacity—the capacity to conceive himself and the bettering of his life as an end in himself—and it is only in the intercourse of men each recognized by each as an end, not merely as a means, that the capacity is actualized and that we really live as persons. Later on Green says:

---

① *Prolegomena*. p. 211.

"*Without society, no person.*" ① "This is as true as that without persons, without self-objectifying agents, there could be no such society as we know. Such society is founded on the recognition by persons of each other, and their interests in each other, as persons, that is as beings who are ends to themselves, who are consciously determined to action by the conception of themselves as that for the sake of which they act. They are interested in each other in so far as each, being aware that another presents his own satisfaction to himself as an object, finds satisfaction for himself in procuring the self-satisfaction of the other. Society is founded on such mutual interest in the sense that unless it is operative,... there would be nothing to lead to that treatment of one human being by another, as an end not merely as a means, on which society even in its narrowest and most primitive forms must rest." ②
While on the one hand there can not be society except as between persons each recognising the other as an end in himself and having the will to treat him as such, on the other, it is only through society that individuality can seek actualisation. It will be seen, then, that Green is neither a blind worshipper of society, nor an advocate of anarchistic individualism.

This sketch of Green's metaphysical and ethical doctrines, however short, serves a definite purpose. It points out that according to Green, man is not natural. In intelligence he is a "free

---

① *Prolegomena.* p. 218.
② *Prolegomena.* p. 218.

cause." In willing he is a free man. He is free in the sense that he is not subject to the determination by external forces. He is self-determined; and in that determination in which he is himself both the subject and the object, there is no "necessity", but freedom. With a free will he is capable of moral action, and with his freedom in intelligence he is capable of creative effort. With his faculty of reason he conceives the idea of good. With his consciousness of an unity of himself with the others, what Prof. Giddings broadly calls the consciousness of kind, he is capable of good will and the idea of common good. Such, then, is the metaphysical and ethical conception of men.

In order to understand Green's political theory, we need bear this conception in mind. In other words, it is necessary to understand the broad metaphysical and ethical foundation upon which his political theory is built, before we can proceed to discuss that theory proper. It may be objected that nowhere is attention paid to what is embodied in conventional morality, such things as virtue, courage, truthfulness, etc. The answer is that they form the content of morality. While they are related to Green's ideas of laws, institutions and customs—which will be dealt with later on—they are not strictly within the sphere of political action. Moral duties are not capable of legal enforcement. In Green's own words, "There is moral duty in regard to obligations, but there can be no obligations as to moral duty."[1]Since

---

[1]  *Principles of Political Obligation.* p. 34.

political action is chiefly directed towards maintaining conditions under which morality becomes possible, it is not within the sphere of this treatise to elaborate on that which properly belongs to moral content.

# Chapter II   The Theory of
# Natural Rights


Green's political theory may be divided into two parts, namely, the principle of political obligation and the principle of state interference. The first includes the theory of natural rights and the theory of the true basis of the state. We will begin with the theory of natural rights.

It is easily seen that Green agrees with Aristotle that man is by nature a social being. There is, therefore, no such separate and isolated man as that described by Rousseau. Even if there is such an animal, it can not be the possessor of rights; for every right involves always two elements, ① a claim on the part of the individual and a recognition of that claim by other individuals. Therefore, if there are any such rights worth speaking of, there is already a society. The idea of men's possessing rights in the sense of rights prior to the formation of society is entirely unfounded.

The theory that society came into existence by contract implies that prior to the institution of the contract, the contracting

---

① *Principles of Political Obligation.* p. 45.

parties were separate and isolated individuals. According to Green, there were no such individuals. The same theory implies that these isolated individuals had fundamental natural rights. According to Green, there were no such rights. Furthermore, social contract assumes that in forming such a contract men were free and equal. "But if freedom is understood in the sense in which most of these writers seemed to understand it as a power of executing, of giving effect to one's will, the amount of freedom possessed in a state of nature, if that state was one of detachment and collision between individuals, must have been very small. Men must have been constantly thwarting each other and thwarted by the powers of nature. In such a state, those only could be free, in the senses supposed, who were not equal to the rest, who in virtue of superior power could use the rest. But whether we suppose an even balance of weakness in subjection to the crushing force of nature, or a domination of a few over many by means of a superior strength, in such a state of nature no general pact is possible."①It is clear, then, that social contract is not only historically non-existent but also logically impossible.

That does not mean, however, that there are no such things as natural rights if rightly understood. Let us first of all state the traditional conception of natural rights more fully. Human beings are supposed to be born into this world with such rights as of life,

---

① *Principles of Political Obligation*, p. 70.

liberty and property.① These rights are natural because they existed for man prior to his forming and joining the social contract and are retained by him after he entered into it. Social contract made political action possible and political action gave rise to legal and civil systems of duties and rights. It is only easy to conclude that these legal or civil rights, being dependent upon natural rights, should base their justification upon their compatibility with those natural rights. Hence the question whether a given civil duty is justifiable or not is determined according as it is or is not compatible with natural rights. But Green asks if civil or legal rights are justified in accordance with their compatibility with natural rights, how are these natural rights to be justified? There is the same necessity of reducing natural rights to something more fundamental, for the question why should these rights be maintained at all has not been answered. They certainly can not exist by themselves. They can not exist without a society, that is, they exist in virtue of there being a society. If their existence is relative to society, their existence is dependent upon something other than themselves. As to what that something is, the traditional conception of natural rights is unable to give us a satisfactory answer, The Utilitarians indeed have made an improvement in that they regard rights and duties as relative to pleasure and pain. To them rights and duties should be enforced according to their consequences; that is, if their enforcement re-

---

① The French and American Declarations differ in specific rights.

sults in more pleasure enjoyed and less pain sustained, then that enforcement is commendable. This theory avoids the necessity of reducing secondary rights to primary rights which are logically non-existent. To Green, of course, this theory is not acceptable since he does not accept the utilitarian premise. Pleasure and pain are not that to which rights and duties should be considered relative.

In order to understand Green's own theory, we have to refer back to his Ethics. We learn from the previous chapter that there are such things as good will, common good and moral ideal. Moral ideal is the one factor to which others are relative, to which rights and duties are relative. The word "natural" may be used to qualify certain rights, but in the sense in which alone it can be used, it does not mean "primary", or "previous to the formation of society" or "pertaining to a state of nature". "Natural" as employed by Green means necessary and necessary for a given purpose. Natural rights are therefore necessary rights for the purpose "which it is the vocation of human society to realise"①. In other words natural rights are not themselves an end but a means to an end, just as laws are also means to an end. A law is not good merely because it enforces natural rights; it is good because it contributes to the realisation of a certain end. That end is the fulfillment of men's vocation as moral beings, the moral ideal. This conception of rights is necessarily based on what should be,

---

① *Principles of Political Obligation*, p. 34.

rather than what actually is, possessed by men in society. It implies an ideal, unattained condition of one's self to which these rights are necessary. Without such an ideal there can be no natural rights in the sense just discussed; for if the end is not held in view, the means has no excuse for existence.

It will be seen from the above that there are two necessary conditions①under which alone we can possibly speak of rights. No one could begin to think of rights if, first, he is not a member of a society, and, second, of a society in which some common good is recognised by the members of the society as their own ideal good. The capacity of being determined by the idea of good so recognised is what constitutes a moral being. Since rights exist, the realization of a moral ideal, only men of moral capacity are entitled to rights. Not only are they entitled to them, they must also actually possess them. Moral capacity "implies a consciousness on the part of the subject of the capacity that its realisation is an end desirable in itself."②Rights are the conditions of realising that end. Only through possessing rights could a man realise that which is recognised as good for himself and society. That does not mean that rights make any positive contribution to one's realisation in the sense that they actively and actually help him to realize. But it does mean that they are the conditions under which the positive realization of moral capacity is made

---

① *Principles of Political Obligation*, p. 44.
② *Principles of Political Obligation*, p. 45.

possible.

The question as to why it is necessary that a person in order to have rights must be a member of a soceity, is answered by the inherent qualities of both the persons and rights. The chapter on the Metaphysical and Ethical Background reveals the necessary relationships between persons and society. Though society can not exist apart from persons, a person in the sense in which Green designates him to be can not exist apart from society. Persons and the society are mutually dependent. Rights just as much as persons must also be considered from the individual as well as the social side. They involve a claim on the part of the individual and the recognition of that claim on the part of the rest constituting the society. The individual claims the capacity to conceive a common good as his own and direct his energies in the light of that common good. The society recognizes his claim as necessary, for each and every one of the society for the purpose of furthering that common good. Without either this claim or this recognition there can be no right. With these two considerations as necessary ingredients, rights can not belong to any isolated being, any being existing apart from society. Natural rights are therefore necessary conditions for the realization, of the moral ideal, the fulfilment of the moral capacity. In this sense and in this sense alone therefore there are such things as natural rights, always bearing in mind that by natural is not meant "primary" or "previous to the formation of society" or "pertaining to the state of nature".

What are, then, some of the conditions for moral life, or

rather conditions under which moral life may be possible? What are some of these rights? There are two great divisions, the private and the public. Private rights are those that exist for a man as one in society and public rights are those that come to be attached to a man as a citizen of a state. Of the private rights there are three classes, namely, the personal rights, the rights of property and the rights of private relations. The first term may be somewhat misleading, since all rights are personal, since it is only by virtue of a person that they are rights at all. By personal rights are meant the rights of life and liberty, that is, "of preserving one's body from the violence of other men and of using it as an instrument of only one's own will."①In other words, the right to free life, including both the right to liberty and life, is essential to the fulfilment of the moral capacity of man and it is only duly claimed and recognized that it becomes a right in the sense in which we have already defined it.

Let us next consider the rights of property. Since property is the center of our modern controversy, we are probably entitled to go more into detail than is warranted in our consideration of personal rights. The fundamental action involved in the acquisition of property is appropriation, and appropriation according to Green is an expression of will, of the individual's effort to give reality to a conception of his own good. Whether it is an instinctive act or not as applied to ants or bees, we do not know, but as it is applied

---

① *Principles of Political Obligation.* p. 155.

to men it certainly is not an instinctive act. The act of appropriation, like every other act of that sort, reflects a self consciousness capable of distinguishing itself from its wants. This self consciousness says in effect, according to Green, "this ( or that )
shall be mine to do as I like with, to satisfy my wants and express my emotions as they arise." ① Property thus appropriated,
instead of remaining a mere external material necessary for
bodily sustenance, has become interwoven with the personality
of the man who appropriates it. Appropriation can not therefore
be merely instinctive.

But appropriation as described above is only a claim and a
claim alone does not constitute a right. It has to be recognized before it acquires validity. Of the various explanations urged for the
validity of property rights, none is entirety satisfactory. Grotius
attributed the right of property to a contract, but according to
Green②contract presupposes property. Hobbes regards the right
of property as dependent upon the existence of a sovereign power
of compulsion who grants such a right.③But the sovereign power,
if merely a strong force of compulsion, can not be the source of
rights, and, if a representative maintainer of rights, implies or
presupposes rights. Locke returns to the law of nature and law of
reason in his consideration of the right of property.④Just as a man

---

① *Principles of Political Obligation.* p. 213.
② *Principles of Political Obligation.* p. 214.
③ *Principles of Political Obligation.* p. 214.
④ *Principles of Political Obligation.* p. 216.

is entitled to his body, so he is entitled to the results of the work of his body and the labor of his hand. Property is the result of labor and necessary for the maintenance and expression of life. Locke has the merit of pointing out the intricate relationship between personal rights and the rights of property, but he does not explain the exact grounds upon which the rights can be rights in any sense. According to Green, the basis of the recognition of the claim to property is the same as that of the other claims to rights. Just as society recognizes the claims of a free life as themselves necessary conditions for moral realization and for the common good of the whole, so also it recognizes the claim to property as necessary for that common good. Just as the foundation of the rights of free life lies in the human will, so also the foundation of the right of property.[1]

Green is fully alive to the results of the historical development of the institution of property. He recognizes the divergence between the rational justification and the actual consequences of the right to property. Theoretically, indeed, all may have property, but as a matter of fact he sees that great numbers do not get it. At least they do not get it in the measure in which alone it is of any value; that is, they fail to get a sufficient amount of it to enable them to give expression to their moral life and to facilitate the realization of their moral ideal. He recognizes

---

[1] *Principles of Political Obligation.* p. 217.

that a man who has nothing①but his labor to sell for a bare subsistence is factually denied the right of property in the ethical sense, the only sense in which property is at all desirable. According to Green, however, this miserable condition is only incidental to and not inherent in the right of property. That right itself is necessary for a moral purpose. The fact that many who have property do not use it for that purpose is no ground for believing that it can not be used for that purpose and therefore should be abolished. Only is it condemnable when the possession of it by one interferes with like possession by another. Only when property of one is used to prevent the acquisition by another does Green subscribe to the Proudhonian declaration that property is theft.②The right of property should accordingly carry with it two conditions.③First, labor, and, second, the respect for the same right of the others, in order that it may not defeat its own purpose.

How shall the right of property thus considered be reconciled with the freedom of trade and the freedom of bequest with all their consequences? Freedom of trade involves the game of buying in the cheapest and selling in the dearest market and in so buying and selling, the merchant often absorbs the legitimate share of labor. Freedom of bequest permits wealth to be

---

① *Principles of Political Obligation.* p. 219.

② *Principles of Political Obligation.* p. 220.

③ *Principles of Political Obligation.* p. 220.

transmitted from its creator to his offspring who may not have labored at all towards creating and possessing that wealth. On the whole, however, Green is not antagonistic towards these policies merely because they give rise to inequality of wealth; for he argues that wealth, given the purpose for which it alone can be claimed and recognized as a right, will be just as unequal as men are unequal. Green, to be sure, is not the kind of hero worshipper as, for instance, Carlyle, though he is quite given to admiration for great men. Neither does he believe in the doctrine that "all men are created equal". Furthermore, in equality of wealth is not necessarily the cause of misery; for wealth is not a fixed stock[1]of which more for one means necessarily less for the other. On the contrary, production can be increased and distribution improved. Though he deplores the condition of a large number of men in England at his time, he has pointed out that many, while working at factories, are the owners of shares of stock. It is evident that what he hopes to see is an eventual diffusion of income, a result which many economists confidently expect. Green has very decided opinions on property in land, but that can better be discussed in connection with the principle of state interference.

Lastly let us consider briefly the rights of private relations. These rights are logically based on the same ground as are the other rights. But there is an important difference. The rights of

---

[1]  *Principles of Political Obligation.* p. 224.

life and liberty are primarily related to the person himself. The right of property is a right over things. But the rights of private relations are rights over persons other than the claimer and possessor of these rights. Husbands and wives have mutual rights over each other. Without going into all the details we may profitably examine two or three points. What, for instance, is it in men that makes them capable of family life? How has there come to be recognition of mutual rights and duties? Is monogamy justifiable? The answer to the first question can be guessed from Green's ideas in other connections. The formation of family supposes a like effort on the part of the parties concerned to give reality to a conception of their own good. It also supposes that this conception of a good is shared by others in the society whose well being is interwoven with their own. The claim of husband over wife and of wife over husband is recognized as conducive to the realization of a common good. Whatever the historical development may be, the rational justification of the rights of private relations is the same as that urged for other rights.

According to Green, all men and all women are entitled to marry and form households and within the households the claims of husband and wife are throughout reciprocal. Polygamy is therefore incapable of justification for several reasons. "It is a violation of the rights first of those who through it are indirectly excluded from regular marriage and therefore from the moral education which results from it, second, of the wife who is morally lowered by exclusion from her proper position in the household and by being used, more or less, as a mere instrument for the husband's pleasure, third, of the children who lose the chance of that full moral training which depends on the concerted action of mother and father." [1] The first stipulation is evidently based on the supposition that the number of women and men is about equal. Just as polygamy is properly condemnable, so also are all the subterfuges that unhappily exist in some countries where monogamy is legally required. Green goes into a somewhat detailed consideration of the historical process through which family has come to be what it actually at present is, and of the problems of divorce, but since the former is purely historical and the latter a matter of policy, either of the two will be out of place for the specific topic with which we are dealing.

The above is both the theory and substance of natural rights. It may be asked as to just what is the connection between this theory and the principle of political obligation. It will be observed that the theory of natural rights centers around our moral ideal. It is indeed because of our moral ideal that they exist. And when we speak of the principle of political obligation, what we are getting at is really a principle by which we justify our obedience to political authorities. If we obey, we obey by virtue of our moral ideal. Now, political authority as represented by the state exists for the purpose of maintaining our rights and giving fuller reality to

---

[1] *Principles of Political Obligation.* p. 237.

them.[1]In other words, it exists for the purpose of maintaining the conditions under which moral life may be possible, bearing always in mind our definition of natural rights. The existence of the state is therefore relative to our moral ideal, and it is in connection with that ideal that the relation between the theory of natural rights and the principle of political obligation becomes evident.

---

[1] *Principles of Political Obligation.* p. 138.

# Chapter III   Green and His Predecessors

According to Green, the principle of political obligation has never been satisfactorily formulated, although many have tried it. The contract theory is ingenious but it is fallacious. Green saw clearly, however, that that theory can not be overturned on merely historical ground; for it is intended to explain the logical and philosophical presupposition of political authority. In order to demolish it to the satisfaction of its advocates, objections must be based not only on historical but also on logical and philosophical grounds. Furthermore, the contract theory and the traditional theory of natural rights are inseparable. Green has to attack both in order that his own theory of natural rights may prevail. It is with these two reasons in view that he elects for criticism Spinoza, Hobbes, Locke and Rousseau. Austin is chosen because Green's conception of sovereignty is a combination of Austin's with that of Rousseau.

1. Spinoza. According to Spinoza, natural rights are merely natural powers. "Whatever the individual does by the laws of his nature, that he does by the highest right and his right toward

nature goes just as far as his power holds out."①Human beings are subjects of passions and as such are natural enemies, each struggling for his self interest and preservation. This condition is of course far from being satisfactory; hence society is formed as an arrangement whereby peace and order are made secure. Since the power of the rest put together is greater than that of the individual the right of the individual is lessened in the state. On the other hand, the right of the state depends upon the power to effect the hopes and fears of the individual. Whatever can not be achieved by threats or rewards is beyond the power and therefore the right of the state.②

Green considers erroneous Spinoza's conception of natural rights as being enjoyed by an individual apart from the society. It is evident from what has been presented before that, according to Green, natural rights can only exist for man as a member of a society. If one is isolated and apart from society he is incapable of having any right whatsoever. He may indeed have power, as Spinoza says, but power can not be considered as right in any sense. This error is made worse by Spinoza's rejection of final causes. He regards man as determined by material and efficient causes and as himself a material and an efficient cause. Thus considered, according to Green, man is only capable of power. He is not capable of right; for rights are not material attributes of

---

①  *Principles of Political Obligation.* p. 49.

②  *Principles of Political Obligation.* p. 53.

a man. They are ideal attributes which the individual possesses as means for the realization of an end. "It is not in so far as I can do this or that, that I have a right to do this or that, but in so far as I recognize myself and am recognized by others as able to do this or that for the sake of a common good."①If there is no such an end in view, natural rights, as has been pointed out, are quite meaningless.

2. Hobbes. Since Hobbes is a materialist and Green is an idealist, they can be expected to disagree. Let us state Hobbes' idea in the fewest words possible. Human actions can be reduced to the antithesis of appetite and aversion. Before there is society men are isolated and solitary; they live in a state of nature. There is constant, actual or potential warfare, since every one is seeking for his own interest; there is competition, distrust and love for personal glory. Under such circumstances, there is neither right nor wrong, neither justice nor injustice. Man has natural rights, that is, the liberty or power to do anything he deems necessary for his preservation. This constant warfare is evidently not the kind that affords much comfort, neither is it conducive to the success of preservation. Therefore men come together to form a social contract by which the right to govern is vested in a man or a group of men. Society is thus formed and with it men surrender their natural rights. It will be noticed that the ruler, the sovereign, is not a party to the contract but that his

---

① *Principles of Political Obligation.* p. 56.

designation by the voice of majority is a stipulation of the contract. Since contract is binding and since it calls for obedience, the minority has no right to resist the power of the sovereign. Thus Hobbes has reached his goal, that is, the absolutism of the sovereign power. It can not justly be resisted, for to resist it amounts to a violation of the contract. It can not be accused of a similar violation because it is not a party to the contract.

Green's criticism can be fore-told. He can not accept the Hobbesian theory of human conduct. His criticism of the theory of natural rights is about the same as that on Spinoza. There is no right in the proper sense prior to the act by which sovereign power is established. There is only power. If there is no right before, there can be no right after, the establishment of the sovereign power; for a power can not create a right. Nor is the power of the sovereign a natural right; for " if natural right means natural power, then upon successful rebellion it disappears " ①. But if there are rights other than mere power, there must be the possibility of a conflict between the power of the sovereign and the natural rights that may justify resistance.

Green, of course, does not believe in a social contract, but his objection is not so much based on historical grounds as on the others. In fact, even if the contract were historically nonexistent, it would be defendable, if only it served to formulate a

---

① *Principles of Political Obligation.* p. 66.

true conception of the moral relations of men. Not only it fails in this, but it positively confuses the theory of natural rights in permitting these rights to be considered as capable of existing apart from the society. Those who contract must have rights. If there is a social contract, it implies that a system of rights has already existed, and rights that are not merely power.

There is one point in Green's criticism to which his followers will probably welcome a modification. Hobbes draws a distinction between jus natural and lex naturalis with one as the propelling and the other as the restraining force.[1] If Green had sufficiently distinguished these two, he probably would have been appreciated to a greater extent.

3. Locke. While Hobbes wrote to condemn the rebellion, Locke wrote to justify the revolution. It is no wonder that they differ so radically, though both believed in a social contract. Locke's state of nature has none of the horrors of that of Hobbes. In it people live to try to live according to the laws of nature. That does not mean that there is no dispute whatsoever; for if so the contract would not be formed at all. The purpose of forming a political society is threefold. First, it is to formulate a settled law instituted by common consent; second, to recognize a known and disinterested judge; third, to grant powers to some persons to enforce the decisions of such a judge. The powers thus granted can

---

[1]    Hobbes. *Philosophical Rudiments concerning Government and Society*. Chap. 14, Sec. III. Dunning, *History of Political Theories*, Vol. II, p. 272.

be with drawn and thus the government established can be over-turned. Social contract establishes a civil society but does not have to have the same government. In fact the powers delegated to the government are in the nature or a fiduciary trust. They can be revoked by the grant or whenever the trust is violated. After all, then the people themselves are the final source of authority. In other words, they are the sovereign. If there is a collision between the people and the government, it is the will of the former that ought to prevail. The right of revolution is justified.

To Green, as has been pointed out, state of nature and social contract are a logical contradiction in terms. These terms imply a transition from a non-political society to a political society. The state of nature must be purely negative; it must be non-political or else it need not be differentiated as such. But if it is a state of war, as Hobbes has supposed it to be, then there can be very little freedom, for if freedom means the power to do as one wills, it must be necessarily diminished through constant warfare. Human beings are not equal, and if they are not, there is very little equality in freedom.[1]The strongest will subdue the rest. Such being the case, a social contract is impossible; for it implies both equality and freedom.

On the other hand, it may also be said, though Green does not say it, that if human beings are exactly equal there will not be war, for there is nothing to gain but everything to lose; hence

---

[1]   *Principles of Political Obligation.* p. 70.

there is no necessity for social contract. In the former case, contract is impossible and in the latter case, it is unnecessary. If, however, the state of nature is one of peace and human beings are unequal, according to Green it presupposes a guiding influence which prevents them from constant warfare. That guiding influence, according to Locke, is the law of nature. Now the law of nature involves no imponent. If it exists at all, it exists in the consciousness of men, not by command of a superior. If it exists in human consciousness[1]and to the extent of exerting a constraining force, it must exist along side a conception of natural rights, or rather mutual rights and obligations. If so, they are already members of a political society. There is then already a political society. Social contract can not create a political society out of a state of nature, for contract presupposes a political society. Therefore the whole doctrine of the state of nature and social contract is logically unsound.

Green is a democrat, hence Locke's doctrine of popular government is more acceptable to him than Hobbes' defense of absolute monarchy. But he does not permit his feelings to get the better of his intellect; for he sees that Locke's theory carried to its logical conclusion involves difficulties. In the matter of revolution, if it is to be justified at all, it must be justified in Green's opinion on the ground that the will of the people demands resistance to the government. But the question is, how can any one

---

① *Principles of Political Obligation.* p. 71.

know exactly or even roughly whether or not a particular revolution really represents the will of the people. On this point Locke offers no guide. The easiest way to find out is, according to Green, some sort of a national referendum, but revolutions are never carried on with that as a basis. Furthermore, they do not succeed merely because they represent the people's will, nor do they necessarily fail if they do not represent that will. If referendum is legally possible, then an overturn of the existing government is no longer revolutionary. Even referendum does not tell much. Government based strictly on the consent of the governed has some inherent defects.①

These criticisms do not seem to be exactly to the point. What we are getting at is evidently the principle of political obligation and these criticisms do not seem to touch that principle. To formulate the principle of political obligation is really to rationalize political obedience. It is to seek for a moral duty for political submission. As far as that goes, the writers criticized above are equally eager for a solution. All this talk of natural rights, of the state of nature and of social contract, however different the conclusions may be at the hands of the different philosophers, reveals a definite aim to offer a rational justification for political obedience, or, if necessary, for political disobedience. And it is also with this purpose in view that Green offers his criticisms, however disconnected they may seem to be from the main theme.

---

① *Principles of Political Obligation.* pp. 78, 90.

Since those writers just now dealt with are on the whole materialistic or at best empirical, their doctrines can not be particularly congenial to that of a man as idealistic as Green. Their theories of political obligation seem to Green to be hopelessly inadequate.

In Rousseau, however, a different element is found. Generally when one thinks of social contract, the three men most often thought of are Hobbes, Locke and Rousseau. To be sure, all propound the theory of social contract, but each does it in a different way, and what is more important for us in this connection, also for a different purpose. With Hobbes, the contract creates an absolute sovereign; with Locke, it renders possible the establishment of a government revocable by the sovereign people, but otherwise detached from them; and with Rousseau, it becomes an instrument through which people become sovereign not as a final source of authority ordinarily held in reserve, but as an active spring of political power, necessitating the conception of a general will as perpetually functioning.

4. Rousseau. According to Rousseau, some pact takes place when men realize that the hindrance to their preservation is too strong for the isolated individuals to combat with. Hence "each of us throws into the common stock his personal and family relations under the supreme direction of the general will, and we accept each member as individual part of the whole.... There results from this association, in place of the several persons and several contracting parties, a collective moral body composed of as many members as there are voices in the assembly, which body

receives from this act of association its unity, its common self, its life and its will.... It is called by its members a state when it is passive, a sovereign when active and a power when compared with other bodies. The associates are called collectively people, severally citizens as sharing in the sovereign authority and subjects as submitting to the laws of the state." ① Such a man becomes also a moral agent. He attains moral freedom which consists of obedience to a self-imposed law. Since law of the state is but the expression of the general will to which he contributes, he is merely obeying himself when he obeys law. Soverignty thus considered is totally different from a supreme coercive force. It has the attributes of pure disinterestedness, of reason, of a common ego which wills nothing but what is for the common good. But Rousseau does not consistently speak in this manner, thus lapsing, according to Green, into dangerous grounds.

Let us examine further Rousseau's conception of sovereignty and government. Sovereignty is not power but will. Power can be delegated, but will can not be delegated. Being the exercise of general will, sovereignty can not be alienated since it can not be delegated. Will by definition is indivisible, so must also be sovereign will and sovereignty. The only exercise of sovereign power, properly so-called, is in legislation, and there is no proper act of legislation except when the whole people comes to a decision with

---

① *Principles of Political Obligation.* p. 81, as quoted by Green from Rousseau.

reference to the whole people. The question decided is as general as the will which decides it, and that is how there has come to be law. Law, being the expression to which every one contributes, can not be unjust; for no one can be unjust to himself, and therefore the whole people can not be unjust to the whole people. Since laws are the expressions of their own will, people can submit to them and yet be free. A mere decree from the government is not law; for government is not sovereign at all. The function of the sovereign is legislative, that of the government is executive; the effect of the former is general, that of the latter is particular.

We need not present Rousseau's views in regard to the different forms of government. The important point to remember is that whatever its form, it is not instituted by contract, and therefore it is revocable by the sovereign without incurring the charge of a violation of the contract. In fact, according to Rousseau, in order that authority may not fall in abeyance, it must be constantly exercised even though it can not be exercised except in assemblies of the whole people. Such assemblies must periodically meet to decide whether or not the present form of government shall be maintained, whether or not authority shall be left in the hands of those now charged with it. At such meetings laws can be revised and repealed. General will can make itself felt only in such a way.

There, according to Green, comes the trouble. What is the general will and how are we to ascertain it? General will is not the will of all, Rousseau says, but the will common to all. The will of all is the totality of wills, the will common to all is the general will. This general will, according to Green's interpretation of Rousseau, may be tainted by special interests, it may lack enlightenment, but it is none the less right and pure. How can it be ascertained? Does unanimity of the votes in the assembly of the whole people alone represent the general will? The social contract in order to be valid requires unanimous consent and the ones who refuse to join it are not citizens. If they are not citizens, how can the state exact their obedience? And after the passing of those who are parties to the contract, how is it to be ascertained whether anyone coming later on is a party to it or not? Rousseau says residence proves him willing to submit to sovereignty. That, Green points out, hardly answers the question, for residence is no indication of consent, and if by residence in a given area one is morally bound to obey the sovereign, then his obedience is not necessarily based on consent. Rousseau does not require unanimity in the assembly of the whole people for expressing the general will after the contract is formed. But if he does not, how can the minority be bound to obey the rulings of the majority? Rousseau says that if anyone finds himself in the minority, he is bound to suppose that he is mistaken in his views of the general will, therefore he is bound to obey. There is no explanation of the rule of the majority if the minority sincerely doubts the wisdom and integrity of the majority. Rousseau is probably more consistent than others in basing political obligation on consent, but it seems to Green, his efforts are none the less futile. The contribution that is really valuable is the conception of sovereignty as representing a general will.

5. Austin. But the general idea of sovereignty, according to Green, has come to be more or less Austinian. It is conceived as a supreme law-giving and enforcing power, and if necessary, it also implies coercive force. According to Austin, "the notions of sovereignty and independent political society may be expressed concisely thus: if a determinate human superior, not in the habit of obedience to a like superior, receive the habitual obedience of the bulk of a given society, that determinate superior is sovereign in that society and the society including the superior is a society political and independent."①" In order that a given society may form a society political and independent, the two distinguishing marks which I have mentioned above must unite. The generality of the given society must be in the habit of obedience to a determinate and common superior; whilst that determinate person or body of persons must not be habitually obedient to a determinate person or body. It is this union of that positive with this negative mark which renders that certain superior sovereign or supreme and which renders that given society political and independent."②Green notes that, according to Austin, law is a rule laid down by one intelligent being having power over other intelligent beings for the purpose of guiding them. Laws are di-

---

① Austin. *Lectures on Jurisprudence.*
② Austin. *Lectures on Jurisprudence.*

vided into two kinds, those set by God to men or the law of nature, those set by men to men or human laws. Of the latter there are again two kinds, firstly, laws established by the sovereign over his subjects, the positive laws, secondly, laws not established by sovereign but enforced through custom and morals, viz., positive morality. Laws are often spoken of as commands and as such they fit in with the conception of sovereignty, since they necessarily proceed from determinate persons.

The Austinian theory of sovereignty is, in Green's opinion, different from that of Rousseau in two important respects. In fact, in those respects the two conceptions are diametrically opposite. First, Austin regards sovereignty as residing with determinate person or persons, while Rousseau regards it as inalienable and solely retained by the whole people. Second, Austin considers the essence of sovereignty as power of such determinate person or persons over subjects, while Rousseau regards it as representing general will of the citizens. In fact, it will be recalled. Rousseau expressly declared that sovereignty is not power but will. Power can be delegated but not will. While, however, the two views are mutually exclusive, each really has its own merit.

According to Green, Austin is right when he regards sovereignty as essentially resident with determinate person or persons; for political facts, historical as well as contemporary, bear out his contention. No matter how complicated the political systems of the different countries may be, there is always some person or a body of persons in whom the supreme power is vested. That is, there are some persons whose authority knows no legal limitation.①

The king in Parliament is the sovereign of Great Britain. There is no legal limit to the action of the king together with House of Lords and Commons. It may, of course, be argued that in Great Britain common law, which is not any command of any determinate person or persons, has been and is an influential body of rules to which people may be said to render habitual obedience. True, but common law may be overruled by statutory laws, and if it is not so overruled, it stands by legislative acquiescence. This state of affairs is by no means limited to Great Britain. Supreme legal authority is also found in the United States where political structure is a complicated system of federal, state and local governments. The federal government is indeed not supreme, that is, it has legal limitations. The Constitution is the supreme law of the land, and legislation contrary to its provisions can be and often is declared unconstitutional. But the Constitution can be amended and the amending power is viewed by many, including Austin himself, ② as the sovereign power as far as the United States is concerned. Therefore, as a matter of fact, sovereignty involves in most cases its residence with determinate person or body or bodies of persons who are thus vested with legally unlimited power to make and enforce laws. Since the term sovereignty has acquired this legalistic implication in

---

① *Principles of Political Obligation.* p. 98.
② Austin. *Lectures on Jurisprudence.*

general, Rousseau, according to Green, is somewhat mislead-ing①in attributing general will to it as its essence.

It seems to Green that this legalistic conception is not entirely satisfactory. It is liable to mistake effect for cause. The reason that sovereign power is supreme and habitually obeyed is not that it is capable of coercive force. Force alone does not explain the supremacy of sovereignty. If we examine more closely and emancipate ourselves from this purely legalistic conception, Green argues, we must look for the source of power, which is not and can not be the power itself, It is here that Rousseau's ideas apply to better advantage. The real cause of habitual obedience is not found in any determinate person or persons, but in "that impalpable congeries of hopes and fears of a people bound together by common interests and sympathy which we call the general will."②These influences, which for the sake of brevity we call the general will, have been operative historically. Sir Henry Maine says in his *Early History of Institutions*: "The vast mass of influences which we may call for shortness moral, habitually shapes, limits, or forbids the actual direction of the forces of society by its sovereign."③In other words, there is a source from which power is derived. Nominally the power of the sovereign may be characterized as supreme, but factually it is only effective

① *Principles of Political Obligation.* p. 98.
② *Principles of Political Obligation.* p. 98.
③ Maine. *Early History of Institutions.* p. 359.

when sanctioned by the good will of the people. The determinate person or body of persons is only able to exercise their power in virtue of an assent if not consent of the people. This assent is not based upon any definite expression of the people; rather is it based upon the desire, the common desire of a common good for a common end to which observance of law and obedience to the sovereign may contribute. There may be person or persons who wield greater powers than the rest, who exact habitual obedience and who probably possess coercive force. Call him or them sovereign if you will, but don't explain their supremacy by their force. That force will come to nothing when opposed to the people's desire. Let this desire, which may be properly called the general will, cease to operate, or let it come into general conflict with sovereign commands, and the habitual obedience will cease also.①In other words:

"There's on earth a yet auguster thing,

Veiled though it be, than Parliament and King."②

① *Principles of Political Obligation.* p. 97.

② *Principles of Political Obligation.* p. 82.

# Chapter IV   The Basis of The State

Being a democrat and an idealist, Green leans to Rousseau more than he does to Austin, believing that political obedience is a matter of will rather than power or force. It may of course be urged that this view of general will as the real determinent of the habitual obedience to sovereign power is applicable only to democratic communities, where governors are elected by the people and government is based on the consent of the governed, and is quite inapplicable to despotic countries where despots both reign and rule supreme. This sounds plausible, but according to Green, it is not true.

That the doctrine under consideration applies more directly to the democratic communities is not denied. But in a despotic country in which there is a sovereign, understood in the Austinian sense, general will, Green holds, is equally if not so directly a potent factor in the habitual obedience. There is always a body of cuatoms, conventions and mores which the sovereign, in order to exact obedience, will find it profitable not to ignore. The Russian Tzars, for instance, found it advisable to worship at Moscow often contrary to their will, and the Chinese Emperors thought it worth while, even against their own inclinations, to pay their respects to the memory of Confucius. There may be communities where coercive force has been successfully employed against the will of the people. In such cases there are generally two conditions worthy of our notice; either there is no sovereign power in the sense of a law-giving and law-enforcing power and therefore also no habitual obedience; or the coercive power of oppression, though constant and recurring, touches the people only at a few points and the obedience thus rendered, though habitual in a sense, is never continuous and is therefore different from the rational and moral obedience to political authority.

The conditions of a so-called tax-collecting despotism offer a fairly satisfactory contrast to the democratic communities. The despots exercise coercive force over their subjects, but exercise it only for a certain specific purpose and only at certain times. They do not legislate in the modern sense, nor do they invade the field of the judiciary, nor do they concern themselves much about customary laws. The subjects render obedience only in regard to those specific things. They are practically left free so far as the laws, institutions, customs and manners are concerned. Life in general is not much affected. They still pay their respects to their patriarch, their priest and their warrior. There is in such a case hardly any sovereign.

The same results can be found in the case of foreign domination over a country which has a highly organized community life. The foreign power is not a sovereign in the sense of a law giver or law maintainer. The subject country has inherited a body of laws and customs which enable it not only to govern itself but also to emancipate itself from foreign domination. North Italy under Austria was in such a condition and the Chinese Empire under the Mongols and Manchus was even more to the point. In both cases, the sovereign, if sovereign at all, is not so in the Austinian sense.

Again there may be aristocratic rulers who are real sovereigns in the sense defined, but in such cases, the power of the rulers is due to a large extent to the good will of the people. Green cites the example of the early Roman Empire①in which, he says, the people lived under a system of rights and obligations better than their own. Although they did not vote or expressly give their consent in any form, they by implication assented to the Roman rule. Even the Russian autocrat did not depend upon absolute coercive power for the habitual obedience he exacted from the people; for, it is contended, he conformed to a complicated system of relations, of written and unwritten laws, from which he was by no means independent.

Austin, according to Green, is in a sense right in his theory of sovereignty; so also is Rousseau. How can these views be harmonized? The trouble with both of them is, he says, that when they emphasize one aspect they forget the other. If sovereignty is the power to maintain rights, it has the elements of both force

---

① *Principles of Political Obligation*. p. 101.

and will. If it sometimes exercises coercive or even tyrannical power, it is not because it is tyrannical or coercive that it receives habitual obedience. On the other hand, sovereignty defined as power and as vested in determinate person or persons may profitably be allowed, according to Green, to retain its legalistic meaning. In that case, it may be misleading to speak of general will as the sovereign. It is however, equally misleading to attribute to sovereignty omnipotence; for if not sustained by general will, it ceases to exist. It is better, according to Green, "to say that law, as the system of rules by which rights are maintained, is the expression of the general will than that the general will is the sovereign. The sovereign being a person or persons by whom in the last resort laws are imposed and enforced, in the long run and on the whole is the agent of the general will, contributes to realize that will." [1] In so far as the sovereign does so contribute to realize that will and is an agent of it, he is in possession of supreme power. On the other hand, if he does not so contribute to realize that will, mere power does not command habitual obedience.

It is only fair to record that Rousseau recognizes the difficulty of his theory of sovereignty and general will as applied to actual political affairs. While in principle he sticks to his conception of sovereignty as consisting in representing general will, he does not, in Green's opinion, altogether avoid the notion that

---

① *Principles of Political Obligation.* p. 104.

there is supreme law-making and law-enforcing power distinct from the will. Though Rousseau does not expressly differentiate a sovereign de jure from a sovereign de facto, such a differentiation can be justifiably inferred from *Contract Social* and is so inferred by Green.①But such a differentiation, according to Green, can not in any way be justified; for strictly speaking, sovereign de facto can not be other than sovereign de jure. Confusion between the two generally comes as a result of a confusion of meaning in the conception either of the term sovereign or of the term jus.②A sovereign is often described as such without being actually such in the real sense. Thus an English King who is called sovereign, but who is not the determinate person or persons entrusted with the supreme law-making and law-enforcing power, may be said to exercise sovereign power de facto, when he raises money without the consent of the Parliament. He may be said to be sovereign de facto and not de jure, since his conduct is contrary to the will of the people as embodied in the laws, customs and conventions. But that is only true as far as the King is only a nominal sovereign, one entirely different from sovereign in the real sense. A real sovereign de facto③is always a sovereign de jure. Given the definitions, the conclusion is inevitable; you can not change it without changing the definitions.

If the sovereign is a real one in the strict sense, Green

---

① *Principles of Political Obligation.* p. 91.
② *Principles of Political Obligation.* p. 105.
③ *Principles of Political Obligation.* p. 105.

argues, the terms de jure and not de jure are not applicable.[1] When one speaks of de jure or not de jure, one necessarily has a definite idea of jus in mind. Now what is meant by jus? If by jus is meant ordinary statutory law, then sovereign de jure is a meaningless expression, for such law proceeds only from the sovereign. If by jus is meant natural law or natural rights or chaims inherent in human beings as members of a society, then indeed a sovereign may not be de jure, but then he is not, in Green's opinion, at the same time a sovereign in the real sense, i. e., the supreme law-making and law enforcing authority. In other words, sovereign de jure is a contradiction in terms. A supreme imponent of law is not limited by the law he imposes. He may formulate rules to limit himself but then he is always at liberty to change them.

This process of reasoning facilitates the understanding of the different points of view. When Hobbes says that laws can not be unjust we have to ge back to the definition of injustice. If by injustice is meant the violation of contract, and the sovereign is not a party to the Contract and therefore can not break it, it necessarily follows that a sovereign can not be unjust. If the sovereign can not be unjust, laws which are laws by reason of their being enacted by him can not be unjust. But, according to Hobbes, laws can be inequitable and pernicious; for by "inequitable" he means that which conflicts with the law of nature, and by "pernicious" that

---

① *Principles of Political Obligation.* p. 106.

which tends to weaken the individuals and the community. ①

Rousseau's argument, Green shows, is similar but on different grounds. His sovereignty is general will, his general will, the will common to the whole people. Since, then, the whole people can not be unjust to the whole people, the sovereign can not be unjust to its subjects.

Green sees that Hobbes thinks of sovereignty as essentially power, and Rousseau thinks of it as essentially will. But whether power or will, sovereignty can not be said to be either de jure or not de jure. If it is power, as we have seen, these terms de jure and not de jure are not applicable to it. If it is will, they are equally inapplicable. "A certain desire either is or is not the general will. A certain interest either is or is not an interest in the common good. There is no sense in saying that such desire or interest is general will de jure but not de facto or vice versa." ②

Confusion comes, according to Green, when sovereignty is made to combine the notions of general will and the supreme law-making and law-enforcing power. It is through this confusion that there is the necessity of making the law-making and law-enforcing power dependent upon the vote of a majority of the citizens and identifying that vote with the general will. It must be understood that general will, though called general, is yet will; and will, being itself unnatural, that is, pertaining to consciousness rather

---

① *Principles of Political Obligation.* p. 107.

② *Principles of Political Obligation.* p. 108.

than to the physical world, can not be so mechanically ascertained by the "natural" process of a majority vote.① While Rousseau's conception of a general will is a valuable contribution, his identification of that will with the vote of a certain number of persons can not be accepted.

The defect of Rousseau's theory, as Green sees it is basically one of his theory of natural rights. If natural rights meant fundamental rights, rights that existed prior to the formation of the society and were retained by individuals after it, then they are above all political interference whatsoever, and the only way to justify political obligation is by the theory of consent. As long as consent is the sole source of authority, the difficulty of the justification of the submission of the minority can not be escaped. According to Green, there is in truth no natural right apart from the society. much less the right to do as one likes irrespective of the society. A right, it may be repeated, is a condition claimed and recognized as necessary for the realization of the moral ideal and common good of men as members of a society. It can not exist in one individual without relation to society, just as force of gravity of one body can not exist in that body without relation to other bodies. Therefore, no one has the right to resist law or government merely because it requires him to do that which he does not himself approve, or not to do that which he desires. The only question, according to Green, is as

---

① *Principles of Political Obligation*. p. 109.

Rousseau has put it: is a given measure in accordance with the general will? In other words, whether that given measure is in accordance with the general will or not, is the real problem. That is a very big problem, and it seems that Green has offered no practical solution. After all, he says, an interest in the common good is the ground for political society, for without that interest "no body of people will recognize any authority as having any claim on their common obedience. It is so far as a government represents to them a common good that the subjects are conscious that they ought to obey it, that is, that obedience to it is a means to an end desirable in itself or absolutely."[1]

It will be remembered that in his Metaphysics and Ethics Green believes in the interdependence of men and society so that each in fact does not exist without the other. Rights and duties must be considered with this view in mind. "It is only as members of a society, as recognizing common interests and objects, that individuals come to have these attributes and rights, and the power which in the political society they have to obey is derived from the development and systematization of those institutions for the regulation of a common life without which they would have no rights at all."[2]Or again, the demand for a justification of any submission to authority presupposes some standard of rights recognized as equally valid for and by the person making

---

[1]  *Principles of Political Obligation*. p. 109.

[2]  *Principles of Political Obligation*. p. 122.

the demand, and others who form a society with him. Such a standard of rights would be quite meaningless, if it does not possess institutions through which dealings with each other are regulated. These institutions are to the consciousness of right just as language is to thought. They are the expressions, with which that consciousness becomes real.①They embody the system of rights and obligations through which men restrain themselves. Primitive or conventional morality, which is essentially the observance of rules and obligations, can not exist without these institutions. In a certain sense, then, the body of laws, institutions and customs embody what Rousseau calls the general will.

Rousseau speaks of social contract as the foundation not only of society and sovereignty, but also of morality.②Through it men become moral beings. By it, submission to power and to the forces of nature, to greed and appetite is transformed into the moral freedom of subjection to the self-imposed law. If such is the ease, he should have seen that natural rights can have no pre-social existence, since they can only exist for the purpose of realizing our moral ideal. Had he seen that, he would have avoided a grave error.

According to Green, morality in the conventional sense and political subjection in the sense of having rights thus secured proceed from the same source. "That common source is the rational

---

① *Principles of Political Obligation.* p. 123.
② *Principles of Political Obligation.* p. 124.

recognition by certain human beings of a common well being which is their well being, and which they conceive as their well being, whether at any moment any one of them is inclined to it or no, and the embodiment of that recognition in rules by which the inclinations of the individuals are restrained and a corresponding freedom of action for the attainment of well being on the whole is secured."①There proceeds from this source, according to Green, an antagonism to some inclinations and a consciousness that such antagonism is founded on reason and on the conception of some adequate good. This antagonism to or constraint of an inclination, whether in relation to an external law or to a self-imposed law, is generally expressed in the term "must"②. I must register for the army. Or I must volunteer for the army. The former may have the element of compulsion in view, if the law is not complied with, but the latter certainly represents nothing of the kind if there is no law for conscription whatsoever. But in both cases there is a certain element of consciousness of a common good which is at the bottom the driving force. Simple fear does not constitute political obligation, neither does force compel it.

It may be objected that such an idea, however pleasing it may sound, is far from representing the fact. In place of good will, some thinkers will say, there is often hatred, and in place of a common good there is class interest; where cooperation alone

---

① *Principles of Political Obligation.* p. 125.
② *Principles of Political Obligation.* p. 125.

will ever produce desirable results, competition holds sway. Instead of happiness being the rule, it becomes the exception, and
instead of misery the exception, it becomes the rule. People
vote, but they do not necessarily elect their governors or decide
issues. Representative government governs but it does not necessarily represent. Law is instituted for the good of all, but it is
often twisted for the benefit of the few. Judges are appointed for
the purpose of maintaining justice, but often they become mere
guardians of legality. Under such circumstances, is it not a waste
of words to indulge in the high-sounding phrases of common good
and moral ideal? If the idea of common good prevails to the
extent to which it is claimed as prevailing, there should not and
there can not be such misery, such poverty, such conflict of
interests and such violence. These undesirable conditions can not
be conducive to the realization of the so-called moral ideal,
neither do they lead to the observance of rights and duties upon
which political obligations are based. If people obey political authorities in spite of this conspicuous absence of the idea of a common good, they must obey on other grounds. It may be more correct to say that they obey by force of habit, or necessity, or for
fear of consequences rather than by reason of a mutual
recognition of rights and obligations.

　　That the actual is far from being the ideal is readily admitted
by Green.①But it is easy, on the other hand, he points out, to

---

　　① *Principles of Political Obligation.* p. 128.

exaggerate the difference, and those who exaggerate it are probably unnecessarily loaded with pessimism. We should bear in mind that every action on the part of the citizen involves more or less the idea of a common good. Some have more of that idea in view, others have less, but none is entirely without it and none, Green admits, has it in all its fullness and completeness. For an ordinary citizen, that idea has probably very little abstract significance, but it is invariably present in his concrete interests. "He has," according to Green, "a clear understanding of certain interests and rights common to himself and his neighbors, if only such as consist in getting his wages paid at the end of the week, in getting his money's worth at the shop, in the inviolability of his own person and that of his wife. Habitually and instinctively, that is, without asking the reason why, he regards the claim which in these, respects he makes for himself as conditioned upon his recognizing alike claim in others, and thus as in a proper sense a right—a claim of which the essence lies in its being common to himself with others."[1] The reason that this manifestation of the idea of a common good is not so easily discerned is, not that it is not discernible, but that the supreme coercive power has been and is the outward visible sign. Just as a man is often taken to be what he seems, so a state is only too generally identified with its outward visible sign. But if we go deeper than mere appearances we shall find that the unifying principle of the state is really the

[1] *Principles of Political Obligation.* p. 129.

promotion of a common good. In other words, will and not force is the true basis of the state.

But institutions grow and are not made, many will say. Whatever our conceptions of them may be at this present moment, their origin and development involve natural conditions and tendencies and therefore also inevitable results. Rationalize and idealize as much as you please, you can not escape the fact that our political and social institutions are materially conditioned. Given certain conditions, and there will be certain results. In order to understand these results you have to consider all the material conditions—the climate, geographical position, sea coasts, bays, rivers, mountains and the like.

That these influences are instrumental in the development of particular institutions is not denied by Green. But what would these influences be, were it not for the synthetic unifying consciousness? Material conditions may and do condition human efforts, but they do not point to the particular direction in which human development has come to be what it is at present. In other words, the creative capacity of human beings should not be minimized, since after all it is the driving force in the advancing march of civilization. It is because men are moral beings that they have this creative capacity, that is, they have it only because they are capable of being determined to action by the conception of an end absolutely desirable, because they are capable of free will and are themselves free. Right here it may be argued that to be human is not necessarily to be moral. While human efforts may have been indispensible for the formation, for instance, of modern states, these efforts are by no means moral. In fact, many will assert, egotism has been the more effective incentive than altruism. There are the Alexanders, the Caesars and the Napoleons. To attribute, for instance, the idea of common good to the "blood-thirsty Corsican" is to ignore an indisputable historical fact.

When we speak of such a historical figure as Napoleon, according to Green, we must not judge him purely by his selfishness, but also by the movement he led and the results attained.[1] This is not to minimize his personal conduct. He was selfish; but it was not his selfishness alone that led him to overrun all Europe. His egotism was subject to all sorts of social influences, among which may be counted national aspiration. The French in those days were utilizing him for certain definite purposes, for instance, the aggrandizement of France. The establishment of a centralized political order on the basis of social equality, the promulgation of the civil code and the like were quite definite purposes. If these results are desirable, then the conduct of Napoleon, though bad, may be "overruled for good"[2]. The same can be said of Alexander and Caesar. Citing merely the selfishness of these leaders is no ground for denying the idea of some common good, since the directions in which these leaders

---

[1]  *Principles of Political Obligation*. p. 133.

[2]  *Principles of Political Obligation*. p. 134.

moved were influenced by that very idea. They may have been wrong in their judgment, but the idea of a common good was, after all, the driving force.

According to Green, there seems to be a prevalent confusion between the state and sovereignty. Since the outward and outstanding characteristic of sovereignty is power, it is generally inferred that the essence of the state is force. But, as has been made clear, the sovereign power, in order that it may remain as such, must be exercised in accordance with what may be conveniently called general will. In other words, it must be exercised for the maintenance of rights. It would be altogether meaningless if considered in the abstract, that is, apart from the state. It is the supreme law-making and law-enforcing power, to be sure, but it is such a power only when exercised in and over a state. And it is, after all, the state that makes sovereign and not sovereign that makes the state. A slave owner may have all the supreme power over all his slaves, but he can not be styled a sovereign. A sovereign may indeed alter his laws, but he can only alter them according to law, that is, according to higher law. If he fails to do that, he can not remain sovereign. It seems, then, necessary to ascertain what a state is.

According to Green, "it is a mistake, then, to think of the state as an aggregation of individuals under a sovereign; equally so when we suppose the individuals as such, or apart from what they derive from society, to possess natural rights, or suppose them to depend on the sovereign for the possession of rights. A state presupposes other forms of community, with the rights that arise out of them, and only exists as sustaining, securing and completing them. In order to make a state, there must have been families of which the members recognized rights in each other; there must further have been intercourse between families, or tribes that have grown out of families, of which each in the same sense recognized rights in the other. The recognition of a right being very short of its definition, the admission of a right in each other by two parties, whether individuals, families, or tribes, being very different from agreement as to what the right consists in, what it is a right to do or acquire, the rights recognized need definition and reconciliation in a general law. When such a general law has been arrived at, regulating the positions of members of a family towards each other and the dealings of families or tribes with each other; when it is voluntarily recognized by a community of families or tribes, and maintained by a power strong enough at once to enforce it within the community and to defend the integrity of the community against attacks from without, then the elementary state has been formed."[1]

Force may have been a necessary factor in the maintenance of rights, but it is only a factor and as such it is subordinate to right. "There is no right but thinking makes it so"[2]none that is not derived from some idea that men have about each other.

---

[1]  *Principles of Political Obligation.* p. 139.

[2]  *Principles of Political Obligation.* p. 140.

Nothing is more real than a right; yet its existence is purely ideal, if by ideal is meant that which is not dependent on anything material, as existing solely in consciousness. It is to these ideal realities that force is subordinate in the creation and development of states.

It will be seen that Green is fighting against two theories at the same time. In the first place, he shows that sovereignty can not create rights, for it implies them. Secondly, he painstakingly points out the futility of basing political obligation on the theory of consent. In this connection he denies the existence of natural rights prior to the formation of society, and declares that the individual has no right against the state merely because it does something against his own inclinations.

Such a position as Green takes renders him a good deal of an absolutist. And he may be, to a certain extent, but his theory is certainly not so sweeping as it may sound. When one speaks of an individual's right against the state, one has to ascertain first what he means by right. As has been a number of times repeated, a right is, in Green's thought, a necessary condition for an individual to realize a moral ideal. It involves on the part of the individual a claim of a capacity to advance the common good, to identify it as his own, and it involves on the part of the society a recognition of such a claim. A right is therefore essentially social, since its important element is the recognition by the society. It exists only relatively to a common good. If the State passes a law for the common good, there is no right on the part of the citizen to

第
五
卷

resist it merely because it is against his own inclinations. That does not mean that the individual has no right to resist for any reason whatsoever. The ground for the resistance to the state must be the same as the ground for the existence of the rights of the individual, that is, resistance must be on social grounds and on the ideal of common good.

# Chapter V  The Principle of State Interference

In the preceding chapters it has been shown that Green disapproved both the absolutist theory that rights are granted by the sovereign power and the prevalent theory that government is based on the consent of the governed. Further, we have noted his conclusion that, while coercive force may be an occasional manifestation of sovereign power, it is, after all, the will that forms the basis of the state. In the present chapter, it is the aim to set forth the principles upon which political actions are based. In other words, the earlier chapters deal with the principle according to which the individual obeys, and the present chapter deals with the principle according to which the state acts. It may be said that they are different directions proceeding from the same principle, for both are related to the moral ideal and the conception of a common good. It is on moral grounds that individuals obey and it is to maintain conditions under which moral life becomes possible that the state acts. But while there is an identity of source, there is really no identity in the intrinsic nature of the two. Political obligation on the part of the individuals may be and is a moral duty, but interference on the part of the state is not in itself a moral act. "There is," in Green's words, "a moral duty in regard to obligations, but there can be no obligation in regard to moral duties."[1] For the sake of clarity, a separate treatment seems to be warranted. This is especially necessary, since in dealing with the different topics, Green does not himself distinguish the two principles involved.

Before proceeding to the principle of state interference, let us first recall to our minds the idea of our moral life. In Green's words, "the condition of a moral life is the possession of will and reason. Will is the capacity in a man of being determined to action by the idea of a possible satisfaction of himself. An act of will is an act so determined. A state of will is the capacity as determined by the particular objects in which the man seeks self-satisfaction; and it becomes a character in so far as the self-satisfaction is habitually sought in objects of a particular kind. Practical reason is the capacity in a man of conceiving the perfection of his nature as an object to be attained by action. All moral ideas have their origin in reason, i. e., in the idea of a possible self perfection to be attained by the moral agent."[2]

But ideas are not ordinarily shaped in the abstract expression embodied in the above statement. That expression can only be arrived at upon analysis of concrete experience. There is

---

[1]  *Principles of Political Obligation.* p. 34.

[2]  *Principles of Political Obligation.* p. 31.

a sort of primitive or, later on, a sort of conventional morality which is instrumental in the historical development of mankind. That morality is, in the Hegelian sense, embodied in the laws, customs and institutions[1]which help human beings in their struggle for improvement. Only when they have gone through a process of actual self-improvement can the idea of self-perfection find its abstract expression. This does not mean that the moral ideal is derived from experience, since the possibility of experience involves an idea from which all other ideas of morality proceed. It does mean that the original ideal can not find its expression without having the other ideas embodied in the social institutions. That is, higher morality is only capable of expression after conventional morality attains concrete reality. When Green speaks of will and reason and perfection, it must be understood that it is morality in the higher sense that he means.

Morality in the higher sense, however, is incapable of enforcement.[2] Moral duties can not be enforced by law. Moral duties are indeed duties to act, and actions, to be sure, are capable of legal enforcement; but moral duties are duties to act from a certain disposition and for a certain motive, both of which are incapable of enforcement. In fact, if moral duties are actually enforced, they lose their moral quality, since they lack the necessary disinterestedness of disposition and motive. The province

---

① *Principles of Political Obligation.* p. 32.
② *Principles of Political Obligation.* p. 34.

of political action is therefore not morality. It only covers outward or external acts. Rights and obligations, whether as ideal or actual, are distinct from morality in the proper or higher sense. However, political action, moral ideal and rights are really related to each other. In fact, without moral ideal, rights are superfluities, as we have already seen from Green's theory of natural rights. "Nothing but external acts can be matter of ' obligation' ( in the restricted sense ) ; and in regard to that which can be made matter of obligation, the question what should be made matter of obligation—the question how far rights and obligations, as actually established by law, correspond to the true jus naturae — must be considered with reference to the moral end, as serving which alone law and obligations imposed by law have their value."[1]

Should laws be strictly limited to external act? And after all, what is meant by an external act? It must be remembered that when we are punished we are not merely punished for our external behavior. Much else is involved. When a man kills somebody unintentionally, he is charged with manslaughter, but if he kills intentionally, he is charged with murder and is punished more severely. In other words, intention from within is just as much a subject of punishment as the external action. It may indeed be argued that intention and action are inseparable, that without the former the latter can not be. When we say that some-

---

[1] *Principles of Political Obligation.* pp. 34–35.

thing is done against our will, according to Green, we generally mean any of the following situations. First, an act may be done by someone using my body as a means through force. There is an act, but it is certainly not mine. Second, an act may he caused by a natural event through the instrumentality of my body doing damage to some one else. Third, an act may be done by the influence of a strong inducement, though it is done against a very strong wish. In the last case, however, it is indeed an act but it is no longer an act against my will. It is therefore evident that in punishing outward acts, intention is likewise punished, for without intention on the part of some one there can hardly be an act that deserves severe punishment.

But if action necessarily includes intention, what is the sense in calling it external as if it were divorced from all intention? According to Green, "an external action is a determination of will as exhibited in certain motions of the bodily members which produce certain effects in the material world; not a determination of the will as arising from certain motives and a certain disposition."[1]What the law does is to prohibit certain determinations of will as exhibiting certain physical motions affecting the material world. It may present a motive for its being obeyed, for it is capable of exciting fear in the individual. But motive in this connection is really unimportant; for law requires primarily conformity and conformity can be attained irrespective of motives. If

---

[1]  *Principles of Political Obligation*. p. 36.

an act is performed as is required by law without inducement of any sort, the purpose of the law is satisfied. If an act forbidden by law is refrained from without the fear of consequences of disobedience, the law is as well satisfied as if there were such an element of fear. In a word, motives are not concerned; the business of law is "to maintain certain conditions of life—to see that certain actions are done which are necessary to the maintenance of those conditions, others omitted which, would interfere with them. It has nothing to do with the motive of the actions or omissions on which, however, the moral value of them depends."①  Legal obligations can only be obligations to do or not to do a certain thing, but not duties of doing or not doing from a certain motive or with a certain disposition. The question is not whether or not law should be limited to outward acts. It can not be otherwise; for with all the weapons it has at its command, it is incapable of enforcing moral duties.

The problem needs further consideration, for outward or external acts can not stand by themselves. What kind of external acts should be made subjects of state interference? Green's answer is that "those acts only should be made subjects of legal injunction or prohibition of which the performance or omission, irrespective of the motive from which it proceeds, is so necessary to the existence of a society in which the moral end can be realized, that it is better for them to be done or omitted from that

---

① *Principles of Political Obligation.* p. 37.

unworthy motive which consists in fear or hope of legal consequences than not to be done at all." ①There are actions and omissions which should be made legal obligations, and when once
made legal obligations they serve a certain moral end. "Since the
end consists in action proceeding from a certain disposition, and
since action done from apprehension of legal consequences does
not proceed from that disposition, no action should be enjoined or
prohibited by law of which the injunction or prohibition interferes
with actions proceeding from that disposition, and every action
should be so enjoined of which the performance is found to produce conditions favourable to action proceeding from that disposition, and of which the legal injunction does not interfere with
such action." ②

No effort is made to paraphrase Green's language here for
fear of losing the actual and the exact idea. This, then, is the
principle of state interference. Because political action is a complex phenomenon, such a principle can only be stated in general
terms. Specific difficulties there are. Situations vary and circumstances differ, but the principle is capable of giving real
guidance. Whatever may have been the development of law in the
past, this should be the rule for the future.

We have stated the principle according to which individuals
obey and the principle according to which the state acts. It may

---

① *Principles of Political Obligation.* p. 38.
② *Principles of Political Obligation.* p. 38.

be asked whether, after the state has acted, it is always the duty of the individuals to obey.

This question has been touched before, but it must be admitted that it could only be answered in general terms. According to Green, "so far as laws anywhere or at any time in force fulfill the idea of a state, there can be no right to disobey them; or there can be no right to disobey the law of the state except in the interest of the state, that is, for the purpose of making the state in respect of its actual laws more completely to correspond to what it is in tendency or idea, that is, a reconciler and a sustainer of rights that arise out of the social relations of men." ①Accordingly no one can resist the state merely because his freedom of action has been obstructed, or because the management of his own affairs has been interfered with, or because he is not allowed to do as he likes with his own.

A prevalent fallacy is that whatever is permitted is taken to be a right. But there can be no right in that sense. Spitting in public was once permitted and probably taken as a right, but when it became generally recognized as detrimental to the health of the community, the state was perfectly justified in prohibiting it, and there can not be any justification whatsoever for resisting the state on that account. Drinking alcoholic liquors will probably come under the same category. Individuals can only spit and drink when the social judgment permits, but when the social

---

① *Principles of Political Obligation.* p. 147.

judgment concludes that spitting and drinking are positively detrimental to the common good, individuals have no right to disobey.

But the social judgment may, from the individual's point of view, be mistaken. He may claim that a law enacted is based on a mistaken or an imperfect view of the common good, and therefore he may claim justification for resistance. Green admits that one may differ with the wisdom of social judgment, but he denies anyone the right to resist the state without having his views shared by his fellow citizens and implicitly acknowledged by them as conducive to the common good. One has a right to resistance only when either some action or some forbearance is implicitly acknowledged by society as conducive to the common good, but explicitly denied or ignored by the state.①

Take, for instance, the case of slavery. Suppose that in a state where slavery is legally permitted, a law is passed prohibiting the education of slaves, has the citizen no right against such a law? As a general rule even bad laws ought to be obeyed, for disobedience is often more detrimental to the common good than bad laws. "But there may be cases in which the public interest... is better served by the violation of some actual law. It is so in regard to slavery when the public conscience has come to recognize a capacity for right... in a body of men to whom legal rights have been hitherto refused, but when some powerful class in its own interest resists the alteration of the law. In such a case

---

① *Principles of Political Obligation.* pp. 148, 150.

the violation of the law on behalf of the slave is not only not a violation of the interest of the violator; the general sense of right on which the general observance of law depends being represented by it, there is no danger of its making a breach in the law-abiding habits of the people." [1]

It is argued by some that a certain condition is here assumed which helps to evade the real difficulty. The really difficult question is what is to be done when no recognition of the implicit rights of the slaves can be elicited from the public conscience? Is there, then, any justification for resistance?

This question, it will be noticed, can be answered from two different points of view. The slaves themselves have rights and obligations arising from social relationships among themselves and with other men. The state may not admit them into citizenship, but it can not deprive them of their social rights. Other men may have claim on them, but the state refusing to recognize their claims has itself no claim on them for obedience. The obligation to obey law does not exist for the slaves.[2] But the men who are befriending them are in a different position. Unlike the slaves, they are generally under the obligation to obey the law, and if they want to resist it they need social recognition. According to Green, if they fail to get recognition from their fellow citizens, they may get it from the slaves and thus are enabled to proceed

---

① *Principles of Political Obligation.* p. 151.
② *Principles of Political Obligation.* p. 152.

with their activity.[1]

However, any such attempt at resistance must be handled with care, for the consequences on the political and social fabric may be more detrimental to the public welfare and common good than the wrong which it is the purpose of such resistance to correct. Practically speaking, certain cautions need be considered and certain difficulties overcome.

In a case where the legal authority of a command is doubtful, it is advisable, according to Green, to regard right in the political issue as not yet formed, and sovereignty as in abeyance, The individual, then, should join the side whose success seems most likely to work towards a common good. Where a vicious law is passed without means of legal amendment or repeal, resistance to authority is not only of right but also of duty.

Resistance to authority is not a matter of majority or minority. Majority has no right to resistance merely because it is a majority not in power, neither is minority prevented from resisting merely because it happens to be a minority represented or unrepresented in the government. There are distinct cases in which minorities are justified in their revolt even if their chances of success are rather slim. The claim to disobey any particular law needs the general recognition of others in order to render it a right, but it does not necessarily become a right by mere decision of a majority.

---

[1]  *Principles of Political Obligation.* p. 153.

It must be said, however, that there are no precise rules to be laid down as a guiding principle for the resistance to despotic governments. Green suggests three questions which may be serviceable in that connection. "A, What prospect is there of resistance to the sovereign power leading to the modification of its character or the improvement in its exercise without its subversion? B, If it is overthrown, is the temper of the people such, are the influences on which the general maintenance of social order and the fabric of recognized rights depend so far separable from it, that its overthrow will not mean anarchy? C, If its overthrow does lead to anarchy, is the whole system of law and government so perverted by private interests hostile to the public, that there has ceased to be any common interest in maintaining it?" [1]

---

[1] *Principles of Political Obligation.* p. 118.

# Chapter VI   Applications of The Principle of State Interference

After having stated the principle of state interference in theory, it remains necessary to inquire into its application in practise. One of the hardest problems in political philosophy is the reconciliation between the individual and the state, between liberty on the one hand and law on the other. This problem is the result of the traditional conception of both liberty and state interference. If liberty is considered as the absence of restraint and state interference is considered as a restraint, then they are necessarily opposed to each other. Green's idea is totally different. Having discussed at length his principle of state interference, we shall present his conception of freedom so as to ascertain the way in which the two are reconciled. Green prefers the term freedom to liberty; probably the word freedom is more adequate in ethics and his conception of freedom is essentially ethical.

It has been shown in the chapter on Metaphysical and Ethical Background that in intelligence man is a "free cause". In willing he is a free man. He is free in the sense that he is not subject to the determination by the external forces. He is self-determined; and in that determination in which he is himself both the subject and object, there is no "necessity" but freedom. With a free will he is capable of moral action; and with his freedom in intelligence he is capable of creative effort. With his faculty of reason he conceives the idea of good. With his consciousness of a unity of himself and others he is capable of good will and the idea of common good.

The above, then, is the basis of freedom. It contains all the elements contrary to the traditional conception of liberty. That conception is merely a negative one; that is, liberty means absence of restraint, of compulsion and obstruction. Green's conception of freedom is positive. It is not the absence of restraint. It is not to do as one likes, irrespective of what others like. It is not an instrument used by one man or one class of men at the expense of the others. It is "a positive power or capacity of doing or enjoying something worth doing or enjoying, and that, too, something that we do or enjoy in common with others."[1] The whole passage following is worth quoting. "When we measure the progress of society by its growth in freedom, we measure it by the increasing development and exercise of those powers of contributing to social good with which we believe the members of the society to be endowed; in short, by the greater power on the part of the citizens as a body to make the most and the best of them-

---

[1] *Works*. Vol. III, p. 371.

selves. Thus, though of course there can be no freedom among men who act not willingly but under compulsion, yet on the other hand, the mere removal of compulsion, the mere enabling a man to do as he likes, is in itself no true contribution to true freedom." [1]

If the above is a true account of freedom, then freedom in all forms of doing as one wills is only as a means to an end, and that end is freedom in the positive sense, the liberation of all powers of all men for the social good. No one has any right to do as he likes, if what he likes and does is detrimental to this end. With such a conception of freedom, Green can not be expected to remain an individualist as far as political action, that is, as far as state interference, is concerned.

Let us take freedom of contract and discuss in turn the different topics involved. It should be remembered that Green was writing in a period the legislation of which was characterized by Professor Dicey as a collectivist. The spirit of the age must not be ignored. There has been much legislation interfering with the freedom of contract and yet meeting the approval of the liberals who in days gone by stood for freedom of contract against restraints. There is therefore an inconsistency somewhere between the earlier attitude and the later one.

According to Green, the attempt to interfere with freedom of contract in the late seventies is essentially the same as the earlier

---

[1]  *Works.* Vol. Ⅲ. p. 371.

attempt to remove the restraints from freedom of contract. In the early days the liberals fought the fight of reform in the name of individual liberty against class privilege. They are at the time of Green's writing fighting the same battle of reform for social good in a different name and under a different banner, but the object of the reformers is the same. As far as contract is concerned, the early efforts to remove its restraints and the later efforts to interfere with its conditions of operation have the same effect of enhancing the freedom of the contracting parties, if we bear in mind the meaning of freedom just defined. We will examine into the concrete circumstances of the contracting parties so as to ascertain whether state interference is justifiabe.

As regards public health and sanitation, the state has passed laws and ordinances compelling people to conform to certain healthful conditions of living. Education in England at the same time has been made compulsory, though the plan was to be carried out only gradually. Factory legislation was started somewhat earlier, but the earlier attempt was far from being satisfactory, neither was it effectual. The early regulations applied to the cotton industry alone and even there the enforcement was quite loose. They aimed for one thing at limiting the hours of labour for children as well as for young persons. Gradually, however, these regulations became enforced and even extended to other industries, and the limitations of hours formerly applicable to children only were made to cover also women laborers. By the seventies those regulations were extended to most industries and were rigidly enforced. The regulation of the hours of labour, important though it is, is not, according to Green, the whole industrial problem. The conditions of labour, the installation of safety appliances and other measures of securing safety and health should be subject to legislation. They are the legitimate objects of state interference. State interference in such cases can not be objected to on the ground that it interferes with freedom of contract, for freedom in the correct sense does not mean absence of regulation.

State interference with freedom of contract is indeed not to serve moral purposes directly. That is beyond the function of the state, but it has the duty to maintain conditions under which alone human capacities can be liberated and morality may become possible. There are some who always have an enormous amount of confidence in human nature. They think people ought to be left to themselves. Industrial conditions may not be desirable, but the people, they argue, are not dummies. Left to themselves, to their own resources, they would of themselves awaken to the realization that reform is necessary, and, in that case, reform is a voluntary act. The instinct of self-preservation is capable of taking care of itself without the help of legislation. But Green says we must take people as we find them. [1] Many, to be sure, are capable of taking care of themselves, but others are not. State interference is not a burden to the conscientious and self-relying man, but it is a decided help to those who happen to be in less

---

[1]　*Works*. Vol. Ⅲ, p. 375.

favourable circumstances.

The objections raised against state interference seem to Green to have missed the point. Some of them, indeed, were based on a sort of individualistic philosophy, but others were directed against something quite different from state interference as such. Some people ridiculed the so-called "grand-motherly government", but what they objected to was centralization more than anything else. There was, as a matter of fact, a tendency to centralize, to turn over municipal and local government business to the central government. This tendency has its defects as well as its merits. One can, however, approve or disapprove centralization without giving any satisfactory reason against state interference. It is one question whether the central government is unnecessarily invading the legitimate area of local governments and quite another whether the state is unnecessarily interfering.

The term freedom of contract has its chief significance in connection with industrial and commercial enterprise. Because it is a part of the property rights, it is closely interwoven with the present economic order. What more important problems in that economic order are there than the relations of land, labour and capital? Green is hostile to land, friendly to labour and capital.

Property, as has been pointed out, in the chapters on the principle of political obligation, has a rational justification. According to Green, it is necessary to the free life and to the fulfilment of our moral ideal. He realizes that accumulation of property by a few men, when it becomes excessive, may lead to disastrous consequences. However, the blame is not properly chargeable to the institution of private property as such, but rather to its incidents or accidents. The existence of a proletarian class is not necessarily connected with the institution of private property; for we must bear in mind that the increased wealth of one man does not automatically mean the decreased wealth of another. Wealth is not a given stock of which a large part can not belong to one without taking away a share that should go to another. On the other hand, it is every day increasing in proportion to the surplus of production of new wealth over the amount necessary for consumption in the process of production.

It is true, according to Green, that wherever industries congregate, there also one will find large numbers of cheap labourers, untaught, underfed and quite incapable to freely contract. They have no intention to save, or if they have the intention, they have nothing to save from, since they live from hand to mouth. They seem to breed and actually do breed in many cases according to the Malthusian formula, without consideration as to the possibility of bringing these young visitors into proper environment and education. But their condition, deplorable as it is, is not necessarily the result of private property as an institution. They are traceable, at least in England, to two causes.[1] In the first place, when capital was applied to mining or manufacture or any other industry, it attracted and absorbed men who were either

---

① *Principles of Political Obligation*. p. 226.

themselves serfs or descendents of those who were trained in serf-dom. Their life was one of forced labour, relieved by church charity or poor law. They were always dependent, with no sense of responsibility, and incapable of taking care of themselves. The landless people of the past were the fathers of the proletarians of the nineteenth century. Secondly, this deplorable condition of the working class is due to the fact that privileges have been granted to the land-owning class which are incompatible with the principle on which property rights rest. However, this will be referred to later.

As far as we can see, Green does not condemn capital. In fact he has very little positive idea about wealth as capital. But judging from his broad principles, we may safely conclude, that if concrete evidence of the crushing nature of capitalism should be offered, he would be quite open to conviction. When convinced, he would probably denounce it as severely as he attacked the particular kind of land ownership.

He was friendly to labour. The following passage will make his position clearer than I can state it in my own words: "Labor, the economists tell us, is a commodity exchangeable like other commodities. This is in a certain sense true, but it is a commodity which attaches in a peculiar manner to the person of man. Hence restriction may need to be placed on the sale of this commodity which would be unnecessary in other cases, in order to prevent labor from being sold under conditions which make it impossible for the person selling it ever to become a free contributor to social good in any form.... Society is, therefore, plainly within its right when it limits freedom of contract for the sale of labor, so far as is done by our laws for the sanitary regulations of factories, workshops, and mines. It is equally within its right in prohibiting the labor of women and young persons beyond certain hours. If they work beyond these hours, the result is demonstrably physical deterioration; which, as demonstrably, carries with it a lowering of the moral forces of society. For the sake of that general freedom of its members to make the best of themselves, which it is the object of civil society to secure, a prohibition should be put by law, which is the deliberate voice of society, on all such contracts of service as in a general way yield such a result." ①

In a later passage, he urges state intervention in behalf of labour, not trusting to leave it to itself. "Left to itself or to the operation of casual benevolence, a degraded population perpetuates and increases itself. Read any of the authorised accounts, given before royal or parliamentary commissions, of the state of the laborers, especially of the women and children, as they were in our great industries before the law was first brought to bear on them, and before freedom of contract was first interfered with in them. Ask yourself what chance there was of a generation, born and bred under such conditions, ever contracting itself out of them. Given a certain standard of moral and material well being, people may be trusted not to sell their labor, or the labor of their

---

① *Works.* Vol. Ⅲ, p. 373.

children, on terms which would not allow that standard to be maintained. But with large masses of our population, until the laws we have been considering took effect, there was no such standard. There was nothing on their part, in the way either of self-respect or established demand for comforts, to prevent them from working and living, or from putting their children to work and live, in a way in which no one who is to be a healthy and free citizen can work and live. No doubt there were many high-minded employers who did their best for their work people before the days of state interference, but they could not prevent less scrupulous hirers of labor from hiring it on the cheapest terms. It is true that cheap labor is in the long run dear labor, but it is only in the long run, and eager traders do not think of the long run. If labor is to be had under conditions incompatible with the health or decent housing, or education of the laborer, there will always be, plenty of people to buy it under those conditions, careless of the burden in the shape of rates and taxes which they may be laying up for posterity. Either the standard of well-being on the part of the sellers of labor must prevent them from selling their labor under those conditions, or the law must prevent it. With a population such as ours was forty years ago, and still largely is, the law must prevent it and continue the prevention for some generations, before the sellers will be in a state to prevent it for themselves." [1]

---

[1]  *Works.* Vol. Ⅲ, pp. 376–377.

As far as land is concerned, Green speaks without reserve. In connection with the existence of a proletarian class, he has pointed out that privileges have been granted to landlords that are incompatible with the true principle upon which property rights are based. No one has the right to do what he likes with his own, especially if what he has as his own happens to be land. Land, like labour, is not a commodity in the ordinary sense. "It is from the land or through the land that the raw material of all wealth is obtained. It is only upon the land that we can live; only across the land that we can move from one place to another."①"It is just as much an original natural material necessary to productive industry as are air, light and water, but while the latter from the nature of the case can not be appropriated, the earth can be and has been."②The only justification for this appropriation is that it is used towards contributing to social good. That justification disappears when appropriation of land does not serve this purpose. Landowners have been given too much privilege in the past. They were permitted to do what they liked with their own, even if what they actually did decreased productive capacity, endangered the health of the farmers and increased their misery and poverty. Misery and poverty of the farmers affect the public welfare. The state in the interest of public freedom which it is its business to maintain can not allow the individual owner to deal as he likes with

---

① *Works*. Vol. Ⅲ, p. 377.

② *Principles of Political Obligation*. p. 227.

his land to the same extent as it permits him to deal with other commodities that he may happen to own.

One of the practical aspects of the land problem is the bad system of settlements. Under that system, the land invariably goes to the eldest son. It has at least two bad effects. First, it prevents the division of an estate into a number of small holdings. Here Green seems to uphold one of the traditions of Jeffersonian democracy; for he unhesitatingly declares that the small proprietors who till their own land are the mainstay of social order. Second, it keeps land in the hands of persons who are too much burdened by personal as well as family debts and therefore unable to improve the land in any way. As a result, land is not half as productive as it ought to be, given the necessary improvements. Various remedies have been suggested, but they do not solve the problem. The problem will not be solved as long as this system of settlement remains in force. It is against public interest to permit landowners to transfer property in such a way as to prevent improvement. If property is not used according to the principle upon which alone property can be justified, then state has every right to step in. In this case, then, state should with hold legal sanction from the kind of land settlement under discussion.

The relation between landlords and tenants demands attention. Generally speaking, freedom of contract should be allowed so as to facilitate any voluntary action for good and the initiative of the citizens to fulfil their moral ideal in the positive sense. But Green's warning is that we must not sacrifice the end

to the means. There are certain contracts which affect public convenience, but in respect to which the contracting parties directly
concerned are not capable of taking public interests into consideration. Such contracts ought to be invalidated by law. Take, for
instance, the agreement between landlords and tenants reserving
game grounds for the former. It involves the reservation of large
tracts of land for no other purpose than that the landlords may occasionally hunt. Hunting is not of itself objectionable, but in this
particular case it takes away agricultural land from legitimate agricultural purposes. Not only do landlords make reservations, but
they can and often do prevent land from cultivation so that there
might be a forest in its stead for their amusement. The tenants
who are used to such treatment by their superiors will generally
enter any agreement by mere force of habit. But again, it is not a
matter that affects the farmer alone. Public interests are also at
stake. The country can not afford to see good land for food production turned into a game resort or a sort of garden for mere
amusement of a few. In this case, again, the state finds it necessary to resort to interference.

Individualists always claim that, left to itself, everything
will be all right. The farmers will in time be conscious of their
own interests, and the landlords will be enlightened enough to
take public interests into consideration. Perhaps this will happen.
Green wishes that it might, but derives from the facts the conviction that it will not. The great majority of English farmers can be
turned out without compensation at six months or a year's notice.

Under such conditions, farming does not attract sufficient capital for improvement, since landlords are spendthrifts and tenants can be kicked out at any time. Best farming is generally done where there is a lease, and the worst farming is generally done where tenancy relies upon the honour of the lords. It is true that a good landlord is as good as, if not better than, a lease, but not all of them are good, and if any one is good, he is not immortal. Agriculture can not be made dependent upon the whims of a few. In order to secure proficient use of land, the farmers need protection, so that necessary capital may as a result be directed towards agriculture. When such a problem confronts the state, the state must take people and situation as it finds them to be and must act accordingly. In this ease the state can not wait, since the subsistence of the population depends upon its action.

As to the complete and comprehensive programme in regard to land reform, Green does not say anything definite. Conditions vary in different places, hence any hard and fast plan can not be formulated. However, we are sure that he does not believe in either single tax or the confiscation of unearned increment. To him "the great objection is that the relation between earned and unearned increment is so complicated, that a system of appropriating the latter to the state could scarcely be established without lessening the stimulus to the individual to make most of the land, and thus ultimately lessening its serviceableness to society." ①

---

① *Principles of Political Obligation.* p. 229.

# Chapter VII  Applications of The Principle of State Interference ( Continued )

The greatest and the obvious interference with free life in history as well as at the present time is certainly war. However German his ideas may be in other respects, Green's idea of war is far from being Teutonic. War, he says, is a violation of the right of life, even if it should not be considered as "multitudinous murder". It is not murder in either the legal or the moral sense. It is not legal murder because murder is unlawful killing and war is lawful killing, if by lawful is meant conforming to man-made laws. Neither is war a "multitudinous murder" in the strict moral sense; for, taken in that strict sense, murder necessarily involves ill will between those killed and those who do the killing. In war there is no particular personal ill feeling. Again, a murder, as generally understood, involves the violation of determinate person or persons. It generally implies that a scheme has been planned by a murderer who is responsible for the murder. But there can hardly be any definite person or persons who may be said to be entirely responsible for any war. No doubt there are wars in which one or a few determinate persons is or are especially blamable, or at least more so than others, but they can not have willed a war as a murderer is capable of willing someone's death. They ate not murderers in the strict sense, however selfish they may be. However wrong or disastrous war may be, it is not murder.

But the above statement should not be taken to mean that war is not a violation of the right to life it is.[1]And it can not be argued that because there is a lack of intention on the part of one soldier to kill any particular enemy, there is, therefore, no ground for characterizing war as a violation of the right to life; for killing in war is caused by human agency and is on the whole intentional in the sense that it is preventable but not prevented. It matters not whether any particular soldier has a definite intention to kill any one in particular he is violating the right to life just the same. Nor does it avail to argue that in killing another, one soldier is just as irresponsible as the lightning that occasionally takes its tolls from among mankind; for in the latter case no right is involved. There is no human relationship between man and lightning, neither is there any mutual claim and recognition. If there is no right involved there certainly can not be any violation of right.

Modern warfare admits both the method of conscription and voluntary service. If a man volunteers to the colours, he takes the

---

[1]  *Principles of Political Obligation.* p. 162.

chance of being killed on his own initiative, and therefore has given up his right to life of which there can not be any violation. It is argued that he is in the same position as a man who works in a dangerous mine for a certain wage. The answer is, that if both— the volunteer and the miner—are killed, the right to life is violated in both cases. The right to life can not be voluntarily given up in either case; for it always involves both the individual claim and the social recognition. Society has an interest in the right to life which the individual representing one party can not disregard.①The same is true of industrial work. If a man works in a dangerous pit and is killed, there is a violation of the right to life, no matter whether the man works voluntarily or not. War is therefore no less wrong when a soldier volunteers to fight. Besides, whatever system may be adopted by the state, whether conscription or voluntary service, there is always an element of compulsion.②Conscription is of course compulsory. Though under a system of voluntary service there is not compulsion exerted on particular persons, yet there is an element of compulsion in the fact that the state decides on war and compels a certain number of lives to be deprived. After all, then, war is a violation of the right to life.

It may yet be argued that war is justifiable in case of self-defense. The right of life, it may be said, is important, but there

①　*Principles of Political Obligation.* p. 163.
②　*Principles of Political Obligation.* p. 163.

are yet more precious things at stake when one is subject to un-provoked attack. The existence of society and of state guaranteeing the whole system of rights and obligations is more important, it is often urged, than the maintenance of the particular right to life. Hence war in the defense of society and of the state has justification in the greater purpose it serves, even if in serving that purpose, it results in killing.

Green answers that this argument is really not to justify war per se, but rather to remove blame from those who resort to it for the purpose of defense.[1]As a matter of fact, we are only told that the state in sending soldiers to the field may be compelled to do so against its will, hence responsibility for destruction of life and property is not chargeable to those who have no other alternative than to resort to force. But war is not a natural recurring phenom-enon that can not be avoided. It has come about through human effort and human energy. If one party is exempt from blame, some other party is not. War as a violation of the right to life is none the less wrong even if the blame is transferred from one party to another. Thus a war for the defense of freedom, or for liberation, or for the existence of a nation is just as wrong as any-thing that violates the right to life, but it is a wrong chargeable not to defenders but to the aggressors. Historically the records are most disappointing. Few wars in Green's opinion can be said to be waged for the purpose of political liberation. Most of the wars

---

[1]  *Principles of Political Obligation.* p. 164.

are waged for the purpose of aggrandizement, brought out by personal jealousies and dynastic ambitions. With the growth of nationalism, patriotism has taken place of dynastic loyalty. Somehow or other, the fallacious notion that advantage to one nation is always a disadvantage to some other nation has been generally accepted by people at large, and as a result all nations are at potential if not actual warfare with one another.

War is wrong no matter who is blamable for it. It is wrong whatever may be the result. That there are good results arising out of war Green does not deny, but the claim that they transform the character of the war Green can not concede. "Wrong doing is a voluntary action, either proceeding from a will uninfluenced by the desire to be good on the part of the agent, or it is an action that interferes with the conditions necessary to the free play and development of a good will on the part of the others."[1] "If an action, so far as any results go which the agent can have in view or over which he has control, interferes with conditions necessary to the free play and the development of a good will on the part of others, it is not the less wrong doing because, through some agency which is not his, the effects which he intended, and which rendered it wrong doing, come to contribute to an ulterior good. Nor, if it issues from bad will (in the sense explained), is it less wrong (in the moral sense) because this will is itself, in the view of some higher being, contributary to a moral good which is

---

[1] *Principles of Political Obligation.* p. 167.

not, in whole or in part, with in the view of the agent. If then war is wrong doing in both the above senses..., it does not cease to be so on account of any good resulting from it in a scheme of providence."①There are probably desirable results from Caesar's wars with the Gauls, from English occupation of distant territories, from German and Italian unification, but incident to these results are also innumerable acts which do not cease to be wrong merely because something good and desirable has been achieved.

War then is a wrong, but is it a wrong that is necessarily inherent in the organization of the nation states? According to Green, there can be no war if the states are in any way organized according to the idea back of them. State according to its idea is an institution " in which all rights are harmoniously maintained, in which all the capacities that give rise to rights have free play given to them."②No state thus organized will ever have any inevitable conflict with any state similarly organized. There is no truth in the notion that the gain of one is the loss of another. In fact the better the states are organized the freer is the scope for the individuals to fulfil their capacities. Consequently much less will be the danger of conflict. War is therefore not inherent in states. Its appearance is more due to the defective organization of states.

Green gives full consideration to the division of society into

---

① *Principles of Political Obligation.* pp. 167—168.

② *Principles of Political Obligation.* p. 170.

different classes of people and the different interests they represent. The familiar division into two dominant classes, the privileged on the one side and the oppressed on the other, he shows to be not a matter of internal politics alone, but one that often gives rise to international conflict. "The privileged class involuntarily believes and spreads the belief that the interest of the state lies in some extension without, not in an improvement of organization from within."[1]It looks as if right here Green is somewhat prophetic without comprehending the full significance of his prophecy. We now know that the priviledged class benefits by national expansion. The militarists want conquest, the merchants want market and the capitalists want industrially undeveloped areas.Their gain is not the gain of the state. The state according to its idea does not and should not involve either a privileged class or a suffering class. The sooner they are removed, the better it is for the state and also for international peace.

It is suggested by some that state is not an abstract formula; it is not a complex of institutions consciously established for the purpose of maintaining and harmonizing rights. It is now generally a nation and all that a nation implies. A nation implies a homogeneous people, possessing peculiar institutions, certain dominant passions and a nationalistic psychology. Nations are now existing in the kind of state of nature in which individuals were once claimed to be living by Hobbes. They are independent and sover-

---

① *Principles of Political Obligation.* p. 171.

eign, and they have only themselves to serve. Since their situations are diverse and their interests conflicting, war is inevitable. It can only be avoided by the establishment of a world empire transcending all the nation states, but that is neither practical nor desirable. It is true Green concedes that states at present are nations and nations at present are not free from egoistic passions. But, he says, there is little occasion for pessimism.①Nations may yet become true states. The more truly the nation becomes the state, the greater the scope for national spirit. National spirit has nothing objectionable if it is directed to worthy objects, and it will be, when states become true in the ideal sense. Other things are also facilitated when states become organized more in accordance with the ideal. Frequent trade and communication and better understanding may eventually produce a consciousness of a social bond between nations so that the demand for justice and peace may eventually speak louder than the bugle of war. When that time comes, this sort of wholesale violation of the right to life may be eliminated.

Another phase of state interference with free life is the right of the state to impose punishment on citizens. Free life on the part of the citizens involves the assumption that every man can freely act to contribute to the social good. The right on the part of the state to punish involves the assumption, that it, the state functions in certain ways to prevent such actions as interfere with

---

① *Principles of Political Obligation.* p. 179.

the possibility of free activity contributory to the social good. In other words, in exercising the right to punish, the state is trying to maintain conditions under which it may be possible for the citizens to realize their moral capacities. Thus considered, the right to punish as well as the nature of the punishments in detail can not be satisfactorily presented without an examination into the whole system of rights and obligations. For us, it is unnecessary to go into the details of these rights and obligations, since we need only dwell on the broad principles of punishment. There has been frequent discussion as to whether punishments are retributive in nature, or preventive or reformatory. The true conception, according to Green, is that they are all three.①The following discussion will therefore consist of three divisions starting with the retributive element in punishment.

At the outset, we have to point out that punishment is incapable of having private vengeance as an element.②In fact private vengeance, which in popular expression implies taking law into one's hands, is incompatible with the right of punishment vested in a political authority, much less is there a "right of private vengeance". There is a contradiction in terms in that expression. Private vengeance implies an interest purely individual while a right is always social and in that sense also public. Abstract the social recognition and a claim is not a right. Hence the right of

---

① *Principles of Political Obligation.* p. 181.
② *Principles of Political Obligation.* p. 181.

punishment on the part of the state does not admit of purely individual interest.

But, it has been asked, is a state capable of the feeling of vengeance at all? If it is so capable, according to Green, it is not so in the same way as the individuals are. France may have felt revengeful toward Germany, but in that case it was against a foreign nation that France felt the feeling of vengeance. Vengeance in the sense of the feeling of one individual towards another, the nation is incapable of. As far as punishment is concerned, if there is the element of vengeance at all, it is in the nature of popular indignation. When a child is murdered the public will likely demand that the criminal should have his due, should be dealt with according to his deserts and be punished "justly".

This lead to the idea of the just and justice. According to Green, the just means "that complex of social conditions which for each individual is necessary to enable him to realize his capacity of contributing to social good."① "Justice is the habit of mind which leads us to respect those conditions in dealing with others—not to interfere with them so far as they already exist, and to bring them into existence so far as they are not found in existence."② A punishment would be unjust "if either the act punished is not a violation of known rights, or an omission to

---

① *Principles of Political Obligation.* p. 188. Footnote.
② *Principles of Political Obligation.* p. 188. Footnote.

fulfil known obligations of a kind which the agent might have prevented, or the punishment is not required for the maintenance of rights."①The criminal when justly punished sees the punishment in his own action returning on himself and may as a result become more susceptible of the idea of common and pubilc good. Thus it will be seen that even in this theory of punishment, rignts and obligations are the real nucleus from which its justification is derived. And when Green speaks of rights and obligations, it is necessary to bear in mind the moral idea and the idea of common good. It must be understood that the general principle here laid down does not offer a practical guidance in specific cases. In fact, justice in specific cases can not be determined without having a more complete and a more harmonized system of rights and obligations than at the present time. An intentional violation of right must be punished whether that be a true right or not, since such violation endangers the social well-being more than any wrong punishment."

Let us next turn to the preventive nature of punishment. The argument in this case is that whatever has been done is done, and that no amount of punishment will undo the injury caused by the criminal act. What punishment can do is to prevent further occurrences of like sort. Punishment on the criminal produces a terror in society and that terror, it is claimed, has a restraining effect on those who contemplate similar crimes. In order to have

---

① *Principles of Political Obligation.* p. 186.

the proper quality of preventiveness, it is believed that the greater the crime, the heavier should be the punishment. This Green agrees with, if by heavier punishment is meant that which produces greater terror in popular imagination, and by greater crime is not meant a greater degree of moral guilt.① It is a fallacy, he holds, to identify heavy punishment with great pain to the criminal, for that makes the effectiveness of punishment depend upon the amount of pain, and this varies so from individual to individual as to be incapable of calculation. A given punishment may be extremely painful to one without being so to another, since sensitiveness to pain differs with different temperaments, experiences and circumstances, none of which the state or its agent can exactly ascertain. And even if they could be ascertained, since their difference is undeniable, the punishment will be different for different individuals and a general rule for punishment will necessarily be impossible.②

The fallacy of identifying greater crime with the greater degree of moral guilt is probably a confusion of both the aim and the function of the state. The state has nothing③to do with the moral depravity of the criminal and in punishing him it is not counting the effect on him so much as the effect on others who might be tempted to do as he has done. In fact there may be moral depravity of an equal amount in two criminals, as for in-

---

① *Principles of Political Obligation.* p. 190.
② *Principles of Political Obligation.* p. 191.
③ *Principles of Political Obligation.* p. 191.

stance, the wealthy banker who embezzles and the poverty-stricken tramp who steals, and yet the punishments may profitably be different; for the same preventive effect may be secured by different punishments.

There are other diffculties confronting the attempt to base punishment on moral depravity. In the first place, the degree of moral depravity can not be ascertained. No one can ascertain it for himself, for an action often involves a complexity of good motives mixed with bad ones, and you can not measure the goodness of the good motives just as you can not measure the badness of bad motives. The man himself can not do it, his friends can not do it, much less can a judge or an agent of the state. Secondly, the state has no business to punish wickedness as such. The moment it starts to punish wickedness, immorality or vice, it vitiates the disinterestedness of effort to escape wickedness, immorality or vice and checks the growth of true goodness. To refuse to be wicked for fear of consequences is not the same as to obey disinterestedly the self-imposed laws, which latter alone makes up morality.

It may be argued that crimes committed under the so-called "extenuating circumstances" should be and are generally punished with leniency. The reason claimed to be the determining factor is that such crimes involve less moral guilt, and punishment, being proportionate to the moral depravity of the criminal, is ipso facto light. Hence a man who steals a bottle of milk because he has not bad food for two days is punished differently from a man who does the same thing because he is in the habit of doing it, or because he is maliciously trying to deprive some people of something. Cases of such circumstances are abundant and practice seems to agree with the theory; but according to Green, while the fact may be true, the explanation is not correct. If crimes under extenuating circumstances are punished with more leniency than those not under such circumstances, it is not because they involve less moral depravity, but because it needs less unpleasantness and less terror to prevent alike occurrence.[1] It this as well as in other cases, morality or rather moral depravity is not the measure, neither the ground for punishment. It does not mean that punishment has no moral purpose. It is one of the instruments to maintain conditions under which morality may be possible. It also serves the moral purpose of protecting rights the maintenance of which advances the moral well being.

Generally, according to Green, popular indignation or disapproval is founded on the outward aspects of a criminal's conduct, that is, it comes essentially from a response in men to the stimulation which the outward aspects of the criminal act generally afford.[2] It may even be said that if crimes can not and should not be punished according to the degree of moral depravity of the criminal, they should be, if they are not, punished according to the outward consequences of the criminal act. The

---

[1]  *Principles of Political Obligation.* p. 193.

[2]  *Principles of Political Obligation.* p. 196.

degree of criminality of the individual depends or should depend upon the consequences of his act, that is, upon the relative importance of the rights he violates; and the more disastrous the consequences, the severer should be the punishment.[1] The engine driver who overlooks the signal through carelessness is and should be accused of manslaughter and punished accordingly, though his moral qualities may not be in a worse condition than those of many whose carelessness does not result in such an accident. The difference in punishment can not be accounted for by the difference in kind or degree of the carelessness in the two cases, for it is after all the consequences that ultimately determine the difference. Another example is drunkenness. The man who drinks may not have such moral depravity as intentionally to violate others' rights; but if he does commit a crime the consequences do not become less disastrous merely because he is under the influence of liquor. An intoxicated mother may smother her child by sleeping on it without the least bit of intention to do any harm. None the less she should be punished; for though she has no intention of committing the crime, the condition that causes it is capable of prevention. Punishment in such cases will produce a terror which will make people more careful about drinking and will prevent some accidental violation of the right to free life. It is in connection with the preventive nature of punishment that there is the necessity and actual practice of distinguis-

---

[1]　*Principles of Political Obligation.* p. 197.

hing civil injuries from crimes. According to Green, the belief that civil injuries are "violations of rights when considered in reference to the injury sustained by the individual", while crimes are "violations of rights when considered in reference to their evil tendencies as regards the community at large", is quite misleading. Nothing is punishable which does not violate some kind of rights; and since rights are social, any violation of them can not be regarded as merely an injury sustained by the individual. If the injury to the individual is not an injury to the community, it is not a violation of rights and therefore should not be punishable.

The real distinction between crimes and civil injuries comes from the preventive nature of punishments. Civil injuries can not generally be prevented by arousing terror in the public mind. ①
Let us take for instance the breach of contract. The party who breaks the contract may not know that he is violating its provisions, and therefore may not be responsible for not knowing that he has violated a right. No amount of terror associated with such a violation of rights will prevent similar violations of rights under given circumstances. It may be argued that even in civil cases, the delinquent party may know his obligations but have no means at his disposal to fulfil them, and therefore punishment in such cases may make him providential; but even here it must be conceded that his inability to fulfil his obligations may not be due to forces of his own making, and, if not, terror as a result of pun-

---

① *Principles of Political Obligation.* p. 199.

ishment will not improve the ability of people under like circum-stances. It is, therefore, from the preventive nature of punishment that there has come to be a distinction between civil and criminal offenses. The actual distinction in English law is more or less an accident.[1]

Let us turn to the reformatory character of punishment. Crime involves the violation of rights, but it also involves a viola-tor of rights, namely the criminal. In punishing him, the state may likely forget that he, too, had or will have rights which, though they may be temporarily suspended, are yet his due after serving his term. He must be given a certain freedom of action conducive to an intelligent exercise of rights so that in being pun-ished once, he may not have to be punished twice, and in having served his term, he may not have to meet social ostracism. Capital punishment and life imprisonment can not be justified ex-cept on two grounds: [2] first, when public order will be easily endangered, if the crime committed is not associated with the punishment that produces the greatest terror; second, when the crime is such as to warrant the assumption of a permanent inca-pacity of the criminal for enjoying and respecting rights. But these conditions are themselves unsatisfactory. Given the condition of the criminal, whether the state has the right to presume his permanent incapacity for rights or not may still be open to doubt.

---

[1] *Principles of Political Obligation.* p. 201.

[2] *Principles of Political Obligation.* p. 203.

It may very well be that the state is not entitled to such presumption. And certainly it does not call for greater terror to deep public order when public education has attained its present standard and police force its present efficiency. Considering the rights of the criminal as well as those of the rest of the citizens, punishment should also be reformatory, and if so, capital punishment and life imprisonment can not be justified except in extreme cases.

According to Green, "there is no direct reference in punishment by state... to moral good or evil. The state in its judicial action does not look to the moral guilt of the criminal whom it punishes, or to the promotion of moral good by means of punishment in him or in others. It looks not to virtue and vice but to rights and wrongs. It looks back to the wrong done in crime which it punishes; not, however, in order to avenge it but in order to the consideration of the sort of terror which needs to be associated with such wrong doing in order to the future maintenance of rights.... Thus punishment of crime is preventive in its object... justly preventive of injustice. But in order to effectually attain its preventive object and to attain it justly, it should be reformatory." [1]

Human beings are capable of rights, because they are capable of a conception of a common good which each shares with the other. They act not only with an end in view but also with a con-

---

[1] *Principles of Political Obligation.* p. 202.

ception of that end. They are, according to Green, performing or seeking to perform self imposed duties; they are moral, and in order to facilitate the realization of their moral ideal, they must be allowed a certain spontaneity of action. The state, instead of actually and actively promoting morality, should devote itself to the task of removing obstacles. Compulsory education and prohibition or temperance are state interferences governed by this principle.

However mystic Green may have seemed to many a student at times, he was not merely a closet philosopher. He was elected to the Oxford Town Council, and expressed his idea of a true liberal program as "the removal of all obstructions which the law can remove to the free development of English citizens."①On the two subjects that interested him more than anything else, namely, education and temperance, he often got into heated controversy.

As to education, he stood for compulsory attendance, the maintenance of schools out of public funds and unsectarian instruction.②State interference in education may seem to be an enforcement of moral duties, for education of children is a moral duty. But Green argued, "on the other hand, the neglect of it does tend to prevent the growth of the capacity for beneficially exercising rights on the part of those whose education is

---

① *Works.* Vol. Ⅲ, Memoir CXX.
② *Works.* Vol. Ⅲ, Memoir CXXIII.

neglected, and it is on this account, not as a purely moral duty on the part of the parent, but as a prevention of a hindrance to the capacity for rights on the part of children, that education should be enforced by the state." [1]Nor can compulsory education be objected to on the ground that it interferes with the spontaneous action of the individuals; for so far as those parents are concerned who have the rights of their children in view, the law that compels education does not interfere with spontaneity of action. The man who prevents his wife from overwork and sends his children to school instead of factory and does all this of his own will, suffers no moral degradation from a law which would compel him to do so. He does not feel the constraint. And for the parents who are unwilling to educate their children, it may be said that the state seeks to remove the hindrances to the exercise of rights on the part of the children and does not aim at imposing inconveniences on the part of the parents.

The question of the liquor traffic was the one in which Green was drawn into political controversy in 1872 with Sir William Harcourt. In a letter to the *Oxford Chronicle* he declared that he would not support "a representative who bids for the votes of the politicians by trying to pooh pooh the drinking evil altogether and to run down all the legislative attempts to check it." [2]But Green was not originally a total abstainer. His ideas were probably influ-

---

[1] *Principles of Political Obligation.* p. 209.
[2] *Works.* Vol. III, Memoir CXVII.

enced by personal as well as social relations. The disastrous career of his elder brother constantly weighed upon his mind and the conviction that the political morale was being sapped by drink came later to be added to his personal experience. In fact, he spoke quite vehemently of "the untaught and underfed denizen of a London yard with ginshops on the right hand and on the left"[1]. At any rate he became an ardent supporter of temperance. In 1872, he joined the United Kingdom Alliance, and later, 1875, he joined also the Church of England Temperance Society.

Green's practical policy in this matter was regulation and limitation but not prohibition. The aim was to devise a process of licensing to limit liquor traffic to certain hours, and if possible to enable neighbors to exclude liquor establishments from their area through legislation. On what ground, then, can legislation be justified in interfering with this particular traffic? "We justify it on the ground of the recognized right on the part of the society to prevent men from doing what they like, if, in exercising their peculiar tastes, in doing as they like, they create a social nuisance. There is no right to freedom in the purchase or sale of a particular commodity, if the general result of allowing such a freedom is to detract from freedom in the higher sense, from the general power of men to make the best of themselves.... Excessive drinking of one man means an injury to others in health, purse and capability to which no limit can be placed. Drunkenness in the

---

[1]  *Principles of Political Obligation.* p. 8.

head of a family means, as a rule, the impoverishment and degradation of all the members of the family; and the pressure of a drinking shop at the corner of the street means, as a rule, the drunkenness of a certain number of heads of families in that street." [1]Such an obstruction to free life must be removed by the authority of the state. Tolerance of any particular liberty of action implies that liberty is not and must not be an impediment to social good.

Even in connection with liquor, there is the *laissez faire* argument that state inteference will not do any good. Leave the people to themselves, and as soon as they know the danger of drinking and as soon as they acquire more self respect, they will give up liquor of their own free will. Giving it up voluntarily is much better than giving it up by compulsion; for in the former you facilitate the spontaneity of action and in the latter you compel obedience merely through fear of consequences. But the trouble is, Green replies, we can not wait. The longer you let liquor go, the greater harm it does and the more difficult it becomes for the state to interfere. On the one hand, the interests that are fattening themselves through intoxication of drunkards would be more influential, more deep rooted in their foothold and much harder to deal with; on the other, intoxication is more or less contagious. Aside from the fact that the friends of a liquor fiend may become themselves victims, the scientists claim that

---

[1] *Works.* Vol. Ⅲ, pp. 383-384.

offspring from drunkards inherit the tendency to drink, hence, given the liquor, they will readily victimize themselves. Green seems to have such an idea in view and that is why he urges not only legislation, but also speedy legislation to limit liquor traffic.

# Chapter VIII    Green's Influence

Turning from Green's theories to the views of his followers and his critics, we need bear in mind that modern tendencies, especially after the war, are away from political idealism. The advancement of science makes possible new approaches to the study of politics. Sociology brings out facts hitherto unknown and therefore not within the compass of political speculation in Green's time. The division of society into different groups with conflicting interests was only vaguely guessed at in the late seventies, but it is now a familiar fact. Modern industrialism has produced several tendencies, none of which subscribes to political idealism. Socialism, or more correctly Marxism, involves economic determinism as its philosophic background. Guild Socialism in England and Syndicalism in France represent a revolt against central authority in politics, but in philosophy they are more affiliated with realism than idealism. The war and its consequences have encouraged radicalism, and radicalism, while speaking in the same old name of freedom and justice, never fails to keep its eye on the cold facts of every day life.

Among scholars who are disinterestedly searching for knowledge, political idealism is also fading. Those who are realistic in temperament are apt to look at facts as they are rather than as they should be. Investigation often shows that what they should be is generally far from being what they actually are. Therefore, instead of building castles in the air it is considered more profitable to state the actual facts and to suggest possible remedies. Others feel that political idealism deals merely with the conscious and conscientious part of human nature in politics. The subtle psychology of the group as well as of the individual, the subconscious action of human beings, the influence of heredity and environment, the biological and social inheritance of the people are important factors for consideration, but political idealism ignores them all by mere reference to an all embracing and all pervading consciousness.

The above spells doom for Green and his idealism. Such is the case, but it does not necessarily have to be. Two factors need be considered. First, the political philosophy of Green has little, if any, of the absolutism of the German idealist. The foregoing analysis, it is hoped, has made that clear. Therefore it is not exactly correct to identify Green with the idealists of the German type, though he was a thorough-going idealist. A revolt against political idealism is not necessarily a revolt against Green. Second, some of the new tendencies do not necessarily contradict the broad principles laid down by Green. They may qualify, and they may supplement, but they do not necessarily deny the fundamentals in his philosophy. A radical, for instance, may become his follower to a marked extent without ceasing to be radical. The thing to bear in mind, as Mr. Barker has advised us, is the broad principle and not the detailed application. You can no more blame Green for his leniency towards capital than you can despise Aristotle for his justification of slavery. These two considerations explain the fact that although broadsides have been fired against political idealism, Green has not been the target, and although new tendencies have gained ground, Green's influence has not entirely faded away. In fact, of the writers who have expressed opinions on him, few, if any, reveal any hostility towards him.①Disciples and critics alike may qualify and destroy his doctrines in view of the better understanding of social facts, but none the less they admire him for the able formulation of political principles, at least in English, into idealistic philosophical terminology.

The champions of the idealistic school of thought of the present day England are Messrs, Bosanquet and Bradley. Both are more Hegelian than Green ever was. Mr. Bradley believes that the community and the individual are so, interwoven that the latter's existence implies a comprehensive system of relationship with the former. An individual becomes what he is, by including in his being his relationship with society and state. If morality by definition consists of the realization of the self, it also consists in the

---

① Except H. Spencer, *Essays Scientific*, *Political and Speculative*. Vol. II, p. 332.

realization of these relations with the society. Mr. Bradley believes in a sort of regimentation in society according to which each has his station and therefore also duties, the fulfilment of which constitutes the realization of the self and social relations, that is, constitutes morality. Dr. Bosanquet admits in his *Philosophical Theory of the State* that he follows the footsteps of Green, but that if he has to part company, it is because Green seems to him to have erred on the score of excessive caution rather than carelessness.[1] And he does part company with Green at many points. He maintains, for instance, that society is within the state. If by state is meant not a mere political mechanism, but a general organization over and above other organizations, it is essentially a community of communities. It is above society. This is already different from Green's point of view, but it leads to a greater and a still more significant difference. Green condemns war as a violation of the rights of life and liberty; to that extent, he argues, the action of the state declaring war is itself wrong and therefore not conducive to the end for which state exists. But Dr. Bosanquet has a different point of view. According to him acts of the state and acts of its agents are to be distinguished, and the terms moral and immoral, properly applicable to the latter, are inappropriate for the former. The state as a state can not act within the relations of private life in which organized morality exists. It "is the guardian of our world and not a factor of our organ-

---

① Bosanquet, *The Philosophical Theory of The State*, Introduction.

ized moral world."①It can not be bound by the system of rights and obligations it enforces, nor can it be limited by the social ethics it maintains.

There are two other points of difference which should be mentioned. Dr. Bosanquet writes with the advantage of the new and fashionable theories of the present age. "National spirit", "social mind", and "group consciousness" are more talked about now than in the late seventies and early eighties. Armed with these new weapons, Dr. Bosanquet presents with greater freedom than Green did the conception of general wilt and the idea of a common good as working instruments. Here he makes use of the progress made by psychology and sociology and in so doing, according to Prof. Barker, he approaches quite near to Hegel. Institutions are regarded as the embodiment of living spirits without which they can not be what they are. Green has the same idea but it is not strained to the same extent. State interference can only apply to the externals; what Green calls the removal of obstructions Bosanquet calls the hindrance of hindrances. State action is, therefore, primarily negative with both, but throughout their works there is discernible a difference of degree of negativity. I mention these differences between Green and Bosanquet not for the purpose of indicating a revolt against the former from among the idealists themselves, but with the view of demonstrating that Green has little in common with the absolutists of the

① Bosanquet, *The Philosophical Theory of The State.* p. 325.

idealistic school of thought. As will be shown later, an idealist is not necessarily an absolutist.

Prof. Fairbrother is an outspoken disciple. In his *Philosophy of T. H. Green*[1], he declares in a prefatory note that Green's philosophy is "perhaps the only complete and consistent philosophy which derives and justifies both moral responsibility in the present and hope for the future from a rigorously scientific metaphysic." With this view in mind, he defended Green from the onslaught of Prof. Seth, Mr. Balfour and Prof. Sedgwick. However, the attack as well as the defence deals so exclusively with philosophy and metaphysics that it is entirely beyond our sphere to examine it.

Prof. Ritchie in his *Principles of State Interference* points out that we can not find out one's attitude in politics from one's philosophical speculation. Green is an idealist in philosophy and a liberal in politics. Hobbes is a materialist in philosophy and an absolutist in politics. Locke is an empiricist in philosophy and a whig in politics. There is no mystery involved in any of the cases. In regard to Green's philosophy, Prof. Ritchie sees a mistake in characterizing it as Hegelian.[2] As far as he can see, Green's is a correction of Kant by Aristotle and of Aristotle by Kant. In regard to freedom, Mr. Ritchie points out Green's departure from the traditional conception. Freedom as is generally understood means a removal or absence of obstruction and as such it is merely nega-

---

[1] Fairbrother, *The Philosophy of T. H. Green.*

[2] Ritchie, *Principles of State Interference.* p. 139.

tive. But with Green, it is positive, it is the capacity or power to do or enjoy something worth doing or enjoying. Out of this conception of freedom, Mr. Ritchie argues, the principle of state interference can be predicted. The state necessarily has to maintain conditions under which it is possible for the people to do or enjoy that which is worth doing or enjoying. That is, in interfering, the state in its very act of interference is maintaining conditions of freedom. It is evident that Mr. Ritchie is very sympathetic in his comments and towards the end of the book he praises the democratic attitude that Green maintains both in active work and in writings.

Of the six writers whom Mr. MacCunn considers radical, Green is one. The account is on the whole laudatory, though little of it is devoted to political theory. His comparison between Green and Bentham will voice his sentiment more adequately than any effort on my part. "Bentham's philosophy was a fighting philosophy. When it was given to the world, democracy was still an aspiration and a struggle. What democracy needed was a rallying cry rather than a reasoned justification. It found that in Bentham.... But time had passed. Democracy had won.... It was when democratic citizenship had become actually and potentially a recognized fact of the first magnitude, when it had passed from struggle to success, from aspiration to fruition that Green... began to propound his civic idealism, thereby bringing to citizenship a new dignity and elevation, and it may be added, fresh grounds of confidence and hope. The political philosophy of Bentham at the

beinning of the 19th century was still a prophecy. The civic idealism of Green towards the end of the century was the justification
of the prophecy fulfilled." [1] Many in the present age will refuse to
share the optimism of Prof. MacCunn; they will probably deny
that democracy as an ideal has already become an accomplished
fact.

Prof. Muirhead has a profound respect for Green. In some
instances he attributes to Green what the latter would probably
hesitate to claim for himself. Clearly Green wrote in a period in
which the chief characteristic was said by Prof. Dicey to be collectivism, and the reason why there was not a strong opposition to
state regulation at the time when *The Service of The State*
(1908) [2] was published was not entirely due to Green's effort. In
regard to socialism, Prof. Muirhead points out that if by it is
meant the reality of a social will as practical working principle
then Green is emphatically socialistic. But if by socialism revolution is implied, then Green is opposed to it. He is, as we have
already seen, opposed to revolution; for he maintains that the object sought through revolution may not be worth the disorder and
probable destruction it entails. To the socialism that seeks to
overthrow capitalism Green will undoubtedly also object, since he
sees no defect inherent in capitalistic control of private property.
Any possible connection between Green and socialism can only

---

[1]　MacCunn, *Six Radical Thinkers.* pp. 215—216.
[2]　Muirhead, *The Service of The State.* 1908.

be urged with extreme caution. Socialism can not be divested of its economic origin and its economic significance and as such it can not merely mean "the reality of a social will as a working principle."

Mr. Barker has probably given the best account of Green's theory.[1] He advises us to pay more attention to the general principles than to the analysis of particular doctrines, as, for instance, Green's treatment of capital and of unearned increment. He points out that Green combines Greek and German philosophy with English caution. The individual is nowhere overwhelmed. Not only that, but in Green there is also a recognition of the idea of universal brotherhood. The state is limited internally as well as externally. It must have a guiding principle in order to function properly, and that principle, according to Mr. Barker, is better than the one Mill adopted. The distinction of self-regarding and others-regarding acts is false, for they can not be distinguished, while outward acts and inward will can be distinguished and that distinction is a good criterion for state action. While state action is not itself moral, it yet serves a moral purpose. It is to maintain the conditions under which morality may be possible. "If it does not interfere with morality, it is for the sake of morality that it refrains; if it does interfere with external acts, it is also for the sake of morality that it intervenes."[2]

---

[1]   Barker, *Political Thought From Spencer to To-day*.

[2]   Barker, *Political Thought From Spencer to To-day*. p. 60.

Mr. H. J. Laski permits disagreement of opinions to a remarkable extent; for though he abhors the doctrines of the idealists, he admires their ability, and though he attacks them with all the power he has at his command, he does not hesitate to admit that Green's *Principles of Political Obligation* and Bosanquet's *Philosophical Theory of The State* are the two greatest works in English political theory since Mill's time.[1]While recognizing the differences between Green and the other idealists, Mr. Laski criticises him in the same way as he criticises them; for as far as Green is concerned, it is not what he was, but what he has been understood or misunderstood to be that invites criticism. In other words, it is not Green's doctrines but their consequences that need be corrected. Green, more than anyone else, in Mr. Laski's opinion, is responsible for what Prof. Hobhouse has called the flowing of the Rhine into the Thames, and is on that account blamable.

But after all Mr. Laski's criticism is more or less centered around the conception of "general will"[2]and is by no means a total rejection of Green's theories. The latter's influence is easily traceable in the *Authority in the Modern State*. Mr. Laski is one of those who are now "reviving" the doctrines of natural rights. The word "reviving" is misleading; for what is at present termed natural rights is quite different from the "rights" of *The Virginia*

---

① Laski, *Authority in The Modern State.* p. 66. Footnote.
② Laski, *Authority in The Modern State.* p. 67.

*Constitution of 1776*, or of the *American Declaration of Independence*, or of the *French Declaration of Rights*, and since they are different they need no "reviving." According to Mr. Laski, a right is natural in the sense that the given conditions of society at the particular time require its recognition. It is not justified on grounds of history. It is not justified on grounds of any abstract or absolute ethic. It is simply insisted that if, in a given condition of society, power is so exerted as to refuse the recognition of that right, resistance is bound to be encountered. By right, that is to say, we mean a demand that has behind the burden of the general experience of the society. It is, as Green has said, "a power of which the exercise by the individual or by some body of men is recognized by a society either as itself directly essential to the common good, or as conferred by an authority of which the maintenance is recognized as so essential." [1] It is, therefore, Green's idea garbed in realistic terms.

Again, take for instance the conception of liberty. Mr. Laski quotes Green's definition with approval, [2] and declares that it is more valuable than the negative conception, because it insists on what, in this age, we feel to be fundamental in liberty—the power of adding something to the quality of the common life.[3] In this connection, it may be observed that Mr. Laski is even over-enthu siastic about Green. He claims that Green in the *Prolego-*

---

[1]  Laski, *Authority in The Modern State*. p. 43.

[2]  Laski, *Authority in The Modern State*. p. 55.

[3]  Laski, *Authority in The Modern State*. p. 55.

*mena to Ethics* has answered the question as to what is worth while to do and to enjoy, that is, as to what good is. It is true that Green defines true good as that which satisfies the moral agent,①and a moral agent is endowed with moral capabilities, the realization of which forms the moral good.②But according to Green, we do not know our moral capabilities till their realization and they are not and can not be completely realized. He therefore admits his inability to define exactly what true good consists of.③ He is only able to form general ideas about it. The conclusion is that as true good is or would be complete realization of moral capabilities, so goodness is proportional to one's habitual responsiveness to the idea of there being such a true good in the various forms of recognized duty and beneficent work in which that idea has so far taken shape among men.④If a definition is to render a defined subject definite, then, the conclusion arrived at by Green falls short of a definition.

Mr. Lilly believes in the doctrine of natural rights and adopts Green's definition.⑤ His adoption of Green's idea is not so apparent but the substance of it is there. The foundation of the state is, for instance, declared to be justice.⑥Justice is based on the conception of an absolute order of right which demands a sys-

---

① Green, *Prolegomena to Ethics.* p. 195.
② Green, *Prolegomena to Ethics.* p. 196.
③ Green, *Prolegomena to Ethics.* p. 18.
④ Green, *Prolegomena to Ethics.* p. 207.
⑤ Lilly, *First Principles in Politics.* p. vii.
⑥ Lilly, *First Principles in Politics.* p. 10.

tem of rights and obligations that should be maintained by law whether they are so or not. These rights, to employ Green's expression, "may properly be called natural"①. The definition of the word "natural" is, therefore, admittedly the same as that of Green. The conception of a right as necessarily involving a claim on the part of an individual to a free exercise of some faculty, and a recognition of that claim by society, is also essentially Green's idea. The ultimate foundation of the state is "the law of man's rational nature, in virtue of which he is a person invested with rights and encompassed by duties." ②That is to say, will and not force is the true basis of the state. Thus in broad outline, Mr. Lilly may be considered a follower of Green.

Sir Roland Wilson is trained in law, and lawyers are not generally given to metaphysical speculation. He is, therefore, expected to disagree with the idealists, but he is careful in dealing with the doctrines with which he finds himself in disagreement. He agrees with the idealists that man is by nature a social being, and that he can not realize his full self except in a community, ③ but he doubts and, I think, rightly, that that community is necessarily the state. If, he argues, the principle of state interference is to maintain conditions under which morality may be possible, then it leaves room for all sorts of restrictive

---

① Lilly, *First Principles in Politics*. p. 9.

② Lilly, *First Principles in Politics*. p. 9.

③ Sir Roland Wilson, *The Province of The State*. p. 212.

measures which are not properly within the province of the state.① Sir Roland Wilson clearly distinguishes moral from legal rights, ② but, it seems to me, he contradicts himself in criticising Green's theory of natural rights; for in his criticism he confuses that which should be in principle with that which is as a matter of fact enforced.③ Being a lawyer, he prefers the legal conception of rights in which neither reciprocity nor consciousness of a common good are necessary elements.④ However, when he argues that "to stretch the state so as to cover all these non-official agencies is to debase our linguistic coinage without any compensating gain, ⑤ it must be said, his argument is not applicable to Green. He is decidedly in error when he says that "state" and "sovereign" are by both of these writers (Green and Bosanquet) treated as interchangeable; for as far as Green is concerned, state and sovereign are expressly distinguished.⑥

Even in America Green's influence is noticeable. Prof. Willoughby has few references to Green in his *Nature of The State*, but these few are sufficient to indicate Green's influence. Prof. Willoughby agrees with Green that morality is incapable of legal enforcement⑦ and, in so agreeing, he necessarily accepts also

---

① Sir Roland Wilson, *The Province of The State*. p, 215.
② Sir Roland Wilson, *The Province of The State*. p. 216.
③ Sir Roland Wilson, *The Province of The State*. p. 217.
④ Sir Roland Wilson, *The Province of The State*. p. 219.
⑤ Sir Roland Wilson, *The Province of The State*. p. 223.
⑥ Green, *Principles of Political Obligation*, pp. 136— 137.
⑦ Willoughby, *The Nature of the State*. p. 53.

Green's definition of morality. Like Green, he is dissatisfied with the theory of Social Contract, and his arguments against it are in some ways similar to those of Green. He agrees, for instance, that natural right as "a right in a state of nature which is not a state of society is a contradiction"[①], and in thus agreeing with Green he also accepts the latter's idea of rights as involving both a claim on the part of the individual and also a recognition of that claim by society. Rights thus conceived can only exist in a society, and if they exist in a state of nature at all, that state of nature, as Green has pointed out, is already a political society. Hence Prof. Willoughby comes to the conclusion that the true origin of the state "must be conceived as an act of a people rather than of individuals. The existence of a common or 'general will' must be predicated, and the creation of the state held to be due to its volition"[②].

For the rest of the chapter, I shall content myself with four books recently published. The first is *The Principles of Citizenship*, by Sir Henry Jones. The author declares that the point of view, that he has adopted is neither psychological nor economic, but ethical. In fact, according to his estimation, "the modern economist will now admit that his science is abstract just as the modern psychologist will admit that faculties of the human mind are not separable powers with an empty ego in the back-

---

① Willoughby, *The Nature of the State*. p. 107.
② Willoughby, *The Nature of the State*. p. 123.

ground."①This should be quite encouraging, if in adopting the ethical point of view in treating political theory, Sir Henry Jones has either a new programme to offer or a decided improvement of the old political idealism. He does not seem to have offered either. While following Green in many respects, his philosophy is essentially along the lines of Bradley and Bosanquet. State, to him, is a moral agent and in functioning it should not limit itself merely to the externals as Green has so cautiously preached. According to Sir Henry Jones, externals and internals can not be separated. If the state has to intervene at all, it has to intervene not only with the external action, but also with the supposedly internal motive. In fact, state interference should be positive in nature so as to secure the desired end, that is, "to make human nature in citizens all that it has in it to become"②. "It may and ought to exercise authority over the external conditions of life of its members with the view of changing not only their outward actions and intentions, but their motives and character."③

Sir Henry Jones accepts Green's theory of natural rights, and in so considering rights and duties, he also accords the state the right to act positively. If state action is not merely negative but also positive, what, it may be asked, is the criterion of state action? The criterion is declared to be the positive promotion of

①　Sir Henry Jones, *The Principles of Citizenship*. p. 161.

②　Sir Henry Jones, *The Principles of Citizenship*. p. 132.

③　Sir Henry Jones, *The Principles of Citizenship*. p. 132.

the good life.①This criterion is applicable to war. The state has the right to summon citizens to a just war and to no other; and the citizen, on his part, has a right and duty to fight for a just war, and no other. But, who is to judge as to whether a war is just or unjust? The answer is both state and citizen. The state, being a moral agent, can not delegate its power for judging. The citizen has the right and duty to judge for himself and to act accordingly. It may even be his duty to fight his own country. This sounds quite radical, but— "what can not be his duty is that of taking no sides when the question of right or wrong is being decided by means of war. The pacifist's protest against the war when his country is fighting is the affirmation of the moral principle when it can not be applied.... The good man deals with the present circumstances and finds his duty at his hand."②

I wonder if it may not be inferred from this that if a citizen opposes war, he must leave the country, lest the subsequent circumstances may compel him to discharge fresh duties at his hand. But, then, that leaves the state practically alone to decide whether a war is just or unjust.

In regard to property, the rights of the state and the citizen are, according to Sir Henry Jones, in similar way limited. The four Principles③to be observed are: 1. Rights of free life mean

---

① Sir Henry Jones, *The Principles of Citizenship*. p. 153.

② Sir Henry Jones, *The Principles of Citizenship*. p. 158.

③ Sir Henry Jones, *The Principles of Citizenship*. pp. 165—166 nothing without sustenance; 2. the right of property is sacred on the same ground as the right to life and liberty; 3. state must facilitate the means that helps to exercise this right; 4. right of property is made contingent upon the use made of it.

Sir Henry Jones follows Green, but he follows Bradley and Bosanquet to a much greater extent.

Prof. Watson is confessedly an idealist and as far as political theory is concerned admits his debt to both Green and Bosanquet. He believes of course that the true basis of the state is will. He believes in general will but argues that Rousseau confuses the general will with the Will of all; ① but if there is any confusion at all, it is not Rousseau but Prof. Watson who is really confused. At any rate he believes in general will as a will common to the citizens of a state, a rational will — "that will which the individual in his best mind recognizes" ②. Ultimately it is the general will which is sovereign and it is the duty of the legal sovereign to discover what this general will is.

The general will creates rights and the system of rules for the maintenance of these rights which are necessary for the realization of the good will. These rights may be termed "natural" but they neither belong to men in isolation as the advocates of Social Contract belived, nor are they created by law as Bentham held. They are justified on the ground that if they are not secured, man

---

①    Watson, *The State in War and Peace.* p. 192.

②    Watson, *The State in War and Peace.* p. 223.

is not able to live his own life freely and to contribute his share to the common good. They involve a claim on the part of the individual and a recognition of that claim by either society or the state. Prof. Watson here uses the terms society and the state interchangeably.①The specific rights are life, liberty, equality and property. The last also includes the right to the freedom of contract.

The state is an organized society of men, and is sovereign. Sovereignty is supreme power, but the supremacy of the state is relative and not absolute.②That is, the state has supreme power within a certain sphere to dictate or to prevent the action of others. It has no power to interfere with all sorts of activities. The state is above all other organizations not in the sense that it can make and unmake them at will, but in the sense that it is the high court of appeal through which their conflicting claims are harmonized.③The principle of state interference is to make moral acts possible by regulation, but not to enforce them.④ The morality of the state is different from the morality of individuals. That does not exempt the state from moral responsibility. Like Green, Prof. Watson is against war, but he does not go to the same extent as Green does in denouncing war. His idea of the cause of war is very much Green's; so also is his idea of its pre-

① Watson, *The State in War and Peace.* p. 222.
② Watson, *The State in War and Peace.* p. 198.
③ Watson, *The State in War and Peace.* p. 208.
④ Watson, *The State in War and Peace.* p. 217.

第
五
卷

vention. Likewise he believes in having better political organization internally so as to diminish friction externally. He agrees with Bosanquet that a healthy state is not a militant state.

From the above account, it is only evident that Prof. Watsonfollows Green closely and if there is any divergence of view at all between the two, it is hardly noticeable. On the whole, no improvement is made, and very likely none is intended.

However, the modern tendency is unmistakably against political idealism. Mr. Joad, in his *Essays in Common Sense Philosophy*, launches a well-considered attack on idealistic political philosophy. He points out that political idealism regards the state as self-sufficing and as above morality, and that it believes that the state and individuals are so intimately interwoven with each other that the act of the state is never unrepresentative of the individuals, and the act of the individuals has inseparable reference to the state. One of the shortcomings of idealistic absolutism is that it identifies state with society. But state and society are two different entities. Human society is greater and more comprehensive than a state. In fact, judging from the past, just as families unite into tribes and tribes into nations, it will not be at all surprising to have nations unite into one great society in the future. To confound human society and the nation state is a mistake of the first magnitude.

Mr. Joad feels that the idealist philosophers seem to be in the habit of philosophizing in utter disregard of facts. In the first place, the state, that is, the political organization, is not the only organization in which human beings are interested. The church, to many, is a much more intimate organization; for while the state touches everyday life hardly at all, the church reminds some people of its existence at least once a week. Industrial unions touch economic life at such vital spots and with such intimacy that they arouse much more interest among their members than the state does among its citizens. Furthermore, with churches and trade unions or other voluntary organizations a man identifies himself by choice. The claims of these voluntary organizations may be said to be moral, but the claims of the state seem to be often founded on "topographical accident." One belongs to it "because he happened to be born in a certain bedroom, a phenomenon over which he has no control."①This sounds wildly radical, but Mr. Joad is neither an anarchist nor a syndicalist. He believes in the necessity of a state. Because society is more and more industrialized, because human beings are more and more interdependent, and economic efforts are generally blind, a political association like the state is all the more necessary. But the kind of state he believes in is far different from the utopia of the political idealists.

I have no quarrel with Mr. Joad's arguments which, when directed towards political absolutists, are on the whole sound. But it does not seem to be exactly correct to bring Green almost indiscriminately into the company of Hegel, Bradley and Bosan-

---

① Joad, *Essays in Common Sense Philosophy.* p. 189.

quet as Mr. Joad does in the first part of his chapter. I think there are differences which it will be profitable for us not to disregard. Mr. Joad seems to realize that fact later on in his book when Green's name disappears, but it is not certain whether that disappearance is due to careless omission or intentional exclusion.

Mr. Hobhouse in this respect makes his position unmistakable. He enters into the controversy with a grave purpose.[1] Like his son, he is engaged in a battle to make the world safe for democracy, but unlike his son his efforts run in a different channel. In order that the end may be obtained, not only must the swords be sharpened, but the pen must also contribute its share. While militarism is being destroyed in the world of practice, idealistic absolutism should be repudiated in the world of thought. Thus Prof. Hobhouse takes Hegelianism to task. It is not necessary to examine the specific charges which are brought against Dr. Bosanquet with the strength of reasoning and lucidity of expression generally expected from such a veteran writer as Hobhouse. My purpose in introducing him is to indicate, as he has indicated, that Green is far different from the thoroughly idealistic absolutists.

Prof. Hobhouse thinks that Green has retained his fundamental humanity[2] and that at his hands Hegelianism has been

---

[1] Hobhouse, *The Metaphysical Theory of The State.*

[2] Hobhouse, *The Metaphysical Theory of The State.* p. 83.

transformed into social idealism.[1] He points out that Green is always cautious where the rights of the individuals are concerned and that individuals are not absorbed in the state. He accepts Green's theory of natural rights with the exception of its idealistic ingredients. According to Green, a claim on the part of the individual becomes a right only when it is met with social and presumably conscious recognition, for idealistically speaking, nothing is but thinking makes it so. According to Professor Hobhouse, a right is a right, whether recognized or not, whenever proof is given of its necessity. The general will with Green is really conceived, according to Mr. Hobhouse, in the psychological sense. "It is the impalpable congeries of hopes and fears of a people bound together by common interest and sympathy." [2] "It is the common will and reason of men as determined by social relations, as interested in each other, as acting together for common ends." [3] With Green, general will is not to overwhelm the individual, neither to override the moral law. When he declares that will and not force is the basis of the state, it is the state that is dependent upon will. If the state is not so dependent, it is a state only by courtesy, as Green said of Russia. Professor Hobhouse may not have pointed out all the differences between Green and the other idealists, but he does distinguish

[1]  Hobhouse, *The Metaphysical Theory of The State.* p. 120.
[2]  *Principles of Political Obligation.* p. 98.
[3]  *Principles of Political Obligation.* p. 103.

him from them. Hence in fighting to make the world safe for democracy, he is not fighting against Green so much as against Messrs, Bradley and Bosanquet.

# Chapter IX    Conclusion

The above survey of criticisms and comments indicates that Green has not been properly dealt with. His followers praise him too highly and attribute virtues to him that do not belong to his share, while his critics sometimes reveal a hostility that should not be his due. It is my purpose in this chapter to bring out the distinct merits as well as the defects embodied in Green's philosophy, but before starting on that, one erroneous impression should be cleared off. The belief that political idealism is necessarily political absolutism is entirely unwarranted. The factors leading to such a belief are probably accidental. Locke was one of the most influential advocates of democracy and it happened that he was an empiricist. Hegel was the intellectual leader of German absolutism and it happened that Hegel was an idealist. It might be urged that Locke wrote as a practical politician, and was influential because Englishmen admired the practical; while Hegel wrote as a philosopher, and was followed because the Germans worshipped the profound. But as a matter of fact, empiricism is no more wedded to democracy than idealism to absolutism. We need only bear in mind that the absolutism of Thomas Hobbes proceeded from his materialism and the democratic tendencies of the 18th century attributable to the eloquence of Jean Jacques Rousseau could be traced to the idealism back of his doctrines. Whether or not the "determinism distilled out of evolutionary science"①has surrendered to the tactics of conservatism, as Mr. Hobson claims, it is easy to point out that empiricism has sometimes played into the clutching hands of either autocracy or plutocracy. Neither is it hard to single out instances where idealism has generated centrifugal forces in modern politics. Philosophical labels do not matter much, but a great deal depends upon their application.

A few words need be said of the age in which Green wrote. The years 1776 and 1870 inaugurated different eras. The period of the American Revolution was memorable for many reasons. In the sphere of everyday life, the world had started on its great transformation. Hand industry was about to be replaced by machine industry. The thing we made—to employ the expression of William Morris had begun to "drive" in the beginning of the 19th century. Misery and poverty had gotten hold of the working classes. In the field of intellectual speculation, the year 1776 was memorable. Adam Smith's *Wealth of Nations* and Bentham's *Fragment on Government* appeared in the same year. With physiocratic tendencies and the traditions of the 18th century philosophy the world might be said to have chosen an extremely

---

① Hobson, *The Crisis of Liberalism*. p. 187.

individualistic path. Intellectually and factually, the period between 1776 and 1870 is one of *laissez faire.*

The last quarter of the last century marked a decided change. From 1870 to 1914 we have a period of collectivism, a period which Professor Hayes has characterized as the Era of Benevolent Bourgeoisie. Politically speaking, it is a period of intense nationalism in regard to foreign relations. Competitive armaments, the exodus of capital, and secret diplomacy are the distinguishing marks of international politics. It is a period of statism internally. The bourgeoisie, emerging from what was formerly called the middle class, gained political ascendancy. The successful business men who are proudly described as being "selfmade men" are often remindful of the bitter cup of experience they had once drunk and, thanks to democracy, they have attained success. Success seems to be the magic goal. A few succeed, some are succeeding, all are trying to succeed and in their frantic efforts to attain success, people of all classes, contrary to Marxian prediction, have worked together for "development" and "progress". National consciousness prevails to a much greater extent than class consciousness. In order to have peace within and honor abroad, the state must have necessary power to "regulate", to "adjust" and eventually to guide. That is the spirit of the age and it is with that spirit that Green has formulated his theories.

Obviously, merits are not lacking in Green's philosophy, but unfortunately its Hegelian label has prejudiced its content. Those who have studied him, however, generally deny that he is a Hegelian at all. Mr. Alfred William Benn, in his *History of English Rationalism in the* 19*th Century*, asserts vigorously that Green is not a Hegelian. Professor Barker describes Green's writings as a product of Oxford, immediately influenced by German philosophy, but ultimately traceable to Greek thought.

More specifically Green is more of an Aristotelian than a Platonist, and more of a Kantian than a Hegelian. Professor Barker is not alone in his estimation, for Professor Ritchie has come to almost the same conclusion in different words. The latter is of the opinion that Green's philosophy is a correction of Kant by Aristotle and of Aristotle by Kant. If so, he may be said to be both Kantian and Aristotelian. The same may in a certain sense be said of Hegel, but that in no sense identifies him with Green. In fact, referring to Hegel's work, Green has himself said that it must be done over again. These opinions indicate that Green has really no occasion for borrowing a Hegelian mantle. Love for Hegel should not be cultivated on account of Green and prejudice against Hegel should not be carried over to Green.

Of the merits the first to be mentioned is Green's theory of natural rights. First of all it serves two distinct purposes as far as Green himself is concerned. It discredits the kind of absolutism that attributes rights to the grace of the sovereign, and it proves the falsity of the doctrine of government by the consent of the governed. If consent is a supreme necessity, then vote counting is a necessary part of the government. If vote counting is necessary, then there is always the difficulty of explaining and justifying the obedience of the minority. That justification has not been furnished by anybody and is not furnished by Green; but Green's theory of natural rights decreases the necessity of such a justification to a considerable extent. Green abhors mathematical government. Government based upon a counting of noses may be a practical expedient, but it can not be our democratic ideal. Government is, after all, a means to an end; make your means your end, and you defeat your ultimate purpose in life.

Further, Green's theory of natural rights is in harmony with modern economic facts and sociological theories. Division of labor prevails on a greater scale than ever before and interdependence of individuals is much more in evidence. A breakfast in London today may involve coffee from South America, wheat from North Dakota, tea from Ceylon, sugar from Cuba and probably potatoes from Ireland. Not only is the fact of economic interdependence indisputable, but also, as is claimed by sociologists, there is constantly in evidence a social consciousness working for a social good. We hear a great deal of "the consciousness of kind", of "social mentality", of "social mind" and of "social consciousness", and if we deduce any lesson from them at all, it is that of mutual interdependence and the necessity of cooperation.

Now the old traditional theory of natural rights does not harmonize with these, if not new, at least more clearly defined facts and tendencies. One can not live in a society of mutual interdependence and retain at the same time the kind of natural rights that are supposedly existent in an isolated state of nature. One can not live in a society whose predominant characteristic is co-operation and at the same time assert fully the rights that are supposedly carried over from a state of nature, the chief feature of which is individual independence and isolation. Eighteenth century economics has been tried and found wanting. Eighteenth century political philosophy is equally so, and as far as the theory of natural rights is concerned, Green's correction is very likely in the right direction.

Green's theory of state interference will be found valuable. Mill, it will be remembered, divides human actions into the self-regarding and others-regarding and considers the latter alone as subject to state interference. The distinction is not sound, for hu-man actions are far more often both self-regarding and others-re-garding rather than either alone. A principle that is itself defective offers no guidance to the practice of state interference. Green's distinction between outward acts and inward will is one which, though not ideal, offers guidance to better advantage in view of the complexity of human relations. Outward acts alone are subject to state interference, because inward will not only should not be but also cannot be.

Many will not concede that Green has scored over Mill in this matter; for they say that it is just as hard to decide which of the outward acts should be a subject for state interference as it is to distinguish between the self-regarding and others-regarding. The advantage lies in the fact that by Green's distinction, at least one part of human effort is excluded from the political area. Furthermore, Green's distinction is, after all, a real distinction, while Mill's is not. As to which of the outward acts should be subject to state interference, Green's answer is that only those should be that obstruct the possibility of a moral life. Basically it is to remove obstructions that the state intervenes. Dr. Bosanquet seeks to improve the phraseology by urging the expression, "Hindrance of hindrances". This, being the one Kant[1] used, Green must have been well aware of.

The difference between Mill and Green, as stated above, is fundamentally a difference in the conception of liberty. Mill's conception of liberty is negative, it is freedom from obstruction. Green's conception is positive. It is a positive power or capacity of doing or enjoying something worth doing or enjoying and something we do or enjoy in common with others. The difference is probably natural. Mill's conception is the traditional conception that has the 18th century philosophy at the background. The natural man is the good man. Left to themselves the people will be all right. It was restraint that forced people to be other than good; hence the negative conception of liberty. By Green's time, however, the evils of laissez faire have already become evident. The freedom of contract in commerce, in labor, in factory conditions and in industry in general has produced child and woman labor,

---

[1]　Kant, *Metaphysische Anfangsgrunde der Rechtslehre*, Einleitung XXXV, Sec. D.

misery, poverty and slavery which can not be tolerated by a man of Green's temperament and religious fervor. Something must be done, and who can do it better than the state. The 18th century philosophers were primarily concerned with removing oppression from above. Oppression is obstruction, hence, liberty is freedom from obstruction, primarily from above. By Green's time the problem is to remove the conditions voluntarily imposed by the people themselves that deprive them of any exercise of the power or capacity that is within them. The problem is to remove these conditions, these obstructions, not so much from above as from the stronger who are able to impose their will on the weaker. Therefore if the state intervenes, it does so for the purpose of maintaining rather than obstructing freedom.

Apart from its connection with the principle of state interference, the positive conception of freedom is itself useful. Some disadvantages of the negative conception are the advantages of the positive conception. The negative conception of liberty easily degenerates into license. It is often taken to be the right of doing whatsoever one will with what he is or has as his own. If such is the case, there will be the greatest scramble in society and anarchy may likely result. The positive conception of freedom means creative human effort. By definition it consists of doing or enjoying something worth doing or enjoying. The importance of conscious creative human effort can not be over-emphasized; for there is too much evidence everywhere of blind confidence that the future will be bright or fatalistic submission to the conviction that it will be dark. Either of the two is dangerous and detrimental to human progress, and by identifying freedom with creative human effort, this danger may be, if not avoided, at least lessened. This positive conception, again, has the advantage of implying the idea of a common good. Freedom is not merely the power to do or to enjoy something worth doing or enjoying, but also to do or enjoy in common with others. It is not doing what one likes with his own, for doing what one likes with his own may not be doing in common with others.

Closely related to the conception of freedom and the principle of state interference is the reconciliation of individualism and collectivism. It is no more correct to say that Green is a thoroughgoing collectivist than to say that he is a thoroughgoing individualist. He is neither and both, viz., in him there is a happy reconciliation. Green's conception of reason and of the will to good involves the idea of perfection or of a possibility of perfection. Man is determined to action by this idea of a possible perfection of himself. But along just what lines one will seek his own good and improvement must depend upon his own capacity or power. This brings us back to the conception of freedom.

If by reason in the moral sense is meant a consciousness of a possibility of perfection to be realized in and by the subject of consciousness, and if by freedom in the political sense is meant the power or capacity to do or enjoy certain things worth doing or enjoying; the two taken together will amount to nothing less than "self expression" in the present day terminology. They mean a consciousness in a man of the possibility of perfection in his power or capacity to do that which is worth doing to satisfy himself. This is individualism and it is individualism of the highest order. It is free from anarchistic tendencies, for they are excluded from its constituent elements.

As to collectivism, we need not repeat what has already been said with reference to the principle of state interference. The only point to be singled out is that with Green individualism and collectivism are harmonious with rather than antagonistic to each other. Collectivism under the guidance and application of the principle of state interference facilitates and strengthens individualism. Indeed, what Professor Barker has said of morality may also be said of individualism. If the state does not intervene, it is for the sake of individuality that the state refrains; and if it does intervene, it is also for the sake of individuality that it intervenes.

There is one point in Green's philosophy that is especially in keeping with the spirit of the present time. He distinguishes state from what may be called Great Society. To Green, the state presupposes other associations. It does not, for instance, create rights but gives fuller reality to rights already existing.①But what rights are already existing, viz., what rights existed previous to the formation of the state?

For answer let us refer to Green's theory of natural rights.

---

① *Principles of Political Obligation.* p. 138.

Men by virtue of being in society are in certain relations and conditions that must be secured to them in order that they may fulfil their moral ideal, that is, in order that they may develop their power and capacity. This is in essence the foundation of rights. Do they depend upon the state? According to Green, they "arise out of social relations that may exist where a state is not.... They depend for their existence indeed on society but not on society's having assumed the form of a state" ①. Therefore there are rights that are independent of any state. Not only are they independent of, but in a sense, more fundamental than the state. For in the first place the purpose for which the state exists at all is to give fuller reality to them. Secondly, some of them the state should never violate. Green is positive in his denunciation of war, and the reason given is that it violates the rights to life in the members of both the offending and the defending state. When discussing the question whether or not conflict between states is inevitable, Green says:"No action in its own interest of a state that fulfilled this idea," viz., the idea of a state as a maintainer and harmonizer of rights, "could conflict with any true interest or right of general society." ②Later on he expresses his hope that an idea of justice, as a relation which should subsist among the whole of mankind, as well as between the members of the same state, may come to act on men's minds as independently of all

---

① *Principles of Political Obligation.* p. 150.
② *Principles of Political Obligation.* p. 170.

calculation of their several interests as does the idea which regulates the conduct of a good citizen.①

This differentiation between the state and human society and Green's discussion of the right of the citizens to resist the state reveals his attitude towards the nature of state acts. State acts are not something irresistible and uncontrolled, but something with reference to which the terms right and wrong may be correctly used. The state is not above morality internally any more than externally. Internally, the state may do wrong, and externally, in regard to other states it may also do wrong; Green's doctrine has nothing to indicate that state and society are synonymous, as Mr. Joad seems to imply. In fact, Green expects that with the better and more perfect organization of the state according to its idea, the two will be harmonized. Neither is there any ground for supposing that, according to Green, state can do no wrong, for he has at least shown that the state does do wrong in many instances. The state as Green conceives it is, after all, not the horrible being that indiscriminate critics of political idealism are afraid of.

In the foregoing paragraphs, I have endeavored to present some of the merits of Green's system which seem to be well worthy of acknowledgment. In the following paragraphs, I shall deal with some defects which admirers of Green would like to see eliminated.

---

① *Principles of Political Obligation.* p. 178.

First of all, the theory that institutions are the embodiment of reason①is decidedly dangerous. Eventually it leads to conservatism, to a preservation and justification of the status quo. We are not asserting that institutions do not represent reason or that reason was not instrumental in the origin of institutions. Customs and conventions have reasons working towards their adoption. But we do affirm that the conception that social institutions are the embodiment of objective reason is dangerous, because our tendency to admire reason may be converted into a tendency to admire institutions, and institutions that existed or are existing are not always worthy of our admiration.

The explanation is really two-fold. Firstly, reasons that operated towards adopting a given institution, while sound at the time of adoption of that institution, may not remain sound at the present time in view of changing and changed circumstances. Geographical representation at a time when there is distinctive and individual local life may be an adequate method for representation, but it may not remain adequate when modern industrialism sweeps away local individuality.

Secondly, institutions may have been adopted through reasoning but not through sound reasoning, and as a result they may be as defective today as once they were in the past. The proper spirit is the spirit of improvement. But if we glorify the majesty of reason at the back of institutions, we are liable to lose our spirit

---

① *Principles of Political Obligation.* p. 86.

of improvement and progress. The more we try to admire our past, the more convinced we are that the past really deserves our admiration. Human beings are a curious lot. If they have an ideal and exert strenuous efforts toward attaining it, they may eventually make their efforts their ideal. If they worship reason and believe that institutions are the embodiment of reason, they may eventually worship institutions. The lack of inventiveness in China, for instance, is largely due to this glorification of the past. Progressive people should look forward, and in this connection it should be said in fairness to Green that he looks to the future rather than the past for his inspiration. He himself is constantly looking for a fuller realization and a fuller development of human capacities.

But personal virtue should not be employed to minimize a doctrinal defect. Green in this particular instance evidently follows Hegel. But Hegel did not formulate his theory without a purpose. What he aimed at was the unification of Germany under a benevolent monarch and in order to accomplish that, he had to formulate a system of philosophy that would arrest the progress of the revolutionary doctrines before and after the French Revolution. He had to contend with the intellectuals of his time who knew their business. They knew that a political revolution could not be effected without revolution of other kinds. An atheist did not cut God off for nothing. The critics of the church had a definite purpose to serve. The worshippers of reason did not worship reason for the fun of it. The advocates of science had a definite axe to grind. They knew that a given political system was supported by and interwoven with the whole fabric of social, ethical and religious concepts, and in order to overturn that political system, they had to be iconoclastic towards not only the political but also the social, ethical and religious idols. In order to prepare the people to attain the desired end, they had to start with a general negation of all the existing, they had to demolish all the fondly cherished manners, customs and conventions. Hegel sought to undermine the tactics of the revolutionary generalship by evolving a system of philosophy which read into institutions the function of reason so that the worshippers of reason would worship institutions. The attempt was certainly ingenious for the purpose it was to serve, but it had not the strength to stern the tide of progressivism and radicalism. Since the latter is here to stay, there is very little excuse for resuscitating the former.

Sovereignty is always a thorny problem in political philosophy. Green's discussion, while remarkably to the point in regard to the distinction or rather non-distinction of sovereign de jure and sovereign de facto, seems nevertheless to be a futile attempt to combine Austin with Rousseau. He agrees with Austin to the extent that sovereignty is the supreme law-giving and law-enforcing power vested in determinate person or persons with occasional manifestations of coercive force. But he also agrees with Rousseau that sovereignty is basically will. Accordingly, sovereignty is supreme power, but it is only supreme power when supported by general will. Thus stated, the conception is either a

truism that needs no elaborate polemics or an intellectual subterfuge that gets us nowhere. Those who are not in the habit of
taking refuge in mysticism will ask somewhat realistically not
whether sovereignty is will or power, but whose power it is that is
supreme and whose will it is that supports that power. The privileged persons who wield supreme power in a country are not so
easily ascertainable and may not, therefore, be said to be exactly
determinate. But they form a class and we know whose power is
supreme. We can not, however, generalize so easily as to whose
will it is that supports the power. Absence of opposition by no
means signifies whole hearted support. General acquiescence does
not amount to general will. Indeed, we are tempted to agree with
Professor Hobhouse that "in so far as it is will, it is not general,
and in so far as it is general it is not will"[1]. Neither a purely legalistic nor a purely metaphysical conception of sovereignty is satisfactory; hence, it may be expected, a hodgepodge of the two
will not fare better with the present day political theorists.

The bald statement that will and not force is the true basis of
the state will be encouraging to many as an abstract principle to
be hoped for and attained, but it is hardly an analysis of facts.
While we do not believe that might is right, we are too often reminded that power or force is a strong determining factor in
public affairs in history as well as at the present time. Green is
particularly unfortunate in his arguments to support his assertion.

---

[1]　Hobhouse, *Metaphysical Theory of State*. p. 127.

It is indeed regrettable enough that force, physical as well as economic, has been as unrestrained in directing human affairs as experience indicates; it is far more regrettable that if an end is attained by some means, in fact, by any means foul or fair, there is always some philosopher, true to the assertion of Frederick the Great, to applaud the end attained and to white-wash the means. We will be surrendering to the cynicism of that monarch, if we follow Green in his *ex post facto* justification of Napoleonic wars. If good when incidental to bad should not be "overruled" for bad, then bad when incidental to good should not be "overruled" for good. Green himself is quite aware of the fallacy of his logic.[1] It may be tenderness not to be strict in our moral estimation, but in regard to a guiding principle it is dangerous to permit sympathetic feeling to get the better of our moral judgment. There seems to be a persistent tendency to countenance the vicious doctrine that the end justifies the means. It should be pointed out that instead of the end justifying the means, the means if not consistent with the end destroys the end, however desirable it may be.

In connection with Green's theory of the true basis of the state, there is another point that should not escape our attention. When will is declared to be the true basis of the state, we are easily led to believe that the state is consciously formed of our free will, because the word will generally implies positive effort.

---

[1]  *Principles of Political Obligation.* p. 168.

As a matter of fact the psychologists will be found irrefutable in their contention that subconscious psychological phenomena are just as instrumental as conscious will in maintaining the state. Conscious will is not the sole foundation of the state, and that is probably why Green in several places speaks of assent instead of consent. But if he distinguishes consent from assent, he should also distinguish active, positive conscious will from passive or negative or habitual acquiescence. When he speaks of the Roman Empire as based on will, it may be presumed that what is meant by will is really passive acquiescence. It is only easily imaginable that if the people had been given a free choice, they would probably not have elected to pay allegiance to Rome. If will and acquiescence were distinguished and were both regarded as the basis of the state, the argument against force might be better appreciated and more intelligently understood.

With a large number of people the chief ground for indictment against Green is to be found in his views on economic questions. He is insistent on land reform, but to the single taxers he has rejected the only remedy that would cure the evil systems he so eloquently complains of. His idea of capital is not up-to-date. While he is sensitive to the abuses of capital, he sees no inherent danger in the concentration of the control of capital. Above all his approach to this subject is different from that of a modern liberal. A modern liberal will inquire into the justice of the distribution of wealth, while Green is contented with a paternal interest in the gradual improvement of the material conditions of the workers. The fundamental question with a modern Socialist, for instance, is whether it is just to allow some persons to accumulate as much as they can under the present circumstances, leaving a large number of people, in Green's phrase, without sufficient means to realize their moral ideal. A radical today is not bothered about the relative condition of the workman today as compared with the condition of his kind in the early part of the 19th century. Green's idea of legislation and freedom of contract may be objected to by the individualist as unnecessary interference on the part of the authority, and by the newer brands of Socialism as usurpation of arbitrary power by the state. His economics certainly leaves much to be desired. He does not fit in with any category. If we call him a Christian Socialist, we meet the opposition that he is Christian without being socialistic. If we bring him into the company of Roscher, Wagner and Schmoller and call him a Historical National economist, we are only too well aware that whether or not he is national enough, he is not sufficiently historical. His explanation of the historical origin of the proletariat is plainly influenced by his hostility toward land. The safe conclusion is that he is not an economist at all. He does not have the proper grasp of economic facts. If we criticise the economic portions of his political doctrine, we should be careful to consider his lack of information rather than to impute motives.

The most noticeable defect of Green's political theory is the absence of any discussion of the organization of government. The fundamental questions of the state are, of course, important, but having discussed them at length, the next problem is to formulate a programme of political organization through which alone political ideas can be worked in practice. If political theory does not deal with principles alone but also with their practical working, then it should also indicate the kind of political organization that will be likely to facilitate the carrying out of those principles. If government is to be based upon the consent of the governed, then the problem of getting people to express their approval or disapproval on certain issues is certainly one that deserves attention, and if government of the whole people by the whole people is impracticable, then problems of representation should be considered so as to find out the best possible solution. If government is not to be based on the counting of noses, what is the substitute? Some expedients will have to be adopted, for in practical affairs, some determining device has to be agreed upon through which alone things can be accomplished. If it is not a majority of votes, it must be something else. So far as this problem is concerned, Green has not offered us any enlightenment at all. Elsewhere I have said that Green's theory of natural rights has diminished the urgency of a justification of the majority rule over the minority, but it does not by any means eliminate that problem. In the absence of a suggested substitute, it may be presumed that Green recognizes the majority rule as an expedient that is inevitable. If so, the justification of the subjection of minority remains a problem. And in the absence of a programme of governmental organization, it may be concluded that

that problem remains with Green unsolved.

There are, of course, references to government, but in those cases, it must be confessed, their meaning is rather obscure. The distinction between the state and government is not as clear as might be expected. This obscurity is probably due to English conditions. The King in Parliament is often described as being the legal sovereign in Great Britain. Whatever it may do, it does without legal limitation. If there is not the tendency to confuse government with the state, there is at least no particular necessity for their rigid distinction. But in a country like the United States, for instance, where there is a written constitution limiting the government in some well defined directions, where laws duly passed may be declared unconstitutional and where constitution can only be amended by a certain rigid process, one gets at a glance the difference between state and government; and when one looks at the adoption of the initiative and referendum in some of the states one wonders at the shrinkage of the power of the government and the expansion of that of the state, which in this case is generally called the "people". It may be questioned whether for Green such a distinction is necessary. Personally, I think it is. With regard to the principle of political obligation, for instance, I feel that we are better off if we bear in mind that our obligation is due to the state and not to any particular government. Furthermore, instead of being a reactionary doctrine, the distinction between government and state is highly democratic, in that it affords oftentimes the opportunity and justification for resistance to government, if necessary, in the name of the state.

Finally it may be asked whether Green is not, after all, following the footsteps of those whose one-sidedness he has been attacking. The economists have created the economic man; we agree with Green that there is no such economic man. The Utilitarians described men as pleasure seekers; we know that only too often we do not fit in with their description. The sensationalists reduced us to a kodak; but the objects reflected on the retina of our eyes do not necessarily print pictures. The naturalists regard us primarily as animal organisms; but we are more than mere animal organisms. Green knows that and in his efforts to free us from being merely economic, exclusively utilitarian, mechanically sensational and simply animal, he has rendered us almost pure consciousness. May it not be questioned whether such a conscious human being exists? Will he not share the same fate with the economic man, the pleasure seeker and the mere animal organism?

Logic sometimes drives man mad, but in logic there is beauty. Idealistic as well as materialistic philosophy has its intellectual charms. It has been said of Karl Marx that the Marxian system is a credit to human ingenuity; hence rather than to demolish it piecemeal, it is better to permit its structure to retain its sublimity and brilliance. The same may be said of Green. Besides the intellectual charm out of reading him, one shares his social idealism.He actually confesses to "hoping for a time when the phrase(the education of a gentleman)will have lost its meaning, because the sort of education which alone makes the gentleman in any sense will be within reach of all. As it was the aspiration of Moses that all the Lord's people should be prophets, so with all seriousness and reverence, we may hope and pray for a condition of English society in which all honest citizens will recognize themselves and be recognized by each other as gentlemen."①

Such an ideal is nowadays too often lost sight of.

---

① *Works.* Vol. III. p. 475.

# Bibliography

**Source Books.**

*Works of Thomas Hill Green*, 3 volumes. Edited by R. L. Nettleship.

T. H. Green, *Principles of Political Obligation.* 1917 Edition.

T. H. Green, *Prolegomena to Ethics.* Edited by A. C. Bradley.

**REFERENCES**

AUSTIN. *Lectures on Jurisprudene.*

BARKER, ERNEST. *Political Thought from Spencer to To-day.*

BAGEHOT, WALTER. *Physics and Politics.*

*English Constitution.*

BENTHAM, JEREMY. *Fragment on Government.*

BLACKSTONE. *Commentaries.*

BRADLEY, F. H. *Ethical Studies.*

BOSANOUET, BERNARD. *The Philosophical Theory of the State.*

BUCKLE, H. T. *History of Civilization,*

DUNNING. *History of Political Theories.*

FAIRBROTHER. *The Philosophy of T. H. Green.*

GEORGE, HENRY. *Progress and Poverty.*

GIDDINGS. *Democracy and Empire.*

HOBBES. *Leviathan.*

*Philosophical Rudiments concerning Government and Society.*

HOBHOUSE, L. T. *Democracy and Reaction.*

*The Metaphysical Theory of the State.*

HOBSON. J. A. *The Crisis of Liberalism.*

HUME, DAVID. *Essays, Moral, Political and Literary.*

JOAD. *Essays in Common Sense Philosophy.*

JONES, SIR HENRY. *The Principles of Citizenship.*

KANT, IMMANUAL. *Metaphysische Anfangsgrunde der Rechtslehre.*

LASKI, H. J. *Authority in the Modern State.*

LOCKE, JOHN. *Two Treatises of Government.*

*Essays on Human Understanding.*

LOWENTHAL. *The Ricardian Socialists.*

MACCUNN. *Six Radical Thinkers.*

MAINE, SIR HENRY. *Popular Government.*

*Early History of Institutions.*

MARX, KARL. *Communist Manifesto.*

MILL, J. S. *On Liberty.*

*Representative Government.*

MONTESQUIEU. *The Spirit of the Laws.*

MUIRHEAD. *The Service of the State.*

PEASE, EDWARD. *History of the Fabian Society.*

RITCHIE, DAVID. *The Principles of State Interference.*

ROUSSEAU, J. J. *Social contract. Tozer Translation.*

SPENCER, HERBERT. *Man versus State.*

*Essays Scientific, Political and Speculative.*

SMITH, ADAM. *Wealth of Nations.*

WALLAS, GRAHAM. *Human Nature in Politics.*

WOODWORTH. *Christian Socialism in England.*

# Vita

The writer of this monograph was born in Hunan, China. He studied in Ming-teh, Yale and Tsing Hua preparatory schools before coming to the United States. In 1917 he was graduated from the University of Pennsylvania and in the following year he obtained from Columbia the degree of M. A., for which he wrote "The Financial Powers of the Governors of the Different States". At Columbia he studied under Professors Dunning, Robinson, Hayes, Schuyler, McBain, Powell, Beard, Salt, J. B. Moore, Munroe Smith, Seligman, Giddings and Simkhovitch.

Articles

# Internal and External Relations [*]

## I

It is not easy to say what relations are. They are probably too
fundamental to be defined. At any rate, we are as yet unable to
define them. However we are directly presented with such situations as involving "left and right", "before and after", etc. Relations are all pervasive. The idea of unrelated entities, though in
itself logically free perhaps from contradiction, is as a matter of
fact untenable. We do sometimes say with regard to certain things
that they are totally unrelated, but what is implied in such a
statement is merely a negation of certain specific relation or relations which happens to be the subject of our attention. To be unrelated in any specific way is itself a relation, and from this point
of view nothing is unrelated.

Any and every entity can become a relatum, logical propositions and relational complexes included. These latter are simply
terms in relation. But relations themselves cannot become relata.

---

 * 原刊于《清华学报》第 6 卷第 1 期, 1930 年 6 月。——编者注

Thus, a relational complex such as "I am taller than you" may bear the relation "Therefore" to another relational complex "I am heavier than you". But the relation "Taller than" cannot bear the relation "Therefore" to the relation "Heavier than". Bradley's infinite regress so far as relations are concerned is to us meaningless.

Bradley seems to have entertained another notion that is equally untenable. Not only did he conceive of relations as capable of being related, but also as capable of relating. Without involving ourselves in verbal niceties, we may say that relations do not relate in the sense that relational complexes are created through their activities. They are not active, they simply are; there is no sense in which they can be said to have either succeeded or failed in relating. The question is not whether a certain relation succeeds or fails in relating certain entities, it is rather whether those entities are or are not in a relational complex characterized by that specific relation. Relations therefore are not relata, nor do they of their own choice relate.

## II

We propose for consideration the following three relational complexes to be known as $a$, $b$, $c$, relational complexes embodying $a$, $b$, $c$, relations.

$a$ . "This book is on the table."

$b$ . "$H_2O$" as relational complex.

*c* . "He knows Physics."

Is *a* relation in the *a* relational complex the same as the *b* relation in the *b* relational complex? If so, are relations all of one kind? If all relations are *b* relations, then the *c* relation in the *c* relational complex is also a *b* relation. If relations are of different kinds, then the c relation may be either an *a* or a *b* or something different from both, and it remains for us to as certain which and what it is.

From the common sense point of view, the above does not present much of a problem, since, at a glance, a good many vague and perhaps obvious differences may be pointed out. But philosophical sophistry has made out of the situation a problem of the first importance. It has been maintained that all relations are "internal". It is difficult to find out what an "internal" relation is, but if it supposed to be anything in the nature of a *b* relation, then we are confronted with very grave problems. For in this latter case the *c* relation subsisting between the knower and the known is also internal and therefore has properties which are the characteristics of the *b* relation. Knowing would then make a difference to the thing known, and no form of knowledge, science included, could claim objectivity. While it is not easy to say exactly what "objectivity" means, it is easy to see that if knowing, being internal, modifies the thing known, then knowledge is not objective at least in the following senses.

a. If all relations are *b* relations, then the relation between the knower and the known is a *b* relation. If so, the known is always a relatum, an entity that is not its original self, because it is modified by knowing. It follows that we can never know any entity other than as relatum. Hence "Noumenon" emerges. Whatever the differences may be does not matter in the least, the point is that there are differences between an entity as such and an entity as relatum, and what is even more significant, we are never in position to know what these differences are.

b. But under the above assumption we are not in position to say that there are no entities other than relata, for in that case how could they be said to be different from relata? If we admit differences between the two, then they either exist or simply are, and the denial of either or both would be contrary to the premises. If entities in any knowledge relation were external objects, then these can not be known as they are, they can only be known as they are known.

c. Since what we know is but knowledge-relata, there can hardly be any standard for the validity of knowledge. What we know is simply "what we know". If "what we know" about a certain thing is again questioned, we can only answer by a further assertion of knowledge possibly in the form: "I know that I know", etc. The question can be asked ad infinitum and any answer other than the first is neither better nor worse than the first.

d. The above may be said just as well about the knower who in any capacity other than a knowing faculty or organism would be just as elusive as any external object.

The impossibility of knowing anything as itself under our

assumption may be approached from another angle.

e. If all relations are internal, then such relations as "to the right of", "to the left of", "before" and "after", "above" and "below" are all internal relations. The knower and the known not only bear a specific relation to each other, namely that of knowing, but also involve spatial relations. Here is a table: if all relations are internal in the sense of a $b$ relation, then this table to the east of me is different from this very table when it is placed to the west of me. I myself change with a change of spatial relations. Thus, when I was to the east of the table, my knowledge of it was such as was appropriate to a specific place, a knowledge that should not be confounded with anything I may know of the table when I shifted to the west of it.

Temporal relations would be internal under the same assumption. The relational complex known as knowledge is an event that takes place in finite time. But in finite time, however short, both the table and I change our temporal relations. Thus my knowledge of the table at one time must not be confounded with my knowledge of that very table at any other time. Time, it is poetically claimed, flows, and our temporal relations change with it; the only knowledge that can be said to be valid is the knowledge that is appropriate to instants, just as in the previous paragraph the only knowledge that can be said to be valid is the knowledge that is appropriate to points. But since knowledge as a relational complex and an event takes place in finite time and place, no knowledge is valid, if all relations are internal in the sense of a $b$ relation.

g. At the same time all entities are related and in no time are they free from relational changes. Under the assumption we are making in the present section, if anything involves any kind of relational changes, then it is impossible for us to know anything about it. My little desk here in my room bears some kind of relation to a twinkling star ten thousand light years away; if that star changes in any way whatsoever, even to the slightest degree, the desk becomes different in some way from what it was. Thus, if we want to know this little desk, we have to know that little star as well as the pyramids of Egypt and the trees of Labrador. Since my desk bears relation to anything and everything in this universe, then on the basis of our supposition we have to know the universe in order to know the desk. But we do not know the universe, hence we do not know this desk. And yet with a suitable definition of knowledge corresponding perhaps inadequately to the vague and inarticulate notion of knowledge which we do entertain, we can claim that we know this desk without knowing the universe in any similar sense. Is our common belief a pious superstition? Or rather is the assumption herein discussed basically untenable?

h. Logic has no content, it need not have any; but if it is useful in any practical way at all, it should be applicable to natural events or entities. In other words, in order that logic may be useful, such statements as "A is A", "A is not-A", must not only be logically significant, but also practically so. They may be true or false, or they may be neither, but we have to recognize their validity in some way before we can speak. But if they are known to be invalid to start with, then we can not possibly speak. The only statements that can possibly claim to be true are those that are made at point-instant. At any finite time and in any finite place no proposition concerning matters of fact can be made with any practical significance. Whether pure logic is affected or not need not be considered in the present connection, it is certain that applied logic evaporates into thin air. An ironic situation arises: those who accept the supposition of this section can not say a word in favour of it, while those who argue in favour of it cannot possibly accept it and escape contradiction.

Our supposition, let us recall, is firstly that all relations are internal, and secondly, that an internal relation is a $b$ relation. Thus far we have been arguing that under such a supposition knowledge is impossible in the various senses already discussed. In order to free ourselves from such a dismal consequence, it is only necessary to overthrow either the first or the second part of the supposition. There are quite a number of people who believe that all relations are internal, but if what is meant by an internal relation is not a $b$ relation, then the specific objections herein set forth are not applicable, whether or not there are other objections. But if an internal relation is conceived as a $b$ relation, then we have to show reasons why some relations are external, and a clear distinction between an external and an internal relation is required. If what is meant by an external relation is made clear, then the proposition that there are external relations may be established. In that case it only remains for us to decide as to whether the specific relation between the knower and the known is an external or internal relation or something totally different from both. What we have been arguing thus far is that that specific relation cannot be conceived as being internal in the sense of a *b* relation.

### III

In this section, we shall take up for discussion in the first place the position of Mr. F. H. Bradley, and secondly that of Professor Spaulding. Both may have the misfortune of being misrepresented.

A. a. Mr. Bradley seems to have thought that relations are impossible. If entities are in relation, then the relation between them does not "relate", for somehow they are already related; if on the other hand they are not related, then no relation can possibly relate them. In other words, if entities are in relation, to relate them is superfluous; if entities are not in relation, to relate them is impossible. It is impossible to relate entities not related, because for such a purpose an infinity of relations is required, and an infinity of relations is by definition unattainable. Comparatively detailed criticism will come at a later stage, for the moment, we should like to point out the following:

1. Relations and relational complexes should not be confused

with each other. Relations simply are, but relational complexes may begin or end. The question is never whether a certain relation is, but always whether certain entities bear that relation to each other.

2. Relations should not be regarded as being engaged in activities. There is no sense in which they may be said to succeed or fail in their effort to relate, simply because there is no sense in which they can be said to make any effort at all.

3. Relations should not be regarded as possible terms, so that there is no sense in which two terms in relation can be said to have become three terms necessitating a further relation.

b. Bradley seems to have entertained the idea that all relations modify their terms. If A and B are related, then A is not the original A, nor B the original B. Each, being in relation, is directly influenced in some way by the relation and indirectly influenced by each other. But if A and B were not in relation with each other, then the influence just mentioned would not have been there to affect them. That is to say, relations modify their terms.

c. Since relations modify their terms, some difference is made to them when they are in relation. Terms in relation must be somehow different from those very terms when out of it. If no difference is made to the terms, in what sense could we say that they are modified by their relation? Some differences therefore there must be between terms that are relata and terms that are mere terms. Of what that difference is, very few of us seem to have any clear notion. Bradley has the idea that qualities and relations imply each other, but in so far as I am aware, there is no attempt to regard them in any consistent way as tautological expressions. Later on we shall attempt to show that difference in quality implies difference in relation, but we are not justified in asserting that difference in relation implies difference in quality.

d. Entities in relation form a relational complex which whether or not further analyzable is at any rate not equivalent to the sum total of its parts. Thus, if we are dealing with such a relational complex as "Japan is to the east of China," we can not possibly say that this is equivalent to "Japan", "to the east of", and "China"; for obviously there are a number of possible combinations each of which is distinct from any other. There is therefore something unique about a relational complex, and this uniqueness which is essentially the uniqueness of the whole has been in some obscure way transformed into a uniqueness of the composing parts.

e. For reasons similar to the ones herein stated, some philosophers have come to the conclusion that all relations are internal, and an internal relation is such that the terms in relation are different from those very terms out of relation. Whether the reasoning is correct or not, we shall not examine for the moment, nor shall we concern ourselves with the conclusion as to whether it follows from the different stages of the argument. But if we accept the conclusion and interpret "modification of terms" as qualitative differences being made to them, then the objection raised in the previous section would apply and would thus make knowledge something of a game of blind man's bluff.

B. It is possibly for this reason that quite a few students of philosophy have come to the conclusion that the proposition that all relations are internal can not be accepted. Perhaps "hasty hands catch frogs for fishes", and in an eager attempt to demolish that proposition, ideas have been put forth that could not stand any close examination. Professor Spaulding might be cited as an example of those whose valour has unfortunately become the better part of discretion.

It should however be pointed out that those who are opposed to the internal relationists are not opposed to the idea of internal relation; they are merely opposed to the idea that all relations are internal. Hence what the external relationists want is not to deny that there are internal relations, but merely to affirm that some relations are external.

a. Some relations, according to Spaulding, do not modify their terms. "Above and below", "before and after" are such relations. If I walk around the table, I am not modified by the various positions which I hold in relation to the table. I may be taller or shorter than my friend, but I cannot be said to be thereby either tall or short. Terms related by this kind of relation are such that to say anything beyond their relation is unwarranted and consequently they are related in a way quite different from those that are related for instance by an organic relation.

b. If there are relations that do not modify their terms, it is

411

believed to follow that there are relations by which no difference whatever is made to the terms. Entities that are relata in these relations are the same as those very entities that are not relata in these relations. It is believed, though I have no assurance in saying so, not only that terms before being related by an external relation are the same as they are after it, but also that terms in such a relation are the same as they are out of it. This may seem to be a distinction without a difference, but a difference there is, and in some cases, a very important one.

c. Since terms in any external relation are the same as they are out of it, it follows that they are each independent of the other, and both independent of the relation. What is meant by independence is merely a lack of mutual modification. Independence is therefore not something which entities possess when they bear no relation to each other, it is rather something that represents the state of affairs in which they bear to each other an external relation. Since entities though related are yet independent of each other, it is thought that the whole in which they are the component parts is not such as to give rise to the idea of uniqueness. Thus, while the internal relationists seemed to have confounded the uniqueness of the whole with that of the parts, the external relationists seem to have mistaken a lack of uniqueness in the component parts for the lack of uniqueness in the whole.

d. The conclusion that Professor Spaulding arrived at is not merely that there are external relations, but also that the specific relation between the knower and the known is an example of such a relation. That is to say, though related, the knower and the known are yet independent of each other. The known is not merely relatum. It is that, but it is also something more; it is the original object. The objections raised in the second section of this article are therefore automatically removed.

There are people who are in sympathy with Spaulding's conclusion, but not with his reasoning; and there are perhaps others who are in sympathy to some extent with Bradley's reasoning, but find it by no means easy to swallow his conclusion. If external relation is to be justified, it must be on some basis and in some way other than those adopted by Professor Spaulding. Berrand Russell has something to say on the subject, but what he has said does not amount to very much. Mr. G. Moore to my knowledge has probably the most adequate appreciation of the problem; in my opinion at any rate, he has certainly made the keenest remarks about it. I do not pretend to understand exactly what his theory is, but I have no doubt that I have been greatly influenced by him. At the same time, I must admit differences of opinion which it would be out of place here for me to discuss.

In this section, two views almost diametrically opposed to each other are presented. Which of the two is to be preferred? Before this question can be answered, there should be a general clarification of terms such as "difference", "modification", "influence", etc. This clarification, I hope, will emerge as we proceed.

# IV

We return to the three different relational complexes mentioned in section Ⅱ. What we want to emphasize is the difference between $a$ and $b$ relations, and to decide whether the $c$ relation belongs to either of them, and if so, which.

A. Points common to all relations.

a. There must be relations such as R and there must be a plurality of entities such as A, B, etc.

b. There must be a possibility of such a relational complex as ARB. Given relations and entities, we need not have relational complexes. In the actual world in which we live we are possibly never confronted with relations that are not involved in relational complexes. But from the point of view of analysis, relations are more primitive than relational complexes, and may be studied prior to and apart from a study of relational complexes.

c. There is something unique about such a relational complex as ARB. It is some kind of whole that is not easily reducible to its parts, since these same parts combined in different ways may result in other and quite different wholes. It is not the uniqueness of wholes that can be or should be denied, it is rather the attempt to assign a single pattern to the uniqueness that we are unable to follow.

d. Entities in relation are affected by the relation. To use Moore's phrase, they acquire a "relational property" which they would not have received if they had not been related.

Such being the case, there is a definite sense in which entities in relaticn can be said to be different from those very entities
out of relation. A and B are entities out of relation, but in relation, they are also relata. The specific difference in the case is
the relational property each acquires from the other, and both
from the relation.

These points conceeded to be common to all relations seem
to substantiate the view of the internal relationists. If what is
meant by an internal relation is one that is analyzable into the
state of affairs herein mentioned, then all relations are internal.
But this state of affairs has been by some at any rate perhaps unwittingly confounded with the specific situation of a $b$ relation,
and an internal relation has come to mean much more than is
conceeded to all relations in the preceeding paragraphs. Before
we take up the specific situation of a $b$ relation, we should clarify
a few terms that are needed for the moment.

B. There are different meanings to the term "identity" just
as there are different meanings to the term "equality". We are
not here concerned with the possible meanings which these term
may embody, for our present purpose, the term identity may be
used as a characteristic of relations, and the term equality as a
characteristic of quality. The first shall be symbolized as "I",
and the second as "=", hence "Ī" stands for difference in relation, and "≠" stands for difference in quality or qualities.
Differences in relation are easily graspable. At any finite place

and during any finite time I change my relations, and differences of relations may be asserted irrespective of empirical evidence, because they can always be inferred from our knowledge of mathematics, physics and astronomy, with a suitable construction of time and space. Qualities however are quite a different matter. Their difference or equality is sometimes operational and always empirical, but whereas a judgement of qualitative difference is final with respect to certain operations, a judgement of equality in our sense at any rate is always tentative. The latter can not be final, because the equality asserted is a mere lack of empirical or experimental difference with respect to certain operations which may be replaced by others, and when they are so replaced, we may be confronted with qualitative differences formerly not experienced by us.

We are assuming here that there is some definite sense in which qualities are different and may be detached from relations. As to whether our assumption is justified or not we shall discuss at a later stage. Nor are we concerned here with the specific sense in which qualities and relations are supposed to differ from each other. I can no more define qualities than I can define relations. But common sense considers them different, and in the absence of clear definitions and sharp distinctions we may accept the common sense view for our present purpose.

C. Let us take first the $a$ relation in the $a$ relational complex, namely, "This book is on the table".

a. The book in this particular relational complex receives a relational property, namely, "on the table". If there were no such relational complex, this specific property would not have been ascribable to the book. We are of course not asking whether or not there is a relation "on"; there always is. Our question is rather whether or not there is a relational complex, namely, "this book is on the table". If there is, "this book" receives the relational property already mentioned.

b. Though this book is on the table, it can not be said that because it is on the table, it has changed its colour or increased its weight. It may change its colour, and it may increase its weight, but if it does either or both of these things, it does so independently of the relational property it has just required. There is a question of inference involved in this connection, but the problem of inference will be dealt with in a separate section.

c. Such being the case, we are justified in saying that the book in such a relation to the table is different from any book not in such a relation. The difference asserted is one of relation. We are also justified in saying that the book in such a relation is equal to this very book out of such a relation. The equality affirmed is one of quality.

d. The relational complex "this book is on the table" is a kind of whole, but it is difficult to say what kind of whole it is. The relation between the whole and its parts is not symmetrical, there is uniqueness of the whole which is qualitatively different from other wholes composed of the same parts, but there is no uniqueness of parts which may enter different wholes without becoming themselves qualitatively different. One thing is certain, this relational complex is neither an organic whole, nor such as involves chemical action between its parts. And if "x" stands for either of these kinds of wholes, we can say definitely that the relational complex "this book is on the table" is not "x".

e. We shall employ "$\hat{R}$," to symbolize a relation; "$\hat{R}P$", the relational property of such a relation; and "x", the two kinds of wholes mentioned. The following expression will embody the points herein discussed.

a. $A\hat{R}B$, $A\hat{R}P$, $A\hat{R}P\overline{I}A$, $A\hat{R}P=A$, $A\hat{R}B \neq x$.

D. Let us take up the $b$ relation in the $b$ relational complex, namely, "$H_2O$".

a. This is a relational complex in which the entities related are hydrogen and oxygen. Each acquires a relational property which it would not have, were it not so related to the other.

b. But in this case the hydrogen that is a relatum in this relational complex has changed its qualities by reason of its being a relatum. What can be said about it as an entity no longer applies when it has become a relatum.

c. From the above we are justified in saying that entities related in the $b$ relational complex are different in relation and also unequal in quality to those very or similar entities not so related.

d. This relational complex is a sort of whole with emergent qualities describable in terms that are not applicabe to the component parts separately. It is a kind of a whole that is equivalent to some kind or form of "x".

e. We shall employ "$\bar{R}$" to symbolize this kind of relation, and "$\bar{R}P$", this kind of relational property. The following expression will embody the points herein discussed.

b. A $\bar{R}$B, A $\bar{R}$P, A $\bar{R}$P ĪA, A $\bar{R}$P $\neq$ A, A $\bar{R}$B = x.

# V

The topic for discussion in this section is not an easy one. To start with a few prefatory remarks are needed. Both $a$ and $b$ relations involve ARP ĪA, but whereas $a$ relation embodies A$\hat{R}$P = A, $b$ relation contains just the opposite, A $\bar{R}$P $\neq$ A. This seems to be the most important point of difference compared to which the other points mentioned may be ignored. The question is: What sort of relation, if any, subsists between A$\hat{R}$P ĪA, and A$\hat{R}$P = A, and what relation, if any, between A $\bar{R}$P IA and A $\bar{R}$P $\neq$ A? If the second part can be inferred from the first in each case, then there is contradiction somewhere. What we want to point out is that the essential difference lies in the nature of $\hat{R}$P and $\bar{R}$P, namely, the two relational properties; that A$\hat{R}$P ĪA and A$\hat{R}$P = A are separately inferable from $\hat{R}$P, and A$\hat{R}$P Ī and A $\bar{R}$P $\neq$ A are separately inferable from $\bar{R}$P; but that in no way is A$\hat{R}$P = A inferable from A$\hat{R}$P ĪA, or A$\bar{R}$P $\neq$ A from A $\bar{R}$P ĪA. It is therefore advisable to take up the problem of implication and inference in so far as it affects our discussion. We shall take up three different kinds of implications to be symbolized as " $*$ ", " $\triangle$ " and " $\therefore$ ".

金岳霖全集

第五卷

A. A few words on propositions in general are not out of place here. There are propositions which have no existential import and which may be called purely logical propositions. There are others which have existential significance and which would be meaningless if the existence of the subject terms is denied. The relations of opposition between propositions depend upon the interpretation of the existence of their subject terms. Take for instance, the A and E forms of propositions. These have no relations of opposition if their subject term is not assumed to exist. They are contrary if their subject term is either assumed or asserted to exist. Where the subject term is exist, its non-existence renders the proposition insignificant, but where the subject term is asserted to exist, its non-existence would mean that the proposition is false.

Aristotelian logic as revealed through text books seems to involve itself in self-contradiction. A, E, I, O are said to be categorical propositions implying an assertion of the existence of their subject terms. If I and O are categorical in the above sense, then they are not sub-contrary, and if they are sub-contrary, as they are declared to be, then they are not categorical in the above sense.

Take for instance the familiar proposition that "All men are mortals", (terms interpreted as classes). It might be interpreted as a proposition asserting an abstract and unique relation between "Humanity" and "Mortality" conceptualized and defined with such rigidity that the proposition may be translated into the follow-

420

ing: "Whether there are men or not, if anything is human, he is mortal", just as one might say of an Euclidean straight line that whether it exists or not, if anything is a straight line, it is the shortest distance between two points. The familiar interpretation however of the above mentioned proposition is that all men are as a matter of fact mortals, or that all men are mortals and there are men. With either the familiar or the unfamiliar interpretation, being a man implies being a mortal, but the implication involved in the one case is quite different from that involved in the other.

B. The kind of implication here symbolized as " * " is the kind involved in the first and non-existential interpretation of propositions. It need not have anything to do with matters of fact. From certain postulates and certain definitions, both of which may be quite arbitrary, a number of propositions are said to follow in the sense that they are implied by the given postulates and definitions. To such a process matters of fact are quite irrelevant. Thus, as we have seen, with suitable definitions of humanity and mortality to which the existence of mankind may be considered as irrelevant, a proposition of the form " Whether there are men or not, if anything is human, he is mortal" may be so interpreted that being human " * " being mortal. " p * q " means that the proposition " p " impliesthe proposition " q ", whatever the facts may be. This is still "strict" implication, but it need not involve any empirical evidence.

C. But when the proposition " All men are mortals" is interpreted as asserting at the same time the existence of men, then the implication involved in it is quite different from that of the above. The proposition so interpreted becomes an inductive generalization and can claim no validity apart from experience. If there were no men to start with, or if there were, and they were all or some of them immortals, the proposition would be false, and being a man would not imply being a mortal. Thus, the implication involved in this case can not be divorced from matters of fact. It is possible for us to say at the present moment at any rate that all the citizens of New York are citizens of The United States of America; hence being a citizen of the former implies being a citizen of the latter. But this need not be so, and in the same way men need not be mortals. However, as a matter of fact, the generalization about men is valid; hence as a matter of fact, being a man does imply being a mortal. "$p \triangle q$" means that facts are such that the proposition $p$ implies the proposition $q$.

D. a. These two implications are often confused. The way in which their distinction can be made clear leads me to think that the views presented here are somewhat akin to those of Mr. Moore. Take for instance, "$A>B$, $B>C$, therefore $A>C$", where "$>$" represents "greater than". We may have the expression:

$$A>B \triangle (B>C * A>C).$$

That is to say, if $A$ is in fact greater then $B$, then the proposition "$B$ is greater then $C$" implies the proposition "$A$ is greater than $C$," whether or not there is any $C$ at all. But we can not have the expression:

$$A>B * (B>C \triangle A>C).$$

That is to say, the proposition "A is greater than B" does not imply the fact that B being greater than C, A must have been greater than C also.

b. The relation between " $*$ " and " $\triangle$ " should next engage our attention. Whenever there is a possibility of " $*$ ", there is a possibility of " $\triangle$ ", provided a certain condition is fulfilled. If for instance we have the implication "$p * q$" and A comes within the definition of p, and B, q, we may have the implication A $\triangle$ B. Hence given $\overline{Ap} = 0$, and $\overline{Bq} = 0$, We are justified in saying $(p * q) \triangle (A \triangle B)$. The question as to whether facts will be so good-humoured as to work for our convenience and substantiate our theories is irrelevant, for, in the first place, we do not claim that $(p * q) * (A \triangle B)$, that is, we do not say that there will always be A and B bearing that relation; and secondly, if there are no A and B, or if there are and they can not be subsumed under p and q, the condition is not fulfilled, and the question of implication does not arise.

c. We have seen then that under certain conditions it is possible for us to have $(p * q) \triangle (A \triangle B)$, though never $(p * q) * (A \triangle B)$. It remains for us to see whether given A $\triangle$ B, we are ever justified in arriving at p $*$ q, even if the condition $\overline{Ap} = 0$, $\overline{Bq} = 0$ is fulfilled. Personally, I see no way of arriving at any such conclusion. This is probably one sense in which empirical generalizations are said to be contingent. So far as we can see, there is no way in which A $\triangle$ B can be transformed into p $*$ q. All that we can claim is that given A $\triangle$ B there is a probability in fa-

vour of p * q. It seems impossible to have either( A △ B ) △ ( p *
q ) , or( A △ B ) * ( p * q ) ; the uttermost we can assert is that( A
△ B ).∴ ( p * q ) , and this, only when the condition already mentioned is fulfilled.

E. Let us not take up "∴". To start with, we may point out
that this is not an implication in any strict sense; it might be
called a sort of practical inference, an inference which was originally probably only physiological, but which has since become
highly trained through the influence of civilization. All empirical
knowledge when applied to things not yet experienced involves this
kind of inference; but from the point of view of logical validity, it is
highly problematical. There is in the situation no evidence of any
necessity in any strict sense, all that can be claimed for it is a
high or low degree of probability. It is something which in human
psychology represents expectation, but what is expected need not
be realized.

There is generally no confusion between " * " and "∴",
but there is confusion between " △ " and "∴", arising chiefly
from the view that with regard to matters of fact, there is no necessity. " △ " is an implication that is partly logical and partly
factual. Empirical knowledge has enabled us to classify men as
animals, hence being a man implies being an animal. If we are
actually confronted with an ethereal man we are quite justified in
calling him either a devil or a god. Empirically so far as we
know, it is just as necessary for a man to be an animal as it is for
a green book to be coloured. But a man need not remain a man,

nor a green book either green or a book. There is however a probability that the status quo will be maintained, and that probability
is the source of the kind of inference which we have symbolized
as "∴".

# VI

We shall now apply the above mentioned implications to the
*a* and *b* relational complexes.

A. We have already said that entities in relation are affected
by the relation, they receive a relational property which they
would not have received, if they had not been related. But what
is the relation between A and B's being related and the acquiring
by them of the relational property? With regard to this question,
I confess that I am not sure of my ground. Sometimes I think in
terms of a "△" implication, but for the present I am inclined to
think in terms of a "∗" implication. Possibly I had in mind
sometime ago the notion that the acquisition of a relational
property is a characteristic of an existent entity; possibly I had
felt that the ascription of a relational property to an entity that
may itself be non-existent is meaningless. I am inclined to think
at the present that whether or not there are "A" s and "B" s,
the very assertion of a relation between them implies their acquiring a relational property of some kind. Our notion of a relation,
though vague, contains at least this point: that if a relation is at
all significant, it must give the terms related some kind of

property which they would not have, had they not been so related. This notion of relation justifies us in saying that the proposition asserting or supposing a relation between A and B implies a proposition to the effect that A and B acquire a relational property of some kind. Hence we may have the following expression:

 a. AR̂B * AR̂P.

 b. A R̄ * A R̄P.

B. If A receives a relational property by virtue of its relation to B, then it is relationally different from what it was when it had not had that property. There is again an implication involved, and like the one discussed in the proceeding paragraph, it seems to be one that holds between propositions. Only in this case, it seems to be more obvious. The assertion with regard to any entity that it possesses any kind of property whatever is significant only when some difference is made by the property mentioned to the entity that is asserted to possess it. If the assertion is at all significant as it is meant to be, then some kind of difference is implied; the only question is whether the implied difference is relational. It can not be argued that the difference implied is not relational, for a relational difference in this connection is the minimum implied. And while it may be argued that more than a minimum may be implied, it can not be argued that a minimum is not implied; for the proposition asserting this minimal difference is, when the significance of propositions is borne in mind; tautological with the original proposition asserting a relation between A and B. Hence we have the expression:

a. $A\hat{R}P * A\hat{R}P \overline{I}A$

b. $A\overline{\underline{R}}P * A\overline{\underline{R}}P \overline{I}A$

C. With regard to the qualitative difference, the question is quite other than the above. We have noted qualitative equality in $a$ relational complex, and qualitative difference in $b$ relational complex, namely, $A\overline{\underline{R}}P = A$ in the former, and $A\overline{\underline{R}}P \neq A$ in the latter. These differences may safely be attributed to the inherent differences in the relational properties. But before we take up the question of implication, we have in passing to indulge in a few remarks on qualitative equality and difference. An assertion of qualitative equality as has already been pointed out is tentative; like an assertion of qualitative difference, it is based on empirical knowledge, but unlike the former, it only holds at a certain stage and with certain kinds of experiences or experiments and may therefore be modified, or supplemented, or overthrown by subsequent and more delicate and detailed experiments. If we divide experiments into varying degrees of crudeness and refinement, we may say that an assertion of qualitative equality is final with respect to all the experiments cruder than the one upon which the assertion is based, but tentative with respect to all the experiments that are more refined. A judgement of qualitative difference on the other hand is just the reverse; it is tentative with respect to the crude, and final with respect to the more refined experiments. Strictly speaking, then, judgements of quality, in so far as their equality and difference are concerned, are empirically both final and tentative in opposite directions, and strictly speaking, we have no ground upon which we can justify our preference for either of them. But we have prejudices; somehow or other we have come to believe that the more refined an experiment is, the better it reveals reality. That being the case, we have greater faith in a judgement of qualitative difference, since it is final with respect to all the experiments more refined than the one upon which the judgement is based.

In the case of the $a$ relational complex, we have a judgement of qualitative equality. With the above prejudice in mind, we can not say that our judgement is final. All that can be claimed is that there is a great probability in its favour, especially when repeated experiments confirm it. Psychologically we expect $A\hat{R}P$ to be qualitatively the same as A. They may be different, and their differences can be and often are attributed to other factors than the mere fact of their being related to each other. But we are not sure that the relation does not bring about some kind of qualitative difference not revealed or not yet revealed through further experience or experiment. We may of course define an $a$ relation as one in which no qualitative difference is made to the entities related; hence if any qualitative difference is revealed through further experiment, then the relation involved is simply not an $a$ relation. Such a definition is open to the following objections. In the first place, does the phrase "no qualitative difference being made" refer to an experience or experiment of a specific degree of refinement? If so, a more refined experiment may result in an $a$ relation ceasing to be such. Does the phrase refer to any kind or degree of experience or experiment? If it does, the definition would be entirely abstract, since it does not refer to a particular kind of experience, and qualitative judgements would cease to be experiential. We may in either case claim that $A\hat{R}P$ and A should be qualitatively the same, and if as a matter of fact they are not, we may always claim that some factor other than the relation is responsible for the difference. In such a case we are merely substituting an abstract qualitative equality for an experienced qualitative difference, and while the substitution is justified when such a determining factor is found, it is not justified if such a factor is not ascertained to be there. From all that has been said above, it seems safe to conclude that the qualitative equality between $A\hat{R}P$ and A is not certain but merely probable. That is to say, given $A\hat{R}P$, there is very high probability $A\hat{R}P$ and A are equal. Hence we have the expression:

    a. $A\hat{R}P \therefore A\hat{R}P = A$.

We may of course state the case negatively. Instead of speaking in terms of equality, we may speak in terms of inequality. Instead of saying that we expect qualitative equality, we may say that we do not expect qualitative inequality. The negative statement is probably stronger than the positive one from the point of view of logic. We may say that if A and B are related by an $a$ relation, it does not follow that $A\hat{R}P$ and A are qualitatively different. We may have the expression:

    a. $A\hat{R}P \; \overline{\triangle} \; A\hat{R}P \neq A$.

In the $b$ relational complex we have a judgement of inequality,

429

that is, of qualitative difference. Again with our prejudice in mind, we can say that a judgement of qualitative difference is final. This does not mean that qualitative difference in reality is always revealed in experience, it simply means that whenever it is revealed in experience, it is also there in reality. In the $b$ relational complex the inequality of $A\bar{R}P$ and A is invariably found in experience so that a part of the definition of such a relational complex is that entities that are its relata are qualitatively different from those that are not. Empirically a $b$ relation, since it involves a judgement of inequality that is regarded as final, can always be established; whereas an $a$ relation, since it involves a judgement of equality that is tentative, can not be empirically established though the probability in its favour may be such as to make it practically certain. Since this is the case, a $b$ relation can be defined without reference to any tentative element in our judgement, and the implication in a $b$ relational complex may be considered as one of factual necessity. We may therefore have the expression:

    b. $A\bar{R}P \triangle A\bar{R}P \neq A$.

    E. We may summarize the above as follows:

        a. $A\hat{R}B * A\hat{R}P * A\hat{R}P\bar{I}A$, $A\hat{R}P \therefore A\hat{R}P = A$;

        b. $A\bar{R}B * A\bar{R}P * A\bar{R}P\bar{I}A$, $A\bar{R}P \triangle A\bar{R}P \neq A$.

    So far we have been considering essentially individual relational complexes, at least in so far as $a$ relational complex is concerned. We may have the following modifications:

    a. A and B may be considered as classes, in which case the

relational complex having them as relata would be a class relational complex. The above formulae still hold.

b. So far also we have been comparing $A_{RP}$ with A, either as different stages of one individual, or different individuals of one class. We may compare ARP with anything whatever that has not the relational property which A has. If X represents such a thing or a class of such things, we may transform the above formulae into the following:

a. $A\hat{R}P * A\hat{R}P * A\hat{R}P \bar{I}X, A\hat{R}P\bar{\triangle}A\hat{R}P \neq X$;

b. $A\bar{R}B * A\bar{R}P * A\bar{R}P\bar{I}X, A\bar{R}P\triangle A\bar{R}P \neq X$.

F. The kind of relation that $a$ is is what we call an external relation, and the kind of relation that $b$ is is what we call an internal relation. The clear distinction between them lies in the different implications or inferences concerning qualitative equality and difference.

Those who maintain that all relations are internal in the above sense seem to have been confused about implications as well as about relational and qualitative differences, with regard to the $a$ relation, the internal relationists, without taking notice of the empirical fact $A\hat{R}P = A$, seem to have thought that since $A\hat{R}P$ $\bar{I}A$ is the case, $A\hat{R}P \neq A$ must be true. Their confusion is twofold. They may have inferred in the first place a " $\triangle$ " implication from a " $*$ " implication. But we have seen that that is possible only under a specific condition which must be satisfied before the inference is valid. In the second place, they may have thought that "$\bar{I}$" implies " $\neq$ " since " $\neq$ " does as a matter of fact imply

"$\bar{I}$". We will see in the next section that although "$\neq$" implies "$\bar{I}$", there is no implication the other way around.

a. Since the internal relationists seem to have made the above two-fold mistake, their view on internal relation ( viz. , our $b$ relation) also becomes fallacious. It is true that both relational and qualitative differences are involved in a $b$ relation; it is also true that both are implied by the internal relational property, but it is not true that the former implies the latter. Qualitative difference between A $\bar{R}$P and A is an empirical fact, it is not inferred from the relational difference between them.

The internal relationists seem to have been guilty of the following confusions.

1. "$\bar{I}$" and "$\neq$" are not clearly distingushed.

2. Since "$\neq$" implies "$\bar{I}$", it is thought that "$\bar{I}$" implies "$\neq$".

3. A $\bar{R}$P$\neq$A is considered as being inferred from A $\bar{R}$P $\bar{I}$A and not as an empirical fact.

4. Since under a certain condition, a "$\triangle$" can be inferred from a "$*$", the internal relationists prehaps thought that A $\bar{R}$P $\triangle$A $\bar{R}$P$\neq$A can always be inferred from A $\bar{R}$P $*$ A $\bar{R}$P $\bar{I}$A.

5. Since the latter is true of all relations, the former must also be; hence all relations are internal in the sense defined.

b. Some of the external relationists seem to have made the following mistakes:

1. "$\bar{I}$" and "$\neq$" are also confused.

2. Since "$\neq$" implies "$\bar{I}$", some external relationists prob-

ably draw the conclusion that " = " implies "I".

3. Since they recognize the qualitative equality between AȒP and A, they probably think that they can not help concluding that AȒP and A are relationally also the same.

4. Since the above is the case, the somewhat careless conclusion is drawn that external relations do not result in any difference whatsoever being made to their terms.

## VII

From what has been said above, we can easily see that the two sources of confusion are the different implications and the lack of a clear distinction between qualitative and relational differences. The former has already been dealt with at some length, but the latter needs a little more detailed consideration than has been given in the preceding paragraphs. The whole problem hinges on our view of qualities and relations, and it is to these that we are now again turning our attention.

Bradley said in the third chapter of his *Appearance and Reality*, "qualities are nothing without relations" and further down "relation without quality is nothing." Bradley has always seemed to me to be more literary than lucid, and I can not claim that I understand what he means by these sentences. It seems that the term relation has been used both as relational complexes and as relations pure and simple, and the term qualities has been used both as entities and as qualities pure and simple. It may be that relational complexes are nothing without entities, that Bradley thought that relations are also nothing without qualities; and that, since as a matter of fact entities are related in relational complexes, qualities are always related by relations. It is probably easy to argue from a synthetical dependence of relational complexes upon both relations and entities to the impossibility of an analytical independence between relations and qualities; for it is easy to forget that the whole is related to its parts in a way quite different from that in which parts are related to each other. The whole depends upon the parts for the kind of whole it is, but the parts do not depend upon each other for the kind of parts they are.

Furthermore, even if relations and qualities were mutually dependent upon each other, it does not mean that they are thus identified with each other. However dependent each may be upon the other for the relation that subsists between both, a husband is not his wife, nor an effect its cause, nor yet a son his father. It is the identification that forms the subject of our discussion, and nothing short of such identification would make any difference to the argument herein set forth. If relations and qualities are identified with each other, then relational equality would mean qualitative equality, and relational difference qualitative difference; but if they are not so identified with each other, no such inference is possible.

A. To start with, we have to admit that qualitative differences involve relational differences. Whenever we experience qualitative difference, we can always experience relational difference of some kind at the same time. This is obvious, since qualitative differences can only be experienced in finite time; and in finite time, a change of temporal relations has already taken place. We may use Venn's notation and say $(\neq)(\bar{I}) = 0$ is true. Hence the proposition "$\neq$" $\triangle$ "$\bar{I}$" is also true. Does it follow then that our $a$ relation, namely, external relation, is impossible in the sense that it is contradictory? The answer to this question depends on whether or not qualitative equality implies relational equality, when we grant that qualitative difference implies relational difference. If qualitative equality implies relational equality, then $A\hat{R}P = A$ as an element in our $a$ relational complex would imply $A\hat{R}PIA$. But $a$ relational complex also involves $A\hat{R}P\ \bar{I}A$; hence $a$ relation would be contradictory and thus impossible. The problem then is whether "$\neq$" $\triangle$ "$\bar{I}$" implies "$=$" $\triangle$ "$I$".

B. In order to tackle this problem, we may make use of the following eight propositions employing Venn's notation for the sake of convenience.

A, $(\bar{I})\overline{(\neq)} = 0.$     A' $(\neq)\overline{(\bar{I})} = 0.$

E, $(\bar{I})(=/=) = 0.$     E' $(\neq)(\bar{I}) = 0.$

$\bar{I}$, $(\bar{I})(\neq) > 0.$     I' $(\neq)(\bar{I}) > 0$

O, $(\bar{I})\overline{(\neq)} > 0.$     O' $\overline{(\neq)}(\bar{I}) > 0.$

a. It is possible, that both A and A' are true propositions. If so, qualitative differences and relational differences are identical; Not only does "$\neq$" imply "$\bar{I}$", but "$\bar{I}$" also implies

" $\neq$ "; not only does " = " imply "I", but 'I' also implies " = ". And external relations in the sense defined would be impossible.

b. It is also possible that both E and E'are true. If so, there is no implication between relational and qualitative differences, and our definition of external and internal relations hold.

C. It is possible that qualitative and relational differences are neither identical with, nor non-implicative of each other. If so, it is possible to have the following possibilities:

a. All relational differences are qualitative differences. The following propositions would then be true: 1. $(\bar{I})\overline{(\neq)}= 0$, 2. $(\neq)\overline{(I)}>0$, and 3. $(\neq)(\bar{I})>0$. Since $(\bar{I})\overline{(\neq)}=0$ is true, it follows that " '$\bar{I}$' implies ' $\neq$ ' " is also true. Since " '$\bar{I}$' implies ' $\neq$ ' " is true, it may happen that with a certain condition fulfilled, we can infer from $A\hat{R}P\ \bar{I}A$, $A\hat{R}P\neq A$, and our view of external relations is impossible, since it affirms the former and denies the latter.

b. Relational and qualitative differences overlap, viz., some of the one is some of the other, but neither is entirely the other. In this case the four particular propositions are true, and our definitions of internal and external relations remain unaffected by any of the propositions.

c. All qualitatative differences are relational differences. If so, the following propositions are true: 1. $(\neq)(\bar{I})= 0$, 2. $(\bar{I})\overline{(\neq)}= 0$, and 3. $(\bar{I})\overline{(\neq)}= 0$. From $(\neq)(\bar{I})= 0$, we can infer that " $\neq$ " implies " $\bar{I}$ ", but from $(\bar{I})\overline{(\neq)}>0$, we can not infer that " $\bar{I}$ " implies " $\neq$ ". If " $\bar{I}$ " implies " $\neq$ " is false, then $A\hat{R}P$ $\bar{I}A$ does not imply $A\hat{R}P \neq A$, and there is no contradiction in our view of external relation. At the same time, although "I" implies " $=$ " is true, " $=$ " implies "I" is false, so $A\hat{R}P = A$ does not imply $A\hat{R}P \bar{I}A$, and the contention of some extreme external relationists that external relations do not make any difference whatsoever to their terms can not be admitted.

D. That which is fatal to our view of external relations is the proposition that all relational differences either are or always involve qualitative differences. We have seen that empirically all qualitative differences involve relational differences; hence if we accept the above assertion, we are either identifying quality with relation or asserting that they always involve each other. We are now confronted with the fundamental contention upon which the claim of the internal relationists is based. In fact the proposition $(\bar{I})(\neq) = 0$ is tautological with the claim that all relations are internal. Have we then any reason for accepting this proposition?

a. We may try to answer this question from empirical evidence. Qualitative equality or difference is a question of experience. If we refuse to admit this, we may find that science and scientific procedure will be confronted with difficulties. In experience qualitative difference does involve relational difference, but in experience the latter does not involve the former. What experience can prove is the proposition that $(\neq)(\bar{I}) = 0$, it can not prove the proposition $(\bar{I})(\neq) = 0$. If it is claimed that experience is too crude, we can enlarge the term to include scientific experiments, and the situation would remain the same as it was before. If it is urged that scientific experiments are themselves crude in the sense that infinitesimal differences are not revealed by them, it may be answered that the suggestion is valid only when qualitative equality or difference is abstracted from all its empirical bearings for the purpose of logical construction; but that if it is not so abstracted, if, that is to say, qualitative equality or difference is to be considered as anything that can be affirmed or denied by experience, then the proposition $(\bar{I})\overline{(\neq)} = 0$ can never claim any empirical evidence whatsoever.

Thus far we have been saying that the above proposition can not be proved empirically. Can it be disproved by experience? This question depends for its answer upon whether or not relationsl differences are limited to those that are empirical. So far as our present stage of civilization is concerned, even our empirical relational differences are not accompanied by qualitative differences. Relatively therefore to our present scale of experience, the preposition $(\bar{I})\overline{(\neq)} = 0$ can be disproved empirically. But as we have already pointed out, our present judgements of qualitative equality are tentative with respect to experiments more delicate than those upon which the judgements are based. It is therefore possible to have a line of demarcation dividing the comparartively crude from the comparatively refined experiments such that our judgements of qualitative equality are final with respect to the former, and tentative with respect to the latter. It is possible for us to wake up some day to find our civilization so far advanced, or experiments so delicately adjusted and reliable, that for every empirical relational difference some qualitative difference can be experienced. Thus if we limit ourselves to relational differences that are empirical, our disproof of the proposition $(\bar{I})\overline{(\neq)} = 0$ can never be final. But fortunately or otherwise relational differences are never so limited; some of them are indeed empirical, others are merely inferred, and in so far as some of them are beyond finite experience, those that are so can never be experienced. At the same time qualitative differences are nothing if not empirical. Since experience is a series of finite events, and experiments, no matter how far advanced, must remain finite operations, not only can we never prove the proposition $(\bar{I})\overline{(\neq)} = 0$, but we can also disprove it conclusively from the point of view of our finite experience.

b. We have seen that so far as our experience is concerned there is no reason whatever for accepting the proposition that all relational differences involve qualitative differences. And what is more there are reasons for rejecting it. But empirical reasons need not be always applicable to the domain of logical contruction. What is empirically rejected need not be barred from entering into a theory or a system as a fundamental postulate to which facts may be considered irrelevant as long as it serves the function for which it is invoked. We hope to point out however that even in this sphere of logical construction, we have no reason for accepting the proposition $(\bar{I})\overline{(\neq)} = 0$.

1. In the first place, we have no reason for rejecting the proposition $(\neq)\bar{I} = 0$; hence if we accept $(\bar{I})\overline{(\neq)} = 0$, we are either identifying quality with relation, or else asserting that they involve each other to the extent that each is not without the other.

2. If qualities and relations are identified with each other, then, for reasons stated in section II of this article, we should not be able to know anything whatever. Nature would indeed be a passage, but it would be such a passage that no glimpse of it could ever be stolen. Hence pragmatically, from the point of view of convenience, the proposition $(\bar{I})\overline{(\neq)} = 0$ should not be accepted.

3. Those who accept the proposition $(\bar{I})\overline{(\neq)} = 0$ can hardly say anything in its favour unless the theory of types takes the arguments supporting it out of the universe of discourse of both relations and qualities. Whether such a defense is possible or not, I have not thought sufficiently to say anything definite. If it is open to the internal relationists to invoke the aid of the theory of types, then their arguments may be consistent, but what they say can never be true. If, on the other hand, this defense is not open to them, then they can not argue at all, for their arguments, themselves in the universe of discourse of relations and qualities, would contradict the proposition for which these arguments are called forth.

Logically and pragmatically we see no reason for accepting the proposition $(\bar{I})\overline{(\neq)} = 0$. Since this proposition is rejected, we have no possibility either of " $I$ " implying " $\neq$ " or of " $=$ ", implying " $I$ ", and our definitions of internal and external relation can be established. For the purpose of reminding our readers we repeat the formulae previously given.

a. $A\hat{R}P * A\hat{R}P * A\hat{R}P\ \bar{I}A$ , $A\hat{R}P\therefore A\hat{R}P = A$ , $A\overline{R}P \triangle A\hat{R}P \neq X$ .

b. $A\ \underline{\overline{R}}B * A\ \underline{\overline{R}}P * A\ \underline{\overline{R}}P\ \bar{I}A$ , $A\ \underline{\overline{R}}P \triangle A\ \underline{\overline{R}}P \neq A$ , $A\ \underline{\overline{R}}P \triangle A\ \underline{\overline{R}}P \neq X$ .

# VIII

We shall now return to the problem of knowledge which may be made easier by the above discussion. Knowledge is a relational complex with terms that are themselves relational complexes thus involving a plurality of relations. Epistemology will have to determine how these entities and relations are to be construed; but for our present purpose, we shall consider the knower and the known as wholes united by a specific relation, namely, that of knowing various theories have been put forth as to what kind of relation this specific one is, and some have concluded that it is an internal relation in the sense defined.

A. Is the knowledge relation then internal or external? If it is internal in the sense of a $b$ relation, then all the arguments set forth in Section Ⅱ would render knowledge very much of a fabrication of our brain. Unfortunately we can not prove empirically what sort of relation our knowledge relation is; we can not prove that it is either internal or external. At best we can only interpret it either as the one or the other or something quite different from both. The conclusion arrived at in this article is that it has to be interpreted as external.

a. But if all relations are internal, then the knowledge relation must also be internal, since no other alternative is possible.

b. The purpose of this study is to disprove the proposition that all relations are internal( in the sense of a *b* relation) , and to establish at the same time the proposition that some relations are external. If we are successful in this attempt, we have at least two alternatives open to us for the interpretation of the knowledge relation.

c. We have to stress the point that if we interpret the knowledge relation as internal or external, we can not prove or disprove it to be either the one or the other.

B. Why do we interpret the knowledge relation as external?

a. If it is regarded as internal, then we have no way of meeting the objections of section Ⅱ .

b. If it is regarded as external, then these objections can not be urged against us.

c. We can not prove the knowledge relation to be external for the simple reason that we can never compare any entity as knowledge relatum with that entity as an external object.

C. What we want to make use of in an external relation is simply $A\hat{R}P = A$. If A stands for any external object, K stands for the knowing faculty, then $A\hat{R}A$ stands for the knowledge relational complex and $A\hat{R}P$ stands for a knowledge relatum. If the external object happens to be this book on my desk, then the book in knowledge is relationally different from the book out of it, but that does not prevent us from inferring that the book as an external object and as a knowledge relatum are qualitatively the same. In a word, this book can be known as an external object.

# The Principle of Introduction and A Priori*

In the course of his discussion on cause and effect, Hume proposed and then, perhaps possessed by a sense of futility, almost immediately dismissed the problem whether we have any assurance of the future's resembling the past. The problem does seem insoluble. Mr. Russell, I believe, has somewhere pointed out that the principle of induction can not be inductively derived, since any attempt at deriving it through induction obviously assumes the principle. It is suspected that the same may be said of the problem of the resemblance of the future to the past; if we assume the resemblance we can always substantiate it, but we can not substantiate it without assuming it, and no amount of substantiation will give us any assurance. In the following discussion I shall give reasons for believing that the supposed problem is hardly a problem, that we do have assurance, but that the assurance we have is *a priori* in nature though different from a tautology.

---

* 原刊于《哲学杂志》第 37 卷第 7 期, 1940 年 3 月。——编者注

I shall take for the purpose of discussing the principle of induction as formulated by Mr. Russell. "If in a large number of instances a thing of one kind is associated in a certain way with a thing of another kind, it is probable that a thing of the first kind is always similarly associated with a thing of the second kind; and as the number of instances increases, the probability approaches almost to certainty." Not having a single book on hand, ① I can not vouch for the correctness of the above quotation, nor will I say anything as to whether or not it is an adequate formulation of a weighty principle.

I shall also leave untouched the problem of probability, important though it is, and devote myself entirely to the principle itself and to the Humean problem of whether or not the future will resemble the past. We may reason that if the future does not resemble the past, then no matter how many instances there are of a certain kind of association, there is no probability of its being continued beyond those given instances. The probability does not refer directly to the generality of a certain association; it refers rather to a representativity of the general which the given instances supply under the assumption that there are general associations persisting through time and space. From the point of view of this article, at any rate, the problem of probability is secondary to the problem whether or not the future will resemble the

---

① Professor Chin's university had moved 3000 miles overland from Peiping to the Southwest and was functioning without adequate library facilities, ed. note.

past.

I shall illustrate the above principle by designating by " $a$ " and " $b$ " things or particulars, by " $A$ " and " $B$ " kinds of things and by "——" whatever association is experienced:

If $\qquad at_1$——$bt_1$

$\qquad\qquad at_2$——$bt_2$

$\qquad\qquad \vdots \qquad \vdots$

$\qquad\qquad at_n$——$bt_n$

_then_ $\qquad A$——$B$

The $a$ s and $b$ s, being particular objects or events, either are or take place in particular places and times. We ignore the problem of space in this article. Time is symbolized by adding $t_1$, $t_2$, $t_3$,... $t_n$ to the $a$ s and $b$ s. $A$ and $B$ being kinds of things, $A$ —— $B$ is therefore the generalization aimed at by induction.

The problem whether or not the future resembles the past is supposed to be crucially tested by the contingency of $at_{n+1}$ being similarly associated or not with $bt_{n+1}$. It is easily supposed that if $at_{n+1}$ is not so associated with $bt_{n+1}$, then $A$——$B$ does not hold and the future disagrees with the past. It is true that under the circumstances, $A$——$B$ does not hold, but it by no means follows that the future does not resemble the past. Although when a generalization holds, the principle of induction succeeds, it does not fail with the failure of a generalization. The problem whether or not the future resembles the past is always resolved into the question of the present or the past agreeing or disagreeing with itself.

The following considerations will, I hope, make the points involved clear.

To start with, since $A \text{——} B$ is meant to be general, it obviously could not be treated as a particular in any way. But we are liable to reason in the following manner:

$$at_1 \text{——} bt_1$$
$$at_2 \text{——} bt_2$$
$$\vdots \qquad \vdots$$
$$at_n \text{——} bt_n$$

$$\overline{\phantom{aaaaaaaaaaaa}}$$

$$A \text{——} B$$

$$\overline{\phantom{aaaaaaaaaaaa}}$$

$$at_{n+1} \text{——} bt_{n+1}$$

If we proceed in this way, we should be treating $A\text{——}B$ as a summary at $t_n$ of instances up to $t_n$. Although it is not itself an instance, it is still a particular proposition which is assumed to be true of the $a$s and $b$s from $t_1$ to $t_n$. This proposition, if true, is true forever after, no matter how $at_{n+1}$ and $bt_{n+1}$ are to be associated. No matter what the future is, even if we assume it to be entirely different from the past, $A\text{——}B$ is not thus invalidated. Under the above suppositions, the agreement or disagreement of the future with the past is merely an agreement or disagreement of any instance after $t_n$ with the instances before, including $t_n$. If there is agreement, well and good; if there is not, we may even have to say that after all history does not repeat itself.

The kind of agreement or disagreement which is not just a

question of history is the kind where $at_{n+1}$ and $bt_{n+1}$ not merely agree or disagree with the previous instances, but also substantiate or invalidate $A$——$B$. But $at_{n+1}$ and $bt_{n+1}$ can affect $A$——$B$ only when the latter is not merely a summary at $t_n$ of instances from $t_1$ to $t_n$, but also a generalization meant for any instance whatever including $at_{n+1}$ and $bt_{n+1}$; that is, when $A$——$B$ is meant to be general. When $A$——$B$ is so meant, we have to proceed in the following way:

$$
\begin{array}{cccc}
\text{Either} & at_1 \text{——} bt_1 & \text{or} & at_1 \text{——} bt_1 \\
& at_2 \text{——} bt_2 & & at_2 \text{——} bt_2 \\
& \vdots \quad \vdots & & \vdots \quad \vdots \\
& at_n \text{——} bt_n & & at_n \text{——} bt_n \\
& at_{n+1} \text{——} bt_{n+1} & & at_{n+1} \text{——} bt_{n+1} \\
& \overline{\phantom{aaaaaaaaaa}} & & \overline{\phantom{aaaaaaaaaa}} \\
& A \text{——} B & & A \text{——} B
\end{array}
$$

depending on whether the fresh instance is positive or negative. The agreement of the fresh instance with the previous instances adds to the force of the generalization, while the disagreement invalidates it. But does this mean that the future agrees or disagrees with the past? The above tabulation probably makes it evident that the question must be answered in the negative. However, we shall refrain from any such conclusion for the moment, since we have been discussing merely the generality of $A$——$B$, and have not even touched upon the problem of time and the relation between the enumeration of instances and the generalization. The principle of induction is formulated in terms of the if-then relation. Now take any case of "If $p$, then $q$." Where $p$ and $q$ represent tautologies, or natural laws, or empirical generalizations, there is no question of time either in the validity or in the assertion of the if-then relation, although of course time may enter as an element in $p$ or $q$. Where $p$ and $q$ both represent particular propositions, the problem of time may be extremely complex, at any rate we shall ignore it here. But where $p$ is in time while $q$ is timeless, the validity of "if $p$ then $q$" may or may not be timeless, the assertion of it involves time as a potent factor. The principle of induction, as formulated by Mr. Russell, summarizes all the instances in the antecedent and embodies the generalization in the consequent. Whether the principle is always valid or not (we shall take up the problem later), the assertion of it in connection with any specific case of induction must include all the known or the experienced evidences gathered $up$ to and at the time of the assertion; that is, the assertion of this principle in the case of the $a$'s and $b$'s as evidences for $A$——$B$ must include the last evidence relative to the time when the assertion is made. Thus at $t_n$ we have

$$\text{if} \quad at_1 \text{——} bt_1$$
$$at_2 \text{——} bt_2$$
$$\vdots \qquad \vdots$$
$$at_n \text{——} bt_n$$

_____

$$\text{then} \quad A \text{——} B$$

while at $t_{n+1}$, we have

450

if $\quad at_1 \text{———} bt_1$

$\qquad at_2 \text{———} bt_2$

$\qquad \vdots \qquad \vdots$

$\qquad at_n \text{———} bt_n$

$\qquad at_{n+1} \text{———} bt_{n+1}$

---

then $\quad A \text{———} B$

From this one could readily see that no fresh instance of $a$ and $b$ ever gets below the horizontal line which is the symbol for the summary up to the present. While it is true that at $t_n$ any possible $at_{n+1}$ and $bt_{n+1}$ in future may or may not agree with the previous instances, yet at no time could the future agree or disagree with the past. We must distinguish the present from $t_n$ as well as the future from $t_{n+1}$, The present and the future are variables while $t_n$ and $t_{n+1}$ are particular values for these variables. The present never stops, but $t_n$ is fixed forever. With this distinction in mind, we can easily see that by the time that $at_{n+1}$ and $bt_{n+1}$ agree with the previous instances, the present has moved from $t_n$, to $t_{n+1}$; viz., it is no longer a future instance. It isn't the future that is agreeing with the past, it is $at_{n+1}$ and $bt_{n+1}$ agreeing with the previous instances.

When we have a positive instance such as $at_{n+1} \text{———} bt_{n+1}$, the generalization $A \text{———} B$ is strengthened at least by the additional force of one more instance, but this does not mean that the principle of induction is also strengthened. If the principle were strengthened by a positive instance, it should be weakened by a negative instance, but it isn't. Supposing we are confronted with a negative instance, we have something like the following.

since $\quad at_1 \text{——} bt_1$

$\qquad at_2 \text{——} bt_2$

$\qquad \vdots \qquad \vdots$

$\qquad at_n \text{——} bt_n$

$\qquad at_{n+1} \text{——} bt_{n+1}$

---

$\therefore \qquad A \qquad B$

which is an instance of an implication with the above enumeration of instances as the antecedent and the above generalization as the consequent.

It is true that in the face of a negative instance, the generalization $A \text{——} B$ does not hold, but then we can easily see that the data gathered are not such as to satisfy the condition for a positive generalization required by the principle of induction, which remains therefore unaffected. It is again no longer the future differing from the past, it is $at_{n+1}$ and $bt_{n+1}$ disagreeing with the previous instances. In fact not only is the principle of induction unaffected, but also by making use of it together with other principles some kind of generalization other than the negative of $A \text{——} B$ could be obtained from the above data.

It is now presumably clear that the success or failure of a generalization does not entail a corresponding success or failure of the principle of induction, and the agreement or disagreement of one instance with the previous instances does not entail a corresponding agreement or disagreement of the future with the past. On what evidence then does the principle rest? What assurance have we for the validity of the principle? We shall see that the problem of the future resembling the past is the same problem as the validity of the principle of induction. In order to tackle the problem we have to remind ourselves of the relation "if-then" in connection with time. Time is a passage, a flow, while the if-then relation in the principle of induction is, let us say, a cross-section, and no matter how time may flow, this relation cuts across it. But in doing so, the contents of the antecedent and the truth value of the consequent may have been changed in any specific induction. Let $p$ stand for any specific antecedent, and $q$ its consequent. As time moves forward the content of $p$ changes and with it possibly also the truth value of $q$. The above illustration of both a positive and a negative instance already exhibits this point: while both change the content of $p$ , a positive instance leaves the truth value of $q$ unchanged, while a negative instance alters the truth value of $q$ .

Thus, with regard to any specific induction, time supplies fresh instances only to change the content of antecedent and possibly also the truth value of the consequent, but in doing so, the truth value of the principle remains unaffected. It remains unaffected partly because any specific induction is only a value for the principle, which means that different values may be substituted but the form of the principle remains; and partly because the consequent is so automatically adjusted to the antecedent that the

453

if-then relation between them has always the same truth value no matter at what time. But having a constant truth value is not the same as being always valid. A false proposition also has a constant truth value. We have to analyze further in order to show that the principle is always valid.

Let us take up the generalization $A$——$B$. It is of the form

(1) $\qquad (a, b)\varphi(a, b)$

and since we ignore the problem of space it is by definition equivalent to

(2) $\varphi(at_1, bt_1) \cdot \varphi(at_2, bt_2) \cdot \ldots \cdot \varphi(at_n, bt_n) \cdot \ldots \cdot \varphi(at\infty, bt\infty)$

Now the antecedent of the principle of induction which is a summary of instances at any time $t_n$ is only

(3) $\varphi(at_1, bt_1) \cdot \varphi(at_2, bt_2) \cdot \ldots \cdot \varphi(at_n, bt_n)$

This is obviously incomplete and is never the equivalent of (2). But although (3) is never the equivalent of (2), it is also never such that (1) is false. No matter how many positive instances are added, (3) will retain the same form. That is to say, "if (3) is true, (1) is true" can always be asserted. Time however may bring forward a negative instance the presence of which changes (3) into

(4) $\varphi(at_1, bt_1) \cdot \varphi(at_2, bt_2) \cdot \ldots \cdot \varphi(at_n, bt_n) \cdot \sim \varphi(at_{n+1}, bt_{n+1})$

Now (4) is equivalent to

(5) $\sim (a, b)\varphi(a, b)$

Hence "If (4) is true, (5) is true" always holds: that is what is meant by saying that a negative instance is conclusive. The implication between ( 4 ) and ( 5 ) is both deductive and inductive; it is deductive because pure logic guarantees its validity, and it is inductive because ( 5 ) the consequent as a generalization follows from the presentation of an actual instance. It is true that at $t_n$ we do not know that a possible instance at $t_{n+1}$ is to be positive, or that it is to be negative, but we do know that it is either positive or negative, and whether it is actually positive or actually negative, it enters into the antecedent, and the consequent is also either positive or negative. In either case, ( 3 ) implies ( 1 ) or ( 4 ) implies ( 5 ) , and whichever the case may be, the principle of induction holds.

The principle of induction therefore would not be invalid, neither will the future, if there is any, upset the past. The past and the present are differentiated, integrated, and catalogued like the books in a library which are marked one way or another. They aremere aggregate names for so many broken up experiences which are labelled sometimes accurately and sometimes haphazardly by the enormous number of concepts with which we face whatever is given. The moment the future enters into the present, it loses its slumpiness, and if it does not fall in the line we expect it to, we may be disappointed, but we shall soon find that it falls in line with something else, or if it doesn't fit in with anything whatever, it will merely enrich the past and the present with a new category: one thing that it does not do is to upset the past. It will not, because the moment we can say something definite about it, it ceases to be lumpy and becomes itself a part of the differentiated and catalogued past and present. The line of argument here taken is analogous to that maintained by C. I. Lewis. Our concepts are prescriptive not in the sense of determining what the future is to be, but in the sense of how it is to be received; and however it may come, we have assurance of receiving it one way or another. Take for instance, our attitude toward any possible instance of $a$, $b$, at $t_{n+1}$. In the first place, it is said to be either positive or negative. We may argue that this says nothing, but we have to admit at the same time that conceptually though perhaps not psychologically we are ready for anything. Supposing that an established generalization in the past has been invalidated, we merely say that the generalization has never been true. The supposed generalization suffers indeed, but not the past. Furthermore, the new instance upon closer examination either baffles us or does not; if it does, it is in the process of furnishing us with new concepts; if it does not, that amounts to saying that our conceptual instruments in stock are capable of dealing with it.

The principle of induction is a *priori*, it is valid for any time. The notion of a *priori* here is not that of any transcendental form by means of which experience is made possible, rather is it a form which is valid for any experience; its origin does not involve a transcendental mind, and our awareness of it is not prior to any experience whatever. From what has been said above, the principle of induction, being true of any experience, is an a *priori* principle. Mr. Russell has somewhere suggested that this principle is *a priori* because it is not and can not be inductively derived. This merely says, however, that any induction assumes the principle and to derive it through induction is to assume it in order that it may be derived; this does not show that the principle is *a priori* in the sense here accepted. In order that the principle may be shown to be *a priori*, we have to show that it is valid for any time, or, with reference to the future, the future can not do anything to upset it. And this, I hope, has been accomplished by the previous paragraphs.

Suppose, however, that time stops with some disembodied intelligence still functioning. This may be unimaginable, but it is eminently conceivable. Experience in our sense discontinues but some lumpy state of affairs remains. Tautologies are still valid, they assert no possibility as a fact and every possibility as a possibility, and any state of affairs that is at all conceivable must be within the realm of possibilities. In fact, to say that a certain state of affairs is conceivable means that it is something for which tautologies hold, for if it were something for which tautologies do not hold, it is automatically inconceivable. I shall not discuss the problem whether logic is one or many. I myself believe that there is only one logic. Suppose for the moment, however, that there are many logics. Obviously one can not invoke all of them at the same time, and if one is used, this one becomes the limit as well as the tool of conceivability. One way or the other, therefore, we may conceive a timeless and lumpy state of affairs in place of our

457

present world. With the stoppage of time, there is also no motion, no life, perhaps also no space, no distinction of this and that, neither particular nor individual; all former distinctions are obscured and universals become empty possibilities. Will the principle of induction hold in such a state of affairs?

To take the obvious point first, the principle will be entirely useless. The disembodied intelligence will see that its usefulness depends upon the differentiation through time of what is given into categories; when time stops, no differentiation takes place, consequently there are also no more $a$s and $b$s. Furthermore, $A$——$B$ which was meant to be general in the form given in(2) above can no longer be so regarded; with the stoppage of time, it ceases also to be a natural law, it becomes at most a brief summary of historical facts of the form such as for instance "The ancient Greeks were athletes." This might be interesting to the disembodied intelligence as a historian, but not if he were a philosopher or a scientist. The principle seems to be plainly useless. But admitting that it is useless in such a state of affairs is far from saying that it is invalid. Under such circumstances a tautology is also useless but it is none the less valid. If we suggest that the principle of induction is no longer valid, we have to give more reasons.

Let us remind ourselves that a tautology is valid at any rate partly because it says nothing, it does not assert the existence of a lumpy state of affairs, or describe what it is like; it is valid for such a state quite as uncommittedly as it is true of our present world. The principle of induction, however, is not a tautology, it does say something. Although it is not identified with any specific induction which may be concerned with the objects of inquiry in any specific field, it yet assumes the existence of particular instances, the subsistence of general relations, the subsumption of particulars under universals; and in assuming that the universals with which it deals are not empty possibilities, but are realized in terms of orderly instances, it assumes a world differentiated into the scaffolding of time and space. What it asserts is therefore entirely millified by the supposed timeless and lumpy state of affairs, for the antecedent which is a summary of instances is still true, but the consequent is false, since with the stoppage of time, there are no natural laws of the kind meant.

It must now be understood that with the elimination of time there are no natural laws. A genuine natural law has to have differentiated physical meaning. In a timeless and lumpy state of affairs, general relations may have both mathematical and metaphysical meaning, but no differentiated physical meaning. They may have mathematical meaning, because all the concepts involved in them may be organized into a deductive system in which these relations enter as theorems. They may have metaphysical meaning in the sense that the said state of affairs may be regarded as a whole in which all attributes are reconciled in a Bradleyian sort of way. But they have no differentiated physical meaning, since the lumpy world is not supposed to furnish us with instances, either observational or experimental, upon which the physical meaning of genuine natural laws must be based.

But, no matter how conceivable our supposition is, it is something such that no positive reason, no reason other than that of pure logic, can be given in favor of its ever taking place. Time won't be annihilated, it is the very core of that givenness, that stubbornness, that concreteness, that basis for factuality which pure logic does not provide for, but which is yet what the world is made of. There is therefore always future. So long as there is a moving future, there is always a living present and a past which can not be upset because whatever is presented will be received one way or another. The conceptual reception of the given is epistemological experience, and the principle of induction is a principle of reception. So long as time supplies us with something to be received, the principle of induction will be valid, It is an *a priori* principie, but of a kind different from a tautology.

金岳霖全集
第五卷

# Chinese Philosophy[*]

## I

Of the three main flows of philosophical thought, it has been
maintained that the Indian is otherworldly, the Greek unworldly
and the Chinese worldly. No philosophy is ever plainly worldly;
to say that it is so is merely an attempt to caricature it in order to
bring out certain features into striking relief. To those who know
something of Chinese philosophy the word worldly merely empha-
sizes certain features in comparison with the Indian and the Greek
schools of thought; but to those who do not know anything about
it, that word is liable to be quite misleading. What is meant is
probably that Chinese philosophy sticks to the kernel of its
subject matter; it is never propelled by the instruments of
thinking either into the dizzy heights of systematic speculation, or
into the depth of a labyrinth of elaborate barrenness. Like
machines in an industrial civilization, intellectuality in philosophy

---

[*] This paper was written in Kunming in 1943 and was mimeographed for
limited circulation. ——The author.

原刊于 *Social Sciences in China*, Vol. I, No. 1, 1980. ——编者注

461

drives; and whether it drives us into blind alleys or not, it may lead us far away from the wide boulevards or spacious squares. Intellectually, Chinese philosophy has always been in the open air.

We are accustomed to think of Chinese philosophy as consisting of Confucianism, Buddhism and Taoism. It is rather as religions that these are exclusively mentioned. In the early stages both Confucianism and Taoism were only philosophies, and as such they were in the pre-Qin period members of a whole democracy of different schools of thought, the variety of which during that period was unparalleled in Chinese history. Since terms are inadequate, we shall refrain from any attempt at description. It is misleading enough to apply the familiar philosophical terms to Western philosophy, it is much worse to apply them to the Chinese. One might say for instance that there were logicians in the pre-Qin period; but if so, readers might be led to think that there were people who brooded over syllogism, or the laws of thought, or even obversion and conversion. The Ying-Yang-ists have been described in a recent article as the precursors of science, and not without foundation either, but then they were precursors of something which strictly speaking never arrived: and if as a result of this description readers imagine them to be ancient Keplers or Galileos, they entertain a distorted view of a whole brand of thinkers.

Confucianism and Taoism are indigenous to China, they are properly Chinese. Buddhism, however, was introduced from India and it might be wondered whether it could be said to be

Chinese. The introduction of a foreign philosophy is not quite the same as the importation of foreign goods. In the last century, for instance, the English were alarmed at the invasion of German Idealism. "The Rhine," they declared, "has flowed into the Thames." But however alarmed they might be, their Thames has not since become a mere Rhine; British Hegelianism while acknowledging its origin and impetus from abroad is distinctly English, though it is not so characteristically English as the philosophies of Locke and Hume. Buddhism in China, in the early stages, at any rate, had been modified by Chinese thought: indeed for a time it was robed in Taoistic garbs, and Taoism, it might be said, became its chief agency of distribution. But there was something stubborn in Buddhism which resisted Taoistic manipulations, hence although it became Chinese to some extent, it is not distinguished by the features characteristic of the indigenous Chinese philosophy.

In the following sections we shall single out certain features for discussion. We shall refrain as much as we can from proper names, technicalities or details.

# II

One of the features characteristic of Chinese philosophy is the underdevelopment of what might be called logico-epistemological consciousness. Undoubtedly such a statement has been made frequently, and perhaps too frequently it has been taken to mean either that Chinese philosophy is illogical or that it is not based on knowledge. Obviously this is not what is meant. We needn't be conscious of biology in order to be biological, or of physics in order to be physical. Chinese philosophers could easily manage to be logical without a developed sense of logic; their philosophy could be founded on the knowledge then accepted as such, and yet devoid of a developed sense of epistemology. To be conscious of logic and epistemology is to be conscious of the instruments of thought. Not having a developed consciousness of epistemology and logic, the Chinese philosophers presented their ideas with a barrenness and disconnectedness that might suggest to those who are accustomed to systematic thought a feeling of indeterminateness unexpected of philosophies, and possibly also dampening to the enthusiasm of the students of Chinese thought.

Not that there was no such consciousness. Perhaps inevitably from the nature of the impetus concerned, this consciousness started with what impatient thinkers are liable to dismiss as mere sophistries. The underlying reality behind the so-called sophistries, however, was only a switch of the muses from the problem of ultimate realities to those of language, thought and ideas, realizing perhaps that the latter must be tackled before the former could be solved. Such a switch took place in the pre-Qin period when a number of thinkers started to maintain the distinction between the universal and the particular, the relativity of terms, the separation of hardness from whitenss, the doctrine of infinite divisibility of the finite, of the staticity of quickly moving arrows, etc., in the midst of speculations which were obviously more directly concerned with the problems of that turbulent age. Students of philosophy will inevitably think of the parallel in Greek thought. It was from similar doctrines arising out of reason itself that the intellectual finesse in Western philosophy was obtained; and it was by them that philosophy was in some sense converted into mental gymnastics. In China, however, the tendency was short lived; admirable as it was for a beginning, it yet died a precocious death. The logico-epistemological consciousness remained underdeveloped almost to the present day.

Whatever the causes may be, and a large number may be stiggested, the effect on philosophy and science is far-reaching indeed. Science in the West is linked up in an intimate way with Greek thought. While it is untenable to regard the former as a direct offspring of the latter, it is none the less true that the former owed part of its development to certain tendencies in Greek thought. Technique in experimentation was comparatively a late arrival in the history of European culture, and while it is of the utmost importance to science it is not its only necessary condition. Certain tools of thinking are equally required, and what was actually supplied might be most conveniently called mathematical patterns of thinking. The emergence of calculus was a great impetus to science, thus indicating that the instruments for handling data are just as important as their collection through observation and experiment. The patterns of thought to which Europeans had long been accustomed were Hellenistic. Hellenism is thoroughly intellectual; its intellectuality is characterized by developing ideas and carrying them ruthlessly and relentlessly either to their sublimities or to their absurdities. *Reductio ad absurdurn* is itself an intellectual instrument. It was this element which was responsible for the early development of logic, which on the one hand supplied the tools of early science, and on the other gave Greek philosophy that admirable articulateness which was the envy of later thinkers. If the development of this logico-epistemological consciousness was partly responsible for the presence of science in the West, the lack of this development must be partly responsible also for the absence of science in China.

The effect on Chinese philosophy is equally far-reaching. While Chinese philosophy is not adorned with intellectual frills and ruffles, it is also not burdened or stifled by them. This is not meant to portray earthiness. There is hardly any philosophy less earthy than that of Chuang Tze. John Middleton Murray has somewhere said that while Plato was a good poet, Hegel was a bad one. On some such basis, Chuang Tze should be regarded as a great poet perhaps even more than a great philosopher. His philosophy is expressed in exquisite poetic prose in delightful parables, extolling as lofty an ideal of life as any philosophy in the West. There is a certain whimsicality that yet manages to be robust, a kind of finality that is not dogmatism, together with that liveliness and graspability which appeal to the understanding as well as to the emotion of the readers. And yet to those who are accustomed to the geometrical pattern of thought in philosophy, there is even in Chuang Tze a sort of intellectual bleakness or disconnectedness as well. Although deduction and inference must have been at the service of the thinker, there was no attempt to weave ideas into a closely knitted pattern. As a result, there isn't that systematic completeness which is so soothing to the trained mind.

But ideas that are worked out to their systematic completeness are liable to be such that we have to take them or leave them. Through them the author is irrevocably committed. They could not be eclectically taken without having their pattern revoked as well. Here as elsewhere the advantage or disadvantage is not entirely on any one side. It may be, as it has often been claimed, that the world will always be divided between Platonists and Aristotelians, and that probably in a number of senses; but other reasons aside, Aristotle, in spite of Aristotelians, may turn out to be much more short lived than Plato, on account of the former's articulateness; for the more articulate an idea is, the less capable also is it of suggestion. Chinese philosophy is so brief and so inarticulate in terms of the interconnectedness of ideas that its suggestiveness is almost unbounded. The result is that for centuries annotations and in terpretations never stopped. Much original thought was disguised in the cloak of ancient phi-losophies which were never revoked, not yet, peculiar as it may seem, completely accepted. Whether the numerous Neo-Confu-cianisms or Neo-Taoisms in the different periods in Chinese history were recrudescences of the original impulses or not, they were not at any rate repetitions of the original thought. In reality there was no lack of originality, but in appearance there was an absence of what might be called free adventures of thought. We are not here speaking of the practical reasons why Chinese philosophy stuck to the beaten path from certain periods onward. Even long before some philosophies acquired the intolerance of religions, the tendency to clothe original thought in terms of existing philosophies was already in evidence. Whatever mundane reasons there may be, Chinese philosophy in the form in which it was presented was particularly suited to being made use of by original thinkers in that it could gather original thought into its mold or structure almost without any effort.

## III

Perhaps most people at all acquainted with Chinese philosophy will single out the unity of nature and man as its most distinguishing characteristic. The term "nature" is illusive and the more one grapples with it, the more it slips through one's fingers. In the ordinary sense in which it is most often used in our everyday life, it is not adequate to stand for the Chinese term "tian." Perhaps if we mean by it "both nature and nature's God," with emphasis sometimes on the one and sometimes on the other, we have something approaching the Chinese term. This doctrine of the unity of nature and man is a comprehensive one indeed; in its highest and broadest realization, it is a state in which the individual is identified with the Universe through the merging of the subject into the object or vice versa, by sticking to the fundamental identity and obliterating all obvious differences. To express this idea adequately requires a special set of terms which it is not the intention of this article to introduce. We may confine ourselves to the mundane consequences. If the ideal is approached to any appreciable extent, there won't be that unhealthy separation of a self or an ego from his fellow beings on the one hand, nor a demarcation of things human from things natural on the other. The resultant attitude both in Chinese philosophy and in popular thought towards nature in the ordinary sense is quite different from that in the West: Nature is hardly ever something to be resisted, to be struggled against, or to be conquered.

In the West, there is quite a pervading desire to conquer nature. Whether human nature is regarded as being "nasty, brutish and short" or human beings as angelically cherubic babes in the woods, they seem to be always battling against nature, claiming a sort of manifest destiny over the whole natural domain. The result of this attitude is a sort of anthropocentricity on the one hand and acertain malleability of nature on the other. The effect on science is tremendous. One of the incentives to the advancement of science is to acquire the power needed for the conquest of nature. Nature cannot be conquered without an adequate knowledge of it. It can only be made malleable for human beings by our making use of it through our knowledge of its laws. All the engineering marvels, all the medical achievements, in fact, the whole modern industrial civilization, including the armaments, for good or for evil, may be regarded in one sense at least as the conquest of nature by natural means towards a state of affairs desired by human beings. From the point of view which regards nature as something quite apart from humans, the issue is clear— victory so far belongs to the human beings; but from the point of view which regards human beings as having a nature of their own and therefore also problems of mutual adjustment arising out of it, the issue is not so clear—it may even turn out that the victor is also the vanquished.

The separation of nature and man results in a sort of anthropocentricity which is clearly exhibited in Western philosophy. To say that man is the measure of things, or that the essence of a thing is the perception of it, or that understanding makes nature, reveals the attitude that nature is somehow not simply given. In the language of philosophy, there is a certain constructibility in the concept "nature" in which there is free play of intellect; and in the language of everyday life, there is a certain manoeuvrability over nature which human beings either do enjoy or want to enjoy. We are not speaking here of Idealism or Realism which are after all conscious constructions. We are speaking rather of the difference in attitude between China and the West such that while in the latter the world is almost taken for granted to be dichotomized into nature and man, in China it takes quite an effort to detach man from the nature of things. Of course different schools of thought in China interpret nature in different ways, attach to it different degrees of interest or importance; different thinkers of the same school, and the same thinker at different times may also have different notions of nature. But whatever the notion may be, man is not set apart from nature and in opposition to it.

Thus far we have merely touched on the nature of man. The partial conquest of nature in the West seems to have left human nature more assertive than before, and far more dangerous. The attempt to humanize science and industry is an attempt to temper human nature so that the results of science and industry would not be implements of cruelty, slaughter and general destruction. If civilization is to be preserved some such attempts at individual and social control are necessary and calling attention to them is surely a credit to a number of thinkers. We should however be careful about suggesting a conquest. In a sense and a significant one too, nature whether human or non-human has never been conquered. No natural law has ever been nullified or suspended for human benefit and at human will; what has been done is to bring about a state of affairs such that certain natural laws operate against certain others so that the results desired by human beings are sometimes realized. If we try to conquer nature by damming it up, nature will overwhelm us with vengeance; there will soon be leakages here and there and later there will be floods, landslides and explosions. The same is true of human nature. The doctrine of original sin, for instance, results either in psychological subterfuges which make human beings undignified, or else in explosions which make them destructive or anti-social.

While certain internal restraint through philosophy or religion and certain external restraint through law are required in any society and admitted by Chinese philosophy, it does not advocate the frustration of the functioning of the primary instincts. There is as a result something which, for lack of an adequate term, might be described as natural naturalness or contented contentedness. By these terms we do not mean to insinuate that there are fewer instances of cruelty or barbarity in Chinese history than in that of any other nation; evidences of want on destruction, or bloodthirstiness, or of desires running rampant seem to abound in Chinese history as anywhere else. What is meant is rather that there isn't that unnaturalness which Oscar Wilde saw in the naturalness of a Victorian. The Chinese may have something to say against unnaturalness, but they do not make a fuss over being natural on the one hand, and seem to be quite contented with their contentedness on the other. Perhaps in modern times we are accustomed to regarding contentedness as stagnation, as mental laziness, or as spiritual snuggery. The modern point of view is essentially one that encourages revolts against one's self, producing as a byproduct such psychological wear and tear that ease and equanimity in life can no longer be maintained. It is a point of view that is opposed to the one we are trying here to describe. The Chinese are contented with their contentedness, exhibiting ideologically the attitude that each to himself is something that is given, and therefore something to be accepted; to borrow a phrase so admirably employed by F. R. Bradley, each has his "station and life," and in them or it he has his natural dignity. We are not speaking here of the heightened philosophical state attainable only by the few. Although Confucianism allows everybody the possibility to become a saint, failure to do so does not cause any psychological strain. Given this attitude concerning one's station and life, one is not merely at one with nature, but also at one with society.

## IV

It is but a truism that individuals can not live apart from society. Both Greek and Chinese philosophies embody this point of view. From Socrates to Aristotle there was an extraordinary emphasis on the importance of a good political life, and all of those scholars are political thinkers as well as philosophers. The Underlying idea seems to be that the fullest or the most "natural" development of an individual can only be attained through the medium of a just political society. Philosophy touches life just as intimately as literature and perhaps more intimately than a number of other subjects. Those who are born philosophers or those who happen to have philosophy thrust upon them through political or social encroachment upon their liberties are bound to take the above truth as one of the premises or active principles. The attempt to furnish what is now called *Lebensanschauung*, to understand life, to give it its meaning, and to lead a good life was a more primitive incentive to philosophy than what is currently valued as pure understanding. Since a good life was desired, the principle of the inter-relatedness of life and politics led philosophy straight to political thought and philosophers became directly or indirectly connected or concerned with politics.

This tradition wasn't entirely carried on in the West, and one of the reasons why it stopped will partly be the subject of discussion in the next section. But in China the tradition persisted almost to the present day. Quite without exception, Chinese philosopy is at the same time political thought. One might say that Taoism isn't, but saying so is like saying that those who advocate economic laissez faire are not advocating an economic policy or not formulating economic thought. Surely anarchism is political thought even if anarchy sometimes means the absence of government. In political thought, Taoism might be said to be negative in what was advocated when compared with Confucianism. It regarded political measures of the kind advocated by the Confucianists as artificialities which created problems rather than solved them. This negative doctrine was based on something positive. The Taoistic political thought was both equalitarian and libertarian; it might even be said to be both carried to the extreme. With the doctrine of universal relativity carried to the sphere of politics, it was opposed to any kind of imposition of standards and political measures are in one way or another standardizations. Standards there may be, and yet standardizations need not take place, for the standards that are inalterably given in the nature of things need not be imposed at all, while those that need be imposed must inevitably be alien to the situation that gives rise to such impositions. Taoistic political thought was a sort of political laissez faire and laissez aller, it was negative only in the sense of condemning super-imposed political efforts, not in the sense of having entertained no political goal whatsoever. Like Confucianism, Taoism has its political ideal. That ideal might be described as a sort of equalitarian and libertarian bliss to be attained in a kind of Rousseauistic state of nature with perhaps certain European strenuosity edited out of its naturalness.

Compared to Taoism, Confucianism was much more positive in political thought. Confucius himself was a statesman as well as a philosopher. He abstained very wisely from the role of an original thinker, declaring that he was a transmitter of doctrines already entertained and a describer of institutions that existed in a bygone and somewhat golden age. Whether consciously or otherwise, he succeeded in endowing his creative thought with the objectivity of historical continuity. He might have described himself as a Neo-Confucianist, for in giving his thought the impersonality already mentioned, he succeeded also in rendering it uniquely Chinese. Even without political backing it probably could induce Chines ethought to follow its trail, and with political backing it easily molded subsequent thought into its own pattern. That pattern is both philosophy and political thought woven into an organic whole in which politics and ethics are inseparable and in terms of which the man and his station and life are also united. The unity of nature and man is also a unity of ethics and politics, of the individual and the society.

Philosophy and political thought may be linked up in many different ways. One may erect a metaphysical system and deduce from it certain principles concerning politics, or one may plunge into politics and indulge in political thought which has no systematic bearing with his philosophy. Political thought may be internal to a philosophical system and external to the philosopher, or internal to the philosopher, but external to his philosophy. In either case, there is a sort of dislocation; either philosophy ceases to be politically potent, or political thought loses its philosophical foundation. British Hegelianism, for instance, furnished a political thought internal to the philosophical system, but so external to the philosophers, with the exception of T. H. Green, that neither it nor they could be said to have exerted any influence on English politics.

Confucianist political thought was in ternal both to the philosopher and his philosophy. Through the doctrine that internal saintliness or sagacity could be externalized into enlightened statecraft, every philosopher felt himself to be a potential statesman. It was in statecraft that one's Philosophical ideals found their broadest realization. Since Confucianism has become a sort of unwritten constitution in China, the country has been governed more by flexible social control than by rigid legal discipline; and in such a body politic, the eminent philosopher and teacher was at least as much as, if not more of, an unofficial statesman, as a prominent lawyer in a country that is predominantly governed by law. A prominent Confucianist philosopher was a sort of uncrowned king or an uncommissioned minister of state, if not during his life, at least posthumously, for it was he who shaped and fashioned the Zeitgeist in terms of which life in any society was more or less sustained. It was thus that Chinese philosophers were sometimes said to have changed the customs and manners of the land, and it was thus that Chinese philosophy and political thought were significantly woven into a single organic pattern.

## V

The unity of philosophy and politics lies partly at any rate in the philosopher. Chinese philosophers until very recent times were quite different from Western philosophers of today. They belonged to the class of Socrates and Plato. In his *Soliloquies* in England, George Santayana declared with some vehemence and more than a trace of protestation that he was a modern Socrates. Of all the present day philosophers, he might indeed be singled out as a cultural influence of more than a technical significance, having gone through and beyond the technicalities of philosophy and stepped into the realm of humane letters. But frankly, there can be no more modern Socrates any more than there can be a modern Aristotle. Ever since Herbert Spencer, we have learned to be wise in checking our ambition to unify the different branches of knowledge through the medium of a single scholar. There is so much technique developed in each branch of knowledge that it is well nigh impossible for the Underlings that we are to be the masters of them all. We regret the passing of Socrateses. A living encyclopedia may bring forth a certain unity to knowledge which may be efficacious towards its further advancement, but since knowledge could be nibbled at piecemeal and improved or advanced through the present method of the division of labor, the loss of such an unity need not be regretted. In some sense, the passing of Socrateses is much more regrettable.

Not only is there a division of labor in the modern pursuit of knowledge, there is also that trained detachment or externalization. One of the fundamental tenets in the modern scientific procedure is to detach the researcher from the object of his research, and this can only be done by cultivating his emotion for objective truth and making it predominate over what other emotions he may happen to have concerning his researches. Obviously one cannot get rid of one's emotions, not even a scientist, but if one is trained to let one's emotion for objective truth dominate over his other emotions in his researches, one has already acquired the detachment needed for scientific research. In accordance with this procedure the modern philosopher becomes more or less detached from his philosophy. He reasons, he argues, but he hardly ever preaches. Together with the division of labor, the tendency towards detachment makes him a detached logician, for a detached epistemologist, or a detached metaphysician. Philosophers in former days were never professional. The emergence of professional philosophers may have done some service to philosophy, but it seems to have also killed something in the philosopher. He knows philosophy, but he does not live it.

That something is gained in philosophy after this method of approach is employed, there is no doubt. We do know more of the problems of each branch of philosophy than we did before. Although the personality of the philosopher cannot as yet be entirely divorced from his philosophy, a basis for objectivity is achieved which makes philosophy much more capable of cumulative effort than it ever was before. The advance in this direction is made possible by the improvements in the tools of expression: a kind of technique of articulation is being developed which cannot be ignored. Anyone may still enjoy the privilege of adopting any philosophy suited to his nature or pre-dispositions, but he can hardly express his ideas in any way he wants. Nor is the gain limited to philosophy; the philosopher has also gained an ideal of detachment. It might be described as a sort of sweet skepticism in which, to use familiar terms, Hebraic sweetness is seasoned with Hellenic light and Hellenic light is tempered with Hebraic sweetness. Anyone who is fortunate enough to approach this ideal will acquire the kind of rare charm in which skepticism doesn't make him cynical, nor does sweetness made him effusingly or obtrusively good. He will not be militantly virtuous and may therefore lose that social or sociological efficacy of function expected of him, but considering the evil that militantly good people may do, he is bound to be a negative asset and a positive value. The ideal is difficult of attainment. In being detached and externalized philosophy becomes a rather tortuous and thorny path; it has become so strewn with technicalities that their mastery requires time, training and a certain academic single-mindedness and before these are mastered one might lose one's way or else wither away in the process. Even when he succeeds to any extent, he is hardly a modern Socrates.

Chinese philosophers were all of them different grades of Socrateses. This was so because ethics, politics, reflective thinking and knowledge were unified in the philosophers; in him, knowledge and virtue were one and inseparable. His philosophy required that he lived it, he was himself its vehicle. To live in accordance with his philosophical convictions was part of his philosophy. It was his business to school himself continually and persistently to that pure experience in which selfishness or egocentricity was transcended so that he would be one with the universe. Obviously this process of schooling could not be stopped, for stopping it would mean the emergence of his ego and the loss of his universe. Hence cognitively he was eternally groping, and conatively, he was eternally behaving or trying to behave. Since these could not be separated, in him you have synthetically the "philosopher" in the original sense. Like Socrates, he did not keep office hours with his philosophy. Neither was he a dusty musty closeted philosopher sitting in a chair on the periphery of life. With him, philosophy was hardly ever merely a pattern of ideas exhibited for human understanding, but also at the same time a system of precepts internal to the conduct of the philosopher and in extreme cases it might even be said to be his biography. We are not speaking of the calibre of the philosopher—he might be second rate; or of the quality of his philosophy—it might not be tenable; we are speaking of the unity of the philosopher with his philosophy, The separation of these has changed the social value of philosophy and deprived the world of one kind of colorfulness.

# Philosophy and Life [*]

## I

It is not merely in China that philosopers have been put on the defence from the point of view of the ever growing irrelevancy of philosophy to life. The philosophers' Conference in the Spring of last year indicated that the problem has finally succeeded in attracting general attention in America. It seems however that if there is any solution to the problem, it does not lie merely with the professional philosophers. In the following pages we shall urge that the professional philosophers are not alone to blame, that the organization of and for knowledge is unsuited towards a discriminating life and that it is dangerous to the ideals of democracy.

The reason why philosophy is singled out for attack lies chiefly in the comparison between its present status and its ancient and honorable history. Philosophy used to deal with the fundamental problems of life and philosophers had often been

---

[*] 此文是作者 1943—1944 年访问美国期间撰写的，生前未发表，标题为编者所加。——编者注

great masters, fountains of not merely knowledge but also of wisdom, to whom the less gifted looked for guidance and light. Socrates, Plato and Aristotle were not merely the walking encyclopedias of their time, they were also its statesmen, its priests, its columnists and its radio commentators combined. In China the discrepancy between the ancient and present day philosophers is perhaps even more striking. The philosophers used to occupy a position more significant if not more powerful than that of the great lawyers in American history in times of peace, and in times of emergency they had even appeared as Catos in the defense of their dynasty or their fatherland. The question arises naturally as to what the present day philosophers are doing to meet the needs of an essentially medieval country invaded by a ruthless enemy, impoverished and almost disorganized by seven years of modern warfare. The comparision renders philosophy a natural target for disatisfaction.

Two points might be briefly considered, one of them concerning the scope of philosophy and the other its nature. The fact that the term philosophy has changed its scope is known to everybody and yet the consequencies of such a change do not seem to have been equally borne in mind. Philosophy has become a sort of impoverished country family with its estate partitioned into small lots managed by city agents. What is known as philosophy that is taught in the universities is merely the scanty lot left to the county seat. Shorn of its ancient glory and splender, it is yet on the whole efficiently managed. If one takes philosophy in the sense of the original property including the lots entrusted to city agents, it hasn't lost its relevancy to current problems nor has it failed to meet national emergencies. Washington D. C. represents the greatest concentration of philosophy, if we take it in this wide sense. The great master has indeed disappeared being split into a large number of experts who should nevertheless be known as philosophers. But if we take philosophy in the narrow sense, it is doubtful whether it has ever been potent in shaping the destinies of man.

Perhaps more relevant to our point is that philosophizing has changed its nature. A sort of objective research has taken place rendering the approach to philosophy more closely allied to science than to religion. Skepticism seems to be the key note to the new approach and the most important tenet is to detach the researcher from the object of his research or at any rate to relegate him as much as possible to an irrelevant background. It is easily seen that with this approach there is hardly any principle unconditionally accepted and none unswervingly adhered to by any group of philosophers. Dogma disappears and with its disappearance philosophy ceases to furnish life with any motive force. It does not urge people to do anything, it hardly ever advocates, and if it insists upon the acceptance of certain propositions, it does so with discursive argumentation rather than peremptory indoctrination. If a philosopher advocates any doctrine militantly, it is not philosophy that is motivating him, it is rather the priest or the politician or the social reformer. Academic philosophy has ceased to be a moral force, in the sense, let's say, of Confusianism, and in making whatever training that is required more and more technical, it has also become less and less of an educational discipline.

Whether modern philosophy is useful or not depends upon the view as to what kind of use is to be made out of it. The significant fact is not that epistemology dominates philosophy, it is rather that the whole field of philosophy is organized for understanding of knowledge. Ethics does not teach students to be good, it teaches them to understand goodness; esthetics does not teach students to appreciate the beautiful, it teaches them to understand beauty. Groham Wallas should be sympathized with for his solitude in concerning himself with the art of thinking, for the courses on logic at present supply the students with the knowledge of validity rather than train them for valid thinking or thought. If something is regrettably lost, something is also distinctly gained. The modern approach to philosophy renders it more tangible than before as well as more capable of cumulative effort, and with it knowledge in philosophy is capable of compound interest. Knowledge in philosophy can be willed to posterity whereas philosophical experience or insight can not. It can not be denied that in being organized for understanding and knowledge, philosophy has had a steady progress and as knowledge is always useful whether directly or indirectly, philosophy can not fail to be useful even though its usefulness is transfered to a sphere different from what we expect it to be if we have in mind the example of philosophy in the past.

Nevertheless something is regrettably lost. In being thus organized for knowledge, philosophy has become even for those who philosophize a mere aspect in life, an absorbing profession during office hours perhaps, but nonetheless an aspect detached from life in general. The symthetic unity of the philosopher with the man seems to have disappeared. One gets the impression that among scores of professors of philosophy, there is hardly a single philosopher. In becoming the monopoly of a few experts, philosophy has ceased to be a free commodity either in the rough and tumble of the market or in the politeness and gentility of society tea parties. The old earnestness of purpose in philosophy has been replaced by a kind of skillfulness in the manipulation of ideas and whatever philosophical impulse there is in the layman, it is no longer satisfied by technical philosophy. For him philosophy becomes as shrouded in mystery as science, but unlike science its usefulness is not evident in terms of concrete achievements. Is there any reason why philosophy should take up its present trend? There are a large number of reasons, but we shall take up only one of them.

## II

In taking up its present trend, philosophy is rumply following the example of almost every branch of study. Almost all studies are at present organized for efficiency and in being so organized they are inevitably accompanied by certain characteristics. In the first place there is on the whole a tendency towards further and further subdivision so that a larger and larger number of scholars become experts in narrower and narrower fields of knowledge. Each tiny subdivision becomes a technical retreat and the expert comfortblaly settled in it can not be expected to be the master of a whole branch of study. Great masters have disappered in natural sciences, they are disappearing in economies and sociology, and in the sphere of philosophy there will soon be the logician, the epistemologist, the esthetician, etc., instead of the philosopher. In the second place, in order to obtain results, scholars have to detach themselves as much as possible from the object of their studies. While the attitude is admirable from the point of view of obtaining reliable knowledge or information, it is liable to render the result of the study external to the student. His study is indeed a vital element in his profession, but whether or not it is equally a vital element in his life depends upon whether or not his profession absorbs his life. If it does, he is a single tracked man with a large number of other aspects of life submerged or undeveloped or brushed aside; and if it doesn't, his study becomes external to his life. Other characteristics may be mentioned, but these two alone are sufficient to indicate the flavour of our present day scholarship. What is even more important is that these characteristics act and react upon each other to accelerate the direction in which our knowledge is tending for the more the studies are sub-divided, the more they are externalized, and the more they are externalized the more minute the subdivisions also become.

These characteristics are the direct results of organizing studies on the basis of efficiency and entirely for the advancement of knowledge. There was a time when studies were not so organized, when the educated were almost always the cultural, some of them even living full lives in which a multiplicity of impulses found their natural play. There used to be scholars in China who didn't care to pass examinations and even during the last century in England there were schloars who didn't bother to write books. For them it was quite sufficient merely to have lived a life of discrimination. It is true that under the social and economic conditions then prevailing, few could indulge in any such ideal. But then now that the conditions are improved why not extend the ideal to the masses of people? The reason why such an ideal can not be seriously entertained lies in the fact that for the individual at present, it has no survival value. In a highly industrialized and economically competitive community, each has a function to perform and efficiency in its performance enables and entitles him to survived. The existance of the idle rich should not blind us to the extent as to minimize the prevalence of this tendency toward greater and greater efficiency. It is this tendency that is ultimately responsible for the remarkable strength of the industrial powers exhibited in the present crisis. If this tendency is so prevalent in other spheres of life, we can hardly expect it to be absent in the realm of scholarship and studies.

There is unfortunately an additional reason. Scholarship used to be in China at least an individual and almost private affair. It did not require much property to indulge in, and while scholars constituted a class or a social and political status, scholarship was not a profession. Poverty of course did diminish the possible number of scholars, but those who were so fortunate as to possess the minimum amount of wealth could become scholars and what is more important they themselves owned the paraphernalia with which they worked. In this respect they were somewhat like the artisans of medieval Europe. They didn't have to justify themselves socially or politically. With industrialization and cooporate organization of institutions for scholarship, the paraphernalia for studies have been taken away from the scholars just as with industrialization the instruments or tools have been taken away from the workers. Scientists depend almost entirely at present upon public institutions and while in Humanities one may still indulge in private research if one happens to be comparatively wealthy, the chance for one's doing so is getting shimmer and shimmer everyday. Scholars have become employees and in being paid for their work are constantly put on the defense unless they show reasons continuously why they should be so employed. Scholarship has become professionalized and it is scholars' business to produce knowledge. The emergence of professional tennis players seemed to have aroused both resentment and resistence, but the emergence of professional scholars has take place unheralded and unsung on the one hand and unresisted and uncondemned on the other. Even philosophy can hardly escape professionalized and philosophers are now taken to task as to what kind of product they are issuing to the general public. Philosophers may suffer in comparison with the scholars in the other branches of knowledge, but both suffer from the domination by the same tendency.

Let it be thoroughly understood that we are not here condemning the tendency discribed above. From the point of view gaining knowledge it should be highly praised. Knowledge is useful directly or indirectly and what is even more significant, it is power. It is power whether we use it in our struggle against nature or merely against other men. Nor is it irrelevant to life; it is probably the most potent factor in improving the conditions under which we live and to use an old phrase it is probably the most effective instrument in hindering whatever natural hinderances there may be to the maintainence of the conditions of a desirable life. What is maintained is rather that however relevant knowledge may be to the conditions of life, it is not, or at any rate has ceased to be, a vital element in the main spring of our actual living. It is somewhat like money which assumes different roles to different people depending on whether it is in the hands of the objectly poor or fabulously rich. In the hands of the former it may remove certain undesirable conditions of life, while in the hands of the latters it need not be conducive to a more desirable mood of living. Like money again, knowledge is a sort of currency with which desires and passions are satisfied, and a wealth of knowledge need not raise the quality of living.

Nor are we belittling science. We are not suggesting that those in a limitation to the applicability of scientific method; it may very well be that anything under the sun could be scientifically studied. Nor are we saying that the training involved is useless to the general business of living; it undoubtedly is especially from the point of view that the scientific attitude may be carried over to the other spheres of life. What is maintained is that no matter how much we know of the processes of life in terms of scientific concepts, we still have to live our lives as individual and social experiences with the paticular endowment that is given to us. A thorough knowledge of nutrition may enable a person to choose the food that is good for his health, but it does not necessarily enable him to prefer what is wholesome to what is tasty. A thorough knowledge of sex certainly does not substitute for sexual experience, it is extremely doubtful whether experts on sex are ever expert lovers. A drunkard who doesn't know that alchohol is bad for him is merely miserable when he is dead drunk, he needn't be unhappy; but if he knows that alchohol is bad for him and yet can not resist it, he is a tragedy when he succumbs to alchohol. It is doubtful whether knowledge by itself had ever been a directing influence; if ever it was, it is no longer so for most people; for them it is a commodity like tooth brush and like tooth brush it is liable to be hung up whenever it is not in use. Whether knowledge in some other sense is virture or not and the Greeks claimed it was we needn't try to ascertain, knowledge as

it has come to be today is not a virture. It is too neutral to influence our preferences or tastes, too properly non-committal to enable us to pass on issues outside of its proper sphere, too external
to enable us to act on our beliefs, and too impotent to furnish us
with any, and instead of being the master or co-worker of
emotions and passions, it has become their slave.

# III

With the exception of Germany, the highly industrialized
countries were also democracies. Democracies have been economically imperialistic, but they have not been in recent years at any
rate blatant military aggressors. If the world is to be made safe for
democracy, democracy should be safe for the world as well as for
its own citizens. Since the citizens constitute the ultimate
sovereign of democracy, it is essential that they themselves
should be free, independent and discriminating individuals. In
order that they may not be blindly led, they should live discriminating lives rather than existas mere lubricated parts of well oiled
machines. Since the majority rules, it is essential that majority
decision represents discriminating choice rather than blind impulse. If power politics is to be condemned in international relations, it should be equally so within a nation or a state. If power
politics in international nations leaves the weak states the helpless
spoils of the strong, power politics within a nation or a state
leaves the citizens identified with the special interests practically

without any voice in their government. Internal politics is indeed more fundemental, for if political action within a state represents the resultant force of the pull and push of special interests, there is no guarantee that they will not pull and push beyond the national boundaries. In order to make democracy safe for the world, it should be made safe for its own citizens. The ideal of democracy can only be achieved by having free independent and discriminating citizens who are eternally vigilant over their public duties. It imposes a most strenuous duty on the common man, but for those who believe in democracy, the responsibility assumed by them is well worth their while for it is the only one compatible with the dignity of being human.

In totalitarian countries some special ideology is imposed on all people as that they are whipped into a single purpose resulting in the kind of uniformity of behavior desired by the accepted leader or oligarchy. A certain amount of uniformity of behavior is necessary for any nation. Most nations depend for it upon a common language, a common cultural pattern or historical heritage, as well as upon blood ties. Modern industry contributes to it so subtly that a certain amount of uniformity of behavior is achieved without being suspected that it is imposed, since it is not consciously imposed by a person or a group of persons. In America, for example, industry is probably the greatest unifying force. Industrial efficiency contributes to political efficacy, measures that are difficult to be carried out in China for instance are easily enforced in America. Industrial power is also military power. By itself it is merely military power that is economically imperialistic, but not militarily aggressive, so that it is defensive not offensive military power. It has thus far saved the democracies from being vanquished in war, and although it has enabled them to be economically imperialistic, it has made them safe neighbors compared to the totalitarian powers. Back in the days of 1940 when the Nazis overrun Holland, Belgium and France, some people in China felt that democracies were woefully weak and in efficient. They were indeed vulnerable and when quick decisions were to be made, they certainly were inadequate. Not many of us know that the power of democracies is latent and when not put to the test not actual; but once the decision is made, the whole apparatus of military action is set up, power becomes phenomenally evident. But power is always dangerous; it could be used for good and evil alike; and whether it is used one way or another depends upon the person or persons who wields it.

We are accustomed to couple industry with democracy without suspecting that along certain lines of development, they may turn out to be compatible with each other. What is needed for the citizens of a democracy is the independant and discriminating individual, and what is needed for the workers of any industry is the efficient and mechanically minded expert. Instead of using the terms spiritual and material, let us employ the terms human and mechanical. Democracy requires the human and industry the mechanical. If everything is industrialized or even carried with the industrial spirit behind it, the result may be the destruction of much if not all that is human. Industrialize religion and we may indeed gain imposing churches and even expert preachers, what may also be lost is the old humble spiritual haven and the intimate kind of moral influence. Industralize our creative impulses, we may indeed aim expert craftsmanship, but then we may lose the genuine artist. The industrial method could be applied to any sphere and whenever it is applied without any ameliorating influence, some measurable criterion will be adopted and in terms of that criterion efficiency will be increased and men who are active in that field will become more and more expert as well as mechanically minded. Add competitive economy to industry, and we can hardly excape baneful results. If one works efficiently for eight hours every weekday, the desire to spend the Sunday efficiently is almost irresistable. A sort of gyroscopic activity results, and the free and easy exchange of ideas and feelings, the desire to be whimsical, or to cope with the imponderables, or merely to be lazy will be easily censored off by the desire to fill the hours of leisure with a maximum of activity, and a minimum of adventure in feeling or in thought. The expert in one sphere is liable to be an igfloramus in other spheres and the mechanically minded may be as helpless as a new born babe when confronted with novel human situations. It is difficult to expect people so conditioned to react alertly and discriminatingly to the complicated internal and international politics and when any important decision is to be made, they are liable to make it at the dictates of their profession or their industrial interests. The democratic ideal may be defeated even in a democracy.

These are quite a few astounding assumptions probably unconsciously held by people in the advanced democracies. Probably very few people believe in the exsistence of the economic man, very few believe without qualification the doctrine of economic determinism and yet an enormous number of persons somehow believe or at least act as if they do believe that economic emancipation is a panacea for all social and political evils. It would be for the economic man, but for most people of flesh and blood the solution of economic problems leaves a large number of other problems unsolved. Probably very few people regard human beings as thinking or knowing machines, and yet the assumption that if people only know what to do and how to do things, all their problems would also be solved. For the thinking or knowing machines, knowledge of solutions would indeed dissolve problems before hand so that they do not even emerge as problems, but for human beings with their passions and desires, their loves and hatreds, hopes and fears, and probably a large assortment of complexes, the acquisition of knowledge not only need not solve problems, it may even render them worse confounded than before. There is at present current in the West a new notion of democracy, a sort of state socialism without its old name, whereby the government gathers enormous powers to better the living conditions of the majority of its citizens; it is indeed an admirable notion of a new democracy to be put in practice within the frame of the old; but to urge it upon the rest of mankind who are without democratic institutions is dangerous, for apart from the old political democracy, state socialism would be totalitarianism, and may even turn out to be facism. Some of the Westerners who are now dissatisfied with the National goverment in China on the ground that it is not democratic seem to have switched their sympathy to the Communist set up without realizing that if one is undemocratic as also is the other and of the two the communistic set up is by far the more totalitarian. There seems to be here a preference for the new democracy even in the absence of the old. The assumption's underlying the enthusiasm of the advocates of this new democracy seems to be that human nature is intrinsically good, a proposition which most of the advocates wouldn't accept. Just as a wealthy man may be a corrupt citizen, an intelligent man a depraved animal as Rausseau long ago pointed out, so the leaders of the new democracy may not be public spirited if there are no existing political institutions that condition or compel them to be. More in a democracy than in any other form of government or state, the problem of the human material can not be by-passed.

## IV

While the advancement and requisition of knowledge may be industrialized with advantage, education shouldn't be. Knowledge has become specific and pragmatical, and so far as its advancement and acquisition are concerned, they may properly be made the output of large scale production. Foundations, research institutes and graduate schools may all be looked upon as knowledge advancing industries. On the whole these have been rather efficient, and so long as the criterion continues to be the search for and the attainment of truth, the quality of the products need not deteriorate. The desire for social or political justification for the exsistence of their industries may operate to the detriment of the adopted criterions, but this is a contingency whith need not be entered into in the present connection. The industrialization of knowledge advancement merely means the professionalization of the employees, not their product; knowledge can still be easily marketed for general public use. The marketing of knowledge is indeed a part of education, but it certainly is not equivalent to it. The present method of lecturing to large classes in colleges and universities, of taking notes, of examinations, of accumulating credits, etc., seems to have confounded education with the marketing of knowledge. Education is not merely the preparation of the young for the various vocations of life, it is rather to prepare them to be independent, discriminating, and human individuals. Again the marketing of knowlege could be industrialized with profit and colleges and universities may be regarded at best partly as such industries. There is no objection to this industrialization provided it is not taken to be the whole of education, since in education more than specialized and pragmatized knowledge is involved. The latter may be instrumental for providing the means of earning one's livelihood, it is not and has not been equally germane to the direction and the colors and flavors of ons's life. Education is essentially concerned with the development of the individual; its negative purpose is to prevent the young from being anti-social, and its positive purpose is to bring out to the fullest fruition whatever there is in the individual. It shouldn't be industrialized and strictly speaking it can not be, since there can not be mass production of individuals. Knowledge has become instrument or the servant to desires and passions, and the more we identify the dissociation of knowledge with education, the more likely we are also to leave desires and passions primitive and untutored and with knowledge as their instrument for satisfaction, also more rampant than in the days of blessed ignorance. The main purpose of education is to mould character, to refine away crudities so that strength may be retained, to establish equilibrium among conflicting propensities, to cultivate certain proclivities so that others might be held in check, to modify whatever nature there is by nurture so that the modified nature is cultured and civilized. A system of values must be consciously accepted and a set of beliefs must be consciously avowed. It is not here urged that education should impose values or instil beliefs. But it certainly should discriminate them, it should encourage the young to be conscious of their own predilections in order to articulate what their values and beliefs are likely to be and to convince them that these are not things to be ashamed of. When one is ashamed of his values and beliefs, one either returns to primitive animalism or succumbs to psychological complexes. The

kind of skepticism necessary and conducive to the research of veridical knowledge should be confined to the realm of thought and
ideas concerning knowledge if it is carried over to the realm of
values and beliefs, it merely renders a person either an emotional
anarchy or emotionally at war with his own intellect. A large
number of the generation growing out of the first world war were
emotional anarchies, to them life at best was merely "amusing",
and a world dominated by "amusing" people is the kinds that
makes some people, such as Henry Adams, shudder and look to
the unity of the 13th century for comfort. We are not arguing for any
specific kind of unity, what we are insisting upon is that people
should be educated towards certain serenity and unashamedness
in avowing their values and beliefs for these are after all the motivating influence in their lives. Individuals who are emotional
anarchies however efficient they may be in their chosen
professions are more or less liabilities to a democracy or with
them as citizens great decisions are either made haphazardly or
else not made at all.

A thorough going liberal education is needed. There should
be character building accompanied by the discrimination of
values and unashamed avowal of beliefs. The discrimination of
knowledge remains necessary and for their purposes the prevailing
system of lectures should be continued. There should be supplemented by free, informal and yet serious discussion of ideals, beliefs, values, desires, preferences, hidden assumptions, loves
and hatreds, likes and dislikes; professors who are engaged in

education and not exclusively in the dissimilation of knowledge should have constant contact with the students to exemplify in actual living, whether comformably or otherwise, whether successfully or unsuccessfully, what they articulate in terms of their own Lebensanschauung Universities which have grown big for the purpose of marketing knowledge, efficiently and on a large scale should establish a large number of small colleges with the separate tutors for the purpose of leading the young through the slow process of learning to be human. All the liberal arts should be brought to bear on the formative young characters just as all sorts of veridical knowledge should be brought to bear on the formative young minds. No consideration of expense should be regarded as relevant. it must be insisted upon that no matter what one intends to be, whether an engineer or a doctor, a banker or a longshoreman, a musician or a physicist, the serene dignity, the serious business as well as the spontaneous playfulness of being human and an individual has priority over all the other special interests. There seems to be a wide spread impatience with idea of sweetness and light, perhaps on the score that it is anaemic, wayward in regard to practical measures, hedgingly discoursive concerning principles and totally unrealistic in a thoroughly realistic world. Whether the above evaluation of the idea is correct or not, we need not attempt to ascertain; for the alleged equalities are only vices to racism, they are virtures to a democracy. It is only through the combination of sweetness with light that we may attain to the full height of being human and become masters of our own passions and desires so that knowledge and power may not be disastrously employed. It is only then that human beings become safe to themselves.

# A Freeman's Task [*]

## I

A large number of philosophers in both England and America had allowed philosophy to be so divorced from life that they found themselves in a quandary. Thus in 1943 when the second world war was already won in the East, but still hung in precarious balance in the West, some American philosophers finding themselves powerless in affecting the issue either one way or another also found themselves with the question whether after all their philosophy wasn't socially superfluous. Sophisticated to the extreme theoretically, they found their practical, efforts vain beatings in the bush and their life and station quite untenable. There was a noticible strand of pessimism. I remember talking to Prof. C. I. Lewis about it, and his arguments to the contrary, though intended to be comforting, were by no means effective.

This strand of pessimism wasn't new then. More than 60 years ago, A. J. Balfour spoke of man going into the pit and per-

---

[*] 本文是作者 1957 年 7 月在华沙国际哲学会议上的发言。——编者注

ishing, of the earth tideless and inert, no longer tolerating the race which has for a moment disturbed its solitude, and of that dear old consciousness which has broken the contented silence of the universe being finally put to rest. Temperamentally cold and almost icy, Balfour was judged by some to be merely lonely and aloof, not pessimistic. I myself do not share this opinion. Bertrand Russell was hardly ever cold temperamentally, but he it was who once developed a passionate defiance against the fate of the Solar System and the supposed tyranny of a universe that was yet admittedly unconscious. Amazing! Was it after all the inert matter with which Balfour was disdainfully concerned? Was it this which Russell was so excited about emotionally? Might it not be after all the awakened masses in the great society that were the object of their attention? Was their bifurcation of the world limited to man and nature? Might it not be extended to classes and masses? Long before Balfour wrote the Foundations of Belief, it had been said of the machine: Faster and faster, our iron master, the thing we made now drives. The machine is undoubtedly a piece of matter, but we now know definitely that the driving is a question of political economy, not of nature. Since, however, economics was sometimes mistaken for nature, might it not he that nature was unwittingly used also to cover economics? Might it not be that this pessimism concerning nature was only a disguise for a pessimism concerning social and economic developments which philosophers desire to shape but with which their philosophy rendered them powerless to deal?

Surely there is nothing wrong with the desire just mentioned. Philosophers live in an actual world no less than doctors and lawyers, artists and engineers. They are faced with problems that demand solution, and besides the trivialities of their everyday life, they are as a matter of fact woven into the fabric of the body politic and in whatever push and pull, stress and strain they participate, they are bound to contribute, or to retard, whether consciously or not, towards the general tendencies of political and social development. They may approve or disapprove of these general tendencies, but the fact that they have helped to mould them either in one way or another seems to be undeniable. And yet subjectively they feel that their training and their profession do not help them to participate in the affairs of the world as they should. What they actually did, they fail to be articulate about as philosophers, and in what they desire to do as philosophers, their philosophy fails to satisfy them. They live in the world, but their philosophy is in some obvious and direct sense out of it. In bifurcating the world in various ways, they have also set their own lives asunder.

The trouble seems to lie with philosophy. In academic western philosophy since Descartes or perhaps even earlier, there was an attempt to cramp realities into a geometrical or Euclidean pattern of thought. Realities, however, are stubborn, and nobody has up to the present succeeded in cramping them. This failure which ought to have been a lesson to philosophers has become instead a challenge. Clever people have been attracted to such a challenge and philosophy instead of being a science of the most general laws of nature, society and human thought, has become a study of concepts in their deductive fruitfulness and a manipulation of them in terms of their deductive connections. The systems that spring up may or may not be entirely deductive in form, but the spirit behind them is deduction, and the operation required is the manipulation of concepts in terms of other concepts. Instead of searching for philosophical truth, philosophers become satisfied with systematic consistency or coherence. Public forum philosophizing can not be swept away, being a genuine attempt to answer questions of public interest, but it can be ruled out as being unacademic and strange as it may seem, also as being "unphilosophical". What was vigorous, living and fruitful has been toned down and ironed out into threadbare conceptual web spinning in unfrequented academic corners; it can no longer take place in Hyde Park or Union Square.

The primary function of concepts is to reflect the world and the objective things in it, of their essences, their necessary relations and connections, in a word, of their laws. The valid systems of concepts are themselves the veridical reflections of different kinds of realities. This is what science is and what scientific philosophy ought to be, and in reflecting the objective world veridically, scientific philosophy enables us to deal with it effectively. Preferring consistency to truth, western philosophy at present has lost its effectiveness. Ever since Hume, matters of fact and matters of theory have been so divorced that necessity is denied to the former and concreteness the latter. Facts become merely stuffy and theory, to those given to conceptual manipulation, increasingly vacuous. In order to avoid bumping against inconvenient facts, theorizing has soured up into thin air. Thus in 1932, while in Cambridge, England, I was surprised to find that in the hands of Professor Moore, philosophy had become a study of language. But even this seemed unsatisfactory to some. Language is an objective fact, it has the kind of stubbornness characteristic of other realities, and the study of it for some philosophers is too empirical to be the core of philosophy. Further abstractions are required and when one reaches the formation and transformation of symbolic conventions, one has almost completely divorced philosophy from life. The philosopher has left the man himself almost completely.

Exceptions are only too few. Bertrand Russell the man seems to have survived Bertrand Russell the philosopher. The following passage is refreshing indeed:

"The purpose of words, though philosophers seem to forget this simple fact, is to deal with matters other than words. If I go into a restaurant and order dinner, I do not want my words to fit into a system with other words, but to bring about the presence of food... The verbalist theories of some modern philosophers forget the homely practical purposes of everyday words and lose themselves in a neo-neo-Platonic mysticism. I seem to hear them saying ' in the beginning was the word', not 'in the beginning was what the word means.'

The language is not what Prof. Moore would have been satisfied with, but the idea expressed is perfectly sane. There is in Russell the man something healthily rugged which Russell the philosopher has not been able to polish away, and it is undoubtedly this that enables him to deal with great issues of the world such as the questions of war or peace."

Others are less fortunate. Santayana once proclaimed himself a modern Socrates, but surely he wasn't, and I venture to suggest, he could never be. One can't help feeling that himself a mere concentration of an infinity of essences, he ought to have been nowhere in space and time, it was probably the fallacy of simple location that interpreted his whereabouts as being somewhere in the neighborhood of Rome during the second world war, and I suspect that the heavy cannonading around Rome did not detach him from his Augustine or his Lucretius. There was nothing conative in him whatsoever, with all his sweetness and all his light. He was sweet enough not to regard the world as a tale told by an idiot, he appreciated whatever that was good and beautiful, but promenading on the seashore in evening dress with all his esthetic sensitiveness did not enable him to experience the joie de vivre in swimming, whether or not it prepared him to enjoy more exquisitely the glories of a sunset. He was philosophically too patent leathered and too silk-hatted to mix with the rough and tumble, he was too much the essence of respectability to be a modern Socrates.

What about pragmatism? The question is meant to imply a tautology, but the fact is that pragmatism is not pragmatic to those with a sense of social responsibility. I have to point out that pragmatism is the philosophy of American imperialism, it rose with the rise of American monopoly in the seventies and eighties of the last century. Some of you will differ with me violently, but it can not be denied that pragmatism is the voice of Empire building, of manifest Destiny, of the Big Stick and of the present "position of force". It is historically conditioned and historians of philosophy have already done it justice. In the present context however the question is whether for the academic man with a sense of social responsibility, pragmatism is a better guide to practice than the other academic schools of philosophy. The answer is that it fares no better. We are not concerned with the imperialists here, but with philosophers. Certainly not all philosophers are imperialists. If pragmatism were practically efficacious to Professor Lewis, he would have been more effective in relieving those professors of their strand of pessimism in 1943. I do not know William James personally. I feel however that there were two sides to him, the shrewd man of affairs and the somewhat mystic teacher of philosophy. I am inclined to feel that the mystic teacher of philosophy would have been pained upon being told that his philosophy linked him with Mussolini.

The above is very sketchy. Much might be said, but more

needn't be. Different as the above mentioned schools are, they all point to one thing: the philosopher is bound to be ill at ease with his own philosophy when it leaves him helpless in his dealings with the problems of life.

Objectively philosophers do play a very important part in society. They contribute towards maintaining the status quo or else changing it, either expediting social advance or else clogging its way. There is no time when the role philosophy played was more apparent than at present, there is no time when it was more real. The effects of negative doctrines are easily overlooked, Objectivism for instance, especially in the form of avoiding "metaphysics" at any cost, seems to be a negative doctrine. In affirming the equality of all point of view, it asserts none of them, but in asserting no point of view, it leaves the traditional, the familiar and current doctrine in actual, though not theoretical, predominance. The apparent ineffectiveness of some of the present day philosophies is exactly the real effectiveness of some of the present day philosophers in the role they play in society, namely, by retarding its progress. The philosophy they propound, apparently ineffective, is no less important than the laws legislators write or the songs poets sing.

But subjectively some philosophers in America and England do have a sense of futility, and the strand of pessimism which began more than half a century ago is preserved in various degrees to the present day. The problem with philosophers is whether we continue to ignore society, serve blindly those whose interests are at war with the welfare of the people, or study social problems, make our philosophies articulate on questions of social development and serve the people consciously and directly. If the former, a sense of futility can not be avoided, since we would feel that we are, slavishly serving something which we do not know what. But if the latter, then we are our own masters. The only way to get rid of a sense of futility in life is to be free and the only way to be free is to know the more general laws not only of nature, but also of society and human thought and to act upon our knowledge viz., to be armed in our social practice with weapons of dialectical and historical materialism.

*A Free Man's Worship* was brilliantly written. Some thirty years ago I worshipped it and in worshipping it I fancied myself free. Since 1945 I began to see that I was mistaken. I had an argument with a friend of mine that year, a sociologist, who was in the habit of thinking in terms of social groups. After enumerating the items that constitute my "freedom", I was asked how many of the four hundred millions (estimate in 1945) were in a position to enjoy it. We argued back and forth and the figure finally arrived at was ten or fifteen thousand. Staggering! The proportion was peculiar to China, then, but the nature of the problem was everywhere the same. Since I myself neither delved nor span, the means of my subsistence was supplied by others. My so-called "free" life including fourteen years abroad and various trips across the oceans was maintained, according to the calculation of another friend six years later, by the unremitting toil of thousands of peasant folk for about as long a period as half a century. It would be too naive to argue that the peasants did so out of their own free choice. Together with others, I used to criticize Aristotle for justifying slavery, but while he couldn't be accused of hypocrisy, I couldn't deny it. Since the kind of "free" life I lived was only maintained by forcibly putting others in chains, I wasn't free, being myself in chains as well. There can't be thorough going individual freedom apart from a free society. And a society can be free only when it can change itself in accordance with and by means of our knowledge of the objective laws of social development.

Russell said somewhere that he respected Spinoza, I suspect that he respected him in the sense Confucius advocated concerning spirits: respect them and get out of their way. At any rate, Russell didn't seem to have been profited by Spinoza, his conception of freedom was similar to Rousseau's, it was such that he became intellectually and emotionally at war with himself, he ought to have been free, but in fact he was bound in chains. He couldn't be consoled by nature since nature in the form of the Solar System would itself be smashed to smithereens; he couldn't be consoled by society, for though he contemplated about socialism in the abstract, through books and pamphlets, he recoiled from it in the concrete since in England it was liable to be uncouth and cockney. His conception of freedom was in a word impossible. Freedom in truth is simply objective necessity known and under control. It grows with the growth of our knowledge. The greater our knowledge of nature, of society and of ourselves, the freer we become. We are freer than Pithecanthropus Erectus, freer than Confucius or Socrates, freer than Copernicus and Newton, freer than Darwin. Russell himself is freer today than he was in 1903. The time has come for us to cease talking about freedom metaphysically or worshipping it abstractly, ours is to consider what the task before us is and to exercise our freedom concretely.

Undoubtedly we differ. We who come from China stand openly and squarely for socialism. This entails a series of far reaching differences. We even differ from some of you as to the concrete content of freedom and democracy. But does this matter so far as the main issue confronting us today is concerned? I felt confident that all of us are against war. I am also confident that all our predecessors, certainly your Socrates and our Confucius, were they only alive today, would declare themselves openly and work incessantly for peace. We differ as to the concrete content of freedom, but can't we agree that we struggle to realize it in our different ways? We also differ concerning democracy, but can't we agree to differ and let each of us strive to realize his ideal? We will differ as to what to do with peace or in it, but we agree with each other that it must be maintained. The world must be made safe for life and this is the task of every free man and free woman throughout the world.

515

# Philosophy as a Guide
# to Social Practice<sup>*</sup>

## I

Philosophy has always been intended to be practically efficacious. Even Hegel meant to translate his philosophy from theory
into practice, thus transforming the whole world according to Hegelian principles. This was an illusion. The world never unfolded
itself in accordance with any philosophy before the advent of
Marxism. After Marx, there was an opposite tendency which tried
to give philosophy the appearance of being ultra mundane, and in
its wake the world of practice appeared to be sinking more and
more below the level of philosophical consciousness. At present,
in some philosophies, the emphasis is exclusively laid on the interpretation of the world. This is more apparent than real. But
since emphasis has been articulately laid on interpretation alone,
a large number of philosophers have been led to divorce theory

---

* 本文是作者 1958 年上半年在英国牛津大学一个欢迎会上的讲
话。——编者注

from practice. Some theories are such as to render their advocates split personalities. What philosophy has put asunder, nothing else seems able to unite. As a philosopher, he has systematic view of the world, but in his daily practice he is in a quandary as to how to behave himself; and as a member of the society he carries on a series of activities, but his activities can not be justified by his own philosophy. His articulate philosophy does not guide his practice, and what does guide it, though a part of his philosophy, is yet something which he does not philosophically avow.

Take myself as an example. I had dealt with philosophy for thirty years before our liberation and had even cogitated a system of objective idealism in which the universe was seen to be actualizing logos. I played with abstract concepts to such an extent as to render me subjectively incapable of coping with my daily routine. I used to find myself in difficulties even in such things as to whether or not I should carry an umbrella on cloudy days. I would reason about it for a considerable time without a conclusion and the final decision was nine times out of ten made on impulse. But the thirty years of my former philosophical life was coincident with a period of extreme turbulence in Chinese history. Class struggle was severe to the extreme, and the academic world in which I had lived was of course not free from it. I had to make decisions on various issues. These decisions were not made on impulse, nor were they the implication of my articulate philosophy. I was guided, by something which was the essence of my thought but for which my avowed philosophy was not an articulation. The practical man was divorced from the philosopher. I was lonely in my ivory tower, as I saw the world passing by.

Dialectical and historical materialism is frankly both an interpretation of the world and a guidance to our social practice in changing it. It is a veridical reflection of the objective world in its most general aspects, and as such it is also most generally a system of norms for thinking. Since it points out the distant objective of our endeavors, and helps us to understand the objective conditions of the country at any particular time, it enables us to formulate policies and adopt measures to cope with these conditions so as to bring us step by step to approach our objective. Our program of action is itself under the direction of our philosophy, hence in whatever we do, we see the philosophical thread running through it. Administration which we used to think of as a fool's job is now seen to be work that requires consummate philosophy. We are no longer split personalities. We know that we are ourselves the rational vehicles of social advancement. Generally we know what we do and we do it resolutely. This can be attained only under the condition that the philosophy we profess is one which unifies theory and practice, which is not merely an interpretation of the world, but also a guidance to our social practice in changing it.

## II

It has been said that the Chinese revolution was brought to a successful conclusion not on account of the truth of a guiding phi-losophy, but on account of hard-headed common sense. We were not devoid of common sense, neither had we an excessive share of it, but to deny the role played by philosophy in our revolution is simply untrue. In what follows, I shall show that in both demo-cratic revolution and socialist reconstruction, philosophy has al-ways been our guide.

Our democratic revolution is an example of the application of the general principles of Marxism and Leninism to the special conditions then prevailing in China. To start with, it is a dialecti-cal principle that the general resides in the special and the parti-cular. Some of us may deny this principle, I myself had denied it before 1949 under the subterfuge that the universal is independent of any, though not all, of its particular instances. Others may admit the principle to be a homely truth. It may be homely, but it is none the less profound, especially when it serves as a guide to our thought and action. In the latter capacity, it is not a mere proposition in a philosophical text book, but also a precept that we should never detach the general from either the special or the particular. As a result of such de-tachment, undue emphasis would be laid either on the general or on the special. Excessive emphasis on the former results in dog-matism and excessive emphasis on the latter results in empiricism. Both had caused set-backs to our revolution. It was combatting these tendencies in philosophy that Chairman Mao Tze—tung wrote the pamphlets *On Practice and On Contradiction.*

Without the guidance of dialectical and historical materialism, our revolution could not have succeeded. Without a scientific philosophy, how could we come to the conclusion that the old China was semi-feudal and semi-colonial, that it was ruled by foregin imperialists, by compradore capitalists and by landlords? Without such a Marxist conclusion, how could we single these classes out as the objects to be overthrown by our revolution? It is historical materialism that supplies us with the theory of class struggle, and it was precisely through class analysis that enabled Chairman Mao Tze-tung to tell us as early as 1926 who the people were who would join us in our revolution. Without philosophical guidance, how could peasants and farmers be mobilized to join the revolution to the extent they did? "National Bourgeoisie" is a term that sounds queer in our ears, but it adequately describes a class of people who might and at certain stages did join us. Old China was semi-colonial. This meant that the foreign imperialists together with the compradore capitalists had been oppressing among others also a section of the bourgeoisie who refused to go the way of the foreign imperialists. They were bourgeoisie, but they were also patriotic. They were afraid of the proletarian revolution, but they also desired the overthrow of the imperialists and the compradores. Since they were bourgeoisie, they could not be devoid of the essence characterizing their class elsewhere, but under the concrete conditions then prevailing, there was in them also a revolutionary side. Our dealings with them were a brilliant example of the unity of the general with the special. Nowhere else have we seen capitalists parading in the streets with beating drums to hail the impending socialization of their capital. Surely this could not be accomplished by practice that was devoid of philosophical guidance.

It may be said that ours is a twentieth century revolution and one led by the proletarians and as such it could not but be guided by Marxist philosophy. But we cannot be doing so forever. The time has already come when we are faced with reconstruction which involves quite a different set of problems the solution of which requires engineering, natural science and economics. Undoubtedly such is actually the case. But our revolution does not end with the overthrow of the reactionary regime, it does not end until a communist society is established. Philosophical guidance is required even in a communist society. Although engineering, natural science and economics are more important today than before, it does not mean that philosophy has become less important. This is the case with every branch of our endeavour.

Take agriculture for instance. Almost immediately after liberation, the land reform movement took place. It was a movement in which the peasants themselves took the most active part. Landlords were dispossessed, and their land distributed to the peasants. With the forces of production thus liberated, the increase of production became phenomenal. Historical materialism teaches us that in order to liberate the forces of production, it is necessary to overthrow the relations of production which hamper them. The landlords had to be overthrown, but of course the problem did not stop there. If we left the things at that stage without further measures being taken, we would be committing a serious mistake. The farmers are in a dual capacity: On the one hand they are themselves workers and on the other they are the owners of their produce. They are, therefore, at the cross-roads: They might turn to socialism and they might turn to capitalism. A policy of laissez-faire and laissez-aller would encourage them to take the disastrous road to capitalism. For in that case, big fish would eat little fish. The richer farmers would be able to swallow up the poorer ones. Measures, however, had been taken. Mutual aid societies had been established, in some places long before the land reform movement. Primary and high grade agricultural co-operatives were instituted. The farmers were not easily persuaded by words. These mutual aid societies and co-operatives were the actual examples of a road diametrically opposed to capitalism. Class struggle in the country side, now of a different nature from that between landlords and peasants, continued to be severe. It was a struggle as to which road to take, and by the end of 1955 the issue was decided in favour of socialism. The farmers realized that it alone solved their problems. This is more easily said now than actually grasped then. A large number of people at that time did not grasp the situation. They did not know that socialism had already won. It was only after a wealth of material on agricultural conditions had been gathered and scientific class analysis applied to it that the predominant direction toward which the peasants were tending became clear and distinct. It is plain here as elsewhere that we are guided by the teachings of historical materialism.

The co-operatives are not quite consolidated, but they will be more and more so as time goes on. They are here to stay because they solve problems which, under old conditions, could never be solved.

Such problems are numerous. We will take two trivial examples, on account of their simplicity. In Honan Province there is a slanting fruit tree which has its roots on the land of one farmer and casts shadows on the land of another. It belongs to the first farmer but it shuts out the sunshine needed by the crops of the second. The owner wants to preserve the tree, and his neighbour wants it removed or cut down. The neighbours had been quarrelling for twenty years. The problem, though trivial, had been insoluble. It ceased to be a problem, however, when both farmers joined the cooperative. Another example. In Kiangsu Province, there is a stream that runs through one village to another. The first village uses the water for irrigation. By the time the stream reaches the second village there is little water left. The two villages had been fighting with each other for a long period. This problem entails greater consequences than the first one. But it was equally insoluble. After co-operation the two villages are organized into one co-operative and their old problem no longer bothers them. Such examples can be cited almost ad infinitum.

Socialization in agriculture is now an accomplished fact. That it could be so without philosophical guidance both in theory and practice is hardly conceivable. It is not necessary to cite as examples other spheres of activity, our reconstruction as an organic whole is itself entailed by the laws of social development propounded by historical materialism.

# III

It is a dialectical principle that in changing the world, we change ourselves as well. Those who participated in the revolution before 1949 found themselves changed in the revolutionary process. Some of them were petit bourgeois intellectuals working primarily for the cause of democracy and science brought forward by the May 4th movement of 1919, but by 1949 they had already become seasoned proletarian intellectuals. This self transformation applies to everybody without exception The farmers mentioned above in being converted from the individual to the co-operative way of farming are themselves changed. The ideas to which they were accustomed are no longer valid guides to their actions. Take the two examples given above. The way the apparently insoluble problems were solved or dissolved means that an individualistic or sectionalistic way of thinking has to give way to the socialistic. As the country becomes more and more socialized the old ways of thinking become increasingly inapplicable. In changing the countryside, the farmers are themselves transformed.

The same is true of intellectuals. There have been reports of "brain washing" in a deprecatory sense. I myself find it difficult to understand the deprecation. Some of us have the good habit of a daily bath, ridding ourselves of the accumulations which none of us regard as desirable expressions of our individuality. If physically washing is necessary, why not mentally? As seen above, thought reorientation is not confined to intellectuals. Of course, it is more serious with them, since their minds are dusty piles of mental bric-a-brac, accumulations which somehow come to be regarded as expressive of individuality. This merely renders reorientation more difficult, not less necessary. It cannot however be achieved through meditation behind closed doors, criticism by others is indispensible. Ideas which we do not suspect in ourselves cannot be dragged out by ourselves and ideas, which we profess vehemently but which are really absent in us, can be ascertained to be thus absent only through the criticism of our colleagues. Criticism and self-criticism is a bit painful at the beginning, but not when one is accustomed to it. It is even exhilarating when we see our dusty mental accumulations being washed away.

Reorientation in philosophy is likely to be a slow process. It cannot be separated from thought reorientation in general, nor can it be considered apart from the revolutionary practice since 1949. It is after all social existence that determines social ideas, and since Chinese society was now turned upside down and downside up, repercussions were bound to take place in philosophy as well. So far as my own experience is concerned, it is the standpoint that is fundamental. When someone pointed out in Feb. 1951 that the theory propounded in *On Practice* is epistemology from the standpoint of the working class, I was frankly skeptical, and it took me quite a few months to see the pamphlet in that light. And seeing it in that light, I also saw that the doctrine taught by Chairman Mao Tze-tung has always been and is still the profound truth in epistemology. Our standpoint is often hidden in our fundamental premises. Before 1949 it was "natural" for me to start in epistemology with sensation detached from social practice, with the individual apart from society, with knowing as a cross-sectional relation in the abstract background of time and space variables, apart from the historical development of human knowledge. It was "natural" because I had the prepossession of the leisure class unable to see the role played in epistemology by manual labour in the sense of social practice in production, the prepossession of the individual whose individuality was taken to be a natural phenomenon though in reality it was a social product historically conditioned, and the prepossession of regarding knowing as a static and cross-sectional relation instead of a dynamic and an ever developing and ever advancing process. Reorientation which meant the readjustment of my standpoint enabled me to see philosophy in a new light.

Without the proper standpoint, dialectical and historical materialism is difficult to understand and impossible to accept, since in that case its virtues might be taken to be "vices". It is the philosophy of a whole Class, not that of this or the other individual. It is scientific exactly in the sense in which any branch of science is scientific, namely it reflects veridically the laws of the objective world, only the laws it deals with are the most general. It is systematic as some of the more developed sciences are, but unlike some philosophies, it is not a closed system. It is frankly incomplete in the sense that it is never finished, it will be richer and more complete as we know more and more of the world. These surely are virtues. To be able to regard them as such, however, it is necessary to abandon certain views of philosophy. I myself did not regard these virtues as "vices", but for one or two years after 1949, I regarded them as "shortcomings". Dialectical materialism seemed to me, then, to be somewhat stark and plain, there seemed to be a certain kind of conceptual bleakness. I wanted to "round the system out" with what I then regarded as sharper "conceptual tools". With a readjustment of my standpoint, I began to see that philosophy, not only is, but also must be a guidance to social practice in changing the world. As such it must be true in the strict sense of science. Any attempt to "round out" dialectical materialism would turn something rich into something barren, something alive into something dead and would close the system in a way as to render it unscientific and therefore incapable of guiding us in changing the world.

Without the proper standpoint, without the conviction that the world must change and philosophy must guide us in changing it, we are liable to indulge in a sort of irresponsible metaphysical sophistication through which profound but plain truth might be turned into "untenable propositions". It is surely a profound truth that objective events and things exist independently of our minds and senses. This is surely a truth that has been continually verified in the history of the development of our knowledge. Surely, Dr. Johnson's leg, an objectively existent thing, had in kicking caused an objectively existent event to take place resulting in an impact, another such event, with a piece of stone, another such thing; and the resulting pain or whatever other feeling there was in the doctor's toe surely did not just happen in a vacuum. And yet philosophers argued as if it did. They could only do so through metaphysical sophistication. By detaching sensation from practice which is itself objectively existent, by excluding what is plainly given to sensation in practice from that which is supposed to be given to sensation alone, the impossibility of deducing or inferring objectively existing events and things from the "given" becomes a "philosophical truth" beyond the intellectual capacities of the "man in the street". A plain and profound truth is thus turned into an untenable proposition. Berkeley had his own axe to grind. But with philosophers such as I was before 1949, this kind of intellectual exercise cannot but be regarded as mental legerdemain. With a switch of my standpoint, I was able to see that philosophizing is a very serious business and that no metaphysical sophistication is permissable. Life is earnest and life is real; so also is philosophy.

The present reconstruction in China is a change of our part of the world toward socialism. The task is nowhere simple, but in a country such as China is, it is simply stupendous. There is no line of activity that remains untouched. Nothing can possibly retain its status quo. The forces of production now liberated more than ever before find expression in the creative activities of practically everybody and in almost every line of effort. Enthusiasm for work is unprecedented and millions and millions of people are at it. Tasks which were thought incapable of realization soon become accomplished facts. For instance, one hundred millions of farmers have recently been engaged in irrigation and other water works and what has been accomplished in this sphere during the last few months is estimated to be equivalent to the accumulated achievement of four thousand years. A socialist society is however highly organic and socialist reconstruction is therefore synthetic to a very high degree. What is required concommitantly of education, of culture, of engineering and the sciences is both difficult and urgent. Philosophy is no exception, especially in its role as a guidance to social practice. A materialistic and dialectical view of things and appropriate methods of coping with them are required in every line of endeavour. Here, it is easily seen that no other philosophy satisfies. Research and popularization must go hand in hand, and strange as it may seem, even with philosophers, the time has come when they have to think hard as well as to roll up their sleeves.

Intense activities will soon take place in philosophy. Plans for research will be made in dialectical and historical materialism. It is probable that our main effort here will be directed towards researches on the laws of socialist development, on the nature of various contradictions and the methods for coping with them. Heated discussions will take place on a greater scale than ever before. Great efforts will be given to the research in the history of Chinese philosophy, greater than any ever given to it in any previous period. The same is true of the history of western philosophy and of logic. Although our guiding principle is that theory and practice are to be closely united, it does not mean that the range of problems to be taken up is limited to a closely defined scope. On the contrary, we will be confronted with an enormous number of problems. Old problems will be re-examined, some of them will be found to have been dissolved already, others may still require solution. What is important, however, is that new problems which we have never dealt with before have come up and will continue to come up as we go deeper and deeper in our studies. A Marxist history of Chinese philosophy is surely a new branch of science and while there are a few precursors in the field, most of the philosophers engaged in it find their works almost bafflingly new. The work ahead of us is plainly difficult but to those philosophers who had been philosophizing in ivory towers, such as I was, the task is also inspiring.

Of men, J. M. Barrie said somewhere in Dear Brutus that the trouble is not with their stars, but with themselves in that they are underlings. Taken individually this can hardly be denied. But in our concerted efforts towards building a new society, whatever little we are able to contribute is of lasting value. Buddha was said to have asked his disciples: "What are you going to do in order to prevent a drop of water from being dried up?" The disciples couldn't answer. Buddha answered "Put it in the ocean". Our efforts are indeed little drops of water, but when we put them in the ocean of efforts of sea hundred millions of people, our drops of water will never dry up.

# On The Essence of
# Russell's Neutral Monism[*]

The advance in physics in leaps and bounds from 1913 to 1929 brought with it difficulties amounting to a crisis. Science is materialistic and physics is no longer sufficient, it has to be superseded by dialectical materialism in order to account for the problems the advance raised. The idealists either ignoring or ignorant of the difference between mechanismic and dialectical materialism, mistook the passing of the former for the passing of materialism. The opportunity for idealistic attacks seemed to have arrived. Difficulties in scientific advance are no blemishes, they can always be overcome and once overcome they push science into further advance. But they are also excuses for the attacks of the idealists. It was not by accident alone that Whitehead, Haldane, Broad and others began to weave scientific concepts into their non-materialistic philosophies. Russell is one of them and the excuse he seized is the notion of things in the world of Sensibles.

---

[*] 本文写于 1960 年至 1966 年之间。很可能是 1964 年或 1965 年。——编者注

In the world of sensibles, things are more or less regid, sub-stantial, they occupy shape and are relatively impenetrable; in a word, they are embodies. Here is a table, its brownness and squareness are visual, they cannot be separately moved by hand. But if I move the table into my study, they are both moved there also. The attributes to the table cohere into certain rigidity, certain substantiality and being embodied, they occupy a certain space not occupied by other things. The table is said to be a thing. The existence of things as embodied groups of attributes had been affirmed throughout the ages. It is here that Russell saw his chance of undermining materialism. His neutral monism con-sists of the construction of matter and mind out of and the reduc-tion of them into sense data, and this is rendered possible through the disembodiment of things. In what follows, Russell's neutral monism and his theory of things are treated as if they are one and the same theory and sometimes one and sometimes the other is mentioned depending upon the context.

# I

To the dialectical materialists, the sensation of things presents no difficulty. Scientifically and historically conceived, sensation is on the one hand inseparably connected with social practice and on the other it is unceasing enriched by rational knowledge. With sensation thus conceived, things can be sensed; as a matter of fact, they had always been, and are being sensed everyday. When one carries a book to his study, he not merely sees the color but also feels the thing in his hand.

Not so, however, according to a philosopher with a Humean turn of mind. When sensation is conceived idealistically and metaphysically, it is cut asunder from social practice, it is unaffected by history, it is abstract and pure. Take for example a green apple that is: not guite ripe. The eye sees the green, and the roundish shape, but anything else is not within its province. The nose smells the applish smell, but it has nothing to do with the color or the shape. So on and so forth. The apple becomes a heap of attributes or qualities, with its substantiality or thinghood evaporating into thin air. To Hume, there are merely impressions with their causes unknown.

In 1912, in his *Problems of Philosophy*, Russell admitted causes too, but while Hume professed not to know what kind of entities they are, Russell regarded them as resembling their effects the sense data; like Kant's nonmena, they cannot be sensed or acquainted with, but unlike nonmena, they can be indirectly known. Russell said in 1959 that there was a good deal in the problems in which he still believed. Two points however stood out in striking relief, even in those early days, in the sense that something had to be done about them. One of that objective things cannot be experienced, they are only inferred from sense data through their caused relation of sense data, and the other is that the inference is not well founded hence unreliable. To a dialectical materialist again there is no such problem, but Russell was confronted with it. What is doubtful is whether he was earnestly trying to solve it scientifically. If he were, he would have found his theory of sense data untenable and would have abandoned it. But in sticking to it, he revealed himself to be, to say the least, not genuine.

Put in a nutshell, the above problem is one of the embodiment of things. It is their bodies that render things inexperiencable to Russell and it is their bodies that force him to regard them as being inferred. Could they be disembodied? In 1914, Russell was engaged in the disembodiment of things. One instrument, to achieve his purpose, he was already familiar with, namely Occam's razor. Through a series of arguments against permanence and substantiality, Russell simply shaved things free from their embodiment. The other instrument he borrowed from Whitehead, namely logical construction. The immalleability of fully bodied things to conceptual manipulation lies in their objectivity and substantiality, but disembodied they could be logically constructed out of sense data. The constructions given in scientific method in philosophy and in mysticism of logic were absurd, but the aim was clear: Things thus constructed are experiencable, since they are themselves merely sense data; and for the same reason the unreliable inference is no longer required. Scientifically the problem was not solved, it was merely by passed philosophically.

The construction of the disembodied things; was muddled, inconsistent and absurd, but the effort was heroic, one could see

Russell perspiring with the endeavor. Was the effort merely for the purpose of setting aside the above mentioned problem? One can't help thinking that there was some additional axe to grind. Strictly speaking, the disembodied things are not things, much less objective things, still less objective material things. Russell wanted to construct matter through the construction of things. How could matter be constructed through bodiless things, through things that are themselves sense data? And yet that is what Russell actually did do. Not only the things he constructed are without their bodies but also the matter he constructed is without its independent existence. The essence of matter is its existence, independent of our sensation, of our thinking and cognition. Without this: independence matter there can not be matter. What Russell constructed is merely something fraudulently labeled. He was once opposed to subjective idealism, he could hardly be said to have slipped unconsciously step by step into its quagmire, we are forced to the conclusion that in 1912 he was already heading towards subjective idealism and by 1914, he had taken an enormous stride.

The stuff with which Russell used to construct things and matter is sense data. By 1914, he had already taken the more important of the two steps towards neutral monism, namely the reduction of "matter" to sense data. For a considerable length of time, he was opposed to the kind of neutral monism proposed by William, James. It had not occured to him to give a similar treatment to mind. According to Alan Wood, ( *Russell the Passionate*

*Skeptic.* 117. ) Russell began to think of an analysis of the mind in 1918 and the book under that name was published in 1921. There, mind was less laboriously constructed. Previously Russell had maintained a distinction between sensation and sense data, conceding the former alone to be mental. He had argued against Berkeley with this distinction, even as late as 1912. In 1919, in the Essay On Propositions ( *Logic and knowledge*, 295 ) Russell began to abandon the distinction and by 1921, the abandonment was definite and final. Mind was reduced to sensations, and since the distinction between sensation and sense data was no longer held, mind was also reduced to sense data. Although the causal relations that entered into the construction were different, the stuff out of which both matter and mind were constructed was the same.

By 1921, Russell's neutral monism was completed since both mind and matter were already constructed. The stuff namely sense data, was neither material nor mental, it was more fundamental than either and neutral between the two of them. We have pointed out that Russell was already on his way towards subjective idealism in 1912, he was not then a neutral monist; by 1914 he had already taken the more important of the two steps towards neutral monism, sinking deeper into subjective idealism, and by 1921, in having also constructed mind, he had already completed his nentral monism. Although Russell had always had the habit of invoking scientific author in his philosophical arguments, his neutral monism up to 1921 was mainly an extension of his philosophical prepossession.

Mr. State in his critical essay on Russell's neutral monism did not include the analysis of matter as his survey. We donor share his reasons for doing so, but we agree with him that Russell's neutral monism was already complete by 1921. What role did the analysis of matter play then? How are we to appraise it?

# II

From 1913 to 1929, physics was advancing at enormous strides. Atomic structure, General Relativity, Quantum mechanics and Wave mechanics pushed it onto its most phenomenal progress. The more rapid the advance, the greater also is the number of difficulties. Concepts forever developing receive in such an advancing science their most comprehensive and rapid development. Difficulties abound and while scientists must solve them, philosophers are by no means idle by their side. Many of them seeing the opportunity for idealism start to pull these formative concepts away from materialism. It was in 1919 in connection with the experiment that finally proved the general theory of relativity that Russell's interest was aroused. What was its content?

The concept of things has to have certain modification in terms of microscopic physics with the result that the relativity of the concept to the universe of discourse must be explicitly specified. Entities in the microscopic world do not merely obey the laws of classical mechanics, they embody the effects of relativity and of quantum and wave mechanics and obey a number of other laws as well. This does not mean invalidating classical mechanics, which still applies, its effects are still fore, only other laws operate as well and their effects can not be ignored. In this respect microscopic and macroscopic worlds are different for in the latter microscopic effects are so small that for certain purposes they can be neglected. Cats and rings are things in the world of sensibles and while in staring at the ring, the cat might have produced microscopic effects on the ring, as some philosophers maintained, in the world of sensibles the ring remains as rigid as substantial and as impenetrable as ever before. The concept of a thing becomes relative to the universe of discourse, where the topic of discussion is concerned with one world, the complications of thinghood due to the other, with the exception of very special cases, are on the whole irrelevant.

In view of the above, we have to admit that rigid and substantial things in the world of sensibles are not similarly so in the microscopic world. Microscopically an ordinary apple may be like the Peking Station with its ebbs and flows of closely packed crowds, or like the work day on Tian An Men square with its sqareness and spaciousness. For those whose ideas were some what hide bound to this mundane, the above seemed to be almost inconceivable, much less believable in the days of 1919. Today it has become almost a part of educated common sense. From this point of view of philosophy, we have to insist on the principle of definite spheres and determinate types in order to obviate the confusion in our discourse. We recognize the different conditions of the two different worlds, but we cannot make use of the condition of the one to deny that of the other. In 1919, there were men who argued that a foot is a foot inspire of the speed of its wavering velocity. This is untenable since it is to deny relativity physics on the basis of sensual conditions. But there are others who deny facts in the sensual world on the basis of microscopic physics. Needless to say that this is equally untenable.

In his introduction to the nature of the physical world, Eddington started with two tables, one was the table of common sense, the other he labeled scientific table. The former is the familiar table with its usual rigidity and substantiality, it is sufficent impenetrable as to be able to support our elbows when we write our books on it. The other is mainly empty space with elutions darting back and forth at enormous speed. We can write with our elbows on the table because in elbow and table there are enormous number of electrons pressing down, as well as surging up. Both these tables exist, but why did Eddington label the second one scientific? Doesn't it reveal a prejudice to the effect that somehow first isn't scientific? In a page or so that followed, he came out with the statements that the scientific table is the only one that is really there. At a breathe he also maintained that this conclusion reached by delicate tests and remorseless logic. Eddington was a scientist, what he said in the sphere of science must be respectecd. But in the above, was he talking science?

Russell entertained similar ideas. Everybody knows the story of Dr. Johnson's refutation of Bishop Berkeley by kicking a stone with his foot. Johnson evidently starred with the naive materialism impicit in common sense, to him the stone exists by itself and kicking merely proves it to be so. This is undoubtedly valid, and Berkeley's rejoinder was merely willful insistence on subjective idealism. There was a time when Russell disagreed with Berkeley. But by 1930, he had change his ideas, saying that Johnson wasn't aware that his foot never even touched the stone, both being only complex systems of waves. We don't deny that in the microscopic world, Johnson's foot and the stone are systems of waves. But is it scientific to say that they are only such systems of waves? The story did not say that Johnson's foot failed to kick the stone, presumably it succeeded the kicking. The foot and the stone are things in the World of sensibles and kicking an event in it. Like Eddington, Russell also denied the reality of the things in the sensible world. Is it possible that such a denial is scientific, or that it is demanded by science?

It may be said that Russell merely denied the reality of sensible things, not sensible things themselves. Didn't he recognize the foot and the stone by saying that they never touched? Russell didn't deny "foot" or "stone", because according to him they are constructions of systems of sense data. As "things" they are bodiless, as "matter" they are devoid of independent existence. Hence what he recognized in "foot" and "stone" are only names attached to sense data. Why did Johnson think that by kicking the stone with his foot, he coud refute Berkeley? He regarded his foot and stone as embodied things and matter as existing independently of sensation and of thinking and recognition. Berkeley's rejoinder was that the stone existed because Johnson kicked it, revealing that what he meant by stone and foot were sensations or ideas. In his younger days Russell was also opposed to Berkeley's view, and if he ever referred to a stone or a foot, he would have meant by them something genuine. In the above argument, the thing the reality of which he denied was the thing Johnson had in his mind, namely embodied stone and foot that exist independently of our sensations and thoughts. Was the denial of the reality of such things scientific or demanded by science?

We have already pointed out that philosophically we have to insist on the principle that spheres must be definite and types distinct in order to obviate confusions in our discourse. While admitting the differences of the microscopic and macroscopic worlds, we must not take advantage of the conditions peculiar to the one in order to deny the conditions peculiar to the other.

This is just what Russell did and he was employing this method to attack materialism. The development of the concept of renders the rigidity and substantiality obtaining in the world of sensibles irrelevant to the microscopic world. But surely microscopic physics never denied the reality of rigid and substantial things in the sensible world. Eddington's theory of two tables might have been borrowed from Russell, but why was Russell so keen on demolishing embodied things in the name of microscopic physics. Here we have to return to what has already been pointed out in the previous section. In 1914 Russell was already engaged in disembodying things, in ridding them of their permanence, rigidity and substantiality, and in constructing them out of sense data. And absurd things had already been constructed. Russell was ever in the habit of using concepts borrowed from science to advance his philosophical arguments, but it was not comprehensive or systemetic. Since the phenomenal advance in physics, he saw his chance of comprehensive and systemctic utilization. To him, the problem became bottling up old wine in new bottles, and this was done in *The Analysis of Matter*. The old wine is neutral monism and the new bottle *The Analysis of Matter*, the former is the content and the latter its form. In the previous section we agreed with Stace, now we differ from him in that from our point of view *The Analysis of Matter* did contribute something to neutral monism in that it supplied a new form, a scientific cloak, which formerly it lacked. Hence forward, it wasn't merely that Russell wanted to disembody things, the impression was indelible that such disembodiment was demanded by physics intimidating the less mathematically minded philosophers with a fair d'accompli concerning which hardly anything can be said.

The conception of events as the primary stuff underlying matter was first brought out in the book just mentioned. Enormous number of things was constructed out of events such as points, instants, electrons and protons etc. The concept seemed to have been borrowed directly from physics and in being used in the construction of so many microscopic entities the impression that it came directly from physics became almost a conclusion. But the cat was out of the bag by 1930. In *Philosophy* ( pp. 276 ) Russell said that events aren't "anything out of the way. Seeing a flash of lightening is an event; so is hearing a tire burst, or smelling a rotten egg, or feeling the coldness of a frog." What appeared to have come directly from physics turned out to be merely sensation! The distinction between sense data and sensation once insisted upon was given up in 1921, hence forward, sensation was sense data. In 1930, matter was said to be groups of events with an extremely complicated logical structure. This merely means what was said in 1914 by the statement that matter was a certain complicated structure of appearences or aspects. Whether appearences, or aspects, or sensations, or events, what was meant was the same, namely, sense data, a term which Russell ceased to use after 1921, but evidently the corresponding thought was never out of his mind. What *The Analysis of Matter* advocated was essentially neutral monism already completed in 1921, the only difference was that if it gave neutral monism a scientific cloak.

## III

Was the cloak well-fitting? Russell's neutral monism completed in 1921, did not come from physics, and yet one could ask: is it such that it could have been derived from physics by anybody else provided he is as well equipped as Russell? If so, the cloak would be well fitting. There are two senses in which neutral monism might have been so derived: one is that it is a part of the content of physics, perhaps one of its laws or theorems, and the other is that, it is philosophically implied by physics, though physics does not include it as its own conclusion. In either of these two senses, the dissenting opinion of a physicist would be conclusive evidence that neutral monism is not so derived, since if it were, it would have been agreed to by all physicists alike. Let us see what Einstein, undoubtedly a great physicist, said concerning things.

To start with, let us quote the following: "The belief in an external world independent of the percipient subject is the foundation of all science." This was quoted by Leuzen in his essay *Einstein's Theory of Knowledge*. It is very important, particularly in view of other quotations below. Plainly this is asserting the existence of an objective material world independent of perception or percipient. Leuzen said further: the primary concept for the theory of space and time is that of bodily object and "according" to Einstein, the characteristic property assigned to a bodily object is existence independent of subjective time and of sensory perception. "In his reply to criticisms, Einstein merely thanked Leuzen but denied nothing in what Leuzen said, presumably what is said accurately reflected Einstein's ideas. This great physicist did not conclude from physics that things in the macroscopic world are bodiless, or that objective material things do not exist. On the contrary, from the point of view of physics he emphasized the existence of objective embodied things. He said: "What does not satisfy me in that theory, from the standpoint of principle, is its attitude towards that which appears to me to be the programmatic aim of all physics: the complete description of any (individual) real situation can it supposedly exist irrespective of any act of observation or substantiation." Einstein admitted Mach's influence in his younger days, but he soon found Mach's epistemologieal position to be essentially untenable. He was definitely opposed to positivism and the epistemology of Bishop Berkeley, saying "what I dislike in this kind of argumentation is the basic positivistic attitute, which from my point of view is untenable, and which seems to me to come to the same thing as Berkeley's principle, esse est percipi." Regarding the positivistic interpretation of things, he said "yet there is hardly likely to be anyone who would be inclined to consider it seriously. For, in the macroscopic sphere it is simply considered certain that one must adhere to the program of a realistic description in space and time,...." This means that the reality of things in the macroscopic world including the world of sensibles must be insisted upon. The positivists regard reality, viz., matter, as something to be disregarded as a metaphysical entity. This again Einstein was opposed to. He said: "We represent sense impressions as conditioned by an objective and by a subjective factor....But if this distinction were rejected, we can not escape solipsism." He was going to make use of such distinction "unconcerned with the reproach that, in doing so, we are guilty of the metaphysical 'original

Sin.'" (673). Einstein was quite aware of what Russell did and his criticism was directed towards the latter's theory of things. He felt that owing to excessive fear of me to physics, Russell conceived of things as boundless of "qualities" such that the "qualities" are taken from the sensory raw material. (289) After using Russell's own phrases against Russell, he concluded that he "saw no" metaphysical "danger in taking the thing (the object in the sense of physics) as an independent concept into the system together with the proper spatio-temporal structure." (291) In view of the above series of quotations, the phrase "independent concept" may be unfortunate, but its meaning is unmistakable.

Einstein's opinion is a conclusive evidence that Russell's neutral monism or theory of things is not a part of the contents of physics, nor a conclusion that must be drawn by philosophers.

We still have to consider possibilities. Although physics does not imply neutral monism, isn't it possible that it may possibly imply in future when some missing link at present unknown but when once discovered would enable the former to imply the latter? The answer is again no. The exposition that physics implies neutral monism or its theory of things renders physics self-contradictory. Hence the supposition is impossible. Microscopic physics is the science that reflects microscopic phenomena and their laws. It consists of our physical knowledge of the microscopic world. Whatever the relation between the microscopic and macroscopic worlds may be, our knowledge of the former is dependent upon a part of our knowledge of the world of sensibles. The proof or verification of our microscopic knowledge does not lie wholly in the microscopic world, it has to have experiment. Experimentation involves flasks, test tubes, solids, liquids and gases and the phenomena resulting from experiments. These are things and events in the world of sensibles. That which is proved or verified in microscopic phenomenon, but the process of proving or verifying takes place daily in the world of sensibles. I had witnessed one of these experiments myself and however complicated it may be, it plainly involves the impliments already mentioned. So far as verification is concerned, the validity of our microscopic knowledge depends upon the validity of our sensible knowledge. What could our attitude be towards these sensible impliments? Are they as unreal as Eddington's nonscientific "table" or Russell's "stone" and "foot" ? If they were the experiments themselves would be unreal and the conclusion drawn from them must be invalid. We are thus confronted with a paradox: If physics implies Russell's neutral monism or theory of things, and if the latter were true physics would be false, consequently physics if true would be false. Consequently it must be false, Since the supposition renders physics self-contradictory. No matter how much Russell tried to make use of physics it must be concluded that physics can not possibly imply his neutral monism or theory of things. The scientific cloak for the latter can not but be a misfit.

Although Russell once opposed subjective idealism in his younger days, yet by 1912, he himself already veered towards subjective idealism. In 1914 he was on his way towards neutral monism and by 1921 he had already completed it. During the period of rapid advance in physics, Russell together with a host of others saw the opportunity of attacking materialism and in 1927 he put on a scientific cloak for his neutral monism or his theory of things already completed in 1921. He remained a neutral monist in 1959 and presumably he still is today.

Russell's philosophy, or the technical part of it is mainly epistemology, his epistemology mainly neutral monism, his neutral monism mainly his theory of disembodied things and the latter essentially his theory of sense data, or sensations. His philosophy is mainly Hume's. Although in 1912 he and Kant rubbed shoulders at a tangent, he soon returned to Hume by way of Mach. Machism Was Hume's philosophy with a scientific Garb of the end of the 19th century, and Russellian philosophy is Hume's phitosophy with a scientific cloak of the first part of the 20th. Hume was described by English philosophers as the great skeptic of the 18th century and Alan Wood now describes Russell as a passionate skeptic. What both were skeptic about and sought to undermine was the foundation of science.

# Prolegomena[*]

"Douter de tout ou tout croire" said Henri Poincaré, "ce sont deux solutions également commodes, qui l'une et l'autre nous dispensent de réfléchir". Either one of them precludes also the possibility of philosophy. No matter from what point of view, philosophy should include not only a thorough going as well as a trained skepticism, but also some kind of belief as one of its necessary ingredients since it must have a starting point. Universal nihilism is not so easy in philosophy as it seems to have been in political thought because any negation, whatever, if it does not affirm anything, denies itself and consequently negates nothing. On the other hand, affirmation is equally difficult. If one does not intend to philosophize, he is in a privileged position, since he does not need anything positive with which to lubricate his wheels of thought. But if, when, and as long as, one philosophises—and there is no reason why he should do so—he is confronted with the difficulty of starting somewhere with something, whatever it is, which his skepticism may have accustomed him to deny. And to

* 原刊于《哲学评论》第 1 卷第 1—2 期，1927 年 4、6 月。——编者注

make his position difficult to maintain, almost from the very start, most of the things with which he is conversant in our daily life are beyond our power to affirm in the face of a denial. Even the existence of our world can be denied without affording us any ground for further argument except the cold comfort that something is affirmed which does not happen to be our world. To such a denial no remedy of logic or fact can be applied. To give an inventory of the world or to cite the evidences of our senses avails us nothing.

And yet, we must start somewhere. The difficulty is with what and where. Ordinarily a choice is made for which no reason can be given except our personal prejudice or the interests of the age in which we live. A predilection for mysticism will perhaps decide one person in favour of impassioned passages on eternal consciousness while a robust sense of reality may lead another to start with an examination of our sense data. Not only do different people effect different choices, but different times also present different problems. The problem of evil remains as unsolved as it was in the age of Plato, but few of us struggle with it at the present time. No solution had been arrived at in the middle ages as to how many angels can possibly stand on a pinhead, and yet no efforts that we know of have been directed in modern times towards arriving at any solution. Philosophical problems are rarely solved; oftentimes they are solved for an age; but oftener still they fade away with the fading interest which prompted their emergence as problems. But if one starts a philosophical essay with a thoroughgoing as well as a trained skepticism, then either personal prejudice or the interest of an age needs some kind of justification, failing which neither can serve as a starting point. But justification must be based upon same kind of criterion which itself needs justification. An endless process is thus initiated in which no starting point can be effected other than arbitrary. In the end it is our prejudice which is the foundation of our philosophic thought, though we should bear in mind that prejudices from the point of view of logic may not be prejudices from the point of view of the accumulated experience of mankind.

In this chapter, we shall deal with the relations of logic to philosophy, to life, and to our knowledge of the world in which we live. We shall try to set forth the role which logic plays in all the spheres mentioned, and to see on what criterion our belief in logic is justified. We shall discuss briefly our notion of convenience, of economy and of logic, and we shall try to ascertain their relation. Our discussion is perhaps less organized than it could be, and may appear at times to be beating at a bush where no bird is suspected to be hiding. But a good deal of the accumulated dust may be swept away, and to that extent at least our discussion may not be an utter waste of effort.

# I

In philosophy, perhaps more than in anything else except logic and mathematics, we deal with propositions which stand or

553

fall upon certain criteria, some of which have long been exploded. If we can find a criterion upon which some propositions are ascertained to be undeniable, we can probably employ these as our starting point. A proposition was once considered established when its opposite was inconceivable. But inconceivability is too elusive a criterion. What is inconceivable to one is easily conceivable to another, and instances abound in history of propositions inconceivable at one age turning to be thoroughly conceivable at the next, and vice versa. Again, propositions were once accepted when they were considered to be self-evident. But the same objections can be raised against self-evidence as are raised against inconceivability. Neither is reliable, because both are psychological resistance to strange and unfamiliar ideas and as such are misappropriated for the criteria of logical validity. If we search for a starting point from ideas that are self-evident or propositions whose opposites are inconceivable we are bound to fail.

Prospositions are said to be valid if they are true and they are said to be true, if they correspond with facts. This correspondence with facts is therefore often taken to be a criterion of the validity of propositions. It is easy to see however that here as elsewhere we can hardly derive any consolation. In the first place we have no way of knowing whether our propositions correspond with facts, if both these terms are taken to embody their common sense significance. On the one hand, they are so distinct from each other, and on the other, we are so identified with one of them that we are not in the position of a third party to judge whether or not there is any correspondence. The assertion of such a correspondence is itself a proposition which can only be true, when there is a further correspondence. Consequently, no matter how persistently we assert the truth of a given proposition, we shall find it yet to be ascertained one step beyond. More of this will come to our notice in the third chapter, but for the present it is sufficient to say that even if the criterion holds, we are not in any sense better off in our search for a starting point. The criterion if acceptable merely helps us to discover truths, it does not enable us to select any one of them to begin our discussion. If truths are created equal like the "Americans" of Abrahams Lincoln, we have no reason to select any one truth to start our discussion any more than the Americans had in 1860 to elect Lincoln for their President. If, on the other hand, truths are not created equal, then some particular truth must be selected and a criterion for such a selection is yet to be discovered.

There is one criterion which is generally considered to be irrefutable namely presupposition by denial. It is at any rate strictly logical and self sufficient. There are some propositions which belong to this category such as for instance the propositions "there are propositions," "there is truth," that "we argue", etc. It is generally considered that to deny any of these is to affirm them and that consequently each stands on its own self-sufficient ground. But if one studies the problem closely, one is liable to be led into two or three lines of thought. To begin with, some at least of these propositions are not strictly presupposed by their own denial. Take for instance, the proposition "there is truth." On the face of it, the denial, if true, affirms the proposition and if false allows the original proposition to stand. It is therefore obvious that the proposition "there is truth" is presupposed by its denial. But if we reason in this fashion we imply suppositions which are not here indicated; we imply, for instance, that truth however defined is of universal application, irrespective of the differences involved in logically prior and logically subsequent steps. The truth of these propositions and the truth affirmed or denied by them belong to different types of logical procedure; and if Mr. Russell's theory of types, of the technique of which I admit complete ignorance, applies to all propositions alike, then the use of presupposition by denial as a criterion in the sense herein discussed is limited to a considerable extent.

The above reasoning may or may not be sound, but it indicates the possibility that some of the propositions which are presupposed by their denial involve other propositions implied in neither the affirmation nor the denial.

In the second place, there are other propositions which deny themselves on similar grounds but which some of us may find it necessary to maintain as embodying our sincere beliefs. The problem of the "lie" is trivial compared with the problem of those who conscript the relativity theory of Einstein for the purpose of their philosophy. It is true that the constant velocity of light and the absoluteness of the "interval" are somewhat ignored by those who assert that everything is relative, but if this proposition embodies the sincere belief of its propounders, it is almost heart-breaking to see it fade away through a self-denial that must seem at times to be purely verbal. The theory of types I am told, is intended to remove the difficulties arising from these propositions, and whether or not it has already attained the technical perfection it seeks, it seems to involve the non-technical problem of its application. Wherever it is applied it is likely to resolve the criterion of presupposition by denial into greater complexities than we can see at a glance, and our attempt to find a starting point has so far produced no definite gain.

In the third place, the criterion of presupposition by denial itself presupposes a belief in logic. If one refuses to believe in logic, propositions can never be established for him merely because they cannot be denied by him according to the rules of logic. While logic is conceivably convincing to most people, it need not be effective with children or lunatics or philosophers. The latter can easily believe that there is truth at the same time that they believe that there is not. If one does not believe in logic, there is no logical reason for him to change his mind, though there may be other reasons why he should do so. That there are other reasons will be the subject of this chapter.

Symbolic logicians can justifiably congratulate themselves for having discovered a few primitive ideas from which most if not all of the logical principles can be deduced. A logical pyramid is thus made possible through the technical skill of the mathematicians. It is questionable, however, whether similar results will be achieved in philosophy by introducing into it the same method elsewhere so profitably employed; for philosophy is less restricted in its sphere than logic, it deals with topics of a more heterogeneous nature and its various problems have not been and are not likely to be linked into a gapless chain. The starting point for any system of logic need not be a starting point for philosophy, consequently the success of symbolic logic has not so far been followed by a corresponding success in philosophical thought.

The terms "philosophy" and "philosopher" have been used with extraordinary vagueness. Goethe has been claimed by some as a great philosopher and Shakespeare by others. What is meant by either statement is probably that both men had great insight into human nature and life, but whatever the statement may mean, few of us dispute it. Shelley is regarded as a great philosopher, by no less a thinker, I understand, than Mr. Whitehead, but none of us ever dreams of writing controversial poems setting forth ideas to refute that angel, ineffective or otherwise. If silence means consent in philosophy as it does in law, then Shelley's philosophy may claim universal acceptance. At the same time, all philosophers are said by some to be poets; Mr. John Middleton Murry regards Plate as a good poet and Hagel a bad one. Whether or not poets feel insulted by the sentiment herein expressed, philosophers seem to remain quite undisturbed in their philosophical serenity. What seems to account on this state of affairs is that philosophy is not concerned with ideas quâ ideas; like science, it is interested in the method from which they are derived and through which they are correlated with each other.

The case of M. Bergson is illuminating at this point of our discussion. Here is a man whose poetry is supposed to take the form of philosophy rather than that of the winged words and sonorous phrases of verse, with the result that each suffers from the other. While his É Vital has successfully penetrated into the perfumedatmosphere of pink tea parties, his philosophy is regarded by a large section of his own profession as being vitiated through self-destruction. Had he allowed his reader to derive inspiration from him through intuition, his hold on the public might have been stronger; he might even have become a religious leader, but then he would not have been in the modern philosophical world. Having selected to be active in the latter field, he has to convince people through argumentation and the moment he argues, he is bound by logic to emphasize intellect at the expense of intuition, since as far as his reading public is concerned it is through the former that the latter makes itself felt. One cannot very well argue for the importance of intuition simply because argumentation involves elements with which intuition as differentiated from intellect by definition is incompatible. We hold no brief for intellect, at least not for the moment; for all we know, intellect might very easily be subordinate to intuition; M. Bergson probably feels strongly that it is; but if the less endowed portion of mankind can not share his insight except through arguments, it is naturally to intellect rather than to intuition that they attach the greater importance. Thus only one of two alternatives is open to M. Bergson, not both: either he adopts the method of systematic philsophy, in which case he may have to abandon his philosophical position; or he gives up argumentation in which case he may have to propagate his idea in the style of Shelley or Keats.

A criticism of a veteran philosopher cannot be crowded into one short paragraph, and a lengthy exposition is totally out of place here. What is intended is merely to show that philosophy is mainly concerned with arguments not with random ideas gathered from here and there. Those who believe in God are not in a better or worse position in philosophy than those who do not, for philosophy offers no criteria upon which particular emotional attachment can be justified. The moment a belief is supported by arguments, philosophy begins to have something to say. But arguments involve analysis and synthesis in which premises and conclusions play a great part and if arguments are the main concern of philosophy, then logic is its essence. A large amount of insight is desirable, a robust sense of reality is probably more convincing in modern times than a rich imagination, but a rigorous reasoning power is in any case indispensable. Philosophers are much less criticized for their ideas than for the way in which they develop them, and many a philosophical system has perished on the one rock of logic.

Special definitions aside, philosophy is for most people a sort of Weltanschauung more or less systematized. While the "world", whatever it is, is generally regarded as common to everybody, our reactions against it and our ideas about it are admittedly different

for different individuals. Nature is persistent in her peculiar manifestations, she insists on having her own way; she may not frown
at the courtship of the scientists, but she has shown hardly any
excitement over philosophical systems. She is indifferent alike to
our hopes and fears, our beliefs and doubts, which are after all
the articulate or the inarticulate premises of most philosophical
systems. Nature reveals no preference for any one set of them
over any other, and our preferences are essentially our own prejudices. Our ultimate beliefs about the world are incapable of justification; they do not need any and are therefore not open to argument. That is why, it is just as futile for us to argue with
priests as it is for them to try to convince us. Once, however, our
beliefs are put on a rational basis, as philosophical ideas are supposed to be, then logical validity becomes a question of supreme
moment. Mr. Bradley has every right to believe in his Absolute as
M. Bergson has in his Elan Vital; without arguments in support
of their beliefs, their position is philosophically not worse than
that of a Christian with his belief in God, or better than that of a
commercial traveler with his belief in the number thirteen; but if
both these philosophers regard their belief, as rationally derived,
then their positions must stand or fall upon the soundness of their
reasoning, that is to say, upon logic.

But is logic in better luck than our beliefs? Is it any less
elusive? Obviously, Mr. Bradley's logic is not the same as Mr.
Russell's, the logic of both is different from that of John Stuart
Mill; and in the hands of the Germans, with their unrivaled aca-

demic apparatus and the rich possibilities of their polysyllabic language, the subject has come to be endowed with a wealth of form, of color, and of light and shade, compared to which even modern painting can hardly boast of richness and variety. Logic not only differs with different logicians, but also varies with different ages. Until very recent times, it did not show any capacity for cumulative effort. It seems to be just as chaotic as philosophy itself and it is difficult to see how it can possibly be made a criterion for philosophical criticism.

Factually there are different logical systems, but theoretically there is only one implied logic. The question is obviously not one of the logician. He may be personally as different from any other logician as he can possibly be, but within his subject matter, he must come into some kind of agreement with his fellow logicians. Whenever he advocates his logical system, he must justify it, but he can only justify it on logical grounds since other grounds are totally irrelevant. He can not however justify his own logical system upon the principles of his own logic, since his problem is to justify these as well. He has to justify his logic by some other logic if he can not claim that his logic justifies itself; but if his logic justifies itself, he can not justify his advocacy of it, since logically in that case he has no reason to advocate. If, when, and in so far as, he advocates a system of logic he is bound to suppose that there is some kind of logic which is not entirely his own and which he has reasons for not preferring to his own. Whether factually he has it or not, theoretically he must be credited with the intention either of convincing his opponent or enabling his readers to effect a choice in his favor. If his expectations are to be fulfilled, he must argue with a process of reasoning that is not exclusively his own nor his opponent's logic, for otherwise he can not be theoretically impartial. Consequently wherever two systems of logic are competing for our preference, one logical system is implied according to which our preference is to be made. Without this implied system, not only can neither side gain ascendency over the other but there will also be no ground for argument. If each argues with a reasoning implied in his own logic, he is not merely doing injustice to his opponent, he is also arguing with something to which his opponent finds himself in opposition from the very beginning. Without an implied system of logic, the argument of the logician is very much the same as that of the English lady who claimed that what the French called "pain," and the Germans "Brot," is really and simply bread.

Logic is in fact never self-explanatory. It is generally explained in terms of something which is not quite itself. A system of logic may be forged into a continuous chain; if so, each link can be explained in terms of the chain, but the whole chain can not be explained in terms of the links without extraneous elements, for otherwise it has to repeat itself each time it is called upon to explain and consequently can never explain itself. As a matter of fact our logic is much looser than that. It generally includes elements which can not be explained by its own principles. It must however be logical, but it can not be logical according to its own logic, The question of its ultimate logicality necessarily resolves any given logic into a portion of a greater logic, whatever that is, which fares no better with the question, if it is again raised. A process of infinite regression is thus initiated which logically allows no end. Thus while an implied system of logic is required when the logicality of a given system is questioned, no such implied system is obtainable. The only alternative is not to ask the question at all, regarding it either as meaningless or as unanswerable. The latter alternative is merely an admission of our impotence which some of us are not willing to acknowledge, while the former alternative will eventually result in our putting logic on the basis of belief. That amounts to saying that there is no logical reason why there should be logic except that as a matter of fact those who believe in it will find their belief resulting in a chain of reasoning each individual step of which is not itself a matter of belief.

What is meant by the latter part of the preceding paragraph may be stated in another way. For those who do not believe in logic, the rigorous reasoning which is its essence is by no means compelling. Arguments no matter how well founded are notoriously ineffective with religious fanatics and impassioned lovers. It is not always because arguments are illogical that they are ineffective, often they are so because the persons to whom they are applied are at the moment of application disbelievers in any rigorous process of reasoning. Martin Luther is said to have believed that he preached better sermons when he was angry than when he was not. A number of observations may be made in the present connection, but the one that is relevant to our discussion is that moments of anger are the moments during which reasoning power is suspended because a belief in logic is no longer compatible with the impatience with which emotional excitement such as anger is necessarily accompanied. Historically a belief in logic may be the result of an acquaintance with logic, but logically it can not be so derived, since it is itself a necessary condition for the effectiveness of logical reasoning.

We seem to be now in a dilemma which brings us exactly to the point where we started. On the one hand, in order that logic may be effective there must be a belief in it, on the other hand our belief is irrelevant to its effectiveness, since effectiveness depends upon logical rigour, not upon our belief. But the dilemma is only apparent, and not real. A child must be born of some parents, but once it is born, it can get along without them. The dilemma is thus seen to be no dilemma at all, for the word effectiveness is used in two different senses. The effectiveness in logical rigour to a person who believes in logic, is not the same as the effectiveness of the conviction which logic may carry to a person who does not believe in it. In the one case, it is within the frame work of logic, and in the other, it is totally out of it; the system of reference being different in each. But while the dilemma is dissolved the difficulty still remains. Logic is no more and no less convincing to one who does not believe in it than the existence of God is to an agnostic.

# II

Our search for a starting point is so far admittedly a failure. Perhaps if we start from a different point of view, we may get further than we have been able to up to the present. Thus far we have tried to justify our position before we know exactly what it is. We have searched for an a priori justification for whatever view we take, and we found that a priori, there can not be any justification whatsoever. Suppose however we start from the other way around, and assume for the moment that there is a world, that it is possible for us to know more and more of it, and that whether we can justify it or not we to come into contact as well as to arrive at some kind of working arrangement with it. If we start with such a point of view, the question as to whether the world is chaotic or orderly is meaningless. We may sound the future with Mr. Balfour and learn "that the energy of our system will decay, the glory of the sun will be dimmed, and the earth, tideless and inert, will no longer tolerate the race which has for the moment disturbed its solitude." Or we may prophesy with Mr. Russell and agree "that no fire, no heroism, no intensity of thought and feeling, can preserve an individual life beyond the grave; that all the labours of the ages, all the devotion, all the inspiration, all the noon day brightness of human genius, are destined to extinction in the vast death of the Solar System, and that the whole temple of Man's achievement must inevitably be buried beneath the debris of a universe in ruins." We may predict with Henry Adams that the dissipation of Solar energy will bring us a sure and steady extinction and yet we do not consciously commit suicide in anticipation. We may be doing so unconsciouly, and of course none the less effectively, but on the whole we do not intentionally expedite our journey to our final destination, with the same industry, the same assiduity and the same zeal with which we eat watermelon or play tennis.

As long as we live, we have to come into some kind of working arrangements with the world. If the world is chaotic, we have to create some kind of order by which we may live in harmony. If the world is harmonious, we have to discover what that harmony is. The problem may be different in each case from that of the other, but the practical result is about the same. We are not discussing here either the Practical or the Pure reason, we are simply insisting that some kind of arrangement must be made by which we may be enabled to do the best we can with our lives. The question is therefore whether the world helps or hinders our life. We seek facility and avoid hindrance. In other words we follow the line of least resistance, which however is historically ascertained. It is found that with whatever we are concerned in our dealings with the world, our line of least resistance can only he followed by following certain define relations implicit either in nature or in human thought, that is to say, by following logic. We are not here concerned with the question as to whether logic is the law of nature or the law of human thought, it may be neither and it may be both; what we want to point out is that without logic our life is so thoroughly burdensome as to be almost impossible.

But life, as it is generally thought of, has nothing to do with logic. It is said to be illogical. Reason seldom plays any significant part in it. We come without our consent and we go against our will; while we live, we are slaves to our passions, our desires, our hopes and our fears on the one hand, and on the other, we are now and forever after under the power of the blind forces of nature, of what Mr. H. F. Osborn called a tetra-plasmic environment. We sometimes hate because we love, we often smile because we are sad; we weep for joy and we dance to the music of death; pain is to us occasionally pleasurable, and gaiety is sometimes the expression of our spiritual torment; we strive for what we know to be unattainable, we live and let live, and whether the path we take is spacious and easy or narrow and straight, we have no clear view of our destination.

The donkeys of Peking were once noted for their sagacity; they were supposed to have seen the futility of a gallop; neither the threat of whips, nor the commands of their drivers could persuade them to budge an inch from the green grass of the road side pastures. But they were discovered to be passionately fond of carrots and were sometimes seen galloping after a carrot at the end of a stick held by their riders. The donkeys are perhaps not sagacious enough but then are they less so than we? It is much easier to see the short comings of the donkey than our own. A certain American professor; once saw a water weasel in a lake and paddled his canoe directly after it. Both were going at a rapid rate. "A weasel is only a weasel" thought the professor, "it does not even know how to escape." The idea of the superiority of man is comforting no less to the plain man than it was to the professor, but before the latter had time to enjoy it, his canoe dashed itself into fragments on a piece of rock and he himself was hurled into the water. Is not our life galloping for a carrot or chasing after a weasel and dashing upon a rock? Is it rational?

But to say that life is either rational or irrational, either logical or illogical is probably the result of a confusion of thought. Life with a capital L is an impossible concept. It is too vague to permit of predication in any way. It may be used to advantage in poetry, but in systematic philosophy it indicates mental poverty rather than mystic insight. It is to some of us frankly meaningless. If it means anything at all, it must mean the lives we live, and the lives we live are so different in quality from each other that hardly any general proposition about them can be philosophically valid. But if some general proposition is actually asserted about life, it must be a vague concept, and as such, we have pointed out, it is incapable of any valid predication.

Suppose, however, we waive the point, and regard Life as a concept capable of predication. The question is whether it is correctly predicated. It is asserted here that life is illogical. Now logic has hardly anything to do either with things, or concepts or

569

individual propositions. Things and concepts cannot be related to logic in any way, because logic is strictly speaking a special relation between propositions. That is why disconnected ideas or concepts or beliefs, or propositions are neither logical nor illogical. That is why a belief in the devil is on the same level, from the point of view of logic, as a belief in God, that is why philosophy is not concerned with random ideas. Life is not a group of clearly stated propositions between which any relation subsists. It is on our assumption a concept and as such it can not be predicated in any way by logic. It is neither logical nor illogical.

The statement that life is illogical probably means that there is little logic in life. But in this form, the proposition is extremely vague. It is susceptible of many different interpretations, two of which may be cited for our discussion. It may mean on the one hand, that the people of a community do not generally have one purpose, or having it, they do not take the same steps to satisfy it, or taking the same steps for satisfaction, they do not arrive at the same conclusion, or arriving at the same conclusion, they do not start from the same purpose. In other words, there is neither common aim, nor common effort. On the other hand, the statement may mean that our individual lives are bundles of contradictions. A mentally comfortable person may feel himself in harmony with nature, but a sensitive and striving soul is likely to be constantly at war with himself. Since it is only the mentally restless who are to any extent reflective, it is probably by them that the contradictions of life are the most keenly felt. But whether they are keenly felt by many or only a few, they seem to be recognized by all.

In order to decide whether the above discussion is to the point or not, we have to clear up one ambiguity contained in the statement referred to in the beginning of the preceding paragraph. We have to point out that whether there is little or much logic in life, we are not justified in saying on that account that life is either illogical or logical. The vagueness of the term life and the definiteness of the term logic do not permit such an inference. A room may possibly be asserted to be dusty when "it" contains much dust, because that which contained much dust is presumably that which is asserted to be dusty, and the degree of dustiness of a room bears some kind of a relation to the quantity of dust contained in it. But in the case of life and logic, such a presumption is quite impossible. The "life" that contains little logic can not be the life that is asserted to be illogical; because strictly speaking the term logic does not permit of degrees, so that the expression "more or less logical" is meaningless and the predication of logicality of any subject for our consideration bears no relation to the amount of logic contained in that subject. If life contains little logic, it simply means that life has few aspects that are logical, and many that are not. The "life" that is said to contain little logic is a generic term that includes everything that is life and the "life" that is asserted to be illogical is limited to those aspects of life to which logic is denied.

It now remains to consider whether there is little or much

logic in life. The question can never be statistically answered. Our answer is necessarily a matter of speculation or belief, and like most beliefs, it is likely coloured by our personal temperament. But while a statistical answer can hardly be given, any confusion of thought involved in the instances generally cited for either of the two alternative answers must be removed. It is ordinarily supposed that conflicting desires in life are logical contradictions. Such however is not necessarily the case. Thus the desire to be in Europe and America at the same time is said to be self-contradictory, because presumably a person can not be in two places at the same time. Such a desire may be split into two, which may be put in the form of statements such as, for instance, "I desire to be in A at T" and "I desire to be in B at T" where B and A represent different places and T the same time. These statements are only contradictory by assuming that no one at the same time can possibly desire to be in two different places. But such an assumption is quite different form the more or less recognized fact that one can not be at two different places at the same time. Factual limitations need not have anything to do with our desires. The fact that we cannot visit the moon is no reason why logically we can not desire to visit it.

The satisfaction of one desire does sometimes preclude the possibility of the satisfaction of another desire. But the satisfaction of desires is generally believed to be different from entertaining them; it may be obtained in the sphere of feelings or emotions, or it may result in some reaction from the external world. To desire the Venus de Milo is by no means the same as to desire a lady of flesh and blood. In the former ease no behavioristic response is expected, while in the latter case such response is actively hoped for. The satisfaction of different desires may therefore be different. If it takes place in the sphere of desires, feelings or emotions, the satisfaction of one desire need not result either in logical contradiction to or logical consistency with the satisfaction of another desire. If it occurs in some kind of response in the external world it does not affirm logical contradiction in the sphere of desires, even where these desires are supposed to conflict; it merely affirms a place for logic in the external world. My desires to be in Europe and America at the same time do not logically contradict each other as desires; their respective satisfactions do contradict each other if we assume that we can not be in different places at the same time. But a logical contradiction in the external world does not mean a logical contradiction in the world of desires.

Our discussion thus far has resulted only in this: that we can not say that life is either logical or illogical, that whether life contains little or much logic cannot be statistically determined, that our view concerning it is a matter of belief, and that some at least of the so-called logical contradictions in life are not so in a strict sense. However, none of the above conclusions has any very direct bearing on the important point at issue. The point is that without logic life would be so burdensome as to be almost impossible. One instance alone of the function of logic in life is sufficient to establish its importance. The relation of "if—then" when reduced to its last analysis is a logical relation; it is also a relation which must be reckoned with if we want to satisfy our desire for self-preservation. If our Lebensanschauung does not happen to be either materialistic or idealistic, we are liable to regard our lives as some kind of adjustment between ourselves on the one hand and nature on the other. We may be a part of nature, or nature may be a part of ourselves, each may be inseparable from the other; but the moment we discuss their relation, we are bound to regard them as two entities, at least during the time of our discussion. Our ideals, our purposes, our wiles, and our instincts must be distinguished from their field of satisfaction, a field that must be regarded as beyond what Mark Twain called the remotest frontiers of our persons.

We seem to be gyrating towards the cesspool of free will and necessity from which many a philosopher has never emerged. Fortunately for us, a lengthy discussion of the problem is here out of place. It is only necessary to mention that without some kind of comparatively rigid relationship in nature, our will, whether determined or not, will not be freely satisfied. If we will to be warm in our room, during the Arctic winters of Peking, it is quite obvious to the much maligned plain man that we had better heat our stoves. Only fools and philosophers are puzzled over the relation between our will to be warm on the one hand, and the heating of the stove on the other. Whatever result the philosophers may arrive at in their discussion of this relation, the plain man recognizes that if we want such and such a thing, we must then do such and such other thing. The relation of "if—then" is not less appreciated by the plain man than by the philosopher, only the latter can describe the steps involved in greater detail than the former. At any rate this is the kind of relationship that facilitates our lives. Most of us can see for ourselves that the discovery of such relationships removes the burden with which we are loaded when we happen to have desires concerning which such relations when discovered indicate the direction of our activity.

But is such a relation a logical one? The logical relation. "if A, then B," whatever A and B may happen to be, does not lead us to the knowledge "if such and such a fact, then such and such other fact or facts." The latter is limited to the sphere of facts or events. It is the relation of cause and effect, and as such it is itself burdened with logical difficulties. Whatever the law of causality may be, however it is stated, it must be rigid in order that it may be effective from the point of view of our every day life and it cannot be quite rigid from the point of view of logic. It probably was not invented by nature merely for its service to mankind, but if it is to be serviceable to mankind it must be valid not merely for the facts of the past, but also for possible similar occurrences that are yet to come. It must in other words afford us some ground for prevision. But such a rigidity of relationship cannot subsist between facts and occurrence that are not yet facts. Nothing certain can be said about the future, so that if the law of causality is to be applied to the future, it can not be rigid, and if it is not rigid, its usefulness as an instrument is to that extent, diminished.

Besides, there is a more fundamental difficulty. The abstract relation "if A then B" can never lead us to a knowledge of any particular causal relationship in the world of facts, and the causal relationship discovered to be subsisting between certain facts can never lead us to the abstract generalization of the nature, if A then B. The difficulty is traditional, and whether or not it has been solved by scientists and logicians, if remains unsolved among philosophers. It is a difficulty of the general problem of the relation between à priori and à posteriori reasoning. Inductive generalization always involves something that is not inductive, and a priori ideas, as we have already pointed out, are in the last analysis incapable of à priori justification. Each seems to be dependent in a measure upon the other, and while we are not here concerned with the solution of the general problem of their mutual relationship, we are nonetheless interested in it in so far as it effects the question as to whether or not the relation of "if—then" in the world of facts is such a relation in the world of logic.

The answer to the above question depends to a large extent upon a reconcilliation between the looseness of the factual relation of "if—then" and the rigidity of the logical relation. If the two can be reconciled, there is hardly any reason why one of them should not be considered, for our purpose at least, as the other. Such a reconciliation is possible only by making the logical relation logically less rigid. Factual relations may become less and less loose in the advance of knowledge, but they can never attain to logical rigidity in the traditional sense. But the traditional sense of logical rigidity is very much modified by the introduction into logic of the calculus of probabilities. The development of this comparatively new branch of knowledge is itself a recognition of the uncertainties that seem to permeate the world of facts. At the same time, these uncertainties, once recognized, lead us to regard our knowledge of facts or factual relations as statistical rather than absolute. We have therefore on the one hand, a development of the logic of probabilities and on the other a recognition of the statistical nature of our knowledge of facts.

These two tendencies, or two aspects of one tendency produce the reconciliation desired between factual and logical relations. On the one hand, the more we improve our statistical method, the more nearly certain factual relations become. (We are here dealing with facts that are known and are assuming that our calculation of the future is based upon our knowledge of the past.) On the other, the logic of probabilities is gaining in rigidity day by day and although it can not attain to the rigidity of formal logic, the calculation of probabilities has become a logical procedure. We do not of course claim that the general problem of the relationship between inductive and deductive reasoning is solved; it may be, and it probably remains, as thorny as it ever was before. We merely point out that the factual relation of "if— then," including such concomitant variations as cause and effect can become very nearly certain through an improvement in statistical method and that some logical relations of "if—then" are conceded to be not quite certain by the introduction in to logic of the calculus of probability. We are therefore in position to say that the factual relation of "if—then" may be considered for specific purposes a logical relation and that if such relations remove some of the burdens of life, we are ready to appreciate what role logic plays in it.

We see then that whether life contains little or much logic, it is logic which enables us to live with the least resistance. We may be able to show latter that logic will play a greater and greater part in life as we travel into the unknown future, but it remains for us to point out in this paragraph that logic facilitates life only in the satisfaction of our desires that are given, it does not have anything to do with the value, or quality or quantity of desires as desires, nor has it anything to do with the psychology of their mutual relations. Life, whatever it means, may be just as romantic or poetic, or absorbingly interesting, or just as dull, or prosaic or commonplace with a flourishing sense of logic as it would be with no development of logic at all. Spiritual sufferings or strivings, ambitions beyond one's capacity, emotional excitement centering around one's ego, or imaginations that are uncontioned by time and space, or religious feelings or Freudian complexes are, from the point of view of those who are a part of them, those aspects of life with which logic is not concerned.

# III

While logic has been criticized by most people as irrelevant to life it has been attacked by philosophers as inadequate for and inapplicable to the problem of knowledge. The attacks come from a number of sources, three of which will be discussed here. In the first place, there is the attack from the point of view of science. The fruitfulness of science is undeniable, and even if philosophers were to ignore it, they can only do so at the expense of their own philosophical ruin. In its history, science was constantly at war with tradition, and in its struggle for existence, it received no aid from syllogistic logic. While it involves principles not empirically derived, its progress was mainly a result of experimentation and empirical observation. Since its accumulated data are too complex to be organized and systematized by syllogistic logic on account of its limited range, it is easily, rather too easily, concluded that logic is of no use to science; and for those positivists who regard science not merely as the royal road, but also as the only road to genuine knowledge, logic, because of its inadequacy for science, is further asserted to be equally inadequate for knowledge.

A second line of criticism comes from skepticism. The arguments of some Greeks against the possibility of knowledge were essentially arguments against logic, since epistemology in those days was more closely interwoven with logic than it probably is today, But historically at any rate the light of the Greek skeptics was a dim one compared to which that of Aristotle and Plato shone with dazzling brilliance. Besides, European philosophy was subsequently captured by Hebraic emotionalism and by the Church, any deviation from which was liable to incur unphilo-sophical treatment, and skepticism was not such a doctrine as to stir its adherents into willing martyrs. Thus the skepticism of the Greeks affects us only indirectly, if at all. It was rather the skep-ticism of David Hume that led many to a renewed attack on logic. The philosophy of that great iconoclast implied an extreme inca-pacity of logic not merely by excluding metaphysics and theology from the sphere of philosophy, but also by making science itself irrational. The subsequent development in philosophy might be regarded as replies to Hume, but while the anti-intellectualism of today may be regarded as a survival of Hume's thought, it has its own distinctive elements derived chiefly from the Darwinian theory of evolution.

The third attack on logic comes from the anti-intellectualism of both Pragmatism and Vitalism. Since the world evolves, the Pragmatists are not slow to infer that logic and truths also evolve. Thus by a single stroke, any particular system of logic is deprived of its eternal validity, and any permanent system is a mere con-tradiction in terms. Like everything else, it rises and passes away; it is an instrument adapted to the purpose of life only for a given time, and presumably also only for a given place. Not only is logic considered to be always evolving, but also its evolution is asserted to be its saving grace, for otherwise it would be powerless to cope with the events of a changing world. This is particularly emphasized by the Intuitionism of M. Bergson, who probably feels, as Li Po felt before him, that the world is a hotel, and time, only a passenger. It probably hurts his sensitive soul to see logicians claiming a knowledge of the world by their manipulation of static concepts, terms and relations, when with everything at a flux, and ourselves a part of the stream; the only way to be intimate with our environment and to know its realities is, according to him, to move with its onward march.

These attacks may be met by three lines of argument, in the first place, syllogistic logic should not be confounded with logic; in the second place, logic can account for certain facts or problems hitherto considered unaccountable; and in the third place, the static nature of logic is not an argument against it.

Science is said to have gone far beyond the limits of logic. The statement is hardly objectionable, if the term logic means syllogistic logic. But there is no reason why the two should be confounded with each other. It is true that syllogistic logic is too narrow to meet the requirements of science, but it is also true that science is itself logical. Science, it need hardly be affirmed, is not merely a body of knowledge. Nor is it merely, as it is often claimed to be empirical knowledge. If it is at all different from the practices of the ancient medicine men, or the weather forecasts of uneducated peasants, it must have some quality that is peculiarly its own. It seems to imply order, organization and systematization.

It is not merely what it contains, it includes the method by which its contents are brought into correlation. In fact, it is chiefly its methodology that is entitled to the credit of its success. But scientific method means a very rigid procedure which is none the less logic, even though it is not mere syllogism.

Much of the familiar criticism of logic centers around this confusion of terms. Another instance of it is the claim that logic is incapable of dealing with a number of very fundamental concepts. The problems of Zeno, the antimonies of Kant, as well as the notions of infinity and continuity are problems which logic is supposed to be powerless to solve. What is meant by logic here is again syllogistic logic, the limitations of which, true or false, are not properly limitations of logic. The problems that are deemed logically insolvable are some of them at any rate already logically solved. The notions of infinity and continuity are now firmly constructed through logical analysis and are likely to remain with us, unless a revolution such as that of the theory of Relativity in mathematical physics takes place in philosophy, necessitating a general house cleaning of our fundamental concepts. Our notions of time and space, of change and motion have not yet received any widely accepted formulation, but it is much more probable than ever before that such a formulation will soon be offered for criticism and perhaps acceptance.

What seems to be very generally overlooked by the students of philosophy is that logic has developed far beyond its original confines. It embodies at present a good deal of the methods of pure science. Not only scientific knowledge, but also scientific procedure, is capable of mathematical expression, and through the merging of mathematics with logic, much of what was once exclusively scientific, or exclusively logical is no longer separated by a clear and distinct line of demarcation. A higher synthesis is obtained through the use of symbols so that, as Mr. Russell tells us, it is difficult to say where mathematics begins or where logic ends. Symbolic logic has been criticized by various people on various grounds. But whatever the criticisms may be, it can claim at least one advantage: it is capable of greater expansion than the traditional logic. On the one hand, it is susceptible of greater generalization, on the other, it is reducible to a fewer number of primitive ideas. It is much more of a closed system than ever before, it is perhaps too abstruse and technical to be of general interest, but in ceasing to be a mere plaything for philosophical dilettantes, it has become a more reliable instrument than it ever was for serious philosophical criticism and construction.

The above paragraphs are intended to show that some attacks on logic are based on a confusion of thought, that the logic of today is different from syllogism, and that in its most developed form, it is capable of dealing with the thorny problems of knowledge. It remains for us to meet the arguments of both pragmatism and Vitalism. The argument that logic evolves and that therefore there is no one logic is met by what has been said in one of the previous sections. The different systems of logic that exist as a matter of fact imply one system that may or may not exist. The existing systems may perish, but the implied system is logically applicable to all time and all possible worlds. If one argues about logic, one is obliged, I believe, to come to the above conclusion, whether one believes in it or not. The only way to escape it is to refrain from logical arguments altogether.

The argument that logic is static and that therefore it is incapable of dealing with the facts of a continuously changing world is worth a few remarks in that it is urged with a good deal of persistence.

M. Poincaré has somewhere pointed out that if our idea of evolution evolves with biological evolution, we would not be able to say anything about it. A constancy of concepts, and an inevitability of the sequence of propositions are indispensable to the advance of science. The world may change, but our generalizations about the changing world can not change with it; for if they change with the changing world, they would not have the validity credited to them for more than a mathematical instant of time. That of course does not mean that our ideas of the changing world do not change, it simply means that they do not change at a one-one ratio with the changing world. For a given period of time, some generalizations must be assumed to be valid at least for that period of time, for otherwise there can not be any system of reference in terms of which, the past can be described and the future appraised in large outlines.

It is not only the past and future that present difficulties of the nature described; the very process of description and appraisal of nature will be quite impossible if the terms or names employed in such description change with the ever-changing world. Science is now regarded as a systematic and minute description of nature, rather than an explanation of it. We who are mere students of philosophy, are not in position to dispute the validity of such a view of science, we only accept what is offered and if a large number of scientists maintain the position that science is a description of nature, we may be required to justify their position.

Formulas are according to this view descriptions. As such, the terms used must be either statistical summaries of a general nature of exact equivalents of individual objects in all particulars. The latter is both impossible and useless, its impossibility will be dealt with later, and its uselessness has already been mentioned, viz., it does not enable us to say anything about the world.

The only alternative left is to regard the terms used in formulas as statistical summaries. Regarded as such, the term human being includes the notion that man lives to an age anywhere from one minute to one hundred years and that though some men die the moment they are born and others live to 110 years, the notion contained in the term is not thus invalidated. But if we look at the problem in this light, the terms or names or symbols used in descriptions are only less permanent than concepts, they are by no means the equivalent of objects in all particulars. They do not change continuously with the objects they describe, because the statistical average does not change in the same ratio with the variation of particular individuals contained in a class statistically studied. Statistical descriptions can not therefore change with the objects described, they are relatively permanent. The very notion of a statistical description involves a relative permanence of its terms.

It is probably this tendency of ideas not to change with the changing world that has led some people to emphasize intuition at the expense of intellect. Let us not concern ourselves for the moment with the question of whether or not it is desirable that our ideas should change at the rate of the changing world. Let us merely make one or two brief observations on intuition. Is it dropped out of thin air for us to exercise our religious belief, or is it capable of analysis and consequently of intellectual justification? If the former, we need not say anything about it, since it is no longer a question of argument and conviction. If the latter, it loses its distinctive quality in the sense that it will be discovered to be different from intellect only in degree and not in kind. It is quite possible as some of us maintain that intuition is only a quick process of reasoning where the premises and the sequence of propositions are merged into the conclusions arrived at almost in an instant. Those who know intuitively, if there are such, may not be able to analyse the process by which they obtain their knowledge, but it can be analysed for them by others who are less given to mysticism. The essential difference between intuition and intellect is probably one of speed. If our reasoning is quick, it is liable to involve ambiguous steps which we are far from being sufficiently detached to recognize and analyse when we are identified with our intuition. The steps involved probably do not follow each other with much logical rigour, and some alternatives may very likely have been ignored. That is where intuition is so often unreliable. And that is why the slow and steady process of reasoning is preferred to the dazzling and quick.

Those who believe in intuition are seldom open to argument. By the kind of psychology that attributes evil to the devil and good to God, they attribute success to intuition and failure to mere "feelings". If they feel that it is going to rain in an hour and find that in an hour it does not rain, they merely "felt", but if within an hour it actually rains, they exalt and exuberate and go into ecstasies over the profundity of their intuition. Fortune telling is still extensively practised in Peking and fortune tellers are still objects of curiosity for tourists. Within the short period of six months, I have personally heard a number of remarkable successes in fortune telling, but to my amusement, none of its failures. Nothing seems to succeed more than success either in business, or in fortune telling or in intuition. It is futile to urge that the results are accidental in the sense that so far as we know no logical or statistical relation subsists between future events and intuition, since it is the successful feelings alone that are entitled to the name of intuitional insight.

But at any rate one of the reasons that have led some people to emphasize intuition is that intellect is unable to keep pace with the changing world and that such inability is regarded by them as a limitation of and therefore a disadvantage to our knowledge of that world. Whether or not this is a limitation of our knowledge need not engage our attention for the present, but whether or not it is therefore a disadvantage is worth a few remarks. Try as I may, I for one do not see the advantage of a knowledge that runs side by side with the changing world. If our knowledge of a tree can and does vary with the variation of that tree in every particular from one mathematical instant of time to another we should be in a nightmare, infinitely more puzzled and involved in our daily life than Tristram Shandy ever was in his "Autobiography". Life, if it includes such knowledge, would be not only burdensome but even impossible. We cannot live because we can not even begin to live. We can possibly live if our lives are infinite in duration, but whatever our spirits may do after our bodies are turned to dust, our lives are conceded by everybody to be altogether finite.

In order therefore what our knowledge may be useful to our lives it must be comparatively more static than the world known. Its names, or symbols or terms must be crystallized for a time at least into statistical summaries or rigid concepts and their relations must be generalizations of a comparatively permanent nature so that they may be used as data for further and more elaborate inferences. If our knowledge is absolute and abstract, it involves relations of concepts and sequence of propositions and if it is statistical and descriptive, it involves a calculus of probabilities. It can not escape logic in either way; it may involve different kinds of different systems of logic, but it can not get along without some kind or some system of logic.

## IV

It is thus seen that logic is indispensable to life, knowledge and philosophy, and probably to a number of other things which need not be enumerated. This, however, does not mean that logic is capable of logical justification. In so far as any a priori reason for its being is concerned, we have not advanced a step. And yet as we have already seen, if we want to live with the least resistance, if we want to philosophize, if we want to know the world in which we live, we have to have logic. The position we intend to take is thus, or at least seems thus to be clearly indicated by our discussions if we can not justify logic logically, we have to justify it by the results it yields. Metaphysically we have to be pragmatic, for otherwise we can not start any discussion. There is no reason why we should be logical any more than there is reason why we should know the world, or recognize its existence, or entertain desires and strive for their satisfaction. "I think, therefore I am" may seem to be certain to Descartes, but it is by no means certain to a large number of the rest of mankind.

But what kind of results? Obviously there may be many kinds of results and a choice of any one of them involves again the notion of a criterion with all the difficulties already discussed. We have repeatedly declared quite frankly that any starting point is arbitrary. It is essentially prejudice from the point of view of logic. Some prejudices are more suited than others to the life we live and the world we live in, but they are none the less prejudices. Our particular prejudice is convenience. The fundamental notion with us is that it is convenient to believe in logic, at least more so than not to believe in it. Logic is sometimes said to drive people mad, because it involves complications and ramifications of all kinds which are supposed to be beyond the intellectual naiveté of the plain man. It is seldom recognized as affording us greater convenience than probably any other element in our life. It affords us convenience, because it is probably the greatest economizing agent. It is that which economises our life, our thought, and our knowledge of the world in which we live.

Our notion is beset with difficulties like any other. To begin with, convenience if it is used as a starting point can not be justified until almost the end of the discussion is reached. An a priori procedure requires the conclusion to be dependent in some measure upon the starting point. Convenience as a criterion, however, requires the starting point to be interpreted in terms of the conclusion. Its essential nature seems to be primarily embodied in the effect the choice leads to when once it is made. But here we are confronted with the difficulty of not knowing what the effects will be. We cannot say beforehand, which is convenient and which is not. We have to experiment. But experimentation implies that we know what is convenient even if we do not know which is convenient. We are driven to a definition of convenience, which as we shall see later is quite impossible if it is to be ultimately intelligible. And if our definition can not be thoroughly intelligible, we are driven to admit that although we have selected convenience as a starting point, we do not know exactly what our starting point is.

But speaking roughly, we assume that convenience means something like following the line of least resistance, or the direction of the greatest economy. It remains to say something about either the notion of resistance or the notion of economy. Neither however is easy to grasp. The notion of economy may be worked out mathematically into some kind of formula derived from still more fundamental and primitive ideas, but it is not a notion which can justify itself, for after all there cannot be such a thing as an economy of economy. Economy is generally considered to be relative, that is, there should be something to which economy is related. We may have an economy of thought, or we may have an economy of action, but if we are pushed to the very last limit, we are bound to conclude that the greatest economy is to have no thought in the one case and no action in the other. If so, there is no need for economy at all. Consequently, the very notion of economy involves things for which economy is desired.

Here again we are in diffculty. Those things for which we desire economy can not be logically derived. They are only assumed in metaphysics for the sake of convenience. We are therefore reasoning in a circle. The difficulty may be real, but it may just as well be said that we have not yet recognized logic and that logical objections, whether or not valid, are as yet inapplicable. And even if they are applicable, they may be removed by regarding the terms to a relation on such a basis that neither is logically prior nor subsequent to the other. It is probably easier for most of us to see that the notion of economy involves, if it does not imply, something, for example action and thought, for which economy is a convenience, than to realize that thought would be impossible without economy and action without economy would be such a waste of energy as to be totally self-destructive.

To such ideas as the above that are by no means clear and distinct, we are tempted to bid a speedy farewell, leaving them to their "lucid vagueness." But we are not yet through with the notion of economy as an instrument. Professor Pearson is probably the most recent propounder of the view that Science is but an economy of thought and whether the view is widely accepted or not, it is as plausible as any. In a later chapter we hope to discuss the relation between science and philosophy in which we will set forth, in greater detail views similar to those of Professor Pearson, but for the moment we only want to point out that not only is science an economy of thought, but also thought an economy of life, and knowledge and facts are but economies of nature.

That thought is an economy of life has been recognized almost from time immemorial. The old proverb, "Reflect two times before you act" was probably meant to avoid mistakes, but mistakes, though complicated by our moral notions, customs and mores are from the point of view of our action chiefly those results that are miscalculated towards the realization of our aim. That is to say, they are a waste of effort. Reflection has therefore long been recognized as an economy of activity. The difficulty is not with the horse sense of the hunter and nomads, nor with the common sense of commercial travelers. These have long been acknowledged as having economised our efforts. It is rather with the reasoning of what may be called the higher region of intellectual solitude that the difficulty of seeing its economizing effects in life is so often confronted. Skeptical philosophy seems to be upon its face value much less of an economy than dogmatic belief. Our beliefs are sources of comfort. When they are dogmatic they obviate the necessity of strenuous thought. They may even economize our activities, but unfortunately they do not economize and historically have not economized our efforts toward the realization of our aims for which an advance of knowledge offers a statistically surer guidance. As contrasted with dogmatic belief, skeptical philosophy offers an economy that is more far-reaching and more comprehensive though perhaps less obvious. We need not concern ourselves for the present with the detailed steps in which philosophy, no matter how abstruse economises our activities, we need merely to say that it bears a very close relation to science such that if science economizes thought and thought economizes life, philosophy achieves practically the same results.

That facts are economies of nature will be seen in the next chapter and need not before claim our attention here. Our main concern for the rest of this chapter will be to discuss the role logic plays as an economizing agent and the nature of metaphysical assumptions. We repeat that our business is not to decide as to whether logic is a law of nature or a law of thought. Whether it is nature or thought is a problem in epistemology with which we are not here concerned. The logical way is to start with a definition of logic, but if we resort to such a procedure, we have to admit our ignorance from the very start. Logic has been defined in various ways, and the definitions are generally, perhaps unconsciously influenced by the metaphysical position of the logician concerned. Frankly we do not know exactly what logic is, we can not define it with any degree of rigidity, quite apart from the difficulties involved in any definition; but we are, and perhaps most people are, impressed with the subject matter of the textbooks on logic. We are struck with the fact that whether we call propositions judgements or vice versa, we do not deal with them as such; we only deal with them to ascertain their relationship, to see whether one follows from the other, and to establish their sequence.

Whether logic is nature or thought does not make much difference to our point of view. Both these terms are extremely vague. A certain professor at Johns Hopkins University has gathered forty-eight or forty-nine different meanings of the word " nature" current in Europe from Aristotle onward. The Chinese term for nature may shed some light for us with reference to the above view of logic. Strictly interpreted, it means " itself-so". Such a term suggests objectivity in the sense that if a thing is itself so, it does not depend upon any external agency either to will it so, or to will it otherwise. It also suggests immutability of relations, and a rigidity of its course, in the sense that any other relation or any other course would be incompatible with its antecedents. In other words, it suggests predetermination. But predetermination is not a natural event, it is strictly speaking a logical relation. An event is never predetermined by its antecedent in the rigid sense in which a conclusion it predetermined by its premises. While the term "itself-so", means natural, is suggests that which is logical. It is by no means impossible that nature and logic are one and the same thing with a separation necessitated only by thought.

Whether or not logic is one with natute, it is at any rate that which is itself-so. That which follows is logical. Logic is therefore a sequence of propositions or judgements or whatever one may call them which follow one from the other. But it is not any kind of sequence, or one of a large number of alternative sequences. It is one sequence and only that one. It is a necessasy sequence. The notion of necessity is notoriously difficult, and we shall not stop even for a rough definition. Some definitions such as for instance Mr. Russell's involve the meaning of truth and even if it is to be accepted, it has to wait until the notion of truth is made clear. According to our scheme, the notion of necessity is even more primitive than the notion of truth, and can not therefore be defined in terms of the latter. But an indication of our attitude is desirable, for otherwise we can hardly mean anything when we say that logic is necessary sequence. A sequence is necessary when in the last refinement of the given premises, one and only one conclusion remains that can follow from there premises.

But what do we mean when we say that the conclusion "follows" from the premises? Evidently, the term "follows" has no signification of either temporal or spatial sequence. Like a river that follows its course, it probably indicates the line of least resistance. But the line of least resistance in thought is the line that meets the least objection. It is the line that continues the meaning of the original thought. This is another way of saying what has often been said before that the conclusion is implied in the premise. Such being the case, no objection can be raised against the conclusion, if none is directed against the premises. The line of the least objection in thought is that line which continues the meaning of the premises. That which continues the meaning of the premises is that which "follows". What is meant by "follow" in thought is the continuity of meaning if once it is given in the form of premises. If the meaning of the premises is concise and precise, only one line of continuity can be traced in which case the notion of necessity is involved.

The essence of logic is now somewhat clear. It is of course by no means rigid. A rigid formulation of what logic is probably requires mathematical skill which does not happen to be a gift of most people, students of philosophy included. We will have to be content with a rather vague notion and to see how, as it stands, logic serves as an economizing agent. But that has already been shown in this chapter. We have seen that logic is the essence of philosophy, it is the structure of science, it is that through which sense data are grouped into facts, and it is the practical instrument by which life seeks to satisfy its desires.

There is moreover one economy which has been very summarily mentioned and which, on account of its importance, deserves a little more emphasis. It is the economy of beliefs. A belief in a God does not involve a belief in a Goddess or even a belief in British foreign policy. Each of these requires a separate belief in the sense that a belief in any one does not lead to a belief in any of the others. But a belief in logic involves a belief of the whole logical procedure. If one believes in a group of premises which lead to a conclusion, one believes in the conclusion as a matter of course. Logic economizes belief in the sense that the steps involved in any process of reasoning does not require separate beliefs.

That is one of the reasons why science has gained ascendency over religion. Science economizes our beliefs. Once believed in, it accounts for itself; the theories of individual scientists may be open to doubt, but the accepted truths form a whole, self-consistent body which may be believed in once, and as a whole for any particular period of time. Especially is this true of the procedure science adopts. Religion on the contrary involves no immutable relations between its separate special tenets. The belief in Christianity involves a whole set of logically heterogeneous beliefs such as for instance the belief in creation and the divinity of Christ, neither of which is deducible from the other and logically each requires a separate belief. In other words religious beliefs are based upon emotion whereas a belief in science is supported by intellect. The difference is that with the former separate emotions are required while with the latter, a few fundamental beliefs are sufficient for all. Because a religion involve separate beliefs, it is not a subject for argumentation. As soon as one argues about a religion, he destroys it. When Eduard Zeller went to his class room to construct the idea of God, he destroyed the Creator more effectively than the swords of the infidel.

## V

It is now necessary to say a few words about our basic metaphysical assumptions. If we say that we believe in logic for the sake of convenience, we do not mean that logic can be created by will. Frankly we do not know what creation by will means. If it means creating something out of nothing, then it seems to be impossible. If God created the world in the sense that a Swiss creates a watch, then, as Walter Bagehot has long ago pointed out, he created a world out of something which he did not create. If creation means producing something out of some substratum, then the raw stuff must have long been there and is there beyond our creative effort. Creation in this sense is practically the same as discovery. If we believe in logic for the sake of convenience, we believe in something that is already there for us to believe in, and to believe in it is more convenient than otherwise. This means metaphysical pragmatism.

A pragmatist in metaphysics need not be a pragmatist in any other branch of philosophy. He may be in every other sphere a realist except that he sees no reason why he should be so when he is pushed by persistent questioning into regions where ideas are neither provable nor disprovable and where the method of proof or disproof is itself open to doubt. His point of view is frankly unpoetic and to the pedantic academician, even undignified; he is almost like the American Y. M. C. A. Secretary who believes that honesty is the best policy, because it pays to be honest. Metaphysically he sees no reasons why he should be a realist except his belief, itself unprovable, that to be realist would turn out to be of greater convenience than otherwise.

But if one is a realist should he meddle with metaphysics at all? Is not metaphysics open to all sorts of ridicule at the hands of our modern realist thinkers? The word " metaphysics ", we must bear in mind, is a perfectly good word meaning above or beyond the physical or the natural. But in recent times it has been identified with the trancendentalism of Kant and the idealism of Hegel as well as the theories of recent idealists and theologians and as such it seems to be characterized by Mr. Russell and others as more or less of a London fog carried into the academic world where intellectual lights are so much dimmed as to make us suspect air castles looming at a distance. But such a limitation of the word metaphysics is a waste of a good and useful term. It is used here as a branch of philosophy, which deals with those ideas or concepts which are so primitive as to be neither provable nor disprovable. It is the sphere where assumptions, or postulates or hypothese or fundamental premises or whatever we may call them are examined and analyzed so as to effect a choice with which to serve as a starting point for any kind of philosophical discussion.

But a choice involves the idea of a criterion which if a logical justification is required is beset with difficulties. The only resort left is to effect a choice without any kind of justification. In which case one choice is just as valid philosophically as any. That is why our fundamental beliefs, viz., those that are not deduced from other beliefs, are essentially prejudices. Our own choice of convenience as a criterion is itself a prejudice. It may have advantages over other selections as we shall try to show but these advantages are not its a priori justifications. They bear no logical relation to its being our choice. That is to say, its advantages are seen only after it has been made our choice. They may lead us as a matter of fact to adopt our choice, but they do not justify it as a matter of logic. Besides our belief in logic is itself a matter of convenience.

As we have already said our belief in logic does not necessarily create logic. Logic may be somewhere, just as somewhere a state of affairs may exist known either as the world or the universe. Neither of them necessarily depends upon our belief for its own existence. But its existence for any of us depends upon our beliefs and our belief is a matter of choice. If one refuses to believe in logic, no amount of logical arguments will convince him, and if one refuses to believe in the existence of the world, no amount of empirical arguments will ever convert him. For those who do not believe in convenience, there is probably no argument in its favour but for those who believe in it, there are advantages.

There is at least one metaphysical advantage. Our notion of convenience carries with it the notion of economy. It does not tolerate a multiplicity of assumptions, it need not have anything to do with either the *Zeitgeist* or the world will, either the life force or the *Elan Vital*, either Spencer's unknowable or Kant's thing-in-itself, either the immanent or the transcendent. It makes use of Oakum's razor to cut off all the fundamental ideas that we do not need. It is satisfied with a minimum that is required at any given time, it may add or substract according to the demands of our positive knowledge at any one time, but it does not multiply concepts to suit religious biases or emotional idiosyncrasies. It aims at philosophical economy though it may and as we shall see, it probably will result in greater complications in the sphere of positive knowledge. And it complicates our knowledge for the convenience of our life.

Another advantage is that our criterion fosters positive knowledge. It recognizes a real world with real problems that demand realistic solutions. In other words it encourages science. Neither materialism nor idealism encourages positive knowledge, because each of them tries to account for the world according to its own bias which does not happen to be a bias that is compatible with our positive knowledge as it is historically developed and as it is developing today. That realism is more in accord with science will be set forth in a later chapter. It is only necessary to mention here that the encourgement our position offers to science, once granted, is an important argument in its favour.

There is still another advantage. Our belief in convenience involves as we have seen our belief in logic, and logic, once believed in, is one of the most powerful instruments in philosophy. It is one that justifies some fundamental propositions which through the adoption of the rules of logic may become unassailable. Such propositions are the ones mentioned at the beginning of this chapter. We have mentioned one or two, and others may yet remain to be discovered. Some technical difficulties may be encountered, but they may also be removed by technical devices. With an improvement in logical technique, more and more irrefutable and self-consistent propositions may be discovered upon which a thorough-going, solid firm and withal skeptical philosophy may yet emerge at a not far distant date. It is perhaps just as futile to hope in philosophy as in other spheres of life, but since students of philosophy are none the less human beings, they have about as much need for consolation as the so-called plain man.

Whether the hope is futile or not, the above paragraph is misleading in the sense that an advance in logic is itself taken to be almost an advance in philosophic speculation. Logic is a structure, a sort of link, but it is not itself a philosophical chain. It may help us to decide as to which ideas are consistent with a given set of ideas, but it does not help us to chose the ideas that are to each of us personae gratae. With regard to fundamental ideas, we follow our personal bias, and if they are detached each from the other, there is no question of their logical validity. Logic does not originate ideas, it does not indicate to us what kind of ideas we should form about the world any more than it fishes out the lady whom we should adore. Given a certain reaction against the world in which we live, logic merely indicates the way by which our ideas about it can be linked together into a comprehensive whole. It has hardly anything to do with the direction of our thought. It offers us as yet no criteria for a choice of premises. With the development of logic, different philosophical systems may become somewhat similar to different geometries; the reasoning may be the same, and yet the thought different.

How does logic help philosophy? The perfection of logical technique is an aid to philosophical criticism. Ideas that are vague, or ambiguous or meaningless may be clarified or removed altogether by a strict logical analysis. With an improvement in logic foggy not sentiments may not pass as philosophic profundities. A proposition is first split into its terms to see whether they are clear and distinct, that is, to see whether they have any definite meaning. They are then reorganized into the original proposition to see whether it has significance. It may be significant without being true, that is to say, without being consistent with other propositions. The proposition that men walk on their heads seems to be quite significant, but it is not true in the sense that it is not consistent with a number of other propositions in which "men" are predicated. Logic helps positive philosophy almost to the same extent as it helps critical philosophy, because in so far as philosophy is critical, it is also positive.

It is hardly necessary to point out that we are not logicians. The arguments so far advanced reveal only a superficial, or to be more generous to ourselves, only an amateurish acquaintance with the subject which we are labouring at great pains to emphasize. But while we emphasize logic, we are not trying to produce a Principia Logica, or even a modest textbook setting forth its principles and methods. Our subject matter is primarily a logical analysis of fundamental philosophical ideas, it is not a philosophical treatment of logical concepts. In other words, we are trying to analyse philosophical ideas logically, not logical ideas philosophically.

The following chapters intend to deal with a number of ideas the recognition of which seems to afford us convenience in the fundamental sense we have discussed in the present chapter. We shall first deal with our notion of facts, then with that of truth. We shall assume the world or at least a part of it to be constantly and continuously changing, and we shall analyse our notion of change. Hence we proceed to a discussion of time, space and motion, and will conclude this book by a disquisition, on metaphysics and science.

We are bound to say, however, that the attempt will be on the whole a failure. This is not false modesty, it is a mere recognition of the inadequacy of the means towards the end. The critical part of this book, if any, is mainly a question of logical analysis, and the positive part, if any, is chiefly a question of logical construction. The whole attempt depends, upon logical rigour for its success. But logical rigour is very likely an unattainable ideal in these pages, since we have from the very beginning neither a distinct notion of what logic is, nor a clearly defined method of logical procedure. If our logic is lacking in rigour and definiteness, our analysis can not very well be clear and distinct, and the system of ideas herein set forth may prove to be as muddled as those of which it is intended to be a criticism.

But if the attempt is suspected to be a failure from the very beginning, why indulge in it at all? This is a very fundamental question. It cuts to the very root of life. The answer is already implied in these pages. We do not do things capable of any abstract justification. We do not generally live for a purpose, and the purpose for which we are said to live is itself incapable of justification. While I am thinking, I am smoking the third cigarette in succession, not because I am as yet unsatisfied with a romatic stimulation, but because so long as I am not actively pushing my pen, my hands need be occupied with something, and it might just as well be a cigarette. Some of us philosophize, because we are interested in truth, others philosophize, because we want to derive consolation. Many are tumbled into philosophy, because they have nothing else with which to occupy themselves. If we do not expect philosophies to end in the same conclusion, we can hardly expect philosophers to start from the same motive.

With us, philosophy is frankly a form of play. We may be playing it with a naivete that is at once amusing and exasperating to the experts, but we are trying as far as possible to play the game according to its rules. With either success or failure we are not concerned, for the result with us does not count half as much as the process. That is where play is one of the most serious activities in life. Other activities have too often some kind of axe to grind. Politics is a sphere where people aim at power finance and industry are spheres where people aim at wealth. Patriotism is sometimes a matter of economics, and philanthropy is for some persons the only road to fame, Science and art, literature and philosophy, may have behind them mixed motives, but a game of solitaire in a dingy garret is the pure expression of a soul abandoned to the stream of life.

# Note on Alternative Systems of Logic [*]

The notion of alternatives seems to involve the following, x, y, z, are equally F without being equally P, or S, or T. F is the limiting concept for which x, y, z, are alternatives from among which, if we adopt P as the criterion of choice, x, which is the most "P" is, will be chosen. The choice of x does not render y and z any the less F.

We can introduce L and define it as "chosen P" or briefly as PF. We are then justified in calling x the L, since y and z are simply not L. Since they have never been L, the choice of x does not and cannot "repudiate" their "L" ness.

But suppose as a matter of fact F means exactly L in the sense in which x, y, z, are all or equally F. In this case we have the kind of confusion detectable in Professor Lewis' article [①]. There we are told that the different systems exhibited (he meant systems, though he may have exhibited system-forms) are all true, but that on the criterion of practical ends of one sort or

---

* 原刊于 The Monist 第 44 卷, 1934 年。

① In The Monist, October, 1932——编者注

another, one of the systems might be chosen, and the chosen one is the logic, because the logicality of the rest is repudiated by the choice. The contention seems to be that practical ends determine the meaning of "logicality" and conceptual pragmatism is thereby strengthened.

But what is meant by these systems being all "true"? None of them is true in the sense that the theory of Relativity is true, or the proposition that Paris is the capital of France is true. If there were an ideal book on the American government in which all the statements are true and systematically arranged so that the whole book is a system of truth. I doubt whether even then Prof. Lewis would include it among his alternative systems. The word "true" then is not used in whatever is its usual sense; it means simply "logically true." What is claimed therefore is that all the systems exhibited are systems of tautologies.

Thus, though Prof. Lewis uses the word true, he means that the systems he exhibited are all of them logical. If so, many will not be able to see the magic which any choice based on practical ends does to the unadopted systems, namely, the repudiation of their logicality. Logicality here, it must be remembered, does not mean adopted, or chosen or practical logicality, but true logicality, exactly in the sense in which the systems mentioned are all of them truly logical or logically true. If they were truly logical or logically true before the choice is made, they are also so after the choice is made, and that is why they can be said to be alternative systems of logic. If so, choice does not determine the meaning of logicality.

But at the same time Prof. Lewis has in mind a notion of logicality which has the sense of the adopted, the chosen, the practical, and that enables him to think that the choice of one system results in the "repudiation" of logicality for the remaining systems. In the sense, however, in which logicality is identified with the adopted, the chosen, or the practical, the systems he enumerated are not all of them logical; hence they are not alternatives. In the former sense of the word logical, our choice of one system does not determine the meaning of logicality, while in the latter sense, our choice does determine something, but what is determined is not the meaning of logicality, but the meaning of practical or useful logicality. Neither sense by itself helps conceptual pragmatism.

But a confusion of the two does give the impression that conceptual pragmatism has received additional evidence. If you use the word true but mean by it both true and logical, and use the word logical but mean by it both useful and logical, the word logical has two meanings such that given the systems enumerated by Prof. Lewis, one can glibly argue that any one of them is as "good" or "true" (both true and logical) as any other before any choice is made, but that after a certain choice is made, the chosen system alone is "logical" (both useful and logical). Hence practical choice determines the meaning of "logicality." But stick to one meaning of the word logical, and the above conclusion can not be derived.

While the argument is erroneous as an additional evidence for conceptual pragmatism, it does rule out the possibility of anybody's pointing to one system of logic and asserting that it is *the* logic. This the article accomplishes with richness and scholarship. But the same idea, it seems, can be conveyed in a much simpler way. A system of logic is a system of tautology. Tautologicality is a relational property of the way in which the elements of a system are related, not a quality of the system as a totality or unity. No system of tautology is as a systsm ever tautological; that is to say, no system is ever exhaustive of system possibilities. In other words, there are alternative systems of logic. But this does not mean that there are alternative logics.

# The Financial Powers of Governors[*]

The subject is both wide and narrow, wide because many
and various powers have been conferred on the governor to wheck
the legislature which are slightly financial in nature, and narrow
because strictly speaking the governor does not enjoy any clearly
defined financial power. To emphasize the former, that is, to
deal with the problem in its wider phase, requires a compilation
of all the miscellaneous and quite disconnected functions the governors of different individual states respectively enjoy. To limit
one's self to the latter, there is really very little that can be written. Fortunately public opinion in regard to public expenditures
and their abuses have been sufficiently aroused as to make a
decided turn in American state legislation, though it is to be regretted that more "so-called" and less genuine budget systems were incorporated into statute books. The state legislatures, so it seems,
have copied each other scrupulously so that one system is often
representative of quite a number of other systems with only slight

---

　*　本文是作者 1918 年在美国哥伦比亚大学政治学系的硕士论
文。——编者注

alterations. Differences, however, are readily found, some deserving of special emphasis while others only a passing mention. I shall limit myself to the constitutional provisions in regard to financial powers and to statutary provisions in, regard to budget as it is the predominant thing concerning which the governor may be said to have some financial power granted by law.

To deal with a subject of this kind constitution is naturally the starting point, but with due respect to its framers it is a rather barren place to fish for information as it does not contain much that needs be informed. The constitutions of the old state are short. Almost invariably they contain the Preamble, the Bill of Rights, the Legislative, the Executive and Judicial departments, and oftentimes a Finance and Revenue section, a section for Education, Corporation and regulations for elections. They embody the old philosophy of government. The Preamble makes the government one of devine purpose if not origin. The Bill of Rights generally enumerates what the government can not do, hence we are not informed as to what it and the governor can do. The Legislative section contains a few stipulations concerning appropriation, The Executive is not given any positive power in the appropriation or in the expenditure of public monies or in the formation of a definite financial policy. The Finance and Revenue section does not tell us much and the rest are not germane to the subject. The new constitutions are much more voluminous, but in essential contents they differ only slightly from the old. They are new only in the sense of the date of its creation and not in philosophy.

Appropriation is the first step in regard to public expenditure. Without exception that power is vested in the legislature. It evidently came form the time honored doctrine of the control of purse. It is practiced everywhere and is so much interwoven with popular belief that it can hardly be changed. The constitution does not have thorough trust in the legislature either. It does not mind to provide for restrictions even on the popular assembly as for instance for the differentiation of appropriation bills. Such bills are generally divided into general and special bills. The former consists of the expenditures of the three departments, viz., the Legislative, the Executive and the Judiciary and of schools and interest on debts. They are fairly constant and almost fixed, and to the framers of the constitutions at least special safeguard seems unnecessary. The special bills are legislative acts each embodying a definite subject for which appropriation is sought for. They are to be expressed by a clear title, the purpose being, to prevent any attempt to insert "riders" in such bills. However, it has been pointed out legislative violations of constitutional provisions can hardly be remedied at law as any doubt in such cases is generally construed by the courts in favor of the legislatures. Whatever may be the judicial interpretation, it is safe to say that in no state is the power of appropriation in any way given to the governor though he has come to be even more representative of the people than the legislators.

Having now seen that the governor has no power in the

formal appropriation of public money, we should resolve ourselves into an examination of his influences previous to the passage of such bills and his control afterward. Rather than to dwell on what he can not do we had better deal with what he can do. As his control after is greater than his influence previous to appropriations, we better start with the former. We are led therefore to the executive veto. It is a strictly negative power. It is found in practically all the American constitutions. They are of two kinds, one is called the blanket veto whereby the governor, if he vetoes at all, vetoes all and everything in a bill, the other is called the separate item veto which enables the governor to veto items or parts without invalidating the whole of a measure. Thirty-one of all the states now have separate item veto. They are given below together with the dates of the constitutions consulted. Constitutions framed later than 1908 are not in the list.

| | |
|---|---|
| Alabama | 1900 |
| Arkansas | 1874 |
| California | 1879 |
| Delaware | |
| Florida | 1885 |
| Georgia | 1877 |
| Illinois | 1870 |
| Kansas | 1859 |
| Louisiana | 1892 |
| Kentucky | 1890 |
| Maryland | 1867 |

Minnesota ···················································· 1857

Mississippi ················································· 1890

Misouri ······················································ 1875

Oregon

Montana ····················································· 1889

Nebraska ···················································· 1875

New Jersey ················································· 1844

New York ··················································· 1894

North Dakota ·············································· 1889

Ohio ·························································· 1857

Pennsylvania ·············································· 1873

South Carolina ··········································· 1895

South Dakota ············································· 1889

Texas ······················································· 1876

Utah ························································· 1895

Virginia ···················································· 1902

Washington

West Virginia ············································ 1872

Wyoming ··················································· 1889

Oklahoma

Most of them, in fact sixteen of them, are southern states. The rest of the states, viz., those that are not mentioned in this list have blanket vetoes.

There are a few provisions which may give the governor some influence previous to appropriation. There is for instance the power to present estimates. It should really be implied in the

governor's power to recommend measures. However, it is sometimes expressly specified in the constitution, and other times only
provided for in the statutes. The governor being supposed to execute all laws of the state and therefore an executive, is taken for
granted as sufficiently acquainted with the needs of the
government to recommend a detailed account of the amount of
money necessary for either one or two year period. Alabama, Colorado, Florida, Idaho, Illinois, Maryland, Misouri, Montana,
Nebraska and Texas have this provision in their constitution.

But the governor is quite a new comer as compared with the
veteran senators and representatives, he is not the index to all the
multifarious state needs, he is not the recipient of all executive
powers as the constitution would have us suppose, and the
framers of the constitutions knew it, hence they vested in the
governor the power to compel, if necessary, the other officers and
subordinates to furnish information whenever desired. This provision is found in most of the states very much in the same wording.
Evidently each copied from the other as is the case now true of
state legislatures.

The power to present estimates brings with it the responsibility
of preparing them, and in as much as the governor is not so thoroughly acquainted with the needs of the departments a provision
is sometimes made for him to require the departments to first submit their estimates to him. He is supposed to review and if necessary to revise and submit them to the legislature supposedly making them an embodiment of a comprehensive financial policy

rather a conglomeration of many disconnected items.

Then there are some miscellaneous provisions. It is too tedious to enumerate them, and they are quite numerous. They are absolutely disconnected, and their sum total instead of helping the governor generally overburdens him with excessive routine. He is charged with the duties of a member of many commissions, he is sometimes empowered constitutionally to suspend the treasurer or other officials from their duty until legislature is again in session. This power may seem tremendous but the conditions under which it may be exercised make it rather impotent. He is sometimes entrusted with the custody of a contingent fund which is generally very small. Oftentimes he is to sign warrants which without his signiture are ineffective. A number of other things may be mentioned.

I have enumerated a few constitutional powers conferred on the governor. Are they of any help to him in financial matters? The executive veto is probably the only power that counts, but then it is purely negative. However, the effectiveness can not be minimized. The estimate by Professor Holcombe may be of some service. "In 1915 more than one thousand separate bills or parts of bills failed to become law because of executive disapproval. In thirty-nine states about 7 percent of the total number of bills submitted to the governor for approval were vetoed. The use of veto in some states was very much greater than in others. The governor of California disapproved 225 bills or parts of bills out of the total of 996 bills adopted by the legislature. In New York 223 bills or parts of bills out of 980 and in Pennsylvania 211 out of 1003 were the subject of executive disapproval." This merely shows the extent to which the veto has been employed.

Significance must be attached to the difference between the separate item veto and the other kind. According to the latter the governor can only object the whole bill, even if only a few items do not meet his approval. The danger is that if he does exercise that power his salary as well as that of the other executives, if not constitutionally provided for, may be cut off. Hence he really does not have complete liberty in the exercise of that prerogative. He is less fortunate than the President of the United States for lack of the latter's influential position. When Mr. Taft wanted a post office built in New Haven, he merely let drop his intention to veto the appropriation if the desired building were not provided for. And Congress got busy in building the post office. The state legislatures are less obedient.

Fortunately many states have already adopted the separate item veto. The governor here is priviledged to veto the objectionable items which he does not like to see in statute books. He does not endanger his own pocket nor that of the others. The veto is even more effective. It arouses less opposition on the whole hence the chance of passing over the veto is consequently slight. Besides, appropriation bills are results of much log rolling and wire-pulling hence much of the time is consumed before final passage which is generally near the close of the session. The legislators can hardly fight against the veto as they are too busy with other pressing mat-

ters. Those who are conversant with the working of state legislatures in the last few days of their session are aware of the hasty
work and the eager desire of getting results which render a recon-
sideration of the governor's objections before the session ends.
Again Professor's words may be quoted. "... Doubtless many
factors many factors affect the use of veto by the state governors,
but the most important is nature of the power itself. In the states
where the governor could veto separate items in appropriation
bills there were nearly ten times as many vetoes as in the states
where the governor did not possess that power. In the latter class
of states the governors vetoed on the average about one in
seventy. In the former class they vetoed either as a whole or in
parts on the average about one in seven. The veto power then is
generally effective. In 1915 in only five out of thirty-nine states
were bills or parts of bills passed over the executive veto. Out of a
total of 1066 vetoes, only twenty one were overriden by the legislatures. In other words, 98 percent of all the executive vetoes
were effective."

Then there is the so-called "pocket veto" which leaves the
legislatures no chance to pass over it. This is not true of all the
states. In some of them, law provides that a certain number of
days are allowed the executive to consider a given piece of legislation, but if the legislature adjourns within that period and the
governor fails to approve the bill it stands as vetoed. This is open
to abuses and is being changed. The veto when applied to
financial matters forms the chief financial power the constitutions

granted to governors. It is the most significant though not a strictly financial power.

The power to present estimates seems formidable in that it ostensibly puts the governor on the initiative in matters of appropriation. The executive who does not execute the laws to the extent as is often supposed is taken for granted as capable of formulating a comprehensive policy for the legislature. The legislature is then expected to surrender its active power to appropriate only to remain satisfied with the passive power to see that sound appropriation is made. This is, however, mere speculation that is far from the truth. The governor may present all the estimates he likes, but after all it is the legislature that does the appropriating.Besides, there is a peculiar phenomenon that runs through American politics. The Federal, the state and the city governments generally recruit their chief executives from outside of their own ranks. I believe more governors become the Presidents of the United States than United States senators or Congressmen. The same is true of cities. Philadelphia elected as her Mayor an ex-postmaster a public service commissioner who entered the service for two months so as to qualify himself for the candidacy in the public eye, rather than his opponent an ex-director of Public Safety who was acquainted with the business of the city. A district attorney, a superintendent of education or in one rare case a base player have more chance than state senators or assembly men in their gubernatorial ambitions. The governor therefore does not know as much as the legislators. His recommendations are often immature judgements based on half digested facts. They do not weigh with the veteren senators and assembly men, however closeted or conservative they may be. Legally the governor has the power to present estimates but as a matter of fact he does not get much beyond estimation and presentation.

Let us pass on to the constitutional power of compelling officers to furnish information whenever desired. This is naturally applicable to financial matters. It is a sort of political mockery to declare the governor the person into whose hand the chief executive powers are vested, knowing perfectly well that he is not. The framers of the constitution seemed to have comprehended the complex situation as a result of their favorite system of checks and balances. They seemed to have realized the importance of the governor if his subordinates kept things too much to themselves. This provision is evidently made for the purpose of establishing the chief executive authority over the subordinates. The latter owe a legal duty to furnish information. But legal duty does not give birth to enthusiasm or thoroughness in the work. The power to review, revise and consolidate all the estimates submitted to him by the subordinates does not help him in fact to formulate a comprehensive financial policy for the government. Its effectiveness is very much barred by the political structure and the time element. A governor is elected variously for one, two, three or four years and sometimes inelligible for reelection. The outgoing administration does not pay much attention to the estimates which eventually will be used by the incoming administration which is not infrequently hostile. The new governor is not sufficiently familiar with his work and by the time when he gets familiar another election is due. The period reserved for the governor to exercise his judgement is short and among the multifarious functions and the Christmas and New Year holidays the governor however capable he may be can not be expected to present estimates that are very intelligent. The miscellaneous duties can be dispensed with as they do not contribute towards the governor's financial power.

From the above survey, we are safe to conclude that the governor is appallingly lacking in financial power. In addition there are restrictions provided for in the Finance and Revenue section which are capable to be prohibitive of governmental activities. It is again the remnant of the 18th century political philosophy that preached liberty, laissez faire liberalism and all the other grand doctrines. The best government was thought to be the one that governed the least. Every effort was exerted to frame an ineffective government and the most obvious way was to limit the revenue and indebtedness. There are generally three ways. Firstly, there is the limitation of purpose for which extra revenue may be appropriated or debts incurred. I do not pretend to say that one state has one kind of limitation and that kind alone. Some have all three combined and others only one of them. One of the purposes for which extra appropriation may be made as commonly stipulated in constitutions is that of defense. As to what constitutes the defense of the common wealth is left for the courts to decide. The courts may extend their long arm as to include in that clause many things that the framers of the constitutions never meant to include. In that case the restrictive purpose may be easily defeated. Then for the purpose of paying old debts new loans may be floated. This is true of some cases but as has been pointed out by students in taxation, it does not hamper the government very much because the latter can always float new loans to pay off the old debts, and reserve tax receipts for constructive work if there is any.

A second way of limiting revenue or indebtedness is to establish a definite ratio in respect to the assessed value of property within jurisdiction. That is, tax or debts may not exceed a certain percentage, say for instance four mills on a dollar on the total assessed property of the state. The ratio is fixed hence rigid but the premise on which the ratio is fixed is flexible. Property does not have a fixed value, as it increases the total amount of revenue derivable from that property is also increased. There is another interesting fact about tax assessment in America. It is generally admitted that property is never assessed at one hundred percent, but considerably lower. The Assessors and the localities make differences with their assessments so that the value is hardly representative of the value of the property of the state. If government institute reforms in tax assessment public revenue will again be increased. The second limitation is again not a rigid one.

But many states have the third form of limit, a limitation of amount expressly stipulated in the constitutions. Many forbid revenue or indebtedness beyond $ 200, 000. Under such circumstances many a constructive work can not be taken or undertaken. Mere legislative grant of additional power to the governor will not overcome constitutional difficulties.

Thus we see that constitutions do not help the governors in their financial power. In fact, with many there is hardly anything that can be called financial power. The older constitutions are of course silent and non-committal, busying themselves chiefly with provisions to prevent tyranny or demagogy or any other emergency that will never emerge in modern times. The new constitutions expand much in volume but hardly anything in content. Similar provisions are there with greater details. The governor is not in any way benefitted.

Let us now proceed to the statutes. In dealing with law, judicial interpretation is helpful and oftentimes necessary. But I have not gone into the trouble of digging up the cases as that would be a hopeless undertaking. I ran over the recent laws, and the revised statutes or the codes of different states. A large number of them do not tell much beyond what is constitutionally granted. The budget systems are the only additions. In so far as our chief interest is in budget making, there seems to be no objection to laying special emphasis on that.

It is needless to say that systems differ, but it is necessary to point out that they or most of them only differ in details. The scheme as worked out by state legislatures and incorporated in statute books can be treated in general under several groups. The chief difference is between the legislative and the executive budgets, the former being prepared by legislature with the cooperation of executives differing only nominally from the present system, while the latter by the executive thus giving the executive greater voice in appropriation. As a matter of fact, however, budgets are generally prepared by executives in Europe as well as in America. Only one or two states have provided for legislative budgets. Arkansas, for instance, resorts to legislative budget for cure of evils of mere legislative appropriation without a budget. Hence the law of 1913 provides that:

1. Department heads shall submit statement of expenses to the state auditor.

2. Departments shall receive estimates from the institutions under their charge.

3. The auditor shall give an account of the state revenue based upon the receipts of past years.

4. The legislature shall point five members of the senate and seven members of the house to form the budget committee to prepare the budget.

It seems to me that this piece of legislation is all together unnecessary. It may almost be called a legislative camouflage. First of all there is no way of collecting information that is reliable. The auditor can hardly be the person to do the work as he is not the co-ordinating head of all the executives. Secondly, granting that the estimates are reliable, is there any way of making it sure that they will be made use of by the legislators? If the latter chose to resort to "pork barrel", does the law provide for any safeguard? In a word, is there any budget?

New York has a number of changes in the statute books in regard to budget making. In 1913 the well known efficiency and economy business figured quite prominently. A department was created with a commissioner at its head appointed by the governor. He is to study the functions of the different state departments, and the expenses necessary for their performance. A board of estimates was established with the governor as the president and the commissioner as the secretary of the board. The board was to prepare the budget. This arrangement, however, did not last long for it was abolished in 1915. What causes the repeal I am not acquainted. But in 1915 a new system was introduced. The governor was to prepare the estimates and to submit them to the legislature which at once refers them to the finance committee of the senate and the ways and means committee of the house. These committees shall appoint clerks who shall do the work of preparing the budget. The two committees shall remain in session during legislative recess. They shall formulate a financial policy and embody it in the budget to be introduced to the legislature when it again convenes. This is a peculiar combination of legislative and executive budget. That is why that this system does not exactly fit into the second category. The success of the plan would be dependent upon the personality of the governor and the legislators on the committees. If he is only a mediocre and the lawmakers are not particular about the budget, they will swing around to their former way of doing things as if there has not been such a law. In no case should a government depend for its success upon mere personality.

It is generally believed that an executive budget is the comparatively more satisfactory. As a general rule it may be true, but when applied to American systems it allows exceptions. The budget systems in the states are very varying in character. At least three classes can be found: 1, those that are prepared by the executives other than the governors; 2, those that are prepared by the governor together with other executives; 3, those that are prepared by the governor alone. Some require a close cooperation between the executives and the chairmen of the finance committees of the legislature, but they are not striking enough to form a separate class. There are a few examples of the first, more of the third and by far the greatest number come under the second.

The first includes Arizona and Connecticut. In the former the auditor is to prepare the budget with the usual provision of requiring information from the departments. While the law provides in minute detail as to what should be embodied in the budget, it fails to touch the problem of preparing reliable and scientific estimates. While it provides for the auditor to present the budget, it does not provide for a closer relation between the budget presented and the final appropriation by the legislature. In Connecticut the treasurer was the budget officer to report to the joint committee on finance in 1907. In 1910, however, a board of finance was formed with the treasurer, the comptroller and the tax commissioner as its members. They hold meetings at which public hearings may be had, and they prepare the budget. They are also to hold joint meeting with legislature committees. What has been said of Arizona may also be said of Connecticut. Like many others they are half way measures which do not satisfy the expectations of the reformers.

The second class is the most numerous. It includes California, Colorado, Delaware, Iowa, Maine, Michigan, New Mexico, North Dakota, Ohio, South Dakota, Tennessee, Vermont and Washington. The budget system of California has been described in the class room. The comptroller is really the budget officer legally, though it has been claimed that the system has no legal standing. The governor plays a conspicuous part hence easily taken as the person responsible for the budget. The system has very little of itself to recommend as the success with which it worked is more due to the extraordinary personality of the governor for the last few years more than anything else. He it was who dominated the other executives and the legislature, and the latter could be made to do what he wanted. A less gifted person would have told a different story.

Like California, Colorado does not have a very satisfactory system, although she is generally credited as a progressive state. The law provides for a board to prepare budgets consisting of the

governor, the auditor the treasurer the secretary of state and attorney general as its members. It has control over the contingent
and incidental expenses of the government. The departments are
to submit their estimates but no expenses are to be incurred by
them unless they are first approved by the board. They gives the
board a power over and above the department heads individually.
The board revises them and submit them to the legislature. One
can readily see that Colorado has not gone very far and the
improvement is the granting of greater power to the board.

Delaware is contended with requiring the governor to furnish
to the general assembly a financial estimate and also a statement
of the receipts and expenditures of the last four years, but at the
same time she recognises that the governor should have greater
control over his subordinates hence he is enabled to remove them
if two thirds of the legislature concur. Iowa also takes care not to
overburden her governor beyond requiring him by law to submit a
budget containing a detailed account of estimates of expenditures
as well as of incomes and to recommend the same to the
legislature as a part of his message.

Maine provides for submission from department heads and
heads of institutions to the auditor of estimates of 1, fixed charges
2, other charges 3, unusual charges under their respective jurisdictions. The auditor tabulates the estimates and submit them to
the legislature and at the same time to the governor either on or
before Nov. 15th so as to afford the latter enough time to deliberate
over the matter. The governor submits the final estimates to the

legislature the first day it convenes. There is then a roundabout process which is characteristic of many a democratic institution.

That highly intellectual state of Massachusetts does not seem to be well ventilated with Cambridge air. Intellectual and progressive as she is in many respects, she has not gone very far in the matter of budget making. The state auditor reviews the estimates from various sources on or before Nov. 15 th. He submits the same to the governor who reviews it with the council. He may add or deduct or revise generally. His activities end there, and his influence on the legislature if any is purely personal. Michigan has attempted to build up a budget system. A commission has been appointed with the governor and the auditor as members ex-officer to study and formulate a budget. It provides for a special investigator to do the budgeting in future. So far a system is lacking.

New Mexico seeks to center responsibity on the executive. The governor is to ask for estimates from state officials and heads of institutions, he is to revise these estimates and to hold public hearings on them if possible. The governor, the auditor and the attorney general are to prepare the budget and the governor is to submit it to the legislature within thirty days of it session. Here is something that should not have been left out in the other systems. The provision that legislators are not allowed to increase items though they can cut them is highly praise worthy. Their interest in appropriation is chiefly for local improvement, it is at least one way of checking waste.

North Dakota too tried to harmonise the legislative and the

executive branches of the government by making the governor, the chairmen of the two finance committees in the legislature, the attorney general and the auditor members of the board. The governor is to be the chairman, and the auditor the secretary of the board. The auditor collects data early in October, and present the same to the board which meets on the third Tuesday in Nov. and proceeds to make up the budget. Hearing on the estimates is open to public. Members of the board are enabled to examine the books of the departments and other documents. The failure is again a failure to provide for proper connection with the legislature so that the final appropriation by that body shall not be entirely different from the budget presented. Ohio made similar attempts and attained similar results. The governor is to receive estimates from the heads of the departments and a statement of possible revenue from the state auditor. He makes up the budget and recommends it to the legislature at the beginning of the session. South Dakota has a system quite similar to that of North Dakota. It also has a board with governor, the auditor, the chairman of tax commission and the chairmen of the two legislative committees. The personal as noticed is only slightly different. The statements of desired appropriation are filed with the auditor on or before August 1st. The budget board in order to formulate the budget may order special investigation and hold public hearings. Vermont has a committee on budget, consisting of the governor, the auditor, the treasurer and the chairmen of the two legislative committees very much the same as the systems of the two Dakotas. The committee holds public and private hearings and prepare the budget. There is, however, the further provision that no department heads may ask for appropriation directly from the legislature without first filing a request with the committee. This seems to be a provision that is lacking in the laws of most states. The state of Washington has similar provisions and I believe with much more completeness.

Before proceeding to Maryland and Tennessee, we better take up the third class. It includes Minnesota, Nebraska, Kansas, New Jersey and Utah. Minnesota expressly made the governor the budget officer. He compiles the data consisting of a, expenditure for the year concerned, b, revenue available, c, expenditure of the second year of the biennial period, d, anticipated funds therefore, e, all the information necessary. The law requires that department heads shall hand in estimates on or before Dec. 1st, The governor revises them if necessary and have them ready on or before Dec. 31st. He shall print the same and give it much publicity, then he shall submit it to the legislature not later than Feb. 1st. Nebraska also made her governor the budget officer and the same provisions are found there.

Kansas in 1917 requires the governor to be budget officer. Provision is also made for the department heads to submit their estimates. The governor is further enabled to ask for appropriation not otherwise provided for in the budget. The legislature is not allowed to make statutory appropriations. New Jersey does not expressly confer the honor on the governor, but he in fact enjoyed it. He is aided by the auditor and treasurer who submit a financial statement. Utah also makes the governor her budget officer in 1917. He may compel the attendence of officers and with their help transmit to the legislature a budget for the preparation of which public hearings may be held. Then there is a provision which is quite remarkable, the provision that the legislative body may not add but may cut the items. And in the mean time no other appropriation bill may be passed. This scheme would have attracted wide attention were it not surpassed by that of Maryland as we shall see later.

We have come to what I believe are the best systems now prevailing in the states, that of Maryland and Tennessee. These states are not known as progressive but they have gone farther than most of the other states in the matter of budget making. It does not mean that they are perfect. None is perfect. But the ones I have enumerated are such unreliable devises as to make these two towering over them in every respect. Let us examine into these systems. Tennessee provides for a budget commission consisting of the governor, the comptroller, the secretary of state and the auditor. Secondly, it provides for the department heads, the heads of boards commissions and institutions receiving appropriations from the state to submit on or before December 1st estimates to the commission together with a statement of the revenue of the respective organizations, and a statement of revenue and expenditure of the last biennial period made in the forms the commission prescribes. Thirdly, it provides that the commission shall submit to the governor a statement consisting of

**a.** a credit balance of the appropriation at the end of the last fiscal year;

**b.** Monthly revenues and expenditures of each and all appropriation accounts in the twelve months of the last fiscal period;

**c.** annual revenues and expenditures of each appropriation for each year of the last two fiscal years;

**d.** monthly average of each monthly account of the last two fiscal year and the total monthly average from all of them for the last two years.

Fourthly, it provides that on or before Oct. 1st, in the even year the commission shall make a field survey of all departments, boards, commissions and institutions of the state. The budget shall be prepared between Oct. lst and Jan. 1st. Fifthly, it provides for public hearings at which department heads, members of board, commissions, institutions may attend and defend their estimates and to which the governor elect and members of the legislature are invited. All reports to the commission shall be presented to the governor elect. Sixthly, the budget shall contain:

**a.** estimates for the departments, boards, commissions and institutions,

**b.** emergency fund,

**c.** estimates submitted by the departments, boards commissions and institutions and a statement of the comptroller according to section third.

This emergency fund shall be spent in emergency cases by the budget commission. Seventhly, the law prohibits the creation of deficiencies by state officers. In the eighth place, it further provides the transfer of funds from one to another without the consent of the commission. That consent shall be in writing. In the nineth place, it provides for the inspection of all the state organizations and the governor may compel the attendence of witnesses and the production under oath of such books and papers as may be desired. In the tenth place, the legislative committee in charge of appropriation, shall hold public hearings at which all and everyone interested may be present. The budget commission has the right to sit and to be heard. In the eleventh place, state officers shall pay to the treasurer all the receipts in the previous month under their respective jurisdictions and send an account to the auditor. Finally, all bills introduced in either or both houses shall be in the form prescribed by the budget commission.

I have described this system in detail because it seems to me to be more than other systems. It has at least three points of value which may work for its success in future. 1, The system as described gives the governor elect a chance to embody his policies in the budget which eventually is to guide the incoming administration. The fault with many a system is to allow the retiring executive to make budgets not acceptable to often hostile incoming executives. 2, There seems to have a consistent attempt to centralize in the hands of the commission powers that are essential for any piece of comprehensive work. Take for instance, no deficiency can be created nor transfered of money be made without the consent of the commission. The department receipts are to be turned to the treasurer and an account of the same to the auditor both of whom are members of the commission. Such a concentration of power and of responsibility will most probably speak well for the quality of the budget to be presented. 3, A partial but not entirely successful attempt has been to submit the legislature to public scrutiny and hence to bring it into line with the policies embodied in the budget. This is not entirely successful and hence serves to introduce the Maryland system. It may be seen that what is lacking in one may be the predominent features of the other. The success or failure of the Tennessee system can not be predicted. The law was only passed in 1917. But it is safe to say that it has provisions compared to which the governors of the other states may well be envious.

At the outset, Maryland has adopted an entirely different method from the rest in this matter. Other states have sought to compromise the people by halfway statutes which do not go to the root of things. Maryland, however, realized that her constitution was not the proper sort to start with. Hence she wisely resorts to constitutional amendment. This does not mean that she has accomplished all what She desired by this one blow. She has simply found what seems to me the right method. Revolutionary as it is it still falls short of thoroughness.

The amendment is substantially the following: the general assembly shall not appropriate any money except in accordance with the following provisions.

A. Every appropriation bill shall be either a budget bill or a supplimentary appropriation on bill.

B. Within twenty days of legislature's session or thirty days after the inauguration of the governor elect the governor shall submit two budgets one for each ensuing year. Such budgets shall contain in the main proposed expenditures and estimated revenues together with a statement of possible surplus or deficit. Accompanying such shall be a statement of:

**a.** revenues and expenditures of each of the two fiscal years next preceding,

**b.** current assets, liabilities, reserves and surplus or deficits of the state,

**c.** the debts and the funds of the state,

**d.** an estimate of the financial condition of the state covered by the two budgets thus provided,

**e.** any explanation the governor desires to make.

2. Each budget shall be devided into two parts, the "governmental appropriation" shall be of the following:

**a.** general assembly,

**b.** the executive department,

**c.** the judiciary certified by the comptroller,

**d.** the payment of interest and debt and,

第
五
卷

**e.** salaries payable by state,

**f.** expenses of schools,

**g.** other expenses.

3. General appropriations shall include all other appropriations and their respective estimates. The governor shall introduce the budget known as the budget bill which before final action by the legislature may be in any way amended by the governor. The legislature shall not amend the bill affecting either the debt obligations or the establishment and maintainance of school systems or the payment of salaries required by the constitution of the state. It may increase or decrease items relating to the legislature. It may increase the items in the judiciary. Beyond these specifications it may not alter the bill in any other way than to strike out or reduce items provided the salaries of officers shall not be reduced during the term of office.

4. The governor and the other executives have a right to be heard. When requested by the legislature they have the duty to answer questions.

C. Supplimentary can only be brought up when the budget bill is finally acted upon and must be under the following rules:

1. Every such hill shall be limitted to one single purpose embodied in the bill.

2. Each such bill shall provide for its own revenue by tax.

3. No such bill shall be passed unless an absolute majority of all the members favor the bill.

D. If such budget bills are not passed the governor may extend the session during which nothing else could be brought up. Then comes the usual provision that the governors may require estimates from the department heads and members of boards, commissions and other officials and may hold hearings on them.

This is in the main the Maryland system established in 1916. Obviously this is the most comprehensive system so far. It almost seems ideal as it contains at least six features which are worthy of recommendation. ①The system is embodied in the constitution, and the constitution is almost always more permanent than ordinary legislation. The former can not be easily changed and is therefore not subject to the constantly changing legislators. ②The legislators power to amend is almost entirely curbed. This is very important. You will notice that the general assembly can increase and decrease items for itself. It can only increase that of the judiciary. For all the rest it merely has the power to decrease items. Under this arrangement the legislature will not be able to pass pork bills. It can not disregard the budget and appropriate in its own way. We would have no use for the budget, however satisfactory they may be, if they are not to be incorporated in the appropriation bills. This is clearly seen by Maryland and she has consistently tried to prevent it. ③The chance of passing a suplimentary bill is very slight. The legislators have to provide for their own revenues in their own bills. The burden of higher taxation is on their own shoulders. They have to have the approval of an absolute majority which is not easily obtained. These bills even when passed by an absolute majority are subject to the governor's veto if he does not approve them. It may he presumed that he generally will not approve if the budget submitted is a comprehensive one. And of course there is very little chance of passing over the governor's veto as has been pointed out elsewhers. These supplimentary bills are not to be brought up until the budget bill is finally acted upon. One can readily see that by that time the legislative session is already near its end. There is therefore not much time to tight the governor's veto. ④Further more the failure to pass the bill works more hardship on ths legislature than on the executives many of the latter are enumerated in the constitution, their salaries are determined by the constitution hence they are not subject to any legislative manipulation. The legislature on the other hand may not get what each individual wanted. ⑤There is provision for definite content which makes the budget easy to follow. ⑥The governor can always attend the legislature to amend the bill before final action thtis giving him the chance to insert into the hill what over sight or carelessness has caused to miss. Then the amendment very wisely provides in general for the collection of data by the governor leaving the details to be determind by law. These details should not be incorporated in the constitution, their work ability must be experimented and tried first before they are to established. They should be flexibe enough to facilitate easy change. These in the main are the assets of the system and they certainly speak well for Maryland.

So much for the systems. A few remarks may not be out of place. They are generally five steps regarding budgets, viz., the preparation, the presentation, the vote, the execution and the control. The American systems deal mostly with preparation, less with presentation and least with the rest. With preparation the problem is technical. It is firstly to get scientific information from reliable sources, secondly to arrange or present it in a way as to make it intelligible to the public and scientific and unmistakable for the guidance of the legislators. Success has been claimed for the technical advancement of budget making. In many states and cities, budgets are highly itemized and lump sum appropriation is being gradually remedied. But even the highly itemized account does not tell much beyond bare figures reveal, it does not tell the actual amount of money necessary for the work carried on by the government. Technical improvement should of itself give rise to political optimism. It is only reliable when one takes human nature for granted. If on the contrary human nature is as it was spotted over with ugliness in matters political and especially with regard to finance mere technical devise will not produce the desired results.

It necessarily follows that political reform or revolution is the problem at issue. The budget shall be prepared and presented by somebody, who shall be that somebody? It shall be accepted or rejected by the legislature, if rejected, what happens to the government? And if accepted, who shall see to it that the budget shall be executed in strict accordance with its provisions? Who shall control the execution of budgets? The budget officer is first of all not easily found. The auditor, the treasurer, the comptroller, the tax commissioner or a combination of them can not very well become the budget officer severally or jointly. Sometimes they are elected at different periods. An auditor may be elected in one year, a treasurer in another year and still other officers in other years. The first may be elected for one year, the second for two years and the third for three or four years as the case may be. One can readily see that there is very little chance for cooperation among them. They are unknown to each other as they are elected at different times, and by the time when they get sufficiently acquainted with each other, someone has to go and someone else takes his place. They do not always know the business of the state as they are elected for short periods, and by the time when they do know their business their tenure of office is already at its end.

Then they are collegues to each other. None is superior and none is subordinate. The auditor can not very well, simply by virtue of his authority as a budget officer, compel the other heads of departments to prepare estimates satisfactory to him and also to them at the same time. He has no legal remedy if remedy is needed. Even if he has, he has no way of arousing enthusiasm in the other executives so that they will devote their time and energy to prepare really scientific estimates. He lacks the social prestige of a governor, and therefore also the psychological factor that works to the latter's advantage. The same is true of the other officers when they are called upon to perform the same duty.

They can not be budget officers either. Commission is compromise. Compromise never solves any problem, it merely delays the solution of a problem. Furthermore, the American political system adds to the impractcaibility of the commission plan. It is not entirely surprising that the officials are hostile to each other. Frequently they come from different parties. That makes a difference in their faith. Often they represent different factions of the same party. In the latter case they adhere to different and waring personalities. Cooperation out of political struggle is not to be expected and scientific work amidst unscientific political subterfuges of all sorts is well nigh impossible.

Having now made clear that department heads can not be the budget officer, whom shall we appeal to for that very important work? The governor seems to be the logical person to accept our appeal. Professor Holcombe of Harvard seems to believe that whenever the governor is made the budget officer the budget is the most effective and the responsibility is most effectively fixed. As a general rule or rather relatively it may be true, but when applied to specific cases and speaking absolutely it certainly is not true. In fact, Professor Holcombe admits himself that the governor has not the time to scrutinize the estimates submitted and formulate a policy of his own. He is entrusted with too much trivial affairs that can be handled as well by secretaries or clerks. He is too much of a routineer.

Political tendencies, however, do seem to gravitate towards executive leadership. They are unmistakable in the Federal government. Mr. Roosevelt and to a less degree Mr. Taft are examples of executive leaders. The most conspicuous champion is President Wilson. He has perfect control over Congress. He drives the members into activity. The same tendency is shown in the states. The governor is looming large in the public eye. He does more than his predecessors. He is expected to do more. He enjoys better social prestige and more important political position than formerly. The early conditions detrimental to the governor's career have either been removed or simply ceased to exist. Formerly, governors are often over shadowed by the United States senators. It is especially true of industrial states. New York had her Roecoe Conkling and Thomas C. Platt, and Pennsylvania had her Mathew Stanley Quay and still has Boise Penrose. These gentlemen were the real governors of their respective states. But this state of affairs has disappeared in some places and is disappearing in others. The governor is getting to be a real governor. By virtue of his position he easily gets public hearing. The legislators do not interest the public at present. If he is in any way endowed with personal magnetism, he can safely follow the example of Mr. Roosevelt. He can always shout to the people whenever the legislators get unruly. That explains the success of some systems, though their scientific value comes to nothing when compared with others.

The above remarks should not be taken to imply that legal reform is unnecessary so far as personality works for political good. It would be too dangerous to trust to mere personality for the accomplishment of public affairs. It would be contrary to the spirit of law to government by law. In absence of a healthier and safer substitute law must be maintained. It avails little to be iconoclastic about the existing if a better order is not yet forth coming. The only point is that if we are to be satisfied with law at all it must be rigid enough to prevent political evil and at the same time sufficiently flexible to foster political good. In other words, it should not seek to prevent evil to the extent of killing all initiative for good. It should not start with so many "Thou shalt not" to narrow the field where thou necessarily and correctly shall. Cautious prevention of what must not be done should not degenerate into obstruction of what imperatively must be done. It seems that public law is often too emphatic on the negative.

Legally the governors in the United States can hardly become good budget officers. The constitutions and statutes do not give him the necessary financial powers for the formula of a financial policy. In fact the early political philosophy under which the constitutions were framed was in conflict with the modern theory of government. An executive was a person to execute the laws, that was his chief duty. Only in a negative way was he also to see that good laws were made. In no instance was he given the power of political leadership in formulating policies. He did not lead in legislation. The legislature was also limited. And an independent judiciary was created. The whole structure was one of checks and balances. Though slightly intoxicated with French Jecobinism, the early Jeffersonian democracy was but an American version of British liberalism. That government was best which governed the least. It ran through all the governmental units in the United States. Even Congress was described by an European observer as an ingenius device to prevent legislation.

Out of an antique structure government as we understand it to be is impossible. The system of checks and balances must be entirely abolished. A thorough job is necessary for any business, political reform is certainly no exception. Even granting that public opinion is most of the time rather averse to drastic changes. Yet it can not be said that it is always tenacious in its desire to retain status quo, some fundamental alteration is necessary and possible in the course of time. In future there should be government through the cooperation of all three departments rather than checking each other. The Presidential system is already established. It should be given legal standing. The same holds good for the states.

The governor should be given the power to appoint all the other executives or rather administrative officers. In that respect he is much worse off than the President of the United States. Often the subordinates are hostile to him. An auditor of one faction may be elected to check the governor of quite another faction. The federal government is admittedly more efficient and more responsive to public opinion than state governments. One reason is that the President has greater appointive power than the state governors. The cabinet members are his subordinates. When Mr. Bryan and Mr. Garrison differed with Mr. Wilson, they knew that it was to their advantage as well as that of Mr. Wilson for them to resign. This can hardly be expected of elective officials. The short ballot movement sought to remove the same evil. The success of that movement will help the governor. At least he is unfit to be a budget officer.

It seems necessary for the legislature to give up much of its power even in financial matters. Formerly it was necessary for Parliament to control the purse so as to force the king to terms. It was reasonable for the colonial governments to follow suit, as the governors were often local tyrants, but to apply that antique remedy to modern and entirely different politics where the governors are no more the agents of distant tyrants, but servants of the people would certainly seem stretching farther than the situation actually or possibly demands. So it would seem consistent for the legislature to surrender it active power of legislation and appropriation and to contended with seeing that good legislation and appropriations are made. Among those that provide for a budget in which he is more or less involved none with the exception of Maryland grants him any kind of control over the legislature.

The governor then is totally lacking in financial power. As

far as budgets are concerned, the technical development will not overcome the difficulties caused by the cumbersome political structure.

# On Political Thought [*]

## I

The term "body politic" in this article is used somewhat in the sense of the Greek word *polis*, without implying, however, the notion of a city. It stands for an organic whole having a government as its nucleus and all its non-nuclear parts composed of those elements which function either toward or away from, or more generally in terms of, the behaviour of the whole through the instrumentality of the government. Consequently, it has no fixed agencies in a society, since some elements may function indifferently in relation to the whole at one time and in one place, and quite relevantly at other times and in other places. Thus, while in terms of the present day ideology a given body politic may be capitalistic or proletarian, the rich and the poor have not always been, nor need always be, the integral parts of a body politic. The essence of a body politic is its supreme power; it is

---

    \* 原刊于 *T' ien Hsia Monthly*（《天下月刊》），第 9 卷第 3 期，1939 年。——编者注

through the exercise of this power that some part or parts become the guiding influence of the whole and in extreme cases identified with it.

The term "politics" denotes the inter-play of the different parts of the whole toward certain ways or certain patterns in which the supreme power is to be exercised; it is therefore different from administration which is the functioning of the machinery of a body politic. That which pertains to politics is said to be political. Political thought in this article means thought on or about politics and is to be distinguished from thought on or about political thought. This distinction is fundamental whether the approach to the study of politics be economic (Marx), historical (Stubbes, Maine), legal (Austin), psychological (Wallas), or philosophical (Hegel, Green). Any of these approaches might be either thought on politics or thought on political thought. It is with the former that the present article deals. Thus, the works of Dunning, Barker, a part of the works of Laski, and most of the writings of the political scientists do not constitute political thought in the sense here meant; Dunning, for example, must have spent the major part of his life in studying political thought, but his published works do not indicate that he did any active thinking on politics. In the works of others, for example, those of Laski, the distinction herein proposed may seem somewhat obscure, but it is none the less there, and for the purpose of this article, it must be maintained.

Political thought is also to be distinguished first from

political thinking, secondly from political ideas, and thirdly from political theory or philosophy. Thinking may refer merely to the actual process taking place in space time and therefore may not result in a structure or a system of ideas which is what is here meant by thought. Anyone who has any political thought to his credit must have done political thinking, but those who have done political thinking do not *ipso facto* achieve political thought. This can be easily seen from the example of Chinese officials, English politicians or American bosses. Ideas and thought are of course closely related, but while thought here refers to a system or structure, ideas are the entities which are the elements of this system or structrue. Political thought is a system of political ideas; these ideas are not limited to one system, but can be organized into different systems. Since political thought is a system or structure, it is thought not so much of the way as on the pattern in which political power is to be exercised. Political theory or political philosophy may or may not be political thought, though most of the examples given are cases of political thought as well. If by political philosophy we mean that part of an entire philosophical or metaphysical system which has political ideas as its deduced element, then political philosophy may not be political thought, for in being purely deductive, it may not have the kind of relevence to actual politics which political thought in this article connotes. Thus, while the political philosophy of Plato is, that of Bradly and Bosanquet is not political thought in the sense here meant.

Political thought must always be partial to the ends which it is called upon to serve. It may be couched in formal or abstract terms, but in its historical context it can always be shown to be speaking for certain interests. Plato spoke in the interest of the intelligentsia, and Hegel tried to stem the tide of iconoclastic rationalism which might shake the foundation of the German body politic, hence he may be said to have as his interest the defence of the *status quo*. Just as saints and devils can quote the Holy *Bible* with equal facility, so may the same or similar ideas stand for different interests. The idea of social contract in the case of Hobbes was a defence of Monarchical absolutism, while with Rousseau, it argued in favour of an absolutism of quite a different kind. Dialecticism with Hegel spoke in the interest of a given *status quo*, while in terms of the present day Materialism, it is an instrument in the interest of the proletariat.

Since political thought must have a particular end in view, it is a theoretical version of something that is eminently practical. We might say that although it is formally a system of thought, it is yet impregnated with the kind of emotion that is always accompanied by a desire to see it put into practice. What is meant here may be conveyed by the distinction between the cognitive and the conative. These terms refer to human activities, and while the activity behind mathematics and physics, for example, may be purely cognitive, that behind political thought is in addition conative. Political thought embodies some kind of will, whether it be a general or group will, or the will of recognized political leaders.

It either carries with it, or can be transformed into a programme which when carried out would realize partially certain principles. It is therefore quite distinct from pure philosophy or mathematics or logic on the one hand, and from the natural sciences on the other.

The kind of political thought with which this article deals, may be divided roughly into two main classes: that which seeks to maintain a *status quo*, and that which attempts to overthrow it. To put the idea in more general terms, political thought is either in favour of something or opposed to something, and with regard to it there is always a pro and con. The activity behind political thought being partly conative, the opposition between rival schools is different on the one hand from the opposition between, let us say, Euclidean and Riemannian geometries or between Newtonian and Wave Mechanics, for in these the divergencies may always be said to be due to the different spheres of applicability. Nor, on the other hand, is this opposition logical contradiction, since the realization of one school of political thought does not entail the falsity of its rivals; at most, it merely means their failure. The opposition involved is neither a material difference, nor a formal contradiction: it is always reducible to an antagonism of wills and a clash of interests.

It is the purpose here to show in the following sections that taken in the sense outlined above political thought is a special kind of facade under the cover of which active, capable, and ruthless men lead people to accomplish what they individually or as a group desire.

## II

Political thought arises when a body politic runs out of gear in the sense that external conditions become such that the political centre of gravity no longer oscillates in the beaten path. By external conditions we mean any state of affairs accruing to a period which is not due to any explicit political thought. These conditions are bound to be many and various in terms of events. It may be true that economic factors have always been prominent, it may even be true that from now on economics is going to be the exclusive underlying factor. If so, we may say that for every political change there are always underlying economic cause. But economic determinism, if true, only explains political changes, it does not by any means imply that economic factors constitute political changes. In other words, economic determinism may be a form of political thought, yet economic enterprises may not be political activities. The body politic may be included in the body economic, but they do not coincide: politics may be economics, but not necessarily *vice versa*. The body politic has always its own excuse for existence and political thought its own excuse for being.

For those students of politics who are not economic determinists, it may be necessary to study history in order to ascertain the specific factors that lead to the rise and fall of a given body politic. Interesting facts may be excavated from dusty volumes and workable generalizations arrived at; but these are not what the present article intends to bring forth. Like economics, history is relevant to, but not identifiable with politics. We are not here interested in the specific factors that lead to the specific rise and fall of given bodies politic. What is aimed at in this section is merely to state that a body politic is never permanent, that like any other individual, it has its period of growth, of maturity and of decay. If we analyse it in terms of politics, and do not attempt to explain it in terms of economics or history, we shall find that each of these periods is identified with certain states of a body politic describable in terms of the behaviour of the politically active, capable, and ruthless politicians.

The period of growth of a body politic is a period of political creativeness. It is a period preceded by destruction and through which political unity is either about to be achieved, or else an accomplished fact. The new order in its process of becoming requires creative ingenuity and the politically inventive, capable, and ruthless men are attracted toward it, accept is as an outlet of their energy and adopt it as the vehicle for realizing their ambitions. In other words, these men function through the emerging order. Their rôle however has both a positive and negative aspect. Being creative and capable, they function toward the political creativeness required of them, but if they, or some of them, more specifically their leaders, are in addition ruthless, no obstacle is allowed through sentimentality or other forms of tender-mindedness to impede the political momentum already initiated. Thus, positively, in functioning through the emerging order, these men achieve political construction. But ruthless men are ruthless in constructive as well as in destructive ways, in initiating the new as well as in defending the old; the absorption of these men in constructive work decreases the supply of formidable enemies in destruction. Hence, negatively, in functioning through the new order these men are no longer possible defenders of the old.

The period of maturity is not generally a period of political creativeness, but one of political conservation or preservation. The creative work having been done, it remains for the body politic to conserve it, and what is accomplished is an order which becomes a *status quo* and which gradually gets to be more or less refined, more or less imposing, and so full of checks and balances and delicate adjustments of one kind or another that functioning through it requires a set of persons endowed with what might be called a legal turn of mind and judicious temperament. These persons may be capable and ruthless, but they are not likey to be politically creative, being possessed by too lively a sense of attachment to the then existing institutions. Both the institutions and the persons running them have a tendency towards conservativeness quite irrespective of their nature; even organizations for revolution are conservative in terms of their own institutions. Conservatism is not politically injurious, if the men at the helm of affairs are capable, fair and alert. When such is the case, and the objective state of affairs is not pressing for drastic changes, the potential revolutionaries, even though they are kept out of the government, can always spend their energy elsewhere and seek other spheres to conquer. Civilization in general flourishes when creative human energy is no longer monopolized, and the body politic is in a state of stable equilibrium which is its period of maturity.

But a body politic does not remain perpetually stable. There will be a time when both the powers that he and the institutions become equally incapable of absorbing alert and capable men whether of the creative or of the conservative type. A decaying body politic does not mean a corrupt or inefficient government. A government may be corrupt or inefficient or both and yet the body politic may be otherwise healthy enough to attract capable men to institute reforms. Reformation means that on the one hand part of the existing political institutions can be used as instruments for political changes of one kind or another indicating a healthy body politic, and on the other, capable men are still willing to accept the existing machinery as an outlet of their energy and as the playground of political of their ambitions. Reformation become impossible only when the political centre of gravity is no longer housed in the formal institutions which become thus empty shells incapable of being used as the vehicles through which the ambitions of the active, capable, and ruthless men could be realized. When such is the case, we have a period of decay.

A fuller analysis could no doubt be given, but brief and

probably inadequate as the above may be, it is yet sufficient to indicate what is meant by these periods. Each of these periods has its peculiarity so far as political thought is concerned. During periods of growth, the struggle is mainly concerned with practical measures or programmes intended to substantiate certain principles which have become more or less accepted. These principles may be more or less emotionally moving to the masses, but are generally no longer intellectually intriguing to the élite. In periods of maturity, there usually isn't much active political thought, though there may be scholarly expositions. It should be the kind of period in which text books on politics would flourish, and whatever is not a defence of the *status quo* is likely to be either ignored or benevolently tolerated, or else mere echoes in the political wilderness. But during periods of decay, political thought is more likely than not to be on fundamental principles. The initial step is to dress up in attractive and easily understood forms, and then to pass them as items of mental currency, until some of these ideas emerge through struggle into prominence, partly because of the cogency of their pattern, but chiefly because of the backing they receive from people who have since become powerful politically. When no political thought different from the predominant one remains in political rivalry, a period of growth of another body politic begins.

In a society or a nation of long history such as China, there may be a succession of different bodies politic, and hence also a cycle of the different periods of growth, maturity and decay. As has been mentioned, we are not interested in the causes that led to the rise or fall of bodies politic. We merely state that there are such periods and that upon analysis they may be seen to have certain bearings on political thought. On the whole, political thought in the sense here meant flourishes during periods of growth and decay, while during periods of maturity, it is quiescent, not in the sense of the absence of political theories, but in the sense that these theories, if any, are not engaged in a struggle to master practical politics.

## III

But why political thought at all? It may be argued that among animals there are numerous examples of instinctive leadership; packs and herds achieve collective action without any articulate thought. School children exemplify the same phenomenon when they play in groups. History abounds in evidences for the transference of political power without any articulation in the form of a structure of political ideas. Why, again, political thought at all? In the following paragraphs, attempts will be made to show that for the kind of animals that human beings are, political thought is needed, in spite of the argument that collective action can be achieved without articulate thought.

To begin with, among human beings the craving for sympathy and understanding result inevitably in the desire for justification. Justification is not merely giving an account of one's activities, but also involves the invoking of principles, articulate or otherwise, in terms of which, sympathy and understanding and even approval may be procured. That there is such a desire for justification we need not doubt for a moment, though theoretical account of it may differ in different studies by different persons. Some may account for it by the notion of a consciousness of kind, others may attribute it to what is called instinct, while still others may claim it to be due to conditioned reflexes. Whatever the explanation may be, the fact remains that human beings desire and need justification. Since justification is needed in so many human activities, it is all the more needed in activities which are political. Political thought is a justification of political activities and is itself indirectly a political activity in disguise.

Besides this craving for justification, political thought is also needed for other reasons. Take the most obvious reason first. Political activity is collective among people who have heterogeneous interests in their other spheres of life, and whose support can be gained only through some kind of common programme. What is meant to be achieved by the activity must be communicated and partly, if not entirely, understood by all concerned, if the activity is to gather momentum. But communication to those who are to accept a certain programme requires articulate thought on the part of those who are proposing it, and communication to the intellectually élite requires especially an exhibition in impersonal terms of the urgent desirability as well as the reasonableness and the cogency of the programme proposed. This could not be done without first principles, or a structure of political ideas. Hence, political thought.

A more subtle reason is that political activity must be based on certain group interests to start with and yet must not be identified with them. Perhaps the term group interests is misleading. One is perhaps liable nowadays to think of group interests as being essentially the economic interests of the capitalists, or the proletariat, or industrial or trade unions. This may or may not be so. What is important is that people may combine to form groups and develop their own interests without having any interests to start with other than the strictly political. In other words, political groups may gather strange bed-fellows for purely political reasons. A political activity would be mere abstract yearning, if it were not based on the interests of political groups; but it can not be identified with any given group, for it may cease to be political. The point involved is that political activities should not be limited to group interests in theory, though always so in practice, merely because political activities are supposedly at any rate indulged in for the whole body politic. If they are in theory limited to any given group, they probably won't find support outside the group; but if they are not based on the interests of any group at all, they are merely the merry-go-rounds of people stigmatized by the *real politikers* as idealistic dreams. Political thought, whatever else it may be, is the theory behind political activities.

Political thought is needed for another reason. Political activity is never purely cognitive, if indeed it has to be so at all; it is at any rate conative. If it is to be at all extensive, it involves the imposition of a will either to shape or to reshape certain aspect or aspects of the political environment. In order that that will may be shared by all to any appreciable degree, not to say its full realization, mass emotion has to be aroused. But as such emotion cannot be aroused by specific measures of one kind or another, general principles will have to be invoked so that people can be made emotionally attached to them and prepared to accept them as what we are in the habit of calling "causes". Causes differ from other principles in having with them emotive values which make it difficult for those who are attached to them to accept or even to contemplate any alternative. They are fundamental in this special sense. At present, the principles of dialectic materialism, though far removed perhaps from practical measures, stir the blood of millions of adherents, whereas the principle of relativity or the principle of induction important for other reasons leave people in a normal state of mind. Extensive or far-reaching political activity cannot leave people in a normal state of mind, in spite of the fact that within the system of thought that is a justification of the said activity, there may be constant and untiring appeals to reason. We must not forget that the eighteenth century rationalism is eminently emotive. It is perhaps the fate of human beings that they are on the whole more susceptible to emotional appeals to reason than to reasonable arguments in favour of it. Since the emotive element could not be absent, political activity has to be accompanied by political thought, the principles of which are generally also "causes".

What is needed in politics is neither sheer activity nor mere programme. Human beings including politicians are neither sufficiently naive nor sufficiently sophisticated for that, for extreme naiveté and extreme sophistication have a common meeting ground in unadorned realism, and human beings are never quite so tough-minded as to be thoroughly realistic. To be human is to be inextricably interwoven with the complex fabric of emotion and intellect, to be immersed in that congeries of hopes, fears, doubts, beliefs, aspirations and inhibitions, for which the Zeitgeist in terms of its ideology and valuation charts out the main spring of action. Since some kind of balance is maintained in life between purely impulsive activity and thoroughly controlled behaviour, political thought has to be formulated in terms of this balance. On the one hand, political activity must be accompanied by thought, and on the other, political thought must be such that it stirs people to political activity.

## IV

Political thought must be timely, despite the idea of eternal concepts or principles. Timeliness here refers to the facility with which certain concepts or principles or systems are accepted at certain times, not their validity, nor their mere subsistence. From the point of view of subsistence, ideas are eternal in the sense that they are out of time; but such a sense of eternity is irrelevant to our present topic, since in this sense all ideas are equally timeless. From the point of view of validity, some principles may be said to be eternally valid. However, it is difficult, if not impossible, to find any example of such in the sphere of political thought, and even if it could be found, we can not assert as a consequence that it is always timely.

Political thought has a practical side in addition to the theoretical. The practical side to a given political thought leads us to the history both of facts and of ideas. An examination of contemporary facts account for certain problems taken up, certain measures advocated, and an examination of contemporary ideas account for certain phrases used and certain principles emphasized in a given political thought. Without this historical background, no political thought is quite understandable. This is plain, but what is not quite so plain is the relation between political thought and the *Zeitgeist*. As has been pointed out in the previous section, the main spring of human action that emerges from a congeries of hopes, fears, beliefs, and doubts and what not, is charted out by the ideology and valuation of a given time. In terms of ideology, what is known as the *Zeitgeist* of a given period is simply its predominant over-simplification of the complex issues so that with it the lazy or the stupid are absolved from any active thinking. One who adheres to a prevailing "ism" of any kind is like wearing coloured glasses; he may see as many things as other people, but in seeing them always in a certain light, he allows whatever thinking that is needed to be in practice done for him. In terms of valuation, the *Zeitgeist* of a given period is reflected in the manners in which the people of that period would conduct themselves in all the complexities of life; so that with it the lazy or the insensitive are excused from having to have any active and real feeling beyond its external forms. One who conducts himself in terms of contemporary valuation is essentially a conventional man, though he may be fashionable, since for him how he should and does feel is socially prescribed. The *Zeitgeist* is therefore something which unifies thought and behaviour, it is a whipping rod by which the masses are herded for action. Since political action does involve the masses, political thought must be in consonance with the *Zeitgeist* in order that it may be stirring. It is more specifically in this sense that political thought has to be timely.

Since times differ, the ideology and valuation of different times are sometimes also different. Take the simpler ease of ideology. The cry of "reason" was stirring in the 18th century, the idea of evolution moving in the latter part of the 19th, while at the present the idea of economic determinism or dialectic materialism is like music in the air to millions of young political enthusiasts. These ideas may be either valid or invalid, but during their prevalency they are all of them dogmas of simplification, in terms of which thinking could be minimized, and political thought in consonance with them is also timely at different times. This obviously does not mean that thought not in consonance with the *Zeitgeist* necessarily fails, the very fact that there is succession of predom-

inant ideas at different times indicates that what was once unpopular may emerge to be timely. But unpopular political thought has
an up-hill fight to gain predominance and before some degree of
timeliness is gained, it has no political efficacy, and while it may
be some kind of pattern of political ideas, it is not yet political
thought in the sense here emphasized. Though abstract and fundamental principles of politics may have long periods of timeliness, the kind of political thought here emphasized generally
varies with the passage of time.

The timeliness of political thought is just as much the timeliness of the structure as that of its ideas. The latter is easily seen.
Take for instance, the historical school of political thought. It
could have struggled along without the notion of evolution, but
with the notion, it captured for a time the imagination of the liter-
ate public. Guild socialism prevailed for a short period some
twenty years ago when people in the West were somewhat tired of
the modern mechanical age; as a system, it adds very little to the
already current forms of socialistic thought, but it had at the time
a romantic appeal by being linked up with the notion of
mediaeval guilds. While the cogency of Thomas Hobbes appeals
to the intellectually fastidious, especially among those who have a
tendency towards abstraction, it was never timely and never
stirred the heart of the masses. Perhaps the idea of social contract
offers an example both for the timeliness of the idea as well as
that of structure; it must have had enormous appeal during the
time it flourished, but in the cogent but untimely system of

Hobbes, its power of appeal was much smaller than in the timely system of Rousseau.

Timeliness is a convenient term to cover complexities which are bafflingly difficult to analyze. Perhaps we could say that the facility with which certain political thought is accepted at certain times indicates something in or about its structure or ideas or both which is meant to appeal, and since political thought is not just any current ideas strung together, the thinker behind it must be an artist as well. This of course is true of other systems. Euclid is an artist as well as a thinker. So also are Rousseau and Marx, only they are so in a different sphere. As a work of art, political thought is on the one hand distinguished from other systems of thought in that it is meant to appeal to a large number of persons and to evoke in them a multifarious set of sometimes even conflicting emotions, and on the other, it is distinguished from what is usually called works of art in that it is at the same time a system of thought, and as such subject also to the rigours of logic. It is a pattern of ideas created out of the materials that are historically and contemporaneously given, but so delicately adjusted as to appeal to the intellect of a few, to satisfy the interest of some, and to arouse the emotion of large members. It is purely political thought, and nothing else; it is neither pure thought, nor pure history, nor pure science, nor pure art, but all of these combined into a whole and woven into a pattern, the appreciation of which is not ecstasy in a gallery, but political activity towards the exercise of political powers more or less in accordance with

667

the pattern created. Though difficult to analyse, political thought must yet have a technique of its own. If l' Abbé Sieyeè could develop the art of writing constitutions, some talented person might in future develop the art of generating political thought to suit different conditions at different times.

## V

But who needs political thought? If it is supplied, it must be supplied to somebody. We must bear in mind that the fundamental thing in polities is the control of political power, and the pattern in which this power is to be exercised. If the patten becomes unsatisfactory from the point of view of the objective conditions obtaining at any period so that political rackets would be started with profit, the control will have to be transferred. If the transference could be achieved without revolution, well and good; if it must be achieved through revolution, then revolution will come. In any case, different groups of capable, active, and ruthless men will he pitted against each other. These are the star actors of the political stage, without them there can be no stirring political drama.

The activities of these men cannot be stayed. These men constitute the natural aristocracy of any society. They are found everywhere, in bands as well as in trade unions, among capitalists as well as among the proletariat. If the objective conditions are not ripe for political activities of any extensive scope, they seek other fields to conquer, but if the objective conditions are such that movements of far-reaching political consequence can be initiated, they become political leaders. Ruthlessness is of supreme importance. The meek may inherit the world in other ways, but not politically. Those who have no wish to impose their will upon others will never become politicians, and those who can be prevented from doing so through any form of tender-mindedness could not be successful political leaders. Unswerving devotion to causes is admirable and as often as not a genuine phenomenon, but the psychological reality behind it is always an unflinching determination to impose one's will upon one's fellow men. For these leaders of men, political thought is a sort of Juno-esque facade, a dignified exposure on the one hand, so that followers could be attracted toward them, and an effective cover on the other, so that their energy might be spent, their ambition realized, and their will at last imposed upon their fellow men.

It is to these men that political thought is supplied as a facade for their activities. In order to remove a possible and likely misunderstanding, it should be said that this paper is not an argument in favour of the Great Man theory. The notion of greatness involves valuation of various kinds, one may be valued for what he is, or for what he does, or both, what is valued in one may he quite different from what is valued in another. At any rate, greatness in men refers to prescriptive values, not to descriptive qualities. Great men may exist, but whether the Great Man theory is valid or not is quite another question. We are not concerned with it or them in this article. The kind of men described here as capable, active, and ruthless, are so described as to indicate their function in the body politic, not the values prescribed for them and heaped upon them by society. They may be scoundrels, ignoramuses, rascals, bores, or great men; Chinese history alone abounds in evidences of scoundrels, and great men becoming powerful political leaders, even founders of dynasties. How they are judged according to the different criteria of valuation is immaterial to the purpose of this article, it is their function that counts.

Perhaps if we proceed from another angle, the point involved may be brought out into even more striking relief. The Kind of Great Man theory that is at all significant does not merely assert the existence of great men, but also that they achieve what they desire irrespective of the objective conditions. In other words, leaders lead, and they are in no sense led. Now, while this articles does affirm that capable, active and ruthless men are political leaders, it does not assert that they are never led. Only theorists insist on leaders leading, the leaders themselves are sufficiently realistic as not to be concerned with whether they actually lead or are sometimes led, the important things with them is to seize the occasion when things are ripe, or else to bid for times as Fabius did of old. They may or may not be opportunists; they either achieve opportunity or wait for it, but they cannot ignore it. The ideas they stand for may originate from themselves, or are appropriated from thinkers who are not practical men, or else mere items of mental currency that could be picked up here and there, but once they champion these ideas, they become also the vehicles for the realization of these ideas. If in political thought, it does not make the least difference whether they are the masters or the disciples, it matters still less, whether they are the originators or merely the instruments of the will that is imposed upon their fellow men. The question whether circumstances make men or men circumstances need not be discussed here, for one way or the other, it is only some men who are of any consequence, and in politics it is the capable, active, and ruthless type of men that counts whether they are saints or devils, or else disciples or masters.

As a rule, however, leaders in practical politics are rarely at the same time political theorists. One who is versed in theory is generally not capable of practical work, and vice versa. Marx is undoubtedly the high priest of communistic thought, but he is not its statesmen; if he were given the rôle of Stalin, he might not have the latter's success, and yet in all probability he would have suffered as philosopher. Mussolini and Hitler might have been tragic and therefore in some sense grand, if they had been satisfied with being the instrument of the blind impulses that burst forth from mass inhibitions, but when they attempt to theorize at the same time, they only succeed in being farcical and ridiculous. To combine the two rôles would be on the whole disparaging to either the one or the other. There were exceptions in earlier ages, but in modern times when division of labour has taken place in almost every line of human endeavour, to be a ruler is hardly compatible with being a theorist at the same time. Political theorizing will more than ever go into the hands of intellectuals who beat about the bush for stirring political ideals and attempt to inherit the world through the capable, active, and ruthless men in politics.

To treat political thought descriptively as a facade is not meant to be derogatory to the theorist or to the statesman; each has his function and *raison d' être* in the body politic. To point out their difference is partly the purpose of this article. It may also be mentioned incidentally that being merely thought on political thought, this article is not its own subject matter.

# Truth in True Novels[*]

## I

Novels can be evaluated in a number of ways. One of the criteria upon which they might be evaluated is the truth they embody. It is not the most important element in a novel, some readers probably pay no attention to it; on the other hand, it is not necessarily the least important, since critics do sometimes take it into consideration when they pass judgment upon novels. Probably the term fiction so often used as a substitute enables cosmic laziness to act upon us to such an extent as to ignore the problem most of the time. Certainly it has not up to the present received either the amount or the kind of attention it undoubtedly deserves. The following discussion is an attempt to reveal certain perplexities in which difficulties are encountered when we take up the problem as to what it is that is said to be true when we say with regard to certain novels either that they are true or that they

* 原刊于 T'ien Hsia Monthly (《天下月刊》), 第 4 卷第 4 期, 1937 年。——编者注

are false.

The general problem of truth is not the subject matter of this article. For the purpose of comparison, however, we may enumerate the different kinds of truths with which we are more or less familiar, and ascertain if possible to which of these the truth of a novel belongs. We may start with the truth in logic or rigorously formalized mathematics. It has often been said that nature abhors a vacuum. It might be claimed at least elliptically that logic loves it. The vacuousness of logic is one of the sources of its universal validity. The propositions in logic are such that they assert no possibility as a fact, and any and every possibility as a possibility. Take the simplest case: *this is a hat or it is not.* It is easily seen that one can make such a statement about anything whatsoever and is in no danger of making any mistake. One cannot make any mistake, because in such a statement one says nothing. But while nothing is said, every possibility is considered, and that is why such statements differ from mere collections of symbols or noises. Truth in logic may therefore be described as eternal; it holds in the best possible world of the optimist as well as in the worst possible world of the pessimist, and also in a state of affairs in which there is no "world" at all, whether good or bad or indifferent. Logic does drive a man mad if he tries to escape from its validity, *madder* even than the legendary monkey who could cross over 108, 000 *li* in one somersault and yet always find himself afterward well within the palm of the benignant and ever smiling Buddha.

Truth in the sciences is quite different from truth in logic. The term science here includes only the natural sciences. Poincaré in his *Science and Hypothesis* dwelt succinctly on the difference between history and science:

"... Carlyle has somewhere said something like this:

'Nothing but facts are of importance. John Lackland passed by here. Here is something that is admirable. Here is a reality for which I would give all the theories in the world.' Carlyle was a fellow countryman of Bacon, but Bacon would not have said that. That is the language of the historian. The physicist would say rather: John Lackland passed by here; but that makes no difference to me, for he will never pass this way again."

What is here said about the physicist applies equally to any other scientist. What the scientist seeks after is general truths. These might be called laws of nature, if we take care not to attach to them the awe-inspiring emotions which Europeans at one time were in the habit of attaching to *jus naturalae* or to *lex naturalis*. Nonetheless a scientific truth is much more serious to most of us than the logician's fondly cherished tautology.

Logicians are to some extent like Matthew Arnold's ineffective angels, they arouse in most of us a bit of impatience and occasionally even a bit of ridicule, appearing to be beating about the bush where there isn't any bird to be caught. Scientists, on the other hand, are out for serious business; they are solid, respectable and dignified citizens of the community, engaged in the business of discovering scientific truth for which no suspicion of frivolity can be entertained. Unlike a proposition in logic, a scientific truth says something on the one hand and doesn't entertain any and every possibility on the other, it is restricted to the nature that is given, and what is said about nature is said with an eye towards generality. There are of course degrees of generality as well as differences in the extent of pervasiveness, but whatever else might be said, one thing is certain: a scientific truth is a true general proposition. When we talk of the law of gravitation, or the second law of thermo-dynamics, or the Mendelian law, we are talking of certain general propositions each and every one of which asserts certain general relations.

Truth in the sciences then is the truth of true general propositions. It is the nature of true general propositions that they are always verifiable. In the experimental sciences these propositions are verifiable at any time given the suitable background, and in the observational sciences, they are verifiable with the recurrence of the phenomena covered by them. They are verifiable, because the relations asserted by them repeat themselves. This is probably the most important difference between history and science. Max Beerbohm once remarked that history never repeats itself, only historians repeat each other. This may be an unnecessary dig at the historians, but it isn't at all a dig at history. No general proposition can possibly deal with unrepeating events; and when general propositions are found in history books, as they often are, they are not assertions of facts in history. There are of course laudable attempts at making history a science, but these are nonetheless futile, for the science of history is no more history than the history of science.

Truth in history is the truth of true singular or else particular propositions. It is the truth either about some concrete events such as the battle of Tours, or the Hegira, or the Council of Nicaea, etc., or else concerning once existent individuals such as Confucius, or T'ang T'ai Chung, or Shakespeare, etc. History not only deals with the concrete, but also with the past. There can be no history of the future, nor of the strict present. What is known as "history in the making" probably refers only to the subject matter for future research, not to the present research for a subject matter that is yet in the making. The concreteness and pastness of history lead us to think of historians as musty grandfatherly persons in night-caps and warm slippers, mumbling to people from their accustomed armchairs by their accustomed firesides, and the truth they discover is correspondingly infested with a home like atmosphere in contradistinction to the ruthlessness and externality of scientific truth on the one hand, and to the strenuous precision and beautiful vacuousness of a proposition of logic on the other.

The different kinds of truths are different from each other not merely in what they are, but also in our response to them in which different emotions are called forth. But they have nonetheless something in common; they contain in all of them the truth of propositions. As to whether or not there are individual propositions is a question over which a logician may worry his head off, but with which we need not concern ourselves in the present connection. Suffice it to say, propositions can be taken individually. As a matter of fact, they are so taken. When we claim that we have said something true either in logic or in history or in the sciences, we mean that we have asserted not only a true but also an individual proposition. This is the starting point of our difficulties in connection with what we mean when we say that certain novels are true. What is it in novels that may be true or false? When we say something about a true Chippendale, or a true Sung picture, or a true Adams fireplace, we can easily transform the statement into a proposition. We may have to strain and stretch, but we don't have to mutilate or do violence to the original statement in order to transform it into a proposition. Could we do the same to novels? Before we answer the question, we shall have to analyse what it is in novels that is said to be true when novels are said to be true.

## II

When a novel is said to be true, it is not the sentences in it which are said to be true. Most of them are not propositions; and even if some true propositions are asserted, the truth of these is irrelevant to the truth of the novel. Take any sentence at random;

"Isabel had not seen much of Madame Merle since her marriage, this lady having indulged in frequent absences from Rome." ( *The Portrait of a Lady* by Henry James. )

This is not a proposition. We needn't, however, enter into the reasons why it isn't, because they are irrelevant to our present issue. A novel may be said to be true, when there are in it false propositions; or false, when there are in it true propositions. It seems that our task has hardly anything to do with individual sentences, not because these are necessarily incapable of truth or falsity, but because even granting them truth or falsity, neither would be relevant to the truth or falsity of the novel in which they are found.

The next thing to do is to take up paragraphs. Here we seem to be on rather firm ground. Paragraphs in novels do give us a sense of reality which single sentences do not. Something organic seems to emerge from a collection of sentences; either a picture is given of a place where we have been, or a scene we have experienced, or a description is made of a person with whom we are directly or indirectly acquainted. Take the following from *Mrs. Dalloway*:

"She advanced, light, tall, very upright, to be greeted at once by button-faced Miss Pym, whose hands were always bright red, as if they had been stood in cold water with the flowers.

"There were flowers: delphiniums, sweet peas,

bunches of lilac; and carnations, masses of carnations. There were roses; there were irises. Ah yes—so she breathed in the earthy garden sweet smell as she stood talking to Miss Pym who owed her help, and thought her kind, but she looked older, this year, turning her head from side to side among the irises and roses and nodding tufts of lilac with her eyes half closed, snuffing in, after the street uproar, the delicious scent, the exquisite coolness. And then, opening her eyes, how fresh like frilled linen clean from a laundry laid in wicker trays the roses looked; and dark and prim the red carnations, holding their heads up; and all the sweet peas spreading in their bowls, tinged violet, snow white, pale—as if it were the evening and girls in muslin frocks came out to pick sweet peas and roses after the superb summer's day, with its almost blue black sky, its delphiniums, its carnations, its arum lilies, was over; and it was between six and seven when every flower—roses, carnations, irises, lilac—glows; white, violet, red, deep orange;every flower seems to burn by itself, softly, purely in the misty beds; and how she loved the grey white moths shining in and out, over the cherry pie, over the evening primroses!

"And as she began to go with Miss Pym from jar to jar, choosing, nonsense, nonsense, she said to herself, more and more gently, as if this beauty, this scent, this colour, and Miss Pym liking her, trusting her, were a wave which she let flow over her and surmount that hatred, that monster, surmount it all; and it lifted her up and up when—oh! a pistol shot in the street outside!

" 'Dear, those motor cars, 'said Miss Pym, going to the window to look, and coming back and smiling apologetically with her hands full of sweet peas, as if those motor cars, those tyres of motor cars, were all *her* fault."

He who has visited London, lived there for a while, gone into English flower shops and come into contact with English people might recall scenes in his own experience after reading the above paragraphs. It does not make any difference whether he has ever visited Mulberry's, whether he ever saw any lilac or delphinium during his stay in London, or whether he has ever met Miss Pym at all; all that he needs be concerned with is that he has experienced the misty, fresh, colourfulness of an English flower shop, and seen Pymish young ladies darting back and forth, and Dallowayish ladies, probably in Burberry and tan shoes, trailing after them, and on the whole more visually conscious of the flowers than aurally conscious of the flower attendant. This alone would give him a sense of reality from the paragraphs quoted above. He would be open to ridicule if he stops to ask whether the statement that there were irises is a true proposition based upon historical research.

Take paragraphs which portray single characters:

"My heart warms to a sense of affectionate absurdity as I recall dear old Codger, surely the most unleaderly of men. No more than from the old schoolmen, his kindred, could one get from him a School for Princes. Yet apart from his teaching he was as curious and adorable as a good Natsuke. Until quite recently he was a power in Cambridge, he could make and mar and destroy, and in a way he has become the quintessence of Cambridge in my thought.

"I see him on his way to the morning's lecture, with his plump childish face, his round innocent eyes, his absurdly non-prehensile fat hand carrying his cap, his grey trousers braced up much too high, his feet a trifle inturned, and going across the great court with a queer tripping pace that seemed cultivated even to my naive undergraduate eye. Or I see him lecturing. He lectured walking up and down between the desks, talking in a fluting rapid voice, and with the uttermost lucidity. If he could not walk up and down he could not lecture. His mind and voice had precisely the fluid quality of some clear subtle liquid; one felt it could flow around anything and overcome nothing. And its nimble eddies were wonderful! Or again I recall him drinking port with little muscular movements in his neck and cheek and chin and his brows knit—very judicial, very concentrated, preparing to say the apt just thing; it was the last thing he would have told a lie about.

"When I think of Codger I am reminded of an inscription I saw on some occasion in Regent's Park above two eyes more limpidly innocent than his- 'Born in the Menagerie.' Never once since Codger began to display the early promise of scholarship at the age of eight or more, had he been outside of the bars. His uttermost travel had been to lecture here and to lecture there. His student phase had culminated in papers of exceptional brilliance, and he had gone on to lecture with a cheerful combination of wit and mannerism that had made him a success from the beginning. He has lectured ever since. He lectures still. Year by year he has become plumper, more rubicund and more and more of an item for the intelligent visitor to see. Even in my time he was pointed out to people as part of our innumerable enrichments, and obviously he knew it. He has become now almost the leading character in a little donnish world of much too intensely appreciated characters."

Codger is said to be McTaggart. This may or may not be information. If it is, it may enrich the relevant knowledge of some of the readers concerning McTaggart, such as how he looked at Cambridge, how he walked most of the time, and what impression he gave to the students, etc. But it does not add anything to the readers' relevant appreciation of Codger. In The *New Machiavelli*, Codger is a pencil portrait of a type, a slightly distorted outline of a character who is concrete enough to be described in that individual way, but who is also nonetheless an instance of Mr. Wells' conception of the dons as female old men. One could see Codger lecturing and talking, in cap and gown, or drinking port, or gyrating about in the winding streets of Cambridge, without ever having heard of the existence of McTaggart, the philosopher. The sense of reality that is felt is not obtained from McTaggart the individual, but from a host of dons whom one could experience as Codger.

But are the above paragraphs true? Detach the first from *Mrs. Dalloway* and we find a very peculiar collection of sentences. There was no mention of Mrs. Dalloway, we could have no idea of who the person was who was buying flowers and celebrating at the same time; we don't see Mulberry mentioned, and we shouldn't know what to do with it if it were; there was Pym to be sure, but one reader might see in her a faded blonde and another a somewhat dried brunette, and neither is relevant unless we know what the whole thing is all about. It is perfectly true that if anything is detached from its own context something is bound to be lost, but the amount or the degree of what is lost varies with the nature of the context, and in the case of novels, the loss in intelligibility is so complete that the question of truth of the novel as a whole can hardly be raised at all.

Or take the second quotation above. Detach it from *The New Machiavelli*, and substitute McTaggart for Codger, and the attitude of some of the readers would be quite different from what it was before. To those who didn't know of the existence of McTaggart, the substitution would not make any difference, and with the same unintelligibility still staring at them, they wouldn't know what to do with themselves. To those who know of McTaggart, however, certain questions arise with the substitution. Codger's knowledge of port, for instance, is a part of Codger as well as the other things mentioned, a character is given together with his virtues and vices; but after the substitution is made, the virtues and vices are no longer the creations of the novelist; questions arise as to whether McTaggart knew his port or merely bluffed, whether he was ever a power at Cambridge, whether his face could be described as childish or his eyes innocent, or whether he often lectured walking up and down between the desks. These questions arise, because the sentences which were formerly used to paint the picture of a Codger who might be real or purely imaginary, but whom we have no criterion for treating either as the one or as the other, are now transformed for those who know of McTaggart into propositions which might assert facts concerning that philosopher and might therefore be true or else false.

The second quotation might stand by itself, as shown above, if certain substitutions were made, transforming it into a group of propositions, but without such a substitution or some similar treatment it is no more intelligible by itself than the first quotation. As parts of novels neither can be detached from its own context, and whatever sense of truth it may give us, it does so with the help of the novel as a whole. But what is it in the whole novel that leads us to say that the novel is either true or false?

Since it is not the sentences alone, nor the paragraphs alone, there must be something else. And so far we have not yet discovered it.

## III

It used to be a common practice among critics of novels to analyse a novel into the following elements, namely, the setting, the character and the plot. If we treat these as separate entities we are bound to do injustice to any novel, but if we regard them as analytical terms, they were useful in the days when novels could be so analysed. In modern novels, however, there is something which for lack of a better term might be described as a pattern. Possibly due to the haste with which books are read in the hurricane life of modern days, possibly due to the realization that a voluminous replica of life is no longer the aim of modern novels, thick tomes are mostly replaced by small and handy volumes, and short stories flourish more than ever before. Whatever the cause may be, there has to be in modern novels greater economy and more efficient organization than in the novels of the past, with the result that they become closely knitted patterns in which what would formerly be taken as the setting, for instance, is now replaced by something which could no longer be labeled exclusively as one thing rather than as any other. The plot has become increasingly unimportant; in some cases we still have a concentrated dose of it, while in others it is minimized to the point of extinction.

We have then a pattern of relationships in which certain characters are involved under conditions which are partly the causes of those characters and partly their effects, and which may still be described as the setting or the plot, though it is a setting or plot which is hardly detachable from the characters in the framework of that pattern of relationships. In the ideal form this pattern is concise, closely knit and economical. Instead of a voluminous description of life as it is lived, we have an abridged edition; instead of an exact copy, we have sometimes a distorted view from some singled out perspective; where there is brevity, it means probably that the missing details are irrelevant, and where there is a wealth of detail, it is likely that they contribute towards a preconceived scheme; and the sentences and paragraphs weave themselves into a complex whole in which the scheme is embodied and by means of which it is conveyed to the readers. There are varying degrees of success in the fabrication of such a pattern from the point of view of the novelist, but the presence of such a pattern seems to be quite undeniable. When something is said about any given novel, something is said about its pattern of relationships.

The pattern should be distinguished from the scheme. The term scheme is ambiguous. It might refer to the plan of the pattern, or to the conception of human nature immanent in the pattern. It is the latter which will engage our attention. Every novel has a pattrn, but not every pattern embodies a conception of human nature. Wherever there is a conception of human nature, it is that which in the last analysis determines the shape or form of the pattern, and it is also that which represents sometimes the articulate philosophy of the author and sometimes his personality or individuality in conjunction with what is later on in this article to be labeled as the special sensitivity of the novelist. In very rare cases these two are combined but often they are not, and since they may not be combined, they merit separate discussion.

When the conception represents only the articulate philosophy of the author, it is liable to be a conception of human nature in terms of abstract, detached and therefore unindividualized qualities, and the pattern of relationships is liable to be such that it fits in with certain specific aspects of life rather than with its synthetic concreteness, and consequently may be transformed into a set of assumptions for special sciences or current philosophies. The social problem novelists, for example, weave into their novels certain aspects of human nature in terms of their social or political philosophy. The attempt is often disastrous, because of the two conceptions involved, namely, one dealing with political and social philosophy and the other dealing with human nature are liable to struggle with each other, and since such novelists are generally much more interested in the former, the latter is either twisted or maimed or relegated to such irrelevance that the pattern of relations exhibited becomes the hypothetical and analytical pattern of the social sciences. The characters created by George Bernard Shaw, for instance, are liable to be the capitalists or the proletarians of Karl Marx, or the superman of Nietzsche, or the economic man of Adam Smith. These abstract men are often wrongly criticized on the ground that they are unreal, but it is exactly on account of their unsubstantiality that they function in the social sciences at all; no science can possibly deal with the concrete man.

It is in novels that these abstract men of the social sciences are entirely out of place. Having neither character nor individuality, nor even the rudimentary flesh and blood, they cannot be the elements with which a novelist weaves his pattern of life. If in a projected novel an author deals with the economic man of Adam Smith and nothing more, he may be a good or bad or indifferent economist; if he deals with men and women as being exclusively cases of hysteria, he becomes a pseudo-psychoanalyst; if he deals with the capitalists or the proletarians with only the properties that enter into their definition, he becomes a sort of parlour communist; in any case, he is hardly a novelist. Fortunately the physical man of the physicist or the chemical man of the chemist has not been dragged into the realm of novels, or else we would have a host of authors who probably would be neither physicist nor chemist on the one hand, nor novelist on the other. The point must now be quite clear. Just as the physical man is not a conception of human nature, but at most, if at all, a concept in physics, so the economic man is a concept in economics, and not a conception of human nature.

Here we must guard ourselves against a possible misunderstanding. We are not arguing against abstraction; in fact any kind of conception is abstract, and a conception of human nature is hardly less so than any other. What is being insisted upon here is rather that the kind of conception which enters into a scheme in a novel must be a conception of human nature and not a conception of any single aspect in which human beings function in any special field of activity. It is perfectly true that in arriving at a conception of the former, help may be obtained from the latter. D. H. Lawrence seems to have a conception of human nature with an emphasis on biology, Henry James has one with a bias towards psychology, the notion of cause and effect is probably inseparable from Hardy's view of life, economies is hardly ever absent from the scheme of most novels of the present day. Nonetheless, whatever conception there is in the novels that are considered true, it is a conception of human nature, that is, of human beings as synthetic wholes, not of human beings in any specific aspect, of individual substantives, not of disembodied adjectives, of human qualities either in coherence or in conflict arising out of their mutual dependence or independence or interdependence with each other, not merely of the properties which enter into the definition of featherless bipeds or rational animals.

The last is of supreme importance. It is that which is responsible for the peculiarity of our conception of human nature in novels. As conception, it may be abstract, but the material with which it is embodied must be studied with concreteness. It cannot be merely asserted in propositions, for if concreteness and individuality were left out, the universal would remain unillustrated and might therefore be empty; on the other hand, it cannot be merely described, for if there is an over-emphasis on particulars, the universal might be lost and the individuality and concreteness would be, as it were, rootless. If it is to be successfully conveyed to the reader, it must be intricately woven into the warp and woof of a pattern of human relationships. The latter must be a picture and a system of concepts. If it were merely a picture, there would not be *raison d'être* for novels, some of us would prefer living to a vicarious enjoyment of life through somebody's description of it; and if it were merely a system of concepts, it would result either in science or in philosophy. This is probably what is meant when people say that a novel shouldn't merely copy life, nor itself be merely an abstraction of life.

More often, however, the conception of human nature is not the product of articulate philosophy, but an expression of the individuality or personality of the novelist in conjunction with a certain type of sensitivity necessary to novel writing. Whenever the latter is the case, the novelist is the key to the pattern in his novels. This on the whole is more satisfactory than having an articulate philosophy. The disadvantages of the latter have been discussed in the paragraphs above. Though by no means inevitable, these disadvantages are overwhelmingly probable, so probable that nobody expects good novels from philosophers or scientists. Since most of the satisfactory novels come from persons with a special type of sensitivity, we must next inquire into that sensitivity before we take up the main thread of our discussion.

## IV

The special sensitivity towards creating patterns of human relationships seems to consist of the following elements: conceptual lucidity, perceptual keenness, emotional vividness, capacity for living the rôles, and the power for expressing the ebb and flow of feelings without spoiling them.

A novelist must be intellectually keen. It has often been taken for granted that an artist can afford to be stupid, while a scientist can afford to be dull, and a philosopher can afford to be both. There seems to be a confusion of some sort which it is not the purpose of this article to dwell upon at any length. What seems to be the trouble is that foolishness is often mistaken for either stupidity or dullness. All of us can afford to be fools; in a sense, civilization depends upon fools; but none of us can afford to be stupid, and possibly least of all an artist. Only the kind of intellectual keenness required differs with different professions. There are at least two elements in intellectual keenness which when combined in different ways could make their possessors keen in entirely different spheres and suited for entirely different purposes. In the first place there is conceptual lucidity. This means clarity in ideas. Some of us are capable of dealing with ideas in their pristine purity, defining them in terms of each other without any aid from the possible things that are denoted by them.

But the extent to which conceptual lucidity is required differs with different lines of work. It is alone sufficient to make a man either a logician or a mathematician, but it is not sufficient to turn either a logician or a mathematician into a man; and while being human is not theoretically essential to the logician or mathematician, it is necessary to a novelist. A novelist must have intellectual lucidity, for without it he cannot even use language with discrimination, but conceptual lucidity is not sufficient nor quite salutary if by any chance one has too much of it.

A novelist must be able to temper or soften his conceptual lucidity by what is called here perceptual keenness. That is to say, he must be able to perceive with clarity. He must see and hear and taste where others fail to see and hear and taste. What is perceivable may or may not be common, but what is perceived is not common to all the percipients. Those who are especially endowed perceive more than those who aren't, and the excess over the normal may be divided into various kinds. Mere quantity may be ruled out at once; of qualitative differences, some needn't engage our attention at all; a chemist in his laboratory may see in a given datum qualities which a layman wouldn't be able to experience. The kind of perceptual keenness required for a novelist is essentially a capacity to perceive what is not perceived by most men in terms of human values, —colours, shapes, designs, and patterns which are capable of arousing in the novelist himself as well as in others, joys, sorrows, desires, memories, and hopes and fears. But perceptual keenness is not sufficient, a man may perceive all that is capable of arousing emotions or feelings and yet fail to arouse them. Neither conceptual lucidity alone, nor perceptual keenness alone, nor the two combined will enable a man to become a successful novelist, that is to say, something else is required which is other than intellect.

It seems obvious that in order that certain feelings or emotions may be aroused in others, the novelist must experience or be able to experience them either directly or indirectly. But mere experiencing is not enough, since all of us are capable of experiencing emotions of one sort or another. If they are to be transmitted to the reader, they must be experienced with what is here called emotional vividness. One is emotionally vivid if one is conscious of emotions and can discriminate between them without losing their poignancy or robustness. This is indeed a rare quality in us mortals. It means a capacity to step in and out of oneself without losing anything in the process. Most of us are either one thing or another, or else neither one thing nor the other at any particular moment. When we taste the wine before ordering it, we don't quite enjoy the wine, we are merely trying to be conscious of its qualities; and when subsequently we do enjoy the wine, we are not always nor quite conscious of its qualities. Graham Wallas used to say that when a dog is angry, the whole dog is angry, but when a man is angry, not every bit of him is sunk below the level of consciousness. With most of us, the more we are conscious of our anger, the less angry we become. A concentrated dose of de-light carries with it a certain amount of abandon which when consciously held in check renders the delight considerably diluted; the poignancy of pain or the inevitability of sadness is partly the result of a sort of lack of understanding in lieu of which if light is brought about the pain may not be quite so acute, and sadness may be turned into extenuated pessimism. Some of us, however, are especially endowed with the capacity for discriminating emotions without diluting them in any way and possibly even gaining liveliness through this discrimination. This emotional vividness is what a novelist must have in order that he may transmit to the reader all that he perceives or feels.

But transmission may take various forms. If what a writer aims at is to transmit knowledge through essays on literary criticism, all the qualities discussed so far may make him an essayist, blessed with the kind of sweet cynicism which is achieved by living in the world without belonging to it. But then he probably wouldn't be a novelist. In order that he may be a successful novelist, he has to have the capacity for living his characters just as the actor has to have the capacity for living his rôles. It is out of this capacity of the novelist that active sympathy of the readers is obtained. It is through this capacity that the qualities perceived or imagined by the novelist become synthesized and vitalized into concrete individuals, that the situations he gathers here and there from his own experience or elsewhere are transformed into the living problems of his created characters, thus weaving the relations conceived by him into the vivid patterns synthetically understandable or experiencible by the readers.

Take some of the characters *in SuiHu* (*All Men are Brothers*),
such as Lu Ta, Lin Ch'ung, or Wu Soong. Each one of them
could be described with a string of adjectives, and yet no such
string by itself would be able to move or fight or eat or drink, if
the author hadn't been able to vitalize every such string into living
beings of flesh and blood. But he can not vitalize these characters
if he cannot temporarily become himself any of them, thus absorbing every such string of adjectives into those congeries of his
own feelings, desires, passions and impulses as well as hopes
and fears, and bundle all of these into the characters he creates.
In the ideal case, the novelist must be able to experience all that
his characters are made to experience. That is to say, he must be
able to live his characters.

But while the actor lives his rôle through his behaviour on
the stage, the novelist has to do it through writing. He must have
the capacity to express himself through the instrumentality of language. Mastery over language is obviously essential, for without it
what is meant to be expressed wouldn't be expressed with adequacy,
not to say beauty. This however needn't be dwelt upon at all.
What should be noticed is that expression through language is
partly at any rate intellectual articulation, and intellectual articulation carries with it a danger that is too often neglected or unno-
ticed. However fleeting or settled feelings may be, they are nonetheless processes or activities or ebbs and flows, even the
thinking activity itself belongs to this category; ideas and
thoughts on the other hand are the static cross sections of this

flow and ebb, like the individual photographs which compose the moving picture. Tag these down for a sufficient length of time, the activity or the flow stops. Intellectual articulation therefore carries with it a certain amount of destructiveness. With some persons it merely arrests the thinking or the feeling or the perceiving activity, while with others it even destroys it. Those who are emotionally vivid are more likely capable of articulation without destruction, but they may not be masters of language. It is in this connection that skill in the use of language has not been sufficiently emphasized, if ever at all. The novelist has to have the power for expression without modifying what is meant to be expressed; and where what is meant to be expressed happens to be the flow and ebb of feelings, a novelist must be able to express them without petrifying them into invoices, bills of lading or static inventories. This is probably what is meant by "living language". Since no word is in itself living, "living language" can only mean language used in such a way that it suggests or conveys or arouses something in us that reverberates with the throb of life.

The above qualities or capacities are the necessary if not the sufficient ingredients of that special sensitivity without which a novelist cannot produce first-rate novels. Other qualities which make up the individuality of the novelist count towards the variety or the type of the novel written. We are not concerned here with the variety or the type of the novels, but with the general nature of the pattern devised. The analysis here given of this special type of sensitivity is indirectly and partly also an analysis of the patterns of human relationships. If any such pattern were to be devised by persons, endowed with the capacities discussed in this section, one can easily see that it would be intelligible and filled with concreteness, embodying actions and reactions in terms of emotions and feelings, and presented in a way as to be experiencible by the readers.

## V

We have then in true novels a conception of human nature embodied in a pattern of human relationships. We have dwelt at some length on why this conception had better be woven into a pattern born of the registered experience of the novelist through his special sensitivity rather than in any articulate philosophy which may have been entertained by a writer through either his detached or else reformist interest in life. When a given novel is said to be true, the logical subject of the assertion seems to be the conception of human nature embodied in the given pattern of relationships. It is this which is said to be true or false in novels. Assuming the correctness of this conclusion, we may take up the question as to what it is in a novel that is said to be true, and in what sense it is so said. We shall take up the first problem first.

A novel is said to be true to life. Since no pattern pictures actual life(for if it does, it would be history), the life to which a novel is said to be true must be a life that may possibly be lived.

We shall denote by life those congeries of events, actions, reactions, thoughts, feelings, passions, impulses, wishes, hopes and fears, and what not, which are the kind of thing that constitutes the sum total of our everyday experience. Most of us find no difficulty with the term when it is restricted to this rather prosaic sense and we shall not stop for further elucidation. It is the notion of possibility that needs further analysis. Since it cannot be bare logical possibility, it must be limited by something other than a pure and absolutely free conception.

To begin with, it is obvious that life is limited by laws which govern its natural environment as well as the stubborn facts of that environment. We do not expect people, however hot-headed or inspired, to revolt against the law of universal gravitation, however inconvenient it may be for them to be confined to this earthly world; nor do we expect them to move with the velocity of light in spite of the fact that in one novel at least the characters are made to travel into astronomical space at a speed far greater than that of light. Stubborn facts of nature limit us almost as much as their laws. We may hate the sun, but we do not generally desire to murder it in any full-blooded fashion; we may love the moon, but we do not do so with the kind of ardour with which we love a person of the opposite sex. Our attitude towards the stubborn facts of our natural environment differs from our attitude towards the stubborn facts of our social environment. If one is prevented by his wife from leaving or by his friends from returning to his home, he feels that his freedom is infringed upon; but if he is prevented by rain or storm from doing either, he may be irritated, but he does not generally feel that his liberty has been outraged.

When we speak of wishes and imaginations, the natural environment is no limitation, but then some limitation is likely to be found in the person who does the wishing or imagining. Solid or stolid persons are not expected to wish the actual world a Platonic Utopia, nor are they likely to imagine themselves flying on wings into the rarified atmosphere of some distant nebula. When life is not limited by nature without, it is limited by character and temperament within. And of course it is limited by history and civilization. So far as the last is concerned, a good deal has been said, though very likely a good deal more has yet to be said. We are not here interested in this problem. What should be pointed out is rather that whatever limitation there is, it is known or felt directly or indirectly through our own experience. Possible life in the widest sense is any conceivable life which does not run counter to the accumulated experiences of mankind.

In spite of limitations the possible life is extremely extensive, far more so than our actual life. Consequently human nature can be conceived in a large variety of ways corresponding to which any number of different patterns can be devised. Conceive human nature in terms of spiritual values, the pattern of human relationships may have to be heightened or sublimated from the point of view of the actual and ordinary; conceive it in terms of certain special perspectives, the pattern may have to be distorted; and conceive it in terms of satire, the pattern may have to be exaggerated. Even when human nature is conceived in terms of "realism", the pattern need not be a detailed and naturalistic copy of actual life. Under *Ninety-Nine Degrees* by Lin Hui-yin is for instance one of the most realistic renderings in recent years of the life of Peking, but it is not stuffed with minute and exact description of any section of the ancient capital. Since *Ulysses* may not give to some of us so intense a sense of reality as does *Mrs. Dalloway*, the pattern may not be an exact copy of life, even when the conception of human nature embodied in it is meant to be "realistic".

While patterns may differ from one another in an indefinite number of ways, there are two attributes or qualities in them which cannot be dispensed with, namely, consistency and reality. Where these are present in a pattern, they are present in such a way that they can hardly be separated. Consistency is suggested by experienced reality, and reality is felt when it is guided by experienced consistency. Just as possibility in connection with life is not bare logical possibility, so consistency here is not mere absence of contradiction. A pattern is consistent when given the reality felt for the elements involved in it, a pattern opposed to or in striking contrast with it is likely to contain elements of discord. Perhaps it would be easier if we were to confine ourselves to the characters of the pattern rather than to take the pattern as a whole. A character is consistent, if given an adequate description of him, the accumulated experience of the sensitive reader not only could but also would understand and sympathize with the behaviour ascribed to him in the pattern. We can easily see that this is quite different from bare logical consistency. Imagine Lin Tai-yü. being married to some person other than Chia Pao-yü. Strictly speaking no contradiction is involved in your imagination. From the point of view of bare consistency, she could; and if one fills Ta Kuan Yuan with telephones, automobiles, asphalt roads, and with swimming pools in summer and skating rinks in winter, she may; for then she might have been a different person in some significant aspects, and the deseription of her as it was would have been inadequate. The description being taken as adequate, the Lin Tai-yü with whom most of us are to some extent acquainted cannot think of any person other than Chia Pao-yü in terms of marriage.

A pattern of human relationships must be real, even though it may not be actual. A sense of reality may be obtained from a number of things in the pattern, such as descriptions of familiar places, characterizations which fit in with persons whom we have met, situations with which we are acquainted in our own life, etc. The sense of reality obtained in such a way needn't be an integral part of the sense of reality of the pattern as a whole. The latter does not depend upon the actualities which we have come upon in our own experience, it is a sort of imaginable or experiencible reality, something which might be experienced in terms of the pattern of relationships the consistency of which is an indication or guide. Though not actual a character becomes nonetheless real, if given an adequate understanding of the context in which he is situated, the accumulated experience of one sort or another on the part of sensitive readers not only could but also would enable them to know how he ought to be described. Thus, his reality is in turn involved with his consistency.

But while reality and consistency are inseparable, they are yet distinct, and being distinct, they are distinguishable. Consistency refers more to the relations, while reality refers more to the entities related in a given pattern. While nothing may be actual in a given pattern, the pattern itself is. It is concrete, and just as with regard to concrete square tables, some are "squarer" than others, among patterns of relationships, some are more consistent and real than others. Since there is a question of degrees concerning consistency and reality, there are likely to be two extremes; in the one those qualities may be so present that the pattern is positively true to life, and in the other, they may be totally absent and the pattern then represents an impossibility. Between these limits there are various degrees of plausibility together with an unequal distribution of it so that some parts of the pattern are said to be more plausible than others. We shall, however, ignore the question of unequal distribution altogether, for that would take us far away from our main task. The purpose of this section is to point out what it is to which a novel is said to be true, and since this turns out to be a possible life within the limits discussed, the pattern of relationships has to be both real and consistent in order that the life indicated may be felt to be possible.

# VI

But in what sense is a novel said to be true? It is not true in the sense of logic, nor in the sense of history, and while it involves general relations, it does not assert them in the way in which they are asserted in science. A novel may contain such general statements as "if one is in love, one forgets himself", or "if one is old, one eats less than when one is young", etc., and yet it is not identified with any of them, nor with all of them combined. It may be true when those propositions are false, or false when they are true. It is involved with general relations, but involved with them in a way in which, although propositions asserting them may be inconclusive and fragmentary, the pattern painting them in all their concreteness may yet be consistent and real.

A consideration of consistency and reality of the pattern leads us to a view of the sense in which a novel may be said to be true. The last section is therefore a preparation for the present. We may theoretically begin with consistency of the pattern, and let our experience of life guide us to a feeling of reality for the entities related in the pattern, or else we may begin with the reality felt for the entities related and leave it to our experience of life to lead us to a feeling of inevitability of the relations given in the pattern. In practice these two never proceed separately unless we are capable upon to articulate our appreciation of a novel. We usually slide from the one to the other and back again without knowing that we are doing so; and if we are capabe of moving in consonance with the unfolding of the pattern of relationships, we are somewhere in the novel whether we imagine ourselves to be any of the characters or not. This capacity for entering into the life of the novel depends partly on the readers and partly on the pattern given in the novel. If the pattern were created out of the actual or projected experience of the novelist registered through the kind of sensitivity analysed in the fourth section, it is likely to be woven with consistency and reality and we can enter into it with varying degrees of success.

But the capacity for entering into the novel depends partly upon the readers. Only readers who are endowed with a part of the sensitivity which enables a novelist to create are capable of entering in any relevant sort of way into the life of the novel created. A novelist may gather material anywhere so long as it has been registered in him, but in weaving it into a pattern, he is guided by his own sensitivity which is also partly that of his sensitive reading public. He must create in such a fashion that his sensitive readers may follow his lead, and it is perfectly possible that he succeeds in doing so only by becoming himself alternately an author and a reader. At any rate, it is the same type of sensitivity that is the connecting link between a novelist and his reading public.

Since any novelist who has anything to say and says it well has a group of readers who appreciate his novels, the question of the different schools of thought, or the different schools of writing, or the different schools of appreciation needn't be touched upon at all, for whatever schools there may be, each has its novelists and its reading public and their relation in one school is essentially their relation in any other. Besides, our subject matter in this article is the truth in true novels. With some schools, the question of truth probably never arises; in such cases, it is plain that we are not concerned with them. Whenever the question does arise, we maintain that there is always a question of a conception of human nature, of a pattern of relationships, and of a notion of possible life. It is not necessary to inquire whether the different schools of thought agree on the truth about human nature; they are not expected to, nor does it matter that they don't. They may differ as much as they like on what the truth about human nature is, but the sense in which a novel is said to be true by one school is the same as the sense in which it is said by any other: namely, the conception of human nature in a given novel is such that the pattern in which it is embodied represents possible life.

The criterion as to whether the pattern does so or not depends on whether or not objectively it is woven with such consistency and reality that those who are endowed with the proper type of sensitivity exhibited elsewhere can enter into the pattern, and not merely subjectively on the part of the readers as to whether they do enter into it or not. These are different things. The first is objective in the sense that the reader may enter into the life of the pattern and come out of it with reasons as to why he did it. The second is subjective in the sense that a reader may tumble into the pattern through causes that might not have anything to do with the novel at all. However, when the first is the case, there are always people who do enter into the life of the pattern, even though the number of these may be smaller than that of those who tumble into it through causes of their own or even accidents of the moment.

Readers may enter into the life of a novel in two different ways, either as actors or as spectators. As actors, they have to identify themselves with some of the characters, and this can only be done when characters are thoroughly familiar. Englishmen may temporarily become Squire Weston, or Tom Jones, or Mr. Pickwick, and Chinese boys often behave as if they were Chang Fei, or Wu Soong, or else Chia Pao-yü. This identification has various consequences, some of which are too trivial to be mentioned, while others might be alarming from the point of view of the possibility of having actual life directed by the pattern of a novel even more effectively than by any formal education.

Identification is not easy when the novel is not familiar and the reader has acquired the habit of regarding novels as novels. The more usual sort of thing for him to do is to become a spectator. When the novel is such that the reader is carried away by it, he is always somewhere lurking in the background of the scenes described, he may even become absorbed into the atmosphere, living in it, pulsating, feeling, and perceiving all that there is to perceive, and even more, since whatever is missing is unconsciously supplied by himself. A good and successful novel is never merely read, since in reading it, colours are seen, noises heard, characters come in and out, and their imagined actions and reactions impinge upon the ebb and flow of the undulating feelings, thoughts and impulses of the person who is at the same time the reader. A consistent and real pattern of human relationships is never devoid of its concrete living focus either in the person of the one who creates it, or in the person of those who appreciate it.

A reader may therefore enter into a novel in either of the two ways mentioned, and if he enters into it with the full force of his whole being and comes out of it with his mind receptive towards the untiversal that is embodied in it, he cannot help feeling that its conception of human nature embodied in its pattern of human relationships is true to possible life. This, then, is the sense in which a novel is said to be true. A novel cannot be claimed to be true by persons who have not read it, nor by readers who are incapable of entering into it; and of those who do enter into its pattern of life, only those who come out of it with something registered other than their concrete and discrete experiences in reading it can say anything about the truth of a novel. Thus understood, the truth of a novel is not likely to be confused with the reality of the incidents or the situations of which the novel is composed, nor with the seriousness or sincerity with which it is written. It seems obvious that not every serious and honest writer can say something true through the instrumentality of novels.

# Education in Contemporary China<sup>*</sup>

## I

I Find myself in a very embarrassing predicament. I am a sort of jack of some trades and master of none. My colleagues in this conference are experts, and I am not an expert in any line. My field has been logic and epistemology for a number of years, and I think I may as well say that in that field there is no expert. If there were experts, they probably wouldn't be philosophers.

It happens that this is a rather peculiar subject, and so I feel diffident when I come before you to try to talk about education. From the bottom of my heart I crave your indulgence.

Now, speaking very frankly, I don't know exactly what education is. Mathematical logic—a subject in which I have been interested for some time—is defined by Mr. Bertrand Russell as a subject in which we do not know what we are talking about—or

＊ 本文发表 1944 年，载 *Voices From Unoccupied China*, by Liu Nai-Chen, Tsa; Chiao, C. K. Chu, J. Heng Lin, Fei Hsiao-Tung, Wu Ching-Chao, Chin Yueh-Lin; ed. by Harley FarnsworthMacnair The University of Chicago Press, 1944。

whether what we say is true. I don't know definitely, clearly, in terms of distinct and clear ideas, what education is. I take it for granted that it is the kind of thing that schools and universities are engaged in, and I shall take it up in that sense only.

I have some statistics here which may not be adequately interpreted, since I do not understand them thoroughly. We may divide education into the customary primary, secondary, and higher education. I shall start with quantity. Experts on education may laugh at that term. I couldn't think of any other, so I speak in terms of quantity.

Possibly one of the things that will surprise you is the increase in the numbers of students in China. During your war years, your colleges and schools are somewhat depleted, whereas in China there is actually an increase in the number of students in both middle ( i. e., high ) schools and universities. I do not know whether that is true of students in the primary schools, but I believe it is. The figures here are not comparative as far as primary education is concerned.

From 1936 to 1937, the number of universities and colleges was 36; from 1937 to 1938, 29; from 1938 to 1939, 32; from 1939 to 1940, 36; from 1940 to 1941, 41; and from 1941 to 1942, 45. There is, then, an increase in the number of higher institutions. These figures are for the government universities. There is a decrease in what are known as private universities. We started with 42 in 1936 and we had only 38 in 1941.

The number of students in colleges, universities, and technical schools in 1936 was 41, 922. In 1941 there were 59, 000 students—that is, roughly, the number of university students has increased in five years from 41, 000 to 59, 000. That is a rather big increase in university and college students. I am using the word "university" to cover colleges and technical schools.

For the middle school, there is the same kind of increase. In 1936–37, we had 627, 000 students; in 1940, 41, 768, 000.

The number of students in primary schools in 1941–42 was around 22, 000, 000. This last figure is not comparative. We have no previous figures, so we don't know whether there is an increase or not, but at the time my colleagues and I left Chungking in the latter part of May [1943], the minister of education told us there was quite an increase in the number of primary students also.

So, in primary, secondary, and higher education we have an increase in the number of students.

Now, as to quality: by "quality" I might mean a number of things, but I am speaking of standards. Put it this way: before the war there were certain standards of excellence. As compared with that, the standard has been very much lowered—and, it is believed, the trend is toward a still greater lowering, so that there is a distinct deterioration of quality.

We may start with the primary school. Previous to the war [1937], primary schools were manned by administrators and teachers, many of whom have now, gone into other lines of work. Of those that remain, the quality of teachers is probably not comparable to the quality of the teachers before the war. I do not know personally the conditions of primary schools. Not having children, I suppose I yield to a certain laziness, but I have never bothered about the primary schools with which my friends are concerned.

Take the school in the village where I lived with a friend. I heard my friend complaining all the time about it. I think, even in terms of health education, that that school lags very much behind some of the other schools to which my friends are accustomed. This friend of mine has two children of school age in my village. Both of them attend school; after a few weeks both had two lines of bluish liquid running from their nostrils all the time—a condition which did not exist before they entered the school. Moreover, they are eternally catching cold. Aside from this kind of thing that I occasionally hear my friends speak of, I have no first hand knowledge.

Neither do I have such knowledge of the secondary schools. I think that previous to the war we had very few good secondary schools. I believe my colleagues will bear out that statement. As far as my experience is concerned with entrance examinations and things of that nature, the middle school in Peking attached to the Normal University, the Nankai Middle School in Tientsin, and the Yangchow Middle School were all very good middle schools, at least good preparatory schools for university education.

I don't know where they are now. Somebody in the audience may be able to tell me whether the Yangchow School is still in existence and, if so, where it is. Nankai is still in Chungking. But in the middle schools we have a question that I shall take up a bit later on in connection with higher education.

In the middle schools we also have the problem of teachers. The teachers there are generally young men with a good deal of ambition and possibly with less attachment to their schools and their profession than is the case with some of the university professors. At the same time their salaries are very low, and it is perfectly possible for a teacher in the middle school to be talking about the standard of living and the cost of living instead of mathematics or physics or whatever the subject may be.

Then there is a question of the teachers' leaving. A lot of them enter government service or the factories run by the National Resources Commission or the Ordnance Department or other factories or railroads or other branches of government service. Hence it has been difficult to retain middle-school teachers, except during the last year or so. I think there has been some difference in the last year, but previous to that time it was extremely difficult to retain teachers. From this alone one can easily see there would be a decrease in the quality of secondary education.

Concerning higher education, I have more direct experience. There are a number of things which contribute toward its deterioration. On the whole, I should say that if we continue the war for, let us say, five years, we shall probably need five years for recovery; that is to say, a total of ten years is needed to return to pre-war standards. If we continue over ten years, we shall probably need somewhere around another ten years for recovery.

With the pre-war standard as the starting-point, the war seems to me to have retarded educational progress for a period that is double the period of the war.

One reason which is peculiar to some universities, and not to others, is the lack of books and equipment. Some universities are not so much affected, although they are affected from the point of view of new books. Some universities have moved from their original location to a distant location with their books and some of their equipment. Of course, they are bound to lose certain things. It has been difficult to remove engineering equipment when that consisted of large and heavy machinery. With regard to books, some universities were fortunate in being able to remove a large number to the interior; but other universities, such as Tsinghua University, Peking University, and Nankai University, were not so fortunate. Peking was lost on July 29, 1937, before most of the things could be moved. In fact, we members of the faculty had to sneak out. Most of the things were left in Peking.

Nankai, in particular, has been a sort of battleground, so that the damage to Nankai University is probably much more thorough than to other universities.

There is, for these universities, almost a 90 percent loss of property 95 percent probably, and, I think, in some cases you might as well say 100 percent, loss of property in terms of equipment and books. Even for those who are more fortunate the problem of new books and things is as difficult as for any other university.

In Lien Ta, which is the Southwest Associated University, that is to say, the combination of National Peking University, National Tsinghua University, and Nankai University, there are few books at the present time, and there is generally a fight for those books—a run for them. It is pathetic to see students hurrying through their dinner in the evening to stick around the door of the library trying to get ahead of one another, and stationing themselves as near to the door as possible so that, when the door opens, they may rush to the desk to get hold of their books.

Not being a scientist, I am unable to discuss the matter of equipment; but one can easily see that, for those universities which have lost their equipment, there is no way to replace it, so that there is a general lack of equipment. As a consequence, there is little experimentation going on so far as this particular university, Lien Ta, is concerned. I think in some other universities the conditions are more favorable. This is one element in the deterioration of quality of higher education.

There is another element which is something like this. Previous to the war, Tsinghua University held every year competitive examinations in various parts of China—for instance, in Peking, in Shanghai, in Canton, and in Hankow—in which generally more than three thousand students participated. I believe a little over three hundred were admitted as Freshmen, so that one out of ten, roughly, is admitted to the university. There is, therefore, a choice of the brighter students among the applicants.

Probably the same proportion holds concerning Pei Ta, that is, Peking National University. I do not know of other universities, but after the war was started we did not have that ratio, and the reason is to some extent plain. There were a number of young men who were left behind in the occupied territory. At first, perhaps, they were not of university age. Suppose a person was somewhere around fourteen or fifteen when the war started. After a few years that person becomes of university age. It would be desirable for him to attend the university. Well, he wants to go to a university in Free China, in the unoccupied territory.

Now suppose he takes a very strict entrance examination. Some of these people would not be admitted; they would not be able to get themselves admitted. They will be stranded somewhere, and they will be very much discouraged. It is, accordingly, advisable from a number of points of view—certainly political as well as other points of view—to lower the standards of admittance so that a larger number of young men from occupied territory may study in Free China.

At first communications were rather easy. Students could take boats from Shanghai, or from Peking, or pass by Hongkong, and get to the hinterland. Later the trip wasn't so easy, and latterly we have heard touching tales of young men coming to the universities in Free China. Two of them whom I know traveled all the way on foot from Peking to Chengtu and, finally, I believe, took trucks to Kunming. They traveled from the northeast corner of China to the uttermost southwest. They had to walk practically all the way from Peking to Loyang. These two certainly walked all that way; after that, they walked quite a bit but probably caught a bus or a truck or a train part of the way.

You will agree that such men have to be taken care of in some way. One method of taking care of them is to give them what they want. If they want to study in the university, the university takes them; and, while they were not well prepared in the occupied territory (and after they come to the university they are not likely to be well trained either), on account of the tack of equipment and books and things, they do enter a university in Free China.

In some places—this is not true everywhere—there is the question of air raids and there is the question of the attractions of other kinds of life that might be taken up simultaneously with university education. These elements all tend toward a deterioration of quality, so that, on the whole, I should say, although there is an increase in quantity, there is a deterioration in quality of education.

Quantity is definitely increasing. To what extent—how much—it has increased, I really do not know, although I have read you the statistics. I am inclined to say that these statistics are more or less exact—or more or less inexact! I don't know which to say. I suppose it depends upon your attitude. Anyway, the trend of those figures indicates definitely an increase in quantity.

Of the deterioration in quality I am more convinced. That is to say, I feel definitely that there is a deterioration.

I now take up a point that has nothing to do with quantity or quality. Well, it may have something to do with quality—that is, direction and purpose. I shall not take up quantity and quality again, except as they come out in the discussion. But as far as direction and purpose are concerned, I should say a few words.

I take it for granted that the purpose of education—the kind of thing that schools and universities are meant for—is to produce a certain development in character, a certain rounding-out of individual character development. There are some intrinsic purposes. I, personally, have been interested more in the intrinsic purpose of education.

For instance, I believe someone suggested last evening that an educated person is one who keeps custody of what has been obtained before and then plunges ahead to improve upon it in the future. Well, education has that purpose—has that more or less intrinsic purpose—from the point of view of human civilization. I do not know whether any of you have thought of this supposition: suppose human beings stopped education for fifty years. I mean stopped completely. I don't mean going on with it surreptitiously, but stopped completely—stopped learning, stopped learning how to write, stopped learning how to read books. If you want to do a thorough job, suppose all the books were burned. I am not in favor of it, in actuality, you understand! But suppose that were the case. I said fifty years because I am Chinese, but perhaps we had better make it a hundred years, because I am conscious that English and Americans now live to ninety or a hundred years rather easily. I don't think we Chinese do very often.

Suppose you figure it at one hundred years that education is completely stopped. Then I think we would return to what somebody would call the bliss of Adam and Eve days. We wouldn't be able to know anything about history. The children born after that one hundred years of absence of education wouldn't be able to know anything of history, wouldn't be able to know anything of science, anything of the accumulated knowledge that has been passed on to us from our forefathers.

Presumably they would be able to start inquiries of their own; but, presumably, if education stopped completely for one hundred years, it would take three or four thousand years for mankind to develop again to the present stage of human knowledge. From that point of view, one can see that education has its intrinsic value from the point of view of knowledge. And, then, from the point of view of human character building, of understanding of human beings, of behaving in society, of spiritual or moral development, education has its own intrinsic values.

But, aside from that, there is another value that we can't very well ignore: that is education to answer certain national purposes. I don't think we can dismiss this element. After all, education has to serve some national purpose. Maybe, to some of us, this is not of value; but, to a number of us—especially to those of us in China—you can easily see that it is of value. That is to say, education has to serve national purposes aside from intrinsic purposes, and it is that element of which. I want to speak next.

National defense involves industrialization and mechanization. I can sympathize with most of my countrymen and with the government in wanting speedy industrialization and speedy mechanization of the country. The government feels keenly the responsibility that rests with it of putting China on such a basis that it can be comparatively secure from invasion.

When war finally came in 1937, some of us in Peiping were definitely relieved in certain ways. I want to convey to you how we felt and why. Previous to 1937, from 1931 onward—indeed, throughout that long period—the people in Peiping all had the feeling: What is Japan going to do next? What will Japan do tomorrow? There was always apprehension, always that tension, which is extremely annoying, extremely uncomfortable. It made life tense, so that when war finally came it was a relief. We got the feeling that at last we were going to have a showdown. The government people, too, felt that way, naturally. It was perfectly plain that China could not remain as it was. China must be industrialized and mechanized to some extent, in order to secure a certain minimum of security against invasion at just any moment.

I sympathize with the government and my people for desiring security, that kind of security which can be obtained only by mechanization, by industrialization, and by modernization. Essentially, after all, it is a question of modernization.

Now education must help along that line. The old education

certainly does not work in the twentieth century. I don't think any of my colleagues have gone through the very old style of education. I had a period of it—the classical education. I was taught to recite the four books, the *Book of Rites*, the *Book of Changes*, the *Book of Odes*, and so on. I had to recite those things without understanding them at all. I was taught to read them, and then to recite them. At the end of the year, I had to take the examination on about ten volumes, standing about a foot high on the table on the teacher's desk. I had to turn my back and start from the first line in a book and just go on reciting to the very last sentence of that book—that kind of thing. I know I was rather naughty when I recited the *Book of Changes.* I did something dishonest and was thoroughly punished for it. Otherwise, I think I passed through without a hitch!

But that kind of education—which has been going on for ages—certainly won't make China modern. The kind of education that came as a substitute for that old form of education, which was officially abolished in 1905, isn't particularly suited, either. We have universities that are divided into departments: for example, the philosophy department or the history department, more or less according to the American plan. And it seems that, from the point of view of quick industrialization and modernization, there is a demand for students who go to engineering schools and, possibly, study economics, but chiefly study engineering and subjects allied to engineering.

I understand there is an idea of producing two million engineers within the next ten years—or, I don't know how many years. To do that we have to modify the present system of education to answer the purposes of national defense, industrialization, and mechanization.

The result is at the present time quite noticeable, even in universities, and, I think, in secondary schools, too. That is to say, there is a flocking of students into engineering and some of them into economics. There is comparatively little interest in pure science and very little interest in the arts.

Now it is not merely the arts—not merely literature and philosophy and history—that are affected, but also pure science, such as chemistry and physics. We used to have a very strong department of physics at Tsinghua University near Peking; it generally had the best students admitted to the university. At the present time it is difficult to attract students to the study of physics. I think this is to some extent true also of chemistry and of the other pure sciences.

The tendency for China to go into intensely practical studies in order to bring about a speedy industrialization and mechanization is already here. The tendency is both planned and caused by circumstances. Even if there were no policy to encourage this tendency, the tendency would probably have come about anyhow. The present generation of young men probably feels that there is much more future in engineering and economics than in anything else. If a young man has a personal equation as well as the national interest at heart, he is likely to go into one of those branches.

I say the tendency is probably natural, and even without encouragement young men, from the point of view either of their own personal interest or of national interest, will probably flock to those branches instead of going to other branches. But at the same time there is a policy that encourages the taking-up of engineering and economics.

I have said that I sympathize with the government in its desire to have quick mechanization and industrialization for national defense. I think I myself believe in that, to some extent, and I can see that, if there is no other alternative, we simply have to industrialize and try to mechanize in a great hurry. I don't want to leave the impression that I am opposed to industrialization. I think it is inevitable, and in order to be able to exist as a nation we simply have to industrialize.

But what I do not like to see is the haste in which we are trying to do it. If we want to speed the process within a period of, let's say, ten or twenty or thirty years, I can see consequences which would make me extremely uncomfortable, to say the least, and which, I think, will probably have a rather bad effect not alone in China but elsewhere.

I shall speak of some of those consequences later. I shall at the present time think in terms of the policy of encouraging the kind of education that is intended to speed up industrialization in a great hurry.

I myself think that we shall not succeed in industrializing

ourselves sufficiently to give us the kind of security that we intend to have through the speeding-up of industrialization. I find myself at a loss to express myself adequately. I have this kind of idea in mind: in order to industrialize, we need not only engineers, not only economists. We need, as well, pure scientists and, I think, the arts also, as well as the pure sciences. That is to say, I feel that the whole attempt toward industrialization is a synthetic one.

In order to industrialize or mechanize, what is needed is not merely engineering and all that "practical stuff", but something else as well. I think it is easy to establish that we need pure science, that if we lack pure science we shall not have very good engineering. Physics and chemistry are as much needed for industrialization as for anything else.

Let us take the example of the present war. We trained a bit of an air force before the war started. We got quite a number of planes, some of them from Italy, I think. There were also planes from America. They went in to fight at the beginning of the war. The training of aviators has been continued. During the five years that I stayed in Kunming, I saw a good deal of the air cadets there, and I am familiar with the names of a number of planes— the Hawk, the Douglas E-15 and E-16(which they Call "Buffaloes"), and a large variety of others—but most of them are such that one doesn't hear of them any more. They weren't adequate, with the change of machines of the enemy. At first the Chinese air force could go up and fight a bit, but gradually it couldn't.

Of the air cadets I knew personally, all of them were killed except two. One of them is now somewhat of an invalid; the other is still going on. I think he has the best luck in the world!

One thing, of course, is that we do not manufacture airplanes. We depend upon airplanes from abroad. The question is: can we manufacture airplanes? We might try it. But if we want to manufacture airplanes which are up to date and capable of dealing with airplanes manufactured in other countries, in enemy countries, we must have aeronautical engineering, and you can easily see that that involves physics, chemistry—and a number of other things—and if we do not have good aeronautical engineers we shan't be able to manufacture airplanes of our own.

So you see that, even in that one single line, the question of building an air force or an airplane industry, we require pure scientists. We must encourage pure science as well. We can easily see that other things are closely related. Consequently, I am inclined to think that if we want to industrialize quickly—or at all—it is not merely engineering that needs to be studied, but also an enormous number of other subjects. And if we emphasize engineering too much, or alone, we shall not succeed in mechanizing and industrializing.

The attempt to speed up engineering education for the purpose of national security will not succeed. By attempting this thing in a great hurry, by suiting education to that speedy industrialization and mechanization, we shan't get the kind of security that industrialization or mechanization is supposed to give us.

The policy of encouraging engineering and economics at the

expense of other subjects would not be adequate to give us a quick industrialization and mechanization so as to give us, in turn, the kind of security that we need. I, personally, am inclined to think that as far as education is concerned we have to attempt it more slowly.

This is speaking from the point of view of adequacy—and I think this thing is not adequate. But there is another point of view, and that is whether it is desirable. If we overemphasize certain elements in education, certain branches of knowledge, it is not desirable. If we return to some of the intrinsic purposes of education—for instance, the preservation of knowledge and the encouragement of knowledge, and the building-up of human character—if, I say, we return to some of these intrinsic values of education, we can easily see that too much emphasis, or too much diversion of young men into one or two even admittedly very useful lines, will not give us the kind of citizens that some of us want.

On the whole, I believe that the new tendency in education is inadequate for the purposes for which it is intended. From another point of view, moreover, I consider it undesirable.

In the attempt to bring about industrialization and modernization and to obtain results speedily, I am afraid the whole population will gradually become regimented: regimented in such a way that education may become mere training, and human beings, with free individual characteristics, may be turned into atoms in the social structure—and not free atoms, either. The entire social organization of China may be whipped into something like an organism with very little individual initiative. I don't like to say this, but I can't help it. I think, in the process of attaining very quick industrialization, there is the danger that we may become totalitarian in structure, and that is something which I am afraid of—and it is something which I think Americans should be afraid of, too.

From my point of view, in order that we may prevent that, it seems to me we must have a world plan, a postwar world plan. I don't know what that plan should be—in fact, I have no definite ideas on the subject—but I think we must have a world plan after the war so that security may be given to individual nations from the point of view of the world as a whole; not from the point of view only of an individual nation trying to attain its own security.

I have that subject at heart more than any other subject. I speak of education merely as a road, as a channel, to lead up to that subject.

It has been said, "Some people are born great, some people achieve greatness, and some people have greatness thrust upon them." With regard to nations we have a similar case. I do not know whether America was born a great leader or whether America achieved leadership. In any case, leadership is thrust upon America; and it seems to me that in America we have to think in terms of world plans in order to avoid future wars, and in order to avoid regimentation here and elsewhere as a weapon for security.

I am sure I am not making myself clear. My English gets extremely rusty so that I don't express myself clearly, but I have wanted to present that problem as a problem for the consideration of all present. I thank you for the opportunity to voice a part of my ideas on the subject.